Astoria and Empire

Astoria & Empire

BY

JAMES P. RONDA

University of Nebraska Press

Lincoln & London

The paper in this book meets
the minimum requirements of American National
Standard for Information Sciences
– Permanence of Paper for Printed Library Materials,
ANSI Z39.48-1984.

Library of Congress Cataloging in Publication Data
Ronda, James P.
Astoria and empire / James P. Ronda.
p.   cm.
Includes bibliographical references.
ISBN 0-8032-3896-7 (alk. Paper)
1. Oregon – History – To 1859.
2. Astoria (Or.) – History.
I. Title.
F880.R68 1990
979.5'46 – dc20
89-38464
CIP

FOR

DON JACKSON

Mentor and Friend

Contents

List of Illustrations and Maps, ix

Preface, xi

Acknowledgments, xiii

Chapter 1
Astoria: The Origins of an Imperial Idea, 1

Chapter 2
Planning Astoria, 37

Chapter 3
The Russian Connection, 65

Chapter 4
To Astoria by Sea, 87

Chapter 5
The Overland Passage: Montreal to
the Arikara Villages, 116

Chapter 6
From the Arikara Villages to Astoria, 165

Chapter 7
Life at Fort Astoria, 196

Chapter 8
Astoria at War, 243

Chapter 9
Astoria in Retreat, 277

Chapter 10
Astoria: The Legacy, 302

Appendix
After Irving: Astoria's Chroniclers, 337

List of Abbreviations, 345

Notes, 347

Bibliography, 375

Index, 389

ILLUSTRATIONS

John Jacob Astor, by
John Wesley Jarvis, 3

Captain James Cook, 5

Peter Pond's map of the
Northwest, 1790, 14

Sir Alexander Mackenzie, 17

Alexander Henry
the Elder, 26

Flag of the Russian-American
Company, 67

Gabriel Franchère, 90

Alexander Ross, 92

The *Tonquin*, 95

Trade goods from Crooks's
canoe, 182

Caldron Linn, 184

Fort Astoria, 1812, 203

The *Beaver*, 241

Robert Stuart, 318

Routes of Hunt and
Stuart, 324

Sketch of the Routes of
Hunt and Stuart, 328

Astoria in the late 1830s,
335

MAPS

Wilson Price Hunt's
overland route, 123

Astoria and the mouth
of the Columbia, 198

Preface

IN LATE DECEMBER 1788 a worried Spanish official in Mexico City set down his fears about a new and aggressive northern neighbor. Viceroy Manuel Antonio Florez offered a gloomy prediction about the future of Spanish–United States relations in the West. He already knew about the steady march of frontiersmen toward St. Louis and now came troubling word of Robert Gray's ship *Columbia* on the Northwest coast. All this seemed to fit a pattern, a design for Yankee expansion at the expense of His Most Catholic Majesty's American domain. "We ought not be surprized," warned the viceroy, "that the English colonies of America, now being an independent Republic, should carry out the design of finding a safe port on the Pacific and of attempting to sustain it by crossing the immense country of the continent above our possessions of Texas, New Mexico, and California."

Florez was not the only officer of empire to hear the footsteps of a westering American nation. Canadian fur merchants and Russian bureaucrats also viewed the young republic as a potent rival in the struggle for western dominion. The viceroy's vision of the future proved startlingly accurate. Within the next two decades an American president would authorize a federally funded expedition to find just the sort of transcontinental route Florez imagined. Equally important, a New York entrepreneur would propose and put into motion an ambitious plan to make the Northwest an American political and commercial empire. John Astor's Pacific Fur Company, with Astoria as its central post on the Columbia River, was Florez's nightmare come true.

Astoria has long represented either a daring overland adventure or simply a failed trading venture. The Astorians surely had their share of adventure. And the Pacific Fur Company never brought its founder the profits he expected. But all those involved in the extensive enterprise knew it meant more than stacks of pelts and ledger-book figures. Thomas Jefferson once described Astoria as "the germ of a great, free and independent empire." Jefferson believed that the entire American claim to the lands west of the Rockies rested on "Astor's settlement near the mouth of the Columbia." John Quincy Adams agreed. The expansionist-minded secretary of state labeled the entire Northwest as "the empire of Astoria."

Washington Irving sensed the imperial dimension when he wrote that Astoria might someday become "the watchword in a contest for dominion on the shores of the Pacific." Irving concluded *Astoria* with that line. It is the beginning point for *Astoria and Empire*. This book seeks to explore Astoria as part of a large and complex struggle for national sovereignty in the Northwest. That struggle was the culmination of a battle for American empire that had its beginnings in the Age of Columbus. *Astoria and Empire* argues the case for a wider stage and a larger cast. That stage encompasses action from Montreal, New York, and Washington to Canton, Sitka, and St. Petersburg. Astoria's larger cast includes American politicians, Montreal merchants, Hawaiian sailors, and Chinook headmen. They move through these pages not simply to add dash and color but because their lives are essential to understanding Astoria's drama. The Astorians and their rivals were always engaged in more than trading and trapping. They were advance agents of empire.

If Astoria symbolizes the final struggle of the great powers for imperial sway in North America, it also represents the cultural diversity that increasingly characterized the continent. Astoria's empire reached out to touch the lives of French Canadians, Russians, Yankees, Scots, and countless Indians. Astoria counted among its citizens men like the Hawaiian gardener James Kimoo, the Iroquois hunter Ignace Shonowane, and the Scots partner Duncan McDougall. Homesick voyageurs, footloose adventurers, and scribbling clerks all called Astoria home. On the Columbia, lines of national rivalry, personal ambition, and cultural diversity intersected to shape a larger continental destiny.

Acknowledgments

THINKING BACK on Astoria, John Astor once asked, "Was there ever an undertaking of more merit, of more hazard and more enterprizing, attended with a greater variety of misfortune?" Astor was thinking about all the troubles that dogged his ventures, but his words equally fit the destiny of Astoria's records. Time has not been kind to the remains of the Pacific Fur Company. Fragments of letters, invoices, diaries, and reports are scattered in more than a dozen repositories. Although important materials have survived, much has been lost.

In pursuing the empire of Astoria, I have incurred many debts. As John Astor sought to balance his ledger book, so let me now begin to square accounts. My travels to distant archives have been made possible by generous grants from the National Endowment for the Humanities and the Youngstown State University Research Council. The quest for Astoria's traces was made easier by the help of many able archivists. I am especially grateful to Peter Michel, Missouri Historical Society; Leslie Morris, Rosenbach Library and Museum; Layne Woolschlager, Oregon Historical Society; Mark Mastromarino, Baker Library, Harvard University Graduate School of Business Administration; George Miles, Beinecke Rare Book and Manuscript Library, Yale University; James J. Holmberg, the Filson Club; Richard J. Clifton, Washington State Parks and Recreation Commission; Karen Fox, State Historical Society of Wisconsin; Milton O. Gustafson, National Archives. Staff members at the National Archives, the Public Archives of Canada, the Sutro Library, the Toronto Metro Reference Library, and the Provincial Archives of British Columbia helped in a dozen ways.

Closer to home my research was advanced by departmental colleagues Fred Blue and Lowell Satre. Hildegard Schnuttgen, head of the Reference Department at Maag Library, Youngstown State University, brought me material I thought well beyond my reach. Audrey Nagy, former supervisor of the Microforms Room at Maag Library, made my many hours before the green screen go more pleasantly. I am especially grateful to my able research assistant and word-processor operator, Linda Pondillo. John Astor could not have wished a more faithful employee.

I want to add a special note of thanks to four people. A conversation with Bill Lang early in this project both clarified its direction and deepened my commitment. John Haeger's masterful reassessment of Astor's business practices taught me much. Jim Axtell and I have shared so much over the years that I find it hard to say thanks in a fresh way. His thoughtful comments on each chapter were just what the doctor ordered. My wife, Jeanne, helped me track the Astorians as we had earlier traced Lewis and Clark. Some readers will find her index to be the best part of this book. I could not have asked for a better companion on the trail.

This book is dedicated to my mentor and friend Donald Jackson. His life and work remain a daily inspiration.

Astoria: The Origins of an Imperial Idea

FOR A NATION at war less than a month, the patriotic rituals of the Fourth of July 1812 had more than customary meaning. But no place mounted a stranger celebration than Fort Astoria. Situated near the mouth of the Columbia River, Astoria was both the field headquarters for the Pacific Fur Company and the most distant outpost in a new American empire west of the Rockies. On that day the assembled partners, clerks, and employees raised the American flag, fired guns in salute, and passed around the grog.[1] But most of those enjoying the holiday were not citizens of the young Republic. The Astorians—Scots, French Canadians, Hawaiians, and a scattering of Yankees and Indians—represented a bewildering variety of backgrounds and allegiances. What the gathering saluted was not the shaky future of the American nation. These traders had been captured by another vision: the dream of empire in the West, the heady prospect of personal wealth and national domain beyond the Great Divide. Marking a national day not their own, the Astorians symbolized both the dream and its diverse beginnings.

* * *

John Jacob Astor never kept company with dreamers. Relentless in the pursuit of wealth, he embodied all that was calculating and pragmatic in American capitalism. The squat, heavyset merchant who stares out at us from the portrait by John Wesley Jarvis seemed nothing more than a self-satisfied entrepreneur. Bounded by the ledger book and the balance sheet, Astor's days were hardly like those of explorers Peter Pond, Alexander Mackenzie, and Meriwether Lewis. Little about him suggests any kinship with those visionaries who plotted empires between the Stony Mountains and the Great Western Sea. But John Astor's mind was always more daring, more intuitive, than his contemporaries knew. As Astor embraced business techniques far in advance of his contemporaries' practice, so he became the focus for a powerful western dream.

That flash of imagination first took written shape in January 1808. Addressing a private letter to the New York mayor De Witt Clinton, Astor carefully drew the outlines of what would become the first American empire west of the Rockies. In this and subsequent letters to President Thomas Jefferson and Secretary of the Treasury Albert Gallatin, he proposed a vast trade network extending from western Europe and the American Great Lakes to the Pacific Northwest and on to Russian America and China. He envisioned a complete land and sea transportation system shifting goods, pelts, information, and employees around a global marketplace. The agent for this enterprise would be the Pacific Fur Company, a private venture with close ties to the federal government. In Astor's scheme, posts of the company would stretch from the Missouri to the Columbia, dotting the route pioneered by Lewis and Clark. Fur and flag would join forces to plant American sovereignty along the Great River of the West.[2]

What Astor so persuasively sketched for his correspondents sounded both new and bold. Here was an American plan using American employees to seize the West for the United States. Those carefully crafted arguments seemed able to bring an entire generation's western aspirations to life at little cost to the national treasury. Astor promised profit for the company and empire for the nation. But was this scheme, with all its lure of wealth and national destiny, an Astor original? What inspired the plans he presented to Clinton,

John Jacob Astor, by John Wesley Jarvis. Courtesy of the National
Portrait Gallery, Smithsonian Institution, Washington, D.C.; Gift
of Mrs. Susan Mary Alsop.

Jefferson, and Gallatin? Where were the origins of Astoria and the
Pacific Fur Company?

The traditional answer came from the Astorians themselves and
through their most famous chronicler, Washington Irving. In their
view, it was the discoveries of Lewis and Clark that first sparked
Astor's endeavor. Even Canadian Astorians like Gabriel Franchère
and Alexander Ross emphasized Astor's debt to Jefferson's westering captains.[3] Western historian Bernard DeVoto who gave fullest

expression to this version when he wrote, "Astoria followed from the expedition of Lewis and Clark as the flight of an arrow follows the release of the bow string."[4] From captains to capitalist has the appeal of chronological symmetry and national pride, but the truth is not nearly so tidy. The earliest impulses toward this western fur empire sprang neither from Astor nor from Lewis and Clark.

The roots of Astoria twist through much of eighteenth-century North America, extending north to Peter Pond's Athabasca country and west to the coastal probings of Captain James Cook. Astoria's roots drew on the experiences of sailors like John Boit and Joseph Ingraham, men schooled in the ways of the maritime fur trade of the Northwest coast. Near the end of the century the roots can be found reaching back toward Montreal to entangle the lives of hardy Nor'westers Alexander Henry the elder, Duncan McGillivray, Alexander Mackenzie, and, much by chance, the rising New Yorker John Jacob Astor.

Neither Astor nor any of his future Canadian rivals would have recognized 1778 as a pivotal year, but that was the year two signal events marked the real beginnings of the Astorian idea. That year Peter Pond, a fur trader and explorer, crossed Methye Portage in modern-day northern Saskatchewan to open up the fur-rich Athabasca country. Pond was no stranger to distant voyages of discovery. Henry Hamilton, lieutenant governor of Canada, once described him as a man with "a passion for making discoveries."[5] Born in Milford, Connecticut, in 1740, Pond was apprenticed to a shoemaker but soon abandoned the bench and awl for service in the provincial militia during the Seven Years' War. At war's end, a sea voyage to the West Indies brought more adventure. In 1765 Pond began what would become a twenty-three-year career as a trader and explorer. Traveling first on the upper Mississippi, he was soon attracted to the more promising territories in what is today Manitoba and Saskatchewan. Along with other independent traders called "the pedlars from Quebec," Pond challenged the Hudson's Bay Company and learned the geography of the far northern frontier. By the time he left the north for good in 1788, he had a

Captain James Cook. Courtesy of the Public Archives of Canada, Ottawa, c 17726.

reputation for violent behavior as well as geographic curiosity. Few men could match the experience and knowledge of this Connecticut Yankee gone west.[6]

At the same time that Pond and his men were struggling across Methye Portage, more than a thousand miles to the west Captain James Cook was pressing his search for the elusive Northwest Passage. In late May his ships *Resolution* and *Discovery*, sailing along the Alaskan coast, entered an opening north of the Kenai Peninsula. The shape of the bay and the presumed river beyond it seemed to fit prevailing notions about the passage. After several days of probing, Captain Charles Clerke of the *Discovery* characterized the waterway as "a fine spacious river . . . but a cursed unfortunate one for us." Cook agreed that the river was probably not *the* passage, but like Clerke he thought it stretched deep into the interior and would someday serve as "a very extensive inland communication."[7] It was not until 1794—fifteen years after Cook's death—that Captain George Vancouver found Cook's River to be a deadend, now properly known as Cook Inlet. But throughout the 1780s, published accounts of Cook's final voyage kept the illusion alive.[8] Speculation about the course and use of the river intensified with the rapid growth of the fur trade between the Northwest coast and China. Cook's mysterious river and the immense profits from selling sea otter pelts at Canton tantalized ambitious men like Peter Pond and his sometime companion Alexander Henry the elder.

While fellow Yankees and Cook-voyage veterans John Ledyard and Simon Woodruff plotted oceangoing trips between Boston, Nootka Sound, and China, Pond took up the Cook's River challenge. Just how he learned of it remains a mystery; he may have read an early account of Cook's voyage or received news from Henry, recently back from a trip to London. Whatever its source, word of the river sparked Pond's imagination. In the late 1770s Indians had told him about rivers flowing west from Lake Athabasca to the sea. By 1784 he was certain one of those rivers was that explored by Cook. Wintering at Athabasca, he began to put his notions down in cartographic form. His earliest sketch is now lost, but a map he drafted the next year contains all its essential features. In fact, almost all the Pond maps express the same optimistic vision—that Lake Athabasca and the Great Slave Lake form a giant water hub for the entire Northwest. Pond imagined several great rivers radiating, like spokes in a wheel, toward the north and the west. He was partially right. The Mackenzie, Peace, and Athabasca rivers do indeed head north and west from the lakes, but they do not form the navigable highway Pond sought. His 1785 map shows Cook's River striking inland from the Pacific while several Athabasca streams flow west to join it. In the early 1780s Pond was uncertain about connections between the lakes and the Pacific. He easily confused Cook's River with the modern-day Mackenzie. Pond's last map shows that by 1789 all this wishful thinking had become conviction. Cook's River appears as a direct water link between the Great Slave Lake and the Pacific.[9]

But Pond's ideas were expressed in more than maps. In October 1784 Benjamin and Joseph Frobisher, Montreal merchants and sometime associates of Pond's, declared their readiness to test his theories by sending out an expedition. Most of the Frobisher petition dealt with the need to find a new route from Lake Superior to Winnipeg now that Grand Portage was in American hands. But Pond's stamp was plain in the Frobishers' claim to have "in view another discovery of greater magnitude." The discovery they alluded to was the Cook's River passage to the sea. The Montreal merchants were willing to venture the journey if the crown would grant a ten-year trade monopoly west of Lake Superior. Here was the first sign that partners of the North West Company were prepared to strike west for the Pacific.[10]

In the spring of 1785 Pond launched his own campaign to win government financing to explore Cook's River; the choice of government mattered little to him. Early in March he presented a petition, now lost, to the Continental Congress, meeting in New York. A detailed map of the Northwest that originally accompanied the petition has survived. This map is in two sections, the northern portion differing little from its counterpart in earlier charts. The map shows a direct water connection to the "Mer du Nord West" via Lakes Athabasca and Great Slave and portrays unnamed rivers piercing the Rockies to join the Pacific. Sensitive to his American audience, Pond conveniently repackaged his earlier proposals, shifting his east-west river systems farther south. The southern half of the map contains elements that would be familiar features in western cartography before Lewis and Clark. In territory that would someday become part of the United States, Pond drew a Missouri River pointing to an easily portaged Rocky Mountains. Once over the portage, travelers would find the great river "Naberkistagon,"

Pond's name for the fabled River of the West. Not wanting any in Congress to miss his message, Pond noted that the distance from Pittsburgh to the confluence of the Ohio and Mississippi rivers was a mere 351 leagues. The cartography had been tailored for new customers, but the fabric of the dream remained the same. Pittsburgh to the Pacific, like Montreal to China, was no fantastic voyage. Exploring distant rivers and building posts to the Pacific promised the wealth of the Orient and a lucrative western domain—surely prizes enough to tempt the new Republic. But a congress struggling to secure independence so soon after a costly war had no time for such visionary schemes.[11]

Rebuffed by the Americans, Pond headed back to Montreal and a meeting with Lieutenant Governor Henry Hamilton. During that interview, and in a subsequent petition, Pond stressed the economic and imperial implications of his proposals. He warned that time was moving against British interests. "Positive information" from Indians had confirmed a growing Russian presence on the Northwest coast. Certain New England sources had reported Boston merchants preparing two ships for the coastal fur trade and the China market. Pond's intelligence was indeed accurate. Russian traders, led by Gregorii Shelikhov, were eager to expand their influence. In less than fifteen years, Shelikhov and his rivals would create the powerful, semiofficial Russian-American Company. The Americans were equally aggressive. The *Columbia* and *Lady Washington* were just the first in a growing fleet headed from Boston to Pacific waters. That maritime thrust, combined with the newly drawn Great Lakes borders, stood to give the Americans a decided advantage in any struggle for the Northwest. Never mind that just a month before, Pond had been ready to aid and abet that American advance. What he now proposed was a plan to steal a march on both the Americans and the Russians. The North West Company, backed by crown sanction and funds, would explore the Cook's River route, construct a chain of posts from the Atlantic to the Pacific, and seize a western empire for Britain. From these posts the English might dominate the fur trade, strengthen alliances with Indians, and defeat any imperial rival. Here was an ideal means to recover the honor and initiative lost in the recent colonial rebellion. As Pond or some more literate amanuesis with the North West Company put it, the plan would "be productive of Great National Advantages." It was a phrase Astor would have admired. Forceful as ever, Pond kept insisting that without royal encouragement his passage to India might "very soon fall a prey to the enterprizes of other Nations."[12]

Hamilton proved a sympathetic audience. He plainly valued Pond's experience and quickly recognized the imperial rewards for exploration. "Mr. Pond's discoveries," he wrote, "may prove of infinite utility to this country." The explosive Nootka Sound controversy was several years away, but English ships were already challenging Spain's claims to the Northwest coast. It seemed to Hamilton that the same intense rivalries that had shaped the destiny of eastern North America had now shifted to the Northwest. Britain could have a western empire but the price would be conflict with Russian, American, and Spanish contenders. The royal official stated: "The prosecution of [Pond's discoveries] may lead to establishments, at this period (considering the active and encroaching spirit of our neighbors) particularly necessary. The pre-occupying certain advantageous stations may be highly expedient." Hamilton was enthusiastic, but the same could not be said of official London. What seemed urgent at Athabasca and Quebec was less pressing on the other side of the Atlantic.[13]

Pond's theories might not have found quick favor in government circles but there were always his friends and partners in the North West Company. During the summer of 1787 he was again in the North, this time exploring the Great Slave Lake. Pond was especially attracted to a mysterious river—later known as the Mackenzie River—and its possible course to the sea. He was fully persuaded that Cook's River joined the Mackenzie to provide a direct water route to the Pacific. The map Pond drew that summer illustrates his expectation. Immediately above Cook's River on the map he wrote the following:

Capt. Cook found the water on this coast to be much fresher [hole in ms.] Salt or Sea Water: also a quantity of drift wood no doubt carried thither by the Rivers Araubaska, Peace, & Mountain as they commonly overflow their banks in the months of May and August the former owing to the breaking up of the ice and the latter to the great quantity of snow upon the mountains melting about that time and at each of these periods there arrives down a vast quantity of large wood such as is not to be meet with to the Northward of the abovementioned Rivers.[14]

Pond's wintering companion at Athabasca was the young Alexander Mackenzie. The old trader became Mackenzie's mentor in geography and discovery. Mackenzie's future ventures to the Arctic Ocean and the Pacific were all rooted in Pond's ambitious theories. But not every Nor'wester was impressed with those speculations. Writing to Simon McTavish, a prominent London supply merchant, the Montreal trader Patrick Small ridiculed such notions, labeling them nothing more than "extravagant ideas."[15] Yet Mackenzie and at least some of the company partners were won over. When Pond quit Athabasca for the last time in May 1788, he left behind a powerful legacy for Mackenzie.

It was not until 1789 that Pond's imperial geography got its first test. Sometime in the spring, the North West Company's partners decided to send a small party to the Pacific over the presumed Mackenzie River–Cook's River passage. Pond's unsavory reputation—he had been implicated in the murder of two traders—made him an unlikely candidate to head the expedition. Instead, the leadership fell to Alexander Mackenzie. As he wrote years later, "I went on this expedition in hopes of getting into Cook's River; tho' I was disappointed in this it proved without a doubt, that there is not a North West passage below this latitude [69°15′ N.] and I believe it will generally be allowed that no passage is practicable in a higher latitude the Sea being eternally covered with Ice."[16]

While Mackenzie was spending most of the summer pressing up the river that now bears his name, Pond was in the East, still promoting his western program. He did not yet know that the young explorer would eventually find not the Pacific but the ice-choked Arctic. In June, Pond may have been in Philadelphia. The Spanish ambassador, Diego Maria de Gardoqui, noted the presence of "one of the many enthusiastic Englishmen who roam these western countries inhabited only by Indians." Whoever this much-traveled adventurer was, he claimed to have gone as far as the Continental Divide. More telling, and further suggesting that the ambassador was speaking of Pond, the trader reportedly had asserted "that the furthest nation he reached assured him that about 100 miles from that place was a river which empties into the Pacific Ocean." Like Pond, this explorer had made a map of the western country—a map that has evidently not survived.[17]

By early November 1789 Pond was in Quebec. It was there that he gave the last and fullest expression to the project that had dominated his life for nearly a decade. In the first week of November he had lengthy talks with Isaac Ogden, a prominent Quebec merchant. As he had played mentor to Mackenzie, Pond now sought to explain the essentials of his western geography to Ogden. Pond used his 1787 map as the basis for the tutorial. He began by giving a quick tour of the familiar Great Lakes and the trading routes to the Great Slave Lake. At the Great Slave Lake, Pond's geography slipped from reality to illusion. He confidently reported that a great river ran out of the Great Slave Lake, striking southwest toward the Pacific. Pond was equally confident and mistaken about the extent of the Rocky Mountains. He claimed that the chain stopped abruptly south of his great river, which was thus allowed to freely join Cook's River. Here was an inland, ice-free Northwest Passage destined to bring sixteenth-century dreams of the China trade once again to cities on the Saint Lawrence.

The discussions with Isaac Ogden were more than mere classroom exercises. Pond always intended his discoveries and speculations to have both commercial and national applications. He certainly believed his Pacific route would bring wealth and power to any who ventured it. Such a water passage might easily shape the destiny of the entire Northwest. Pond conjured up an empire populated by more than fur merchants and their native partners. This West, so he claimed, had a rich agricultural future once farmers settled on the fertile lands of Athabasca. Pelts, grain, tea, and silk—all these would flow through a West linked to Montreal on the one hand and China on the other. And all these economic wonders would be under the protection of an expanding British empire. Pond ended this lesson on a tantalizing note. He told Ogden that Alexander Mackenzie was already exploring the Cook's River route and would soon be in London by way of Russia. Still unaware of Mackenzie's discovery that his river went north instead of west, Pond dreamed with all the confidence of any visionary.[18]

Isaac Ogden was not the first to be captivated by Pond's stories. The merchant described the trader as a "Gentleman of observation and Science" and carefully recorded their conversations in a long letter to his father in London. Enclosed in that letter was a redrawing of Pond's 1787 map. In this version, wish became fact as a misdirected Mackenzie River directly joined Cook's River. Both the letter and the map were published in the March 1790 issue of the popular *Gentleman's Magazine* of London. And as fortune would have it, Pond's notions caught the attention of government officials planning Captain George Vancouver's expedition to the Northwest coast. Despite the news, already current in London, of Mackenzie's initial failure, Pond's optimistic geography carried the day. Vancouver was instructed to seek out Cook's River and evaluate its economic and imperial potential.[19]

Nor was Isaac Ogden the only Quebecker taken with Pond's rough charm and appealing ideas. The trader caught the attention of Dr. John Mervin Nooth, a respected physician with an abiding interest in natural history. Nooth corresponded regularly with Sir Joseph Banks, who had been deeply involved in the Cook voyages and eagerly collected any scrap of information about possible northwest passages. Nooth was certain that Banks would want to hear about that "very singular Person of the name of Pond" who had just come to Quebec. Pond repeated the now-familiar Cook's River tale, adding for Nooth some vague stories about new animals and unusual fossils to be found in the Northwest. Pond had no specimens to contribute to Nooth's natural history cabinet, but there was his map, probably the same one he showed to Ogden. The talk and the map were enough for Nooth. He was persuaded that exploring the Cook's River passage would reap an important scientific harvest.[20]

Water connections to the Pacific, dreams of China, trading posts stretching across the Northwest, and money from a national treasury—these were the fundamentals of Pond's imperial geography. They were also the roots of Astoria. Pond's theories first took form in Alexander Mackenzie's voyages of discovery to the Arctic Ocean in 1789 and to the Pacific in 1792–93. Although Mackenzie later did what he could to traduce Pond's reputation, there can be no doubt that the old Yankee trader was what Lieutenant Governor Hamilton called him—a man filled with "a passion for making discoveries." It was Pond's passion that would inspire both the North West Company's Columbian Enterprise and Astor's Pacific Fur Company. Rivals for western domain, both sprang from common ground.

Pond's influence was plain in September 1794 when Mackenzie was returning from his epic trek to the Pacific. Meeting with Lieutenant Governor John Graves Simcoe at Niagara, the explorer presented a grand program aimed at "the entire command of the fur trade of North America." Like his teacher, Mackenzie knew that the plan meant playing for high stakes in an imperial contest. If Pond outlined the grand strategy, Mackenzie filled in the tactical details. Both agreed that Britain had to field a single government-funded company to meet Russian and American competition. Pond thought in terms of money channeled directly to the North West Company. Mackenzie advanced a bolder plan, the kind of scheme that would have appealed to Astor: he proposed the merger of the North West Company and the Hudson's Bay Company. As he saw it, the new conglomerate would be blessed with abundant capital and unrivaled power. Furs from the Northwest would move swiftly to Pacific coast ports along an efficient transport system based at Hudson Bay, not at the American-dominated Great Lakes. One post would be established at Cook's River and a second somewhere to the south. Years

Peter Pond's map of
the Northwest, 1790.
Gentleman's Magazine,
March 1790.
Collection of the
author.

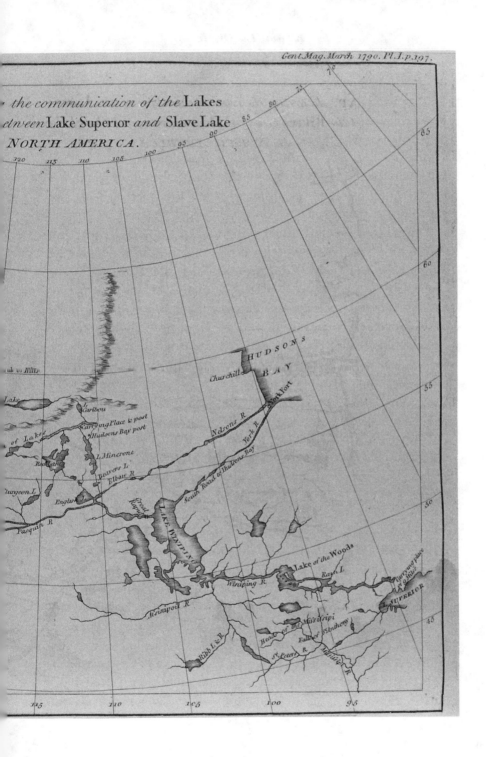

the communication of the Lakes

etween Lake Superior and Slave Lake

NORTH AMERICA.

120 115 110 105 100 95 90 85 80 75 70

65

60

55

50

45

HUDSONS

BAY

Churchill

York Fort

Caribou

Carrying Place & post

Hudsons Bay post

L. Mincrent

Beavers L.

Elbow R.

Red Lake

Sturgeon L.

English

Pasquin R.

Great Rapids

LAKE WINNIPING

Nelsons R.

York R.

South Road to Hudsons Bay

Lake of the Woods

Rain L.

Winnipeg R.

Carrying place of Miss.

SUPERIOR

Sisinapoil R.

Ribb L. & R.

Head of the Missisipi

Falls of St Anthony

St Peters R.

Ouisconsin R.

115 110 105 100 95

later Mackenzie selected a site at the mouth of the Columbia for that
second trading house. Also like Pond, Mackenzie was dazzled by the
prospect of bumper profits in the Canton market. But as Canadian
fur merchants knew all too well, the British East India Company
held a monopoly on the China trade. And without the promise of
China, the fur trade of the Northwest had little attraction. Mackenzie doubted that the company's monopoly would soon end, but
he did hope to secure a permit to bring furs directly from the
Northwest to Canton.[21]

Throughout the next fifteen years Mackenzie stalked the grand
design he called "my favorite project." In petition after petition, he
sought crown support for ventures variously called the Columbian
Enterprise or the Fishery and Fur Company. Whatever corporate
name it bore, the message was the same. Exploration of the Northwest would swell Britain's treasury, defeat her rivals, and extend the
empire. Mackenzie's petitions were like those of Richard Hakluyt in
the days of the first Elizabeth. Both men rang the changes of empire,
promising a new world in the West. For Mackenzie the results were
always the same. He received polite hearings at the Colonial Office
in London but never saw his words become action.[22]

Even though the Mackenzie project gained no official approval, it
did eventually become part of the North West Company's strategy
for expansion west of the Rockies. Partners in the company and
agents from the London supply houses that stood behind the traders had long wanted to break into the Northwest coast fur trade and
the China market. But government restrictions and the British East
India Company monopoly had shut the Nor'westers out. Even if
deception was involved, Montreal was bent on having a share of the
China bonanza. Sometime in 1792 the company hatched a scheme
to use American ships in the China trade. These vessels, manned by
American crews and sailing with United States registration papers,
would be immune from British regulation. The plan may have been
the brainchild of Alexander Henry, an associate of Pond's and sometime business partner with Astor. By December 1792 Henry reported to Canton merchants Hamilton and Reid that two American

Sir Alexander Mackenzie. Courtesy of the Public Archives of
Canada, Ottawa, c 1348.

ships in the covert employ of the North West Company were set to
leave New York in early spring 1794.[23]

Despite these careful plans, the Nor'wester maritime venture was
not especially successful. The Canton fur market was wildly unpredictable. Sudden changes in American citizenship laws in 1795
made the entire scheme less attractive. By 1795 James Hallowell, a
company agent, was suggesting the need for a full-fledged Ameri-

can partner. That partner might have been John Astor had he not been in Europe. As it was, Hallowell urged that no further action be taken until Astor returned and the company could benefit from his expert advice.[24] Despite setbacks and losses, the North West Company continued to seek American means to crack the China market. Early in 1798 Alexander Mackenzie traveled first to New York and then to Philadelphia to purchase an American ship. When the London supply agents heard that the company was persisting in the venture, they urged that all maritime efforts cease. McTavish, Fraser, and Company of London put it bluntly enough: "We can see no prospect of certainty in markets or safety in remittances."[25]

Thwarted in their efforts to develop an oceangoing route to the Northwest and China, the company turned back to plans laid by Pond and Mackenzie. More than anyone else, it was Duncan McGillivray who championed further exploration after Mackenzie left the concern in 1799. McGillivray had been a mere clerk with the company when Mackenzie had first proposed his Pacific plans. But even then he had seen the value of uniting the North West Company and the Hudson's Bay Company for the "general utility" of both.[26]

McGillivray was no easy-chair visionary. By 1800 he had become a partner with enough influence to promote and organize western expeditions. The first of those probes came in 1800. When the company's partners held their annual meeting in midsummer, McGillivray evidently proposed an expedition to locate a route to the Pacific more southerly than that blazed by Mackenzie. Although minutes for that meeting have not survived, David Thompson's journal records, "Mr. Duncan McGillivray was to be early at Rocky Mountain House, about the latter end of September 1800, to prepare for crossing the mountains, proceeding to the Pacific Ocean, the next year." Rocky Mountain House was an ideal base for the North West Company's expeditions. Built in 1799 to forestall competition with the Hudson's Bay Company for the Piegan Blackfeet trade, the post was situated on the banks of the North Saskatchewan River west of modern-day Edmonton. Despite its name, the post was more than sixty miles from the mountains. It was from Rocky Mountain House that McGillivray launched his search for a pass across the mountains to the Pacific and its China trade.[27]

Although the major push to the Pacific would not come until 1801, McGillivray decided in early November 1800 that a preliminary reconnaissance was needed. David Thompson had just returned to Rocky Mountain House from travels along the Red Deer River at the foothills of the Rockies. From Indian information Thompson surmised that a pass might be found southwest of the post. He evidently convinced McGillivray that this pass might lead directly to the upper reaches of the Columbia River. No such pass exists, but McGillivray accepted Thompson's advice. Taking Thompson and four other men, he set off southwest along a trail beside the Clearwater River. The party crossed the Red Deer River and by the end of November camped at Bow River near present-day Calgary. Stretching to the west was what seemed to Thompson an ocean of snow-covered mountains. Finding any opening through that barrier in the winter would have been impossible. McGillivray was already suffering from exposure and rheumatism when the disgruntled explorers straggled back to Rocky Mountain House in the first week of December.[28]

Despite this initial disappointment, McGillivray remained convinced that a track could be found through the mountains to the upper Columbia. But the 1800 misadventure had broken his health. By spring he could barely hobble about on crutches. It was plain that any exploring would have to be led by an abler man. Yet David Thompson, who later became Canada's premier explorer, was not chosen for the task. Instead, the leadership went to James Hughes, a company partner. Thompson would go along, but only as the second-in-command. Disillusioned about finding any pass southwest of Rocky Mountain House, McGillivray settled on following the North Saskatchewan to its source. Both Thompson and McGillivray expected the portage to Pacific waters to be short and easy.

Hughes, Thompson, seven company men, and a Cree guide named Rook left Rocky Mountain House on June 6. Rook claimed that horses could manage the mountain trails and passes without difficulty. But from the beginning the venture was beset by troubles. The explorers' horses, struggling under heavy packs of trade goods, slipped and sank in the swampy muskeg. Rook proved worthless as a guide. By June 9 the expedition was at the junction of the Saskatchewan and North Ram rivers. Here the party followed one of the branches of the Ram west toward the mountains. Rain and cold continued to impede their progress. In the increasingly broken ground, sharp rocks cut the men's feet and crippled their horses. Reaching higher elevations on June 13, the expedition found snowbanks sometimes waist high. Furious that Rook had not warned them of the difficulties in bringing horses over such a trail, they decided there could be no other course but to turn back. But Hughes and Thompson were not about to abandon the enterprise. By June 23 the explorers were back on the North Saskatchewan. Thompson thought that the river might be navigable; what could not be accomplished on horseback might be done by canoe. That strategy was destined to fail. Swelled by the spring snowmelt, the Saskatchewan was too fast and dangerous, no matter how sturdy the canoe and its paddlers. Blocked at every hand, the expedition returned to Rocky Mountain House.[29]

What seemed abject failure had important lessons. In his report "An Attempt to Cross the Rocky Mountains . . . in order to Penetrate to the Pacific Ocean," Thompson was quick to point them out. He had no doubt that the goal was both desirable and feasible. What was needed was better planning and a new route. The expedition, he noted, "has taught us to make a better choice of our men, and take fewer of them, and never employ an Indian of this side of the mountain for our guide." Thompson suggested that canoes provided more reliable transport than horses. Finally, there were the all-important questions of route and schedule. Experience now suggested that the best time to start was in May, well before the mountain snowmelt made rivers treacherous. And the best route traced the North Saskatchewan to its head, "from whence there is said to be a short Road to the Waters which flow on the other Side of the Mountains."[30]

Thompson's analysis of problems and solutions was remarkably accurate. With a little luck the North West Company could have had men and posts across the mountains well before Thomas Jefferson wrote instructions for Meriwether Lewis. But good fortune eluded the Nor'westers. From 1802 to 1804, crucial years in the exploration of the Far West, the company abandoned its search for Pacific waters. Rocky Mountain House was temporarily closed and Thompson assigned other duties. These decisions did not reflect any change in Duncan McGillivray's determination to follow in the tracks of Pond and Mackenzie. But the company was caught up in a ferocious trade war. When Mackenzie left the North West Company in 1799 he founded his own firm, the New North West, or XY, Company. By 1801 the former partners were locked in fierce competition. The sleeping giant, the Hudson's Bay Company, was also fully aroused and was intent on defeating all the "pedlars from Quebec" no matter what company employed them.[31] Men, money, and supplies that might have been used to push beyond Rocky Mountain House all went to the war with more-eastern enemies. At the very time Lewis and Clark were preparing to explore land and water routes to the Pacific, the Canadians temporarily lost the initiative.

Whatever the many successes of Lewis and Clark, their journey to Fort Clatsop did not ensure American dominion along the Columbia. The North West Company still had telling advantages in experienced men, well-located posts, and a vast store of wilderness knowledge. With the union of the XY and North West companies in 1804, some of the fury in the trade war subsided. Once again the Nor'westers could pick up the Pacific challenge. In the next four years the company sent two of its most skilled frontiersmen across the mountains to reestablish British primacy in the Northwest.

When the North West Company's partners met at Fort William in July 1805, they may well have known about Jefferson's westering captains. That unwelcome news and a trading world less splintered by murderous rivalries evidently convinced the company to resume what was now a twenty-year-old project. Records for this meeting have not survived, so it is unclear just how the decision was made. It

is likely that sometime in July the company drafted instructions to
seek the most practical water route to the Pacific. But those instructions contained a crucial misconception. From the time of Alexander Mackenzie, western geographers had confused two great
rivers. The Columbia and the Fraser had roughly parallel courses,
but only the Columbia was navigable to the sea. Any canoes surviving the boiling, churning white water of the Fraser would still be far
from the Pacific.[32]

The trader selected to lead the company's renewed Pacific enterprise was Simon Fraser. Fraser had been with the company as a clerk
since the 1790s and had become a partner in 1801. Young, energetic, and determined, he was a wise choice for what the company
hoped would be its most successful western venture. By August
1805 Fraser was heading west for three years of exploration beyond
the mountains. His plan was to build a series of staging posts and
eventually a major entrepôt on the upper reaches of the Columbia.
In 1807 Fraser and his men put up Fort George at the junction of the
Nechako and Fraser rivers. At the end of May 1808, convinced that
the river that now bears his name was the Columbia, Fraser and
twenty-four men set off downriver to the Pacific. Few rivers in North
America demand more from men and canoes. Steep banks, swift
currents, and miles of terrifying white water severely tested the skill
and nerve of expedition members. Fraser put it bluntly in his journal
entry for June 26, 1808: "I have been for a long period among the
Rocky Mountains, but have never seen any thing equal to this country, for I cannot find words to describe our situation at times. We had
to pass where no human being should venture."[33]

In all those days of harrowing adventure, Fraser never lost sight
of his mission. When Indians suggested a quicker overland route to
the sea, he rejected their advice. As he noted, "Going to the Sea by an
indirect way was not the object of the undertaking." In the first week
of July the expedition was at Musqueam on the Strait of Georgia
opposite Vancouver Island. Here at last Fraser realized that the river
he and his men had braved was not the Columbia. At Musqueam
they were still more than 140 miles from Cape Flattery and the open

sea. Exhausted and confronted with growing Indian hostility, Fraser decided to retrace his steps to Fort George. The journal entry for July 3 captures all his emotion. "Here I must again acknowledge my great disappointment in not seeing the *main* ocean, having gone so near it as to be almost within view." Fraser's river gave Simon and his men a great tale to tell, but the waterway was useless as a route for commerce or a path to empire. Fraser had expanded geographic horizons, but the Nor'westers still lacked their house with a Pacific view.[34]

None of these disappointments were known at Fort William or in the Montreal countinghouses. Confident that Fraser would find a Columbia passage to the sea, the company prepared to send David Thompson to again search out mountain passes west of Rocky Mountain House. Using that post on the North Saskatchewan as his base, Thompson planned an exploring program that would occupy the next six years of his life. By the end of 1811 he not only had discovered two important passes (Howse and Athabasca) but also had comprehended the intricate nature of the upper Columbia. Thompson began his drive to the sea in 1806 by sending Jaco Finley west from Rocky Mountain House to blaze horse trails in what is now Banff National Park. Finley did his work well. In late June 1807 Thompson's expedition reached Howse Pass in the Canadian Rockies. It was a moment he had been waiting for since those early days with James Hughes and Duncan McGillivray. Howse Pass, some eighty miles northwest of present-day Banff, Alberta, was the gateway to the upper Columbia River. As viewed from Rocky Mountain House, the mountains had once been a hazy, distant barrier. Now that barrier had been cracked and the Pacific lay open for the empire of John Bull. On June 30, near what is today Golden, British Columbia, the expedition came upon the Columbia River. Uncertain of the river's true character, Thompson named it the Kootenay. Later in the summer his party went by canoe to Lake Windermere, there to build Kootenay House.[35] With both Thompson and Fraser seeming to converge on the Pacific, the Nor'westers appeared ready to challenge any American advance. But David Thompson did not get to the Pacific until 1811. When he finally did, he was a guest of Astor's men at Astoria.

Just before his death in 1808, Duncan McGillivray began to gather materials for what would become an important company pamphlet. Titling his thoughts "Some Account of the Trade carried on by the North West Company," McGillivray surveyed the history of the Canadian fur trade and its current troubles with American competitors. He was certain that a company-crown partnership in the West would breathe new life into both the company and the empire. "That the spirit of commerce is fertile in expedient and unwearied in pursuit of new sources of wealth, is fully exemplified in the labours of the North West Company. Not satisfied with the immense region on the eastern side of the Rocky Mountains throughout which their trade is established; they have commenced a project for extending their researches and trade as far as the South sea; and have already introduced British manufactured goods, among the natives on the Western side of the Rocky Mountains; intending at some future period to form a general establishment for the trade of that country on the Columbia river, which, as has been already observed, receives and conducts to the Ocean all the waters that rise West of the Mountains." But such an ambitious enterprise could not be mounted by a single company. "All this," McGillivray concluded, "cannot be accomplished without the aid of the British Government."[36] How could an empire be fashioned beyond the Great Divide? It was no coincidence that in 1808 both Duncan McGillivray and John Astor asked that question and came up with the same answer.

* * *

In all this it is easy to lose track of John Jacob Astor and his Pacific Fur Company. But the path from New York to Montreal runs straight and true. The New York merchant had long done business in Montreal. Astor may have made his first fur-buying trip to the city in the fall of 1787; he was certainly there the following year. From then on Astor became a regular part of the Montreal business world, traveling to the city each fall to purchase skins and pelts. Business and social life blended easily in Montreal. Astor, who sometimes brought his family on these journeys, soon enjoyed invitations to dine with prominent members of the North West Company. One of his hosts was Joseph Frobisher, a partner with Peter Pond and a founding Nor'wester. Opportunities to attend gala dinners of the Beaver Club soon followed.[37] Astor was so fully accepted in Montreal fur trade society that when the North West Company was desperately seeking ways to circumvent the East India Company's monopoly in China, he was considered for partnership in the concern. By the same token, at least once in 1798 Mackenzie and Astor had commercial and social dealings in New York. At a time when Montreal and its merchants were filled with talk about the Rocky Mountains, western rivers, and the Northwest-coast-to-China trade, Astor was there to hear it all. He could not escape an atmosphere so charged with the exciting visions of Pond, Mackenzie, and McGillivray.[38]

The business and social contacts Astor made in Montreal were essential to the genealogy of the Pacific Fur Company. Talk in the Frobisher dining room or at the Beaver Club amounted to Astor's education in fur trade geography and strategy. He could not have gone to a better place for his studies. But no matter how important the Montreal climate of opinion, it was not the most powerful influence on Astor's western enterprise. That influence came in the person of Alexander Henry the elder. Like Peter Pond, Henry was an expatriate American. He was born in New Jersey in 1739, but beyond the fact that he received a sound education and had some early business dealings in Albany, little is known of his early years. In 1760, at the end of the Seven Years' War, Henry joined British forces bound for Canada. His was no dream of military glory. Instead, he hoped to gain entrance to the western fur business, long a French trading sphere. For the next sixteen years Henry was one of the "pedlars from Quebec," searching out new fur regions and challenging the Hudson's Bay Company at every river bend. He traveled with Peter Pond and shared winter quarters with Joseph and Thomas Frobisher. Henry recounted these dramatic times in his

Alexander Henry the Elder. From Henry, *Travels and Adventures*
(1809). Collection of the author.

*Travels and Adventures in Canada and the Indian Territories between the
Years 1760 and 1776.*[39]

Alexander Henry was more than an itinerant trader who happened to write an engaging book about his exploits. Like Pond,
Henry became both fur trade strategist and student of western

geography. His earliest thoughts on those subjects were recorded in July 1776 as he and his partners prepared to leave their Beaver Lake trading post. From talks with Chipewyan Indians, Henry had begun to formulate a picture of the relationship among western lakes and rivers, the Rockies, and the Pacific Ocean. As he understood it from Indian sources, Lake Athabasca was the heart of a river system that ran to the eastern face of the mountains. He was told that the distance between the mountains and the ocean was "not great."[40] Henry was in no position to follow up this piece of conjecture, but the image of rivers, mountains, and an ocean temptingly close would remain.

In the fall of 1776 Henry left the Northwest fur trade for the quieter life of a Montreal businessman. Those business dealings eventually led him to make three journeys to England. It was on his final trip (1780–81) that Henry met Sir Joseph Banks. Described by one English explorer as "the common Center of we discoverers," Banks was a gifted naturalist and geographer.[41] More important, he was the most prominent scientist associated with Cook's voyages.

Henry came to a London filled with news about Cook's final voyage. The expedition had returned in October 1780 and first accounts were being rushed to press the next year. Although Cook's tragic death in Hawaii got considerable attention, the geographic and scientific discoveries were not forgotten. Sometime in March 1781, just before leaving England, Henry had a brief meeting with Banks. Daniel Solander, botanist on Cook's first voyage and Keeper of the British Museum's Natural History Department, may have been present as well. Banks and Solander were already busy studying Cook artifacts, including those gathered on the Northwest coast. Like many other visitors to Banks's Soho Square residence, Henry saw a crowded library and an impressive array of natural history specimens. Among the objects were several knives collected at Cook's River. Those blades captured Henry's attention. He insisted he recognized them as trade goods given to Indians around Lake Athabasca. That they had gotten to Cook's River seemed to prove the existence of a water passage from the interior lakes to the Pacific.

Writing to Banks on the eve of his departure for Canada, Henry volunteered to lead an expedition charting the imagined passage. He also left Banks and Solander a preliminary "Sketch of My Travels" and would later dedicate his *Travels and Adventures* to Banks. Henry left England filled with the exciting commercial and national possibilities offered by Cook's illusory river.[42]

When Henry returned to Montreal in the spring of 1781 he began to formulate plans for such a western trek. Those plans must have been refined and advanced by talks with Peter Pond when the trader came east that summer. By October Henry was ready to offer Banks a comprehensive exploration program. He proposed probing the rivers running out of Lake Athabasca, for he was certain that one would connect with Cook's River. Knowing Banks's interest in the economics of empire, Henry claimed that such a venture would "fetch large Profits & a Valuable New Commerce." Henry's letter contained precise travel instructions and a careful estimate of both the cost and the personnel needed for such a reconnaissance. Reflecting the information picked up from Indians at Beaver Lake years before, he predicted that once on a river out of Lake Athabasca, travelers would not "be any very great distance to the Pacific."[43]

Drawing on common sources for inspiration and information, Henry and Pond developed similar ideas and strategies. In 1785, the same year Pond was busy selling his dreams in New York and Montreal, Henry was detailing what he called "my scheme for the Northwest Coast of America." Writing to William Edgar, a New York businessman, he claimed that trade with China from the mouth of Cook's River would "receive more profits than from all the upper posts." Edgar, who later became an associate of Astor's in the American Fur Company, had been preparing to invest in shipping ventures to China. Henry counseled patience, saying his plans would be less costly and ultimately more profitable. A year later he was prepared to spell out the specifics. What had been a simple proposal for exploration in 1781 had now matured into something much more ambitious. Again writing to Edgar, Henry suggested building a chain of posts, positioned to dominate trade, all along the Northwest coast. The Cook's River inland passage would make all this possible and profitable. "I make no doubt," he explained, "but Cook's River has a communication with those parts of the Northwest I was at, by which a road would be opened across the continent." Even after leaving the active trader life, Henry never lost that vision of a road across the continent. It was a vision he would pass on to a new business partner from New York.[44]

Alexander Henry was the personal and intellectual connection between the world of Canadian exploration and John Jacob Astor. As an outsider struggling to do business in Montreal, Astor needed an agent and friend. How Astor and Henry met is not known. They may have been introduced by William Edgar. However the link was forged, Astor and Henry were doing business as early as August 1790. Just how quickly the two men became both friends and associates can be judged by the fact that Astor often stayed at Henry's home on Notre Dame Street when visiting the city. By 1800 Henry described their relationship as a partnership.[45] The two shared profits and projects. It was Henry who introduced Astor to Montreal society and to the fur trade projects that had captured the imaginations of so many in the city. Writing in the mid-1790s, Henry was plain about his dealings with Astor. "Him [Astor] and me has been considerably connected in the fur and China trade this several years."[46] The roots of Astoria ran from Pond and Mackenzie through Henry to finally reach Astor himself.

* * *

The northern lineage was surely Astoria's main branch, but Astor's plans also drew strength from sources more remote. The influence of the Lewis and Clark expedition has often been overstated, but the accomplishments of the two explorers did not go unnoticed in New York. Although the connection from Astor to the captains was not as direct as that to Montreal, it was plainly important.

When Thomas Jefferson read Alexander Mackenzie's *Voyages from Montreal* late in 1802, he was undoubtedly struck by the explorer's enthusiasm for commerce on the Columbia River. "Whatever course may be taken from the Atlantic," argued Mackenzie, "the Columbia is the line of communication from the Pacific Ocean, pointed out by nature." The essential Pond-Henry-Mackenzie theme was unmistakable: "By opening this intercourse between the Atlantic and Pacific Oceans, and forming regular establishments through the interior, and at both extremes, as well as along the coasts and islands, the entire command of the fur trade might be obtained." As Donald Jackson has written, those words "jolted Jefferson back into thinking in terms of hemispheric geography."[47] These ideas triggered a set of decisions that culminated the next year in Jefferson's instructions to Meriwether Lewis. Jefferson's explorers were directed to find an American version of Cook's River, what the president termed "the most direct & practicable water communication across this continent for the purpose of commerce." But unlike his Canadian competitors, Jefferson did not propose a permanent post west of the Rockies. Instead, he placed highest priority on fashioning a St. Louis–based, Missouri River trade system. Jefferson assumed that such a system would draw furs away from the Pacific coast. Hence Lewis and Clark were ordered to find a trading house location somewhere near the headwaters of the Missouri.[48]

Though the captains surveyed trading sites along the Missouri, once on the Columbia they could not fail to see the significance of that river. On his return in 1806, Lewis proposed an American trade empire that differed markedly from Jefferson's original version. The expedition had not found the president's desired "water communication," and the northern Rockies route was neither "direct" nor "practicable." "Still," argued Lewis, "we believe that many articles not bulky brittle nor of a very perishable nature may be conveyed to the United States by this rout with more facility than that at present practical." Without abandoning Jefferson's Missouri River plan, Lewis proposed something more ambitious: a major post on the Columbia. Furs from interior trading houses would be carried to the Columbia River entrepôt no later than August of each year, then shipped directly to Canton. Lewis maintained that the plan would preempt any initiative of the North West Company by giving the United States direct access to the China market. He recognized that the size and complexity of the task required government subsidies but felt certain the financial and political returns would more than justify the expense.[49] Once back in Washington, Lewis went so far as to declare that "the signal Advantage" of the entire expedition "would be the establishment of a trading post at the mouth of the Columbia River, for expediting the commerce in furs to China."[50]

Meriwether Lewis's objectives were much like those of Pond, Henry, and Mackenzie. But in the genealogy of Astoria his proposals mattered little. Lewis's plans were destined for Jefferson alone. A shorter version of the 1806 report, drafted by Lewis but bearing Clark's name, was written expressly for publication. It discussed the possibility of a Columbia River post, suggested a schedule for fur collection from interior houses, and pointed to great profits in the China trade. By early November 1806 the letter had been reprinted not only in western newspapers but in the *National Intelligencer* and the *New York Post* as well.[51] Whether Astor learned about Lewis's plans through such accounts is unknown. He surely knew about the Lewis and Clark overland route but was apparently unaware of Lewis's doubts about its commercial value. In the end, the Lewis and Clark expedition neither created Astoria nor offered Astor any major ideas. Perhaps the relationship was more subtle, something like a catalytic reaction. The expedition may have crystallized thoughts and plans Astor already had developed from talks with Henry and the Montreal Nor'westers. The example of one already successful American endeavor must have made a mark on Astor. Lewis and Clark's journey may have encouraged him to take those Pond-Henry-Mackenzie ideas and test them in his own imperial adventure.

*   *   *

Astoria also had saltwater roots. Astor lived in a world of ship captains and sailors' lore. His commercial life was tied together by the barks and brigantines that plied the trades to Liverpool, Amsterdam, and Canton. Some of Astor's most trusted agents were men like John Ebbets and William Pigot, sailing masters in a wider world. Much of what Astor knew about the Northwest coast and the China trade came from such men. The talk at New York's popular Tontine Coffee House and dockside gossip about the coast and its peoples would not have escaped him. Nor'westers taught Astor fur trade routes and ways, but sailors gave him a Pacific geography.

Two facts of American maritime history shaped Astoria well before Astor began his western plans. In 1784 Philadelphia merchants led by the financier Robert Morris sent the first American ship to China. The *Empress of China* took the lead in what would soon become a great fleet of Yankee ships calling at Canton. Morris hailed this commercial advance, saying it had "opened new objects to all America."[52] And he was right. Goods from China—tea, textiles, and porcelain—soon became an American rage. From architecture to fashion, the influence of China was everywhere. When the Boston merchant Joseph Barrell and his partners sent the *Columbia* and the *Lady Washington* to the Northwest and China in 1787, Americans became part of a trade with fabulous prospects. Each leg of a Pacific voyage—trade goods for the Northwest, furs for China, and Chinese items for American customers—promised immense profits. By the 1790s merchants and captains in nearly every American port were talking about soft gold, the sea otter pelts that might command high prices in Canton. Captain Joseph Ingraham, master of the brigantine *Hope*, summed it up with nautical precision. "The trade to China from the N.W. being lucrative and in its infancy, it was not long neglected."[53] A popular sailor ballad echoed Ingraham's words:

> Come all ye bold Northwest men,
> That plough the raging main,
> Into some foreign country,
> Your fortune for to gain.[54]

But if songs, stories, and shipping reports attracted Astor to the coastal fur trade and China, those same sources warned him of the hazards in the business. Commercial dealings in Canton, the only port open to foreigners, posed enormous difficulties. The Chinese imperial customs bureaucracy moved slowly, and all negotiations had to pass through approved interpreters. Patience and judicious payments were essential for success.[55] But the most serious problem was the market itself. The Canton fur market was notoriously unstable. When Thomas Randall, a resident merchant, appraised the market in August 1791, he found the demand for sea otters and other skins "very great." But by the time Joseph Ingraham got to Canton five months later, all was changed. The American captain found four other ships fresh from the Northwest. He estimated that at the end of 1791 Canton warehouses were filled to overflowing with between seven to eleven thousand sea otter pelts, far in excess of anything the Chinese luxury market could absorb. When young John Boit brought his tiny sloop *Union* to China in late 1795 he reported, "Sea otter skins fell 100 dollars in value since I was here in the *Columbia* [1792] which is a disasterous circumstance to my voyage." Boit was eventually able to sell his cargo, but his jaunty log entry "fortune is fickle" would not have pleased an owner like John Astor.[56]

The Northwest coast itself taught stern lessons that kept their force even when learned secondhand. Astor must have heard the one told of native people and their shrewd trading ways. Coastal people had quickly learned to judge the quality and utility of goods offered for skins. Bargaining skills were sharpened long before the first tall ships came to call. William Bayly, astronomer for Captain Cook, found Indians to be "very keen traders getting as much as they could for everything they had; always asking for more give them what you would." Alexander Walker, a participant in one of the earliest fur voyages to the coast, witnessed the transformation of the natives' taste in goods. On the first trading day, Indians were so anxious for European goods that they offered everything for sale. But on the second day, with curiosity satisfied, the same people were interested only in functional iron and copper. Yet on both days, with such seemingly different economic agendas, the rituals of trade were the same. "They would not part with any thing out of their hands, before they had received an equivalent; they never forgot to examine carefully our goods. Nor were they contented with their own opinion alone, but handing our goods to their friends, consulted with them respecting their quality, and what they should give in return." It was the Yankee skipper Joseph Ingraham who put it best: the people of the coast had "a truly mercantile spirit."[57]

But the mercantile spirit that bound together both sets of traders sometimes brought sailors and Indians to grief. Because captains in the maritime fur trade believed they could easily escape the consequences, they often used unbridled terror to make favorable bargains. Violence bred violence, and some ships and crews fell victim to attack by Indians. The popular ballad "Bold Northwestmen" recounts an attempt by Indians at the Queen Charlotte Islands to seize the brig *Lady Washington*. This was no random fury but an effort to take revenge for unprovoked assaults on two chiefs. The attack failed and the song drew a lesson many in the trade wanted to believe.

> I'd have you all take warning and always ready be,
> For to suppress those savages of Northwest America;
> For they are so desirous some vessel for to gain,
> That they will never leave off, till most of them are slain.[58]

Astor may not have heard that particular piece of sailor wisdom but he did attend to its lesson. In a letter to Captain Jonathan Thorn of the *Tonquin* on the eve of her sailing, Astor warned the master of danger from Indians along the coast. It was a warning the arrogant Thorn evidently ignored, with terrible consequences the next year. The potential for attack was great, and one captain complained, "To be constantly on guard against the treachery of the savages is as disagreeable a situation as I can conceive of."[59] In virtually every case, attacks by natives were prompted by the traders' violence against Indians. One Indian put it simply. "Others come, kill us, and take our property by force; you came, bartered with us, and hurt not a man. You are good."[60]

Not every tale from the coast was a cautionary one. Sailors also had much to teach Astor about the physical and economic geography of the Northwest. Journals and logs of the period are rich in speculation about rivers that might join Pacific waters to Atlantic tides. Robert Haswell, second officer on the *Columbia* for her first Northwest voyage, had evidently heard about a fixture in Far Western geography, the River of the West. When the *Columbia* was at Tillamook Bay on the Oregon coast in August 1788, Haswell imagined that the bay was "the enterence of the river of the West." He continued his geographic theorizing the following summer when the *Columbia* was much farther up the coast, near the Queen Charlotte Islands. Struck by the number of rivers along the coast, Haswell noted, "[Some] may overlap the western bounds of the Lakes that have their vent in our Eastern coast and perhaps Lakes are now discovered that is the source of Large navagable Rivers that emty themselves in the North Pacific Ocean." These arresting lines suggest that Pond and Henry were not alone in their Pacific visions. And like them, Haswell recognized that Pacific exploration would ultimately be a national enterprise.[61]

These same sailor-geographers had also thought about suitable locations for trading houses and settlements. John Kendrick, captain of the *Columbia* on her first voyage, had orders to purchase land on the coast for "a fort or improvement."[62] More elaborate plans were given to James Colnett, the British captain of the *Argonaut*, when he took the ship to the Northwest in 1789. The South Seas Company, backer of the venture, envisioned a "solid establishment" with both English and Chinese employees busy on company time. But it was eighteen-year-old John Boit, then fifth mate on the *Columbia*, who saw the future most clearly. In May 1792 the *Columbia* was anchored in its namesake river, not far from the future site of Astoria. Boit studied the river, noted its resources, and watched the Chinook Indians busily trading alongside the vessel. "This river in my opinion," he asserted, "would be a fine place for a factory." With a post on the Columbia River and one farther north, merchants and their ships could "engross the whole trade of the Northwest Coast." When John Astor wrote De Witt Clinton almost twenty years later proposing what would become Astoria and the Pacific Fur Company, he came to the same conclusions. But John Boit of Boston had already been there.[63]

Alexander Ross, one of the Pacific Fur Company's clerks at Astoria, once wrote that Astor possessed a "comprehensive mind."[64] Ross meant that Astor could see pattern and unity in apparent diversity. What Astor comprehended, what he drew to focus on in his own enterprise, were the visions of others. Pond, Henry, and Mackenzie—their hopes and designs were ones that Astor would have quickly recognized. Their plans provided the form and substance for Astoria. But Astoria exhibited nuances, builder's touches, that not even its architect would have recognized. These came from men like John Boit and Meriwether Lewis. Astoria grew out of the hopes of others. Yet those prospects and hopes needed energy and direction to succeed. Astor never kept company with dreamers, but he freely borrowed from them.

2

Planning Astoria

JOHN ASTOR KNEW what separated a fanciful scheme from a successful venture. He believed the difference was not so much the vision as the astute planning behind each. And though every New York merchant agreed that some planning was essential for commercial success, few made such relentless calculations as Astor. Whether in furs, shipping, or real estate, he ran his affairs with a unique combination of thoughtful caution and stunning audacity.

No enterprise demanded more thorough preparation than the Pacific venture. Astor knew that he would be playing on a very large field for immense stakes. The undertaking required constant attention to detail. And there were bound to be many details. He had to find reliable field agents, recruit seasoned traders, purchase large stores of trade goods, and negotiate for maritime transport to the Northwest coast. All this called for the careful application of the business techniques that had been an Astor hallmark for many years. But these tasks did not by themselves involve something new for the entrepreneur. Astoria would also demand a deft political touch.

Astor understood that his proposals were as much political as commercial. Astoria pushed and shoved its way into the kingdom of politics, both national and international. Like Jefferson, Astor quickly grasped the connection between trade and empire, personal profit and national sovereignty. From Peter Pond to Alexander Henry, all Astoria's prophets agreed that the enterprise could not succeed without firm support from a national government. Gaining such support had eluded even so celebrated an explorer as Sir Alexander Mackenzie. Astor was determined to win some official backing. The federal establishment had hustled Lewis and Clark across the continent; might not much the same be expected for the first American commercial undertaking west of the mountains? Astoria's future depended as much on decisions made in Washington as on those reached in New York or along the Columbia.

Financial considerations and political jockeying all occupied Astor's attention, but no part of Astoria's planning was more intricate than dealings with the North West Company. Astor knew from the start that New York and Montreal might be on a collision course. For their part, the Nor'westers recognized Astor as a powerful and shrewd opponent. The company had had its fill of brutal trade wars. The prospect of waging another, this time for the Northwest, was not welcome. Yet neither Astor nor the Canadians seemed ready to part with the dream of distant empire. Throughout the two years of preparation before Astor sent his men to the coast, both sides pursued contradictory courses. Sometimes they sought a joint venture while at other moments each plotted exclusive domain beyond the Rockies.

* * *

Astoria flickered into life sometime late in 1807. It was then that Astor first mentioned his western ideas to De Witt Clinton. Clinton was an ideal sounding board. Mayor of New York and sometime lieutenant governor of the state, he had important political friends and considerable business savvy. And it was not lost on Astor that Clinton's uncle George was Jefferson's vice-president. No direct record of those earliest talks between Astor and Clinton survives, but it is plain from later correspondence that the mayor urged his friend to pursue the Pacific enterprise. It is equally clear that Astor had been thinking about the Far West for some time.

What had been vague and roundabout now took on sharp definition. Writing to Clinton on January 25, 1808, Astor precisely detailed his "plans on the Subject of a company for carrying on the furr trade in the United States even more extensive than it is done by the companys in Canada." What Astor proposed was an ambitious design aimed at controlling the entire fur trade and extending it to the Pacific. Drawing on his Montreal sources of inspiration, Astor envisioned a series of trading posts from the Missouri to the Western Sea. These houses would follow the route pioneered by Lewis and Clark. Because Astor lacked good connections in St. Louis, he initially selected New Orleans as his principal midcontinent post. Although Astor made no mention of China, Clinton surely knew that he was interested in far more than the domestic fur trade. Canton was the unspoken goal; Russian America was the unexpected opportunity.

Astor was also aware of the expense involved in pursuing such distant horizons. He openly admitted that in the first two or three years the whole venture would not turn a cent of profit. Once over those costly years, the enterprise would surely justify Astor's expectations. The immediate problem was to attract investors and capital. He believed that perhaps ten or twelve shareholders might be found. Astor measured his commitment to the project by promising to allocate some fifty to one hundred thousand dollars of his own funds. Because this was to be so large a venture, Astor decided that incorporation by state charter might be the best means to protect company assets. Knowing Clinton's influence in New York politics, Astor hoped he would support the application.

But more was required than a simple act of incorporation. Astor wanted some sort of connection to the national government. The slippery word he used to describe that relationship was *approbation*. It was a term that might mean anything from mere knowledge and general assent to a full partnership. In the years before the War of 1812 Astor employed the word to mean vague approval. Once the war had begun and Astoria was in grave danger, he acted as if approbation signified a military commitment to either defend Astoria or retake it from the British. Without such official sanction,

Astor was certain the whole effort would collapse. But he believed that such an unfortunate turn of events would not happen. With the confidence that marked all his dealings, he predicted, "Such an undertaking would be pleasing to our government and . . . they would give aid to Insure its success."[1]

Plans, funding, a charter, and some sort of government backing—these were the objects of Astor's immediate concern. But in all of this there was one final worry. If Astoria had been inspired by Canadian explorers, those same Canadians might be the venture's chief rivals. At this early stage Astor wanted none of his Montreal trading partners to know what was afoot. As he put it to Clinton, "The people in Montreal . . . would take it unkind of me to propose an opposition to them." Astor had good reason to fear that retaliation by Nor'westers might doom the Pacific Fur Company even before it was fully launched.[2]

Astor had intended to go to Washington sometime in early February. Once there he hoped to wait on Jefferson and present a full explanation of his plans. Instead, Astor wrote the president a carefully worded letter outlining his proposals. His correspondence with Clinton had been filled with financial details and open requests for political help. Writing to the mayor, Astor had made no secret of his intention to dominate the western trade to the exclusion of all competitors, American or Canadian. But his approach to Jefferson was quite different. Without offering any particulars, Astor announced his intention "to carry on the trade so extensively that it may in time embrace the greater part of the fur trade on this continent." Just how this was to be accomplished went unexplained. The letter's real point came when Astor broached the subject of government support. He made it all sound quite bland and inoffensive. What he sought was "the countenance and good wishes of the executive of the United States." Again using the word *approbation*, Astor argued that without it, the whole enterprise was sure to fail. If the request for official approval was couched in ambiguous language, what Astor promised in return was equally vague. Government agents and private merchants knew that the fur trade was an essential link between Indians and whites. British and American diplomats believed that the fur trade was the foundation for both national power and frontier peace. Astor made a carefully phrased declaration: "Every exertion shall be made to preserve the views and wishes of government with the Indians and it is believed that the trade will in time be made productive and have advantages to the Country."[3]

The letter to Jefferson was remarkable for its silences. What it did not say reveals much about the political calculation Astor employed. He alluded to a grand scheme to engross the fur trade but never offered any details. The merchant skirted any possible cooperation with the Canadians, letting Jefferson think that this might be a wholly American enterprise serving national as well as private goals. But nowhere was there a more eloquent silence than on the question of monopoly. Astor never intended the Pacific Fur Company to be a public venture. Nor did he want any competitors. What he sought was total control of the western trade. Such monopolistic aims would surely have offended Jefferson. Astor knew that and wisely steered clear of even the slightest hint of monopoly. In some ways the letter was a carefully laid trap. Jefferson was being asked to approve a project while knowing nothing about its promoter and little about the plan itself.

Having made at least part of his case known to the president, Astor moved to work the Clinton connection. He thoughtfully suggested that Jefferson talk with the vice-president if more information was needed. Astor now had to make sure that George Clinton possessed the right sort of detail. Vice-President Clinton may well have heard about Astor's western design from his nephew De Witt. Writing to George Clinton in early March 1808, Astor presented a brief progress report. He admitted that plans were taking shape slowly. What was needed now was action from both the federal government and the state of New York. Astor remained confident that a state charter would not be difficult to obtain. The federal assent might be more troublesome but not impossible. Yet the Canadian response continued to worry him. It was one part of the plan he could neither predict nor control.[4]

Letters to Jefferson and both Clintons were essential parts of a strategy aimed at moving Astoria from dream to reality. But Astor knew that it would take more than polite correspondence to fulfill his ambitions. The next step was incorporation by New York State. Astor valued a state charter not just for the financial advantages it offered but also for the air of legitimacy it lent to his efforts. Soon after writing George Clinton, Astor prepared to travel to Albany to seek such a charter. The company Astor wanted the state to approve was not the Pacific Fur Company. Rather, he was aiming at a charter for something grandly called the American Fur Company. This body was intended as an umbrella to cover Astor's many fur trade interests. Whether Astor made the trip to Albany is not clear. What is plain is that his influence with De Witt Clinton paid off. On April 6 the New York legislature chartered the American Fur Company. That charter contained some of the language Astor had used in his earlier letters. The company would eliminate foreign competition, "conciliate and secure the good will and affections of the Indian tribes," and eventually be of "great public utility."[5] What Astor needed now was some sign from Jefferson that the western venture might have at least the semblance of federal sanction.

That eagerly awaited response came within a week. On April 8 Jefferson asked Secretary of War Henry Dearborn to gather what information he could about Astor. The president had never heard of the New Yorker and needed something more than what Astor had included in his letter. Just as Astor thought, Dearborn turned to George Clinton for advice. And Clinton evidently said all the right things. The vice-president, Dearborn reported to Jefferson, "speaks well of Astor, as a man of large vision and fair character and well acquainted with the fur and peltry business."[6]

Although it took Jefferson more than a month to reply to Astor, it was not for want of ideas about American expansion. He had made scattered references to the West before 1803, but it was the preparation for the Lewis and Clark expedition that compelled Jefferson to make his first comprehensive western plans. Like other empire builders of his age, Jefferson linked trade and sovereignty. The

Lewis and Clark instructions were written before the Louisiana Purchase and were of necessity more commercial than political. But the implications were plain. An American trading system would enhance national power at the expense of British and Spanish rivals.

The political aspect of Jefferson's western thought showed itself more clearly after the Purchase. In an important letter to Senator John C. Breckinridge, the president began to clarify the outlines of an extended American empire. Jeffersonian Republicans had long been wary of territorial expansion, arguing that republics were ideally small, compact nations with homogeneous populations. Although he later came to accept some degree of land gain west of St. Louis, Jefferson was not prepared early in the century to see the United States as a single Atlantic-to-Pacific nation. He expected that there would be at least two republics, divided at the Mississippi. They would be friendly neighbors, sharing a common language and political tradition. This would be liberty's empire, shutting the gates against Britain and Spain. Jefferson put his imperial vision in one forceful sentence: "The future inhabitants of the Atlantic and Missipi States will be our sons."[7]

But in all this one question remained unanswered, the very question that Astor most wanted resolved: what part would the federal government play in western expansion after the period of initial discovery and exploration? Jefferson gave a partial answer when he sent Lewis and Clark. The federal establishment would accept responsibility for exploration and scientific discovery. But might the government go beyond spying out the land to support private, commercial ventures on it?

Jefferson answered in a November 1806 conversation with Senator William Plumer. The president was fresh from reading a long, detailed letter from Meriwether Lewis, who had offered his thoughts on a western trade system centered on the Columbia River and reaching across the Pacific to China. Lewis hoped that this plan might receive some official boost. When Jefferson talked with Plumer on the evening of November 29, he was enthusiastic about the possibilities of commerce on the Columbia River. Plumer recalled that Jefferson was eager to have "some enterprizing mercantile Americans go on to the river Columbia and near the Pacific ocean, and settle the land there." The president insisted that no other nation had claims to the region, an assertion bound to raise hackles in any number of European capitals. But would the government organize, fund, and support such settlements? Two years before Astor asked for "approbation," Jefferson gave his answer. Private investors could follow in the tracks of government explorers, but the traders and settlers were on their own. As Plumer recollected Jefferson's words, the president "doubted whether it would be prudent for the government of the United States to attempt such a project." And Jefferson was not talking about an unspecified project. He was replying to Lewis's ideas—ideas very close to those proposed by Astor. Jefferson expected and hoped that Americans would follow Lewis and Clark, but the impetus would have to come from private sources.[8]

When Jefferson sat down on April 13 to reply to Astor, he drew on ideas that had been growing over the past five years. The president registered his pleasure to hear that "our merchants" were busy forming companies to pursue the Indian trade "in our territories." Reflecting his own concerns, he considered it "highly desirable to have that trade centered in the hands of our own citizens." Astor would not have been pleased about Jefferson's notion that many companies might find wealth in the western trade. "The field is immense," wrote the president, "and would occupy a vast extent of capital by different companies engaging in different districts." Astor never mentioned his monopolistic ambitions to Jefferson. The merchant could overlook the president's views of competition. What Astor really wanted was that elusive word of "approbation." What came in the letter was only a vague statement of general support. Jefferson promised "every reasonable patronage and facility in the power of the executive." This was no brush-off, but Astor certainly did not get what he was after.[9]

Many crucial episodes in the history of Astoria remain shrouded in mystery, which is partly the result of Astor's passion for secrecy.

But the loss of important records for the years before 1812 makes any inquiry more difficult. The earliest surviving Astor letter book is for the period 1813–15. Astor may have been dissatisfied with Jefferson's response. Perhaps he had expected a more enthusiastic endorsement of the whole project. And he could not have been heartened by Jefferson's vision of a West filled with rival trading companies. These concerns were evidently enough to push Astor toward a journey to the Federal City sometime between mid-April and mid-July 1808. He often had talked about such a trip and now he felt it necessary.

There is no contemporary record of Astor's meeting with Jefferson and selected cabinet members. What does survive is Astor's 1813 recollection of the gathering. As Astor recalled in a letter to James Madison, the audience with Jefferson took place after the April 6 chartering of the American Fur Company. Considering the contents of Jefferson's April 13 letter, the meeting must have been held after that date as well. Astor insisted that the gathering included not only the president but also Secretary of the Treasury Gallatin, Secretary of War Dearborn, and Secretary of State Madison. At the conference Astor "presented more full in detail the Plan for wresting from the British the trade with the Indians." Jefferson's response to all this must have pleased Astor. The president "apeard to be highly pleasd and expresd a particular Desire that a post might be Established at or near the mouth of the Columbia River." But the purpose of the meeting, at least for Astor, was to get a firm commitment to back Astoria. Astor told the politicians about his fears of opposition from the North West Company. "In case the plan Should promise Sucess and be likely to becom of that Importancs expected the north-west company might by means of aid from there government Destroy us." Here Astor pleaded for some assurances of protection should his posts and employees come under attack. Jefferson's response, so Astor said, was unambiguous. Support against hostile action was promised "in the most Desided and explicit maner."[10]

There are legitimate suspicions about Astor's recollection of this meeting. His account was part of a larger effort in 1813 to gain government approval for a naval expedition to protect Astoria against British attack. There is the distinct possibility that Astor invented the meeting and its alleged promises as a means to pressure President Madison. However, additional evidence now makes the fact of a meeting more likely. Astor would hardly have asked Madison to recall the meeting, at which the secretary of state was supposed to have been present, had the gathering been a product of Astor's imagination. Madison, Gallatin, Dearborn, and Jefferson had all been in Washington from April through July. And Gallatin did allude to the event years later when he wrote that the Astoria project was "communicated to government, and met with its full approbation and best wishes."[11]

But no piece of evidence goes further to validate Astor's claim of a meeting than a letter from Jefferson to Meriwether Lewis. Writing on July 17, 1808, Jefferson demonstrated a grasp of Astor's plans and discussed details present in neither Astor's initial note to him nor his reply to Astor. Plainly, sometime between April and July much had passed between the merchant and the president. That new information may well have come from the meeting Astor described some years later.

Writing to Lewis, Jefferson reported, "A powerful company is at length forming for taking up the Indian trade on a large scale." Jefferson knew the amount of capital invested in the venture as well as other financial details. But more telling, he was aware of something that Astor had not decided until the summer of 1808. In 1806 Montreal merchants had created the second Michilimackinac Company. The company was engaged in the Great Lakes trade—what the Nor'westers called the southwest trade. The company's men did business on American soil and deposited the profits in Canadian pockets. Though profitable, the trade left the company vulnerable to any changes in laws governing foreign traders doing business in American territories. Sometime during the summer of 1808 Astor decided to make the Nor'westers a startling offer. He proposed buying out the Michilimackinac Company, assuming all goods and debts of the concern. Astor further suggested that a boundary line be drawn between trapping areas worked by his American Fur Company and the North West Company. Astor probably saw this buyout as a necessary first step on his grander western plans. Jefferson knew much of this when he told Lewis that the "English Mackinac company will probably withdraw from the competition." Calling Astor "a most excellent man" and "perfectly master" of the fur trade, Jefferson urged Lewis to offer full government cooperation should Astor travel to St. Louis.[12]

The seven months from January through July 1808 were busy ones for Astor. The few extant letters from this period show him working hard to define and advance his Pacific adventure. Correspondence with Jefferson and both Clintons reveal how carefully Astor made his plans and pursued them. The American Fur Company's incorporation was yet another important development. But perhaps Astor's most daring actions in those early months were his probable meeting with Jefferson and his decision to open talks with the North West Company. These were gambles, chances with considerable risk. Astor was willing to expose his plans to official Washington. Now he was prepared to show at least some of his hand in Montreal.

Jefferson thought Astor had travel plans, and indeed the New Yorker was preparing for a journey. But the destination was Montreal, not St. Louis. Astor made a fur-buying expedition to Montreal every fall. But this year he hoped to acquire more than skins and pelts. He was now ready to make an offer for the Michilimackinac Company. By mid-September Astor was fully engaged in the Montreal social whirl, dining at the Frobisher house and enjoying a Beaver Club gala. Sometime during those hectic days he made his proposal. The only reliable source for what Astor had in mind is a letter he wrote to Albert Gallatin at the end of September. Astor claimed that Michilimackinac's partners had lost nearly one hundred thousand dollars over the past two years. And with tensions growing between the United States and Britain, Astor suspected that the partners feared new American trade restrictions. He believed that worries about embargo legislation and financial losses might move the Canadians to accept his offer.

When Astor inquired about the value of the Michilimackinac Company, he was told that the asking price was $700,000. Convinced that this was at least $150,000 more than it was worth, Astor countered by offering $600,000. He further proposed assuming all outstanding company debts. But the offer was rejected at the end of September. It was not hard for Astor to find reasons for the rejection. As he explained to Gallatin, two separate considerations seemed to be at work. Although the Nor'westers did fear American commercial legislation and its influence on the Great Lakes trade, they evidently decided that selling out the valuable southwest trade would be quitting the game before really necessary. Montreal, willing to take its chances, waited to see what would happen next in Anglo-American relations. But the decision to reject Astor's offer was based on more than political and diplomatic considerations. Nationalism and the clash of personalities played their part as well. As Astor put it with his usual bluntness, "I see they did not like to give up to the Americans." He might have been even closer to the mark had he said that the Canadians did not like yielding to him. After years of doing business with Astor, they knew his acumen and tenacity. They may have admired his skill; they surely resented his rapid rise.[13]

Astor always connected the purchase of at least a share of the Michilimackinac Company with his plans for Astoria. At a distance this connection may seem remote. When Astor told Jefferson he wanted to engross the entire fur trade, that meant everything from the Great Lakes to the Pacific Northwest. Controlling the Michilimackinac Company was part of the larger scheme. But there is yet another intriguing connection. At least one historian has argued that Astor went to Montreal in 1808 not only to buy the Michilimackinac Company but also to sell a share in his Pacific venture.[14] There is no surviving evidence to support this conjecture. Astor certainly did his best to convince Jefferson and Gallatin that the Pacific Fur Company would deliver a West for Americans only. But in 1809–10 Astor did begin to negotiate a complex arrangement with the North West Company, one involving the purchase of the Michilimackinac Company and a joint venture beyond the mountains. In 1808, however, all that was yet to happen. For now Astor had suffered a temporary setback.

For all John Astor's thoughtful planning, Astoria's future was in many ways beyond his control. Engaged in an international game, he was subject to what must have seemed the whims of great powers. In early spring 1809, shifts in relations between Britain and the United States gave Astor fresh hope. On March 4 Congress repealed the commercial embargo passed some years before. Hard on the heels of this repeal came a congressional nonintercourse act, opening American commerce to all countries except Britain and France. By using third countries as intermediaries, Canadians and Americans could continue business activities. Such an arrangement was cumbersome, but Montreal merchants were accustomed to the complexities of the trade. The repeal of the Embargo might have convinced the Nor'westers that they could indeed go it alone. But their reaction was just the opposite. The on-again-off-again nature of American trade policy convinced them that they were hostages to the politics of an unpredictable Congress. By mid-March 1809 Astor was hearing rumors suggesting that Montreal was reconsidering his Michilimackinac offer.[15]

In April there was yet another confusing diplomatic development. David Erskine, British ambassador to the United States, misread his instructions from London. Erskine had always been friendly to American interests and now he signed an agreement promising that the Royal Navy would no longer stop, search, and seize American ships in the Atlantic. The bargain would be valid if the United States promised to remove the nonintercourse act aimed at Britain. The Erskine Agreement was "greeted in the United States with universal joy, and hundreds of ships left for British ports."[16] But Canadian traders were much less certain what the agreement meant for them. Being able to buy and sell British goods for the Great Lakes was essential. But once again those merchants saw how vulnerable they were to international events.

The same events that caused confusion in Montreal evidently forced Astor to decide that this was the time to move his Pacific plans from word to action. Hints of possible help from Montreal may have made the decision easier. But Astor could not have missed that the Nor'westers were pressing on with their own western plans. Journeys by Simon Fraser and David Thompson were clear indications of a continued Canadian drive to the sea. Now was the time to act, or Astor would lose any share of the Northwest.

During the spring of 1809 Astoria became more than a paper dream. Astor began by searching for a suitable ship to carry traders and goods to the coast. He wanted to find a ship of "considerable burthen say 300 tons." The ship's company would build an armed post on the Columbia. The traders would then send a party eastward over the mountains to meet those Astorians coming up the Missouri. Astor supposed that the entire permanent Columbian contingent would be about fifty men, of which forty-five would be Americans.[17]

When Astor first wrote to De Witt Clinton in 1808, St. Louis evidently played little or no role in his plans. Although he knew that the city was essential to the western trade, Astor had been largely unsuccessful in entering its business life. He did have a commercial correspondent in Charles Gratiot and did have some contact with the Chouteaus, but Astor was surely no force in St. Louis commerce.[18] Still, much of the success of the Pacific Fur Company would depend on a strong presence in the city. Astor now planned to have his Missouri River expedition leave St. Louis in the spring of 1810. That party would be much larger than the Columbia River group and would contain as many Americans as possible. Choosing the leadership for this expedition was a crucial decision. An experienced Canadian was the best bet. But national concern dictated that the expedition be led by an American.

It is not clear how Astor selected Wilson Price Hunt for this position. Born in New Jersey in 1783, Hunt went to St. Louis in 1803. There he formed a partnership with a fellow merchant, John Hankinson. The two men were general-merchandise agents, selling everything from soap and grain to whiskey and boats. They even dabbled in the fur market, trading with the Chouteaus and Astor's St. Louis agent, Charles Gratiot.[19]

Hunt was no garden-variety city merchant. He never gave his western dreams formal shape in words that have survived, but his actions bespoke an enduring fascination with the West. In late summer 1806, just before Lewis and Clark came back to St. Louis, Hunt got his first taste of western opportunity. He was approached by Manuel Lisa, one of the frontier's most energetic explorers and traders. Lisa was planning an expedition to Santa Fe. Fortunes were to be made in the Spanish territories, but hazards along the trail could not be discounted. Many Americans bound for Santa Fe met death at the hands of Indians or suffered long imprisonment for violating Spanish trade restrictions. Lisa must have thought the young Hunt was ready for adventure and profit no matter the risk. But Hunt calculated the risks and by mid-August let himself out of any southwestern voyage.[20]

No more than four weeks later Lewis and Clark were in town. Like everyone else in the city, Hunt was eager to hear about the expedition. Perhaps he made it a point to attend the festive homecoming dinner and ball at William Christy's tavern on September 25. If he did not get to talk with the explorers on that occasion, he did not have long to wait. Two days later, on September 27, Lewis came to Hunt looking to buy a wide variety of provisions. He eventually purchased some three hundred dollars' worth of goods. Here was Hunt's chance, and it is plain that in the following days he learned much from both Lewis and Clark. Hunt not only talked with the explorers but also saw many of the specimens brought back from the West. Writing to his cousin John Wesley Hunt on October 14, Wilson Price displayed detailed knowledge about the expedition and its route to the Pacific. Hunt was not an experienced frontiersman but he did possess a genuine interest in exploration. Almost more important to Astor, he had the right citizenship. What brought Hunt to Astor's attention remains unknown, but by the summer of 1809 Wilson Price Hunt was ready to follow in the footsteps of Jefferson's captains.[21]

What had started as a tentative proposal in January 1808 was now rapidly taking shape as an impressive enterprise. The steps taken during the spring of 1809 reveal a John Astor possessed with energy, initiative, and imagination. If Astor was bold, he could be equally cautious. From the beginning he had sought some brand of official standing, even if it meant nothing more than tacit approval. With this in mind, he now took Treasury Secretary Gallatin more fully into his confidence. The two men had been growing steadily closer. Astor provided the secretary with important financial information and was in turn rewarded by having an influential friend in the cabinet. In later years both business and family ties drew the two even closer. In mid-May 1809 Astor drafted for Gallatin what amounted to the most comprehensive report to date on his Pacific enterprise. He told Gallatin about the Columbia and Missouri river parties, noting their sizes and routes. And never overlooking the inherent nationalism in the scheme, Astor reported, "Particular attention will be paid to employ and introduce into this trade as many young Americans of respectable connections and of good moral character as possible."[22]

Astor intended that this letter be more than a mere progress report. His correspondence with Jefferson and De Witt Clinton contained short sermons on the text of government-company relations. But it was Gallatin, already a staunch proponent of American economic nationalism, who received full chapter and verse on federal backing for the Astorian enterprise. Letters to others had only hinted at the character of official "approbation." The secretary was told that the word had now taken on sharper definition in Astor's mind. Astor smoothly assured Gallatin that no steps would be taken "without the knowledge of government." Wrapping his private affairs in the cloak of national interest, the merchant declared his intention "to act as much as possible with its [the United States] wishes." Astor had very nearly made the Pacific Fur Company another branch of government, placing himself at the cabinet table.[23]

Astor now made three politely phrased demands. Knowing that his undertaking might spark a less-than-friendly reaction from

Montreal and London, he renewed his request for some kind of official standing. If Astorians were to be at risk, he wanted them seen as agents of the United States, not mere employees of a private firm. Astor also fretted about a new western rival, the St. Louis Missouri Fur Company. With powerful backers like the Chouteaus, William Clark, Manuel Lisa, and Meriwether Lewis's brother Reuben, the company could muster strong political influence. Did the company, Astor queried Gallatin, enjoy any special favor in the halls of government? He hoped not. Finally there was the thorny matter of the federal factory system for Indian trade. That trade monopoly, long a mainstay of government policy, stood squarely in the path of the Pacific Fur Company. How to oppose and dismantle the factory system troubled Astor for years. All these arguments, observations, and demands evidently impressed the shrewd Gallatin. For now the secretary scrawled a note at the bottom of the letter urging President Madison to read the proposal and pass it on to Secretary of War William Eustis.[24]

While Astor was busy with eastern negotiations, his new St. Louis agent, Wilson Price Hunt, may have been equally active. Because the Astor-Hunt correspondence is no longer extant, it is difficult to trace either Astor's intentions or Hunt's pursuit of his employer's instructions. The historian David Lavender maintains that Hunt, prompted by Astor, was indeed hard at work during the summer of 1809 making preparations for the expedition slated for the following spring. It is plain from a notice in the *Louisiana Gazette* that Hunt dissolved his partnership with John Hankinson in early June. Lavender believes that Hunt then made an informal arrangement with traders Ramsay Crooks, Robert McClellan, and Joseph Miller. That bargain called for these adventurers to go up the Missouri, survey suitable post sites, and perhaps even cross the Continental Divide. In return, writes Lavender, Hunt and Astor would provide the necessary trade goods and would guarantee future places for Crooks and his companions in the Pacific Fur Company. Lavender believes Hunt did this partly to give his unemployed friend Crooks work and partly to satisfy Astor that the summer of 1809 would not pass without some real action.[25]

Indeed Crooks and company did go up the Missouri in July. After
a brief trip to Mackinac for supplies, Crooks joined the Missouri Fur
Company convoy heading upriver. The St. Louis company was
charged with returning Sheheke, a Mandan chief recruited by Lewis
and Clark, to his home village. At the end of July Crooks, McClellan,
and their men were camped near the Platte River. There they waited
until the end of August, when Joseph Miller and forty men appeared with a keelboat of trade goods. The force then continued up
the Missouri as far as the James River in present-day South Dakota.
There they were stopped by Teton Sioux warriors intent on exacting
tolls for passage along their part of the river. With their progress
halted, Crooks and his party retreated, wintered over, and returned
to St. Louis in early June 1810.

There can be no doubt that Crooks, McClellan, and Miller—all
future Astorians—made such a journey on the Missouri in 1809.
But whether they did so as advance agents for Astor remains in
doubt. When Astor's St. Louis correspondent, Charles Gratiot,
wrote him in June 1810 he reported that Hunt had been Crooks's
supplier "last fall." A further piece of evidence comes from the
recollections of General Thomas James. In the years immediately
after Lewis and Clark, James was a young trader eager for fortune
and adventure. Writing many years later, he characterized Crooks in
1809 as an Astor agent. To these bits of evidence Lavender adds one
additional supposition. When the Pacific Fur Company was formally
organized in 1810, Crooks was given five shares of stock, more than
the number offered to older and more experienced traders. Lavender asks rhetorically, "Was this extra recognition based on the
enterprise and initiative Crooks showed in pushing up the river in
1809, hoping to found advance posts?" Lacking any substantial
evidence, we must return a Scotch verdict—not proven.[26]

Whatever the course of events in St. Louis, Astor now worked
diligently in both Washington and Montreal. In mid-July 1809 he
wrote a cryptic note to Gallatin. Alluding to his long May 16 letter,
Astor urged the secretary to find opportunity "for reminding the
President on the subject of my letter and if at your convenience you

will please to inform me, of his opinion on the same." Having some response from President Madison was now more important than ever. In July news had come of the repudiation of the Erskine Agreement. It was plain that commercial and diplomatic relations between Britain and the United States were heading into dangerous waters. Perhaps now, faced with the cutoff of trade goods to the Great Lakes, Montreal merchants would be more open to Astor's proposals.[27]

At the end of the summer of 1809 Astor made his now customary trip to Montreal. Once again he made the usual round of merchant dining rooms and the Beaver Club. Sometime during those busy days he renewed his offer to the North West Company. For the first time, surviving documents allow us to see precisely what Astor proposed. If the Nor'westers would purchase a one-third interest in his forthcoming Pacific venture, Astor would buy a one-half interest in the Michilimackinac Company. Astor believed that such a proposal presented real advantages for both parties. The North West Company could have a reliable supply of trade goods for the Great Lakes, thanks to Astor's American citizenship. In return, he could have a lock on the Great Lakes and at the same time avoid any expensive competition in the Northwest.[28] Economic nationalism was the tune sung in Washington, but in Canada Astor's song was cooperation and mutual interest.

Astor must have believed that his notions would be attractive to the Montreal partners. But they were not the only Canadians to be consulted. Each year in July the North West Company's wintering partners gathered at Fort William on Lake Superior to count profits and plot trade strategy. At the July 1809 meeting Astor's offer was yet unknown. But the winterers did have major decisions to make. They decided to press on with their own western plans, sending David Thompson again to the upper Columbia. The partners recognized that the sale of the Michilimackinac Company was probably inevitable but saw no reason for alarm. The prospect of sharing the West with Astor would have prompted angry protest from Fort William's great hall.[29]

When Astor left Montreal sometime in September he brought home no Canadian agreement. Frustrated by this seeming rejection, he wrote a bitter letter to Gallatin. Astor complained that as early as March it had been rumored the Nor'westers were ready to bite on his proposals. But now the current had shifted and Astor was sure the Canadians would not join him. Astor evidently did not know about the differences between the wintering partners and those in Montreal. Indeed, he blamed official British policy for all his troubles. Astor was convinced that the Canadians were "instigated by their government to this step." He reported that when in Montreal the previous year, merchants had been heard discussing the need for London to act against any American incursions into the West. Astor was now sure those appeals had been answered.[30]

There is no evidence to support Astor's claim that his proposals had fallen victim to crown policy. But his plans had caused real alarm in Montreal. The Nor'westers never underestimated Astor. They knew him to be a persistent, energetic, and imaginative competitor. At the end of September 1809 the Montreal partners drafted a long memorial for the British ambassador in Washington. For the first time, the Canadians hoisted the danger flags. "The Americans," they warned, "seem to aim at establishments in trade beyond the Rocky Mountains, and on the River Columbia to which they have no pretensions by discovery, either by water or land." Raising arguments that would become stock-in-trade for the later Oregon Question, the company maintained that Britain's exclusive title to the Northwest was fixed through the efforts of Cook, Vancouver, and Mackenzie. The Nor'westers' concern was plain. "No establishment of the States on that river or on the coast of the Pacific should therefore be sanctioned."[31]

Montreal's worries can be measured by the company's decision to press against Astor in London. In late January 1810 the partners decided it was time Nathaniel Atcheson, their agent in London, began to circularize crown officials about the Astor threat. What prompted this decision was news that Astor was preparing his ship *Enterprise* for a trading voyage to the Northwest coast. The Nor'westers also may have learned that Astor was negotiating with the Russian-American Company. Confusing these preparations with the main Astorian undertaking, the company told its London agent that Astor would be ready to invade the Far West by the spring. Calling all this "an Emergency," the company ordered Atcheson to push for immediate official action, which amounted to a revival of the strategies proposed long before by Alexander Mackenzie. Atcheson was to tell the crown that the time had come to break the East India Company's monopoly in China. Only then could the Canadians freely compete and stop Astor in his tracks. Feeling the pressure of Astor's challenge, the Nor'westers told Atcheson that they needed some response by early spring so that decisions could be made at the July 1810 Fort William rendezvous.[32]

The casual observer might have thought that this flurry of activity meant the Nor'westers had decided to oppose Astor at every turn. In fact there was no clear-cut company policy. The North West Company was never a single, unified corporate body. Instead, there were interlocking, short-term agreements between wintering partners, Montreal merchants, and London supply houses. Faced now with the prospect of spirited opposition from Astor and the certainty of more restrictive commercial legislation from the American Congress, some in Montreal decided to reopen negotiations with Astor. On February 14, 1810, William McGillivray, senior partner in McTavish, McGillivrays & Co., and John Richardson, of Forsyth, Richardson & Co., came to New York seeking a meeting with Astor. They came ostensibly to talk only about the Michilimackinac Company. Richardson admitted that "dire necessity" forced this move and that new embargo legislation meant "utter ruin" unless the Michilimackinac Company could gain an American partner. But there was more to discuss than the Great Lakes. Rumors were flying in Montreal that Astor had "a charter from Congress for an exclusive right to the Indian trade." The always knowledgeable Alexander Henry wrote a Detroit friend that Astor was "to be connected with the North West Company to make settlements on the Northwest coast of America, to communicate with the Inland Northwest trade."[33]

Henry evidently knew a great deal about what had happened in New York that February. Astor was in fact unwilling to deal with McGillivray and Richardson unless they met his conditions. Astor knew that the Canadians were desperate. Richardson admitted, "If we fail with Mr. Astor, a journey to Washington will be requisite."[34] Astor's price to bail out the Michilimackinac Company was what it had been in the fall of 1809—the North West Company would have to purchase a one-third share in his Pacific venture. What had been unattractive to Montreal some months before now seemed a small price for saving the known value of the Great Lakes trade. McGillivray and Richardson offered their tentative approval but noted that final acceptance had to come from both the Montreal partners and the winterers. This meant that no firm decision could be reached until after the July Fort William meeting, which was much too late for Astor. He had hoped to send his Columbia and Missouri river expeditions on their way in early spring. Astor insisted that matters be settled by May.[35] How McGillivray and Richardson reacted to this demand is unrecorded. Evidently both parties believed that some sort of informal bargain could be struck before July.

Convinced that matters with the Canadians were about to be settled, Astor began formal arrangements to bring the Pacific Fur Company to legal life. He had long known that success in any western enterprise depended on having the services of experienced Canadian traders and voyageurs. Astor was perfectly ready to talk with Gallatin and others about an American West, but he knew all along that Canadian hands would fashion the future. Sometime early in 1810 Astor began to recruit Canadian partners. His many trips to Montreal must have helped in that process. The men he selected were Alexander McKay, Donald Mackenzie, and Duncan McDougall. Mackenzie had been a North West Company clerk, and it is probable that McDougall held a similar position. Of the three, McKay was the most experienced. He had joined the North West Company sometime before 1791 and had become a partner in 1793. In the same year he joined Alexander Mackenzie on his epic trek to the Pacific. Alexander Ross, one of Astor's Canadian clerks, believed that the three partners joined the Pacific Fur Company because they were unhappy with their lack of advancement in Nor'wester ranks. However they were chosen, the three gathered in New York on March 10, 1810, to sign provisional Articles of Agreement for the new company.[36]

The provisional articles set out the goals of the new company and the responsibilities of the partners. The Pacific Fur Company was "to make an establishment at or in the vicinity of Columbia River or wheresoever the same shall be found practicable on the Northwest coast for the purpose of carrying on a trade with the Indians." For his part, Astor promised to provide the concern with all goods and equipment required for pursuing the trade, which meant everything from trade items and provisions to ammunition and ships. The agreement also clarified how shares in the company were to be allocated. Of the one hundred available shares, Astor was to have half, with the remaining allotted among the other partners. Although Wilson Price Hunt was surely on Astor's payroll by March 1810, he was not listed as a partner nor did he sign the provisional agreement. McKay, McDougall, and Mackenzie were each granted five shares. Adopting Nor'wester usage, these men were termed wintering partners. As such they were given control of daily trading affairs. Although much of the March agreement was given over to routine financial and legal matters, one clause is of special note. Astor still expected a reply from the North West Company. Provisions had to be made for its purchase of Pacific Fur Company stock. If the offer was accepted, the number of the company's shares would increase to two hundred. This watering of the stock would allow for the one-third Canadian purchase while still preserving Astor's ultimate control. The March agreement was an interim measure, but its meaning was clear. Astor felt confident of success and was determined to press ahead.[37]

By early April his enthusiasm was beginning to cool. There had been no word from Montreal on any part of his proposal. Astor expected George Gillespie, a North West Company partner, to arrive in New York at any moment with a reply. In the meantime Astor queried Gallatin about the current state of commercial legislation. "I am very anxious to know," he wrote, "if in case the non-intercourse is not taking off whether in such case any measures are like to be adopted as will permit the supplying the Indians with goods from Canada in the usual way."[38]

As the May deadline approached, Astor must have worried about the future of a project now nearly two years old. More than ever Astoria's outcome depended on events and decisions far from New York. Activity in London may have seemed remote, but the officials in Whitehall Palace had long played a decisive role in the destiny of the American West. Petitions sent by the North West Company to the Colonial Office in 1809 and those sent in January 1810 had not stirred any action. In March 1810 the Canadians and their allies made a more direct approach. Representatives from the Committee of British North American Merchants paid a call on Lord Liverpool to plead for aid to stop the American advance. The visitors got a polite hearing but no action. Undeterred by what seemed official indifference, the committee drafted a long petition, sending it to the government in early April. The memorial repeated intelligence about American expeditions bound for the Northwest. As before, the crown was urged to move quickly lest the Americans make any permanent establishment on the coast.[39]

Although they had been business rivals at the beginning of the century, Alexander Mackenzie and the North West Company were now aggressively pursuing the same objectives. For many years Mackenzie had persistently filed one petition after another, all looking for acceptance of his Pacific ideas. In the same month that the Canadian merchants sent their memorial, Mackenzie drafted yet another letter. This statement was nearly identical to earlier ones but with one crucial difference: in 1808 he had worried about Spanish influence on the Northwest coast, now the enemy was clearly Astor and the Americans. "Being at variance with the Americans," he argued, "a small Naval Force might be necessary" to protect any British post on the Columbia. The Board of Trade did not consider Mackenzie's petition until August 1811. By then Astoria was firmly planted just where he had feared it would be.[40]

Events in London were bound to have an effect on Astoria, but those consequences were not to be felt for some time. Decisions made in Washington were certain to have more immediate results. From the time of the first nonimportation act in 1806, Congress and the president had experimented with commercial legislation designed both to isolate the United States from the virus of European war and to punish those nations who violated American neutrality on the high seas. Those efforts enjoyed varying degrees of success. Surely the roller-coaster course frightened Canadians who needed free access to the Great Lakes. In 1809 Congress enacted yet another nonintercourse act, this after the collapse of the ill-fated Erskine Agreement. The 1809 law satisfied neither Madison nor Congress. Legislators determined to stop the president from making any trade decisions on his own passed something with the memorable label Macon's Bill Number 2. This was designed to replace the 1809 act, ending trade restrictions aimed at Britain and France. But the legislation was not without its unique features. It stipulated that if either France or Britain ended their restrictions against the United States and the other failed to follow suit, the United States would promptly reinstitute nonimportation against the offending nation. As it turned out, the French did accept American overtures while British actions were less certain.[41]

All these complex political and diplomatic maneuvers could not have come at a worse time for Astor. So long as embargo rules cut off the flow of goods to the Canadians, Astor was certain that his offer would be attractive. During the month of May the Montreal partners were struggling to reach a decision. News of Macon's Bill Number 2 sharpened their arguments. Two groups of partners—McTavish, McGillivrays & Co. and Forsyth, Richardson & Co.—were willing to hazard their fortunes on England's acceptance of the congressional offer. These merchants maintained that once trade restrictions were lifted, goods would flow easily and there would be no need to share anything with Astor. But this view was not shared by all the Montreal partners. James and Andrew McGill and Parker, Gerrard, and Ogilvie, who also owned shares of the Michilimackinac

Company, had had enough of the vagaries of American policy. Convinced that Astor provided a sound alternative, they urged acceptance of his proposal. After what must have been a stiff debate, those who favored Astor sold their shares of Michilimackinac Company stock to those in opposition. The result of all this was that Montreal now decisively rejected any cooperation with Astor. But these unexpected decisions were late in getting to wintering partners at Fort William. The Nor'westers were headed toward two differing policies, both being pursued at the same time.[42]

May was nearly gone when a frustrated Astor wrote Gallatin about these intricate affairs. Astor had been waiting patiently all month for news. But George Gillespie was nowhere to be found. By May 26 Astor was convinced that he would have to act alone in the West, facing Nor'wester opposition at every bend. "I have thus reluctantly been obliged to Declare off the bargain," he wrote bitterly. With characteristic resolve, Astor told Gallatin, "Considering the time which I have lost and other money spent in pursuit of this object on which I feel so deep an interest I cannot abandon it altogether."[43] Now was the time to press on with the Columbia and Missouri river expeditions. Let the Canadians beware.

By late June 1810 Astor was ready to draft formal papers for the Pacific Fur Company. At Lachine outside Montreal his Canadian partners were already busy signing up clerks and voyageurs. In New York the paper work was under way. The March provisional agreement had been signed only by the Canadian partners. Now in June the names of the Americans—Wilson Price Hunt, Ramsay Crooks, Robert McClellan, and Joseph Miller—were added.[44]

But there was one final twist in the planning of Astoria—a twist that once again involved Astor and the North West Company. When the wintering partners met at Fort William in July 1810 they believed that Astor's proposals were still a live issue. The negative decision taken by the Montreal partners was quite unknown to them. Evidence suggests that there was an angry debate at Fort William. The winterers, many deeply committed to expansion west of the Rockies, had always resented what they termed American "pretensions" to the region. Some were determined to have a North-west free of American influence, whereas others recognized that the Yankee invasion could not be halted. All agreed that Astor's plans posed an immediate threat to the company, especially if the crown did not act to support Canadian interests. In the end the argument was settled by instructing William McGillivray, somewhat reluc-tantly, to "accept the third proposed" by Astor. The winterers urged caution on McGillivray, calling on him to keep a close hand on all dealings with the shrewd Astor.[45]

None of the wintering partners thought that joining forces with Astor meant they would share the entire Northwest with him. To make certain that the company's interests were protected, they as-signed David Thompson to meet the Astorians on the Columbia. On July 22 a messenger met Thompson at Rainy Lake. The explorer was heading east for a well-earned rest. Instead he was ordered to turn around and trek west.[46] It has long been a legend in Canadian history that Thompson then raced across the continent hoping to beat the Americans to the Columbia. But once he arrived he found Astoria already built. Some Canadian historians have faulted Thompson for running a poor race and losing an empire, whereas others have worked to clear his record. Thompson did indeed move slowly, dogged by troubles with Indians, desertions, and a some-times wavering will to go ahead. But the evidence now suggests that there was no race.[47]

Thompson left for the Columbia believing that the Americans on the coast were not competitors but new business partners. On July 15, 1811, just before arriving at Astoria, Thompson sent a revealing note to the Astorians. "With pleasure," he wrote, "I acquaint you that the Wintering Partners have acceded to the offer by Mr. Astor, accepting one third share of the business you are engaged in." Thompson was evidently one of those who supported such a joint venture, adding that he hoped "the respective parties *at Montreal* [my emphasis] may finally settle the arrangements between the two companies which in my opinion will be to our mutual interest."[48] Because Thompson's instructions for his western journey have not survived, one can only look to his actions for clues to what the wintering Nor'westers really wanted. Thompson did believe that the Astorians and the Nor'westers were partners. But it is equally plain that he was told to do what he could to limit American influence on the coast. On July 9, 1811, Thompson was at the confluence of the Snake and Columbia rivers near present-day Pasco, Washington. There he met with Walula Indians who asked him, as they had asked Lewis and Clark, to establish a trading post. Thompson obliged by nailing a note to a nearby tree. That note shows the other side of Nor'wester policy—a policy determined to hem in American activity. The notice read: "Know hereby that this country is claimed by Great Britain as part of its territories, and that the North West Company of Merchants from Canada, finding the factory for this people inconvenient for them, do hereby intend to erect a factory in this place for the commerce of the country around."[49]

* * *

Early in 1810 the planning for Astoria was nearly complete. Financial arrangements had been concluded. Astor's agents were recruiting at Lachine. In New York preparations were well under way to obtain a ship, captain, and crew for the ocean journey to the coast. When Astor wrote Gallatin about all this in May, he asked what might have struck the secretary as an odd question. Astor wanted to know if the United States was contemplating any changes in commercial policy toward Russia.[50] This interest in Russian affairs pointed to the last piece of planning before Astoria could become not an isolated trading post but an empire.

3

The Russian Connection

TRADERS AND ADVENTURERS like Gregorii Shelikhov, Alexander Baranov, and Nikolai Rezanov do not spring to mind as prominent actors in the drama of frontier America. Places like Fort Union, South Pass, and the Lolo Trail have quicker recognition in the geography of western expansion than New Archangel, Fort St. Michael, and Kodiak Island. But while British and American explorers and traders were forging empires west of St. Louis and Rocky Mountain House, Russian adventurers were doing likewise on the high frontier of Alaska and the Far Northwest.

By the 1780s Russian traders and their *promyshlenniks* (fur hunters) were busy exploiting the fur resources of the Alaskan coast. The most energetic of those promoters was Gregorii Shelikhov. Beginning in 1783, Shelikhov and his partner, Ivan Golikov, mounted extensive fur voyages to Alaska. Unlike previous Russian efforts, these aimed at founding permanent settlements on the American mainland. Although filled with danger, the expeditions reaped huge rewards for Shelikhov and a growing band of rivals. The promise of even greater profits was behind a major 1788 report to Empress Catherine the Great. Drafted by Shelikhov and Golikov and representing the interests of their American Company, the memorial detailed the rapid expansion of Russian trade along the Northwest coast. The partners claimed to have placed more than fifty thousand native people under imperial rule. Explorers were ready, they insisted, to extend Russian America from the Kurile Islands down the coast to Spanish California. The empress could have this new world for a pittance. A grant of 250,000 rubles, the promise of one hundred soldiers for garrison duty, and the assurance of imperial protection—the polite way to ask for a trade monopoly—would secure an American domain for Russia. The official Commission on Commerce, evidently unmindful that such a state-sponsored action might offend British sensibilities on the eve of the Nootka Sound controversy, urged approval of the plan. But the cautious Catherine balked. Her daring explorers were given nothing more than silver swords, gold medals, and a perfunctory letter of encouragement.[1]

Catherine's lack of enthusiasm did nothing to hinder the growth of Russian enterprise along the west coast. In the 1780s there were seven fur trade companies eagerly chasing sea otters. Over the next ten years intense competition and the dangers of trade reduced that number to three. By 1797 two of the largest firms had combined to form the United American Company. Despite these mergers, rivalries persisted. The largest traders, including Shelikhov's heirs, urged the government to create a semiofficial monopoly company. On July 19, 1799, Emperor Paul signed an order forming the Russian-American Company.[2] Granted a monopoly for twenty years, the company moved quickly to press its advantage. Led by its aggressive field manager, Alexander Baranov, the Russian-American Company began to fashion a genuine trade empire. When Minister of Commerce Nikolai Rumiantsev reviewed the company's progress in 1803, prospects for both business and territorial growth seemed bright.[3]

But Rumiantsev's report was far too glowing. As Baranov made plain in repeated letters to the directors at St. Petersburg, profits were being held down by a range of problems. Perhaps the most serious difficulty was that posed by the increasing number of British and American ships trading in North Pacific waters. Although En-

Flag of the Russian-American Company. Courtesy of the National
Archives, Washington, D.C.

glish vessels had begun the sea otter trade in 1785, American ships
quickly gained the advantage. American merchants had direct access to China through Canton. Between 1787 and 1806 some
seventy-two Yankee vessels were in Northwest waters. The American traders paid high prices, offered quality goods, and consistently
garnered the best pelts.[4] For all their anger at foreign competitors,
what infuriated the Russians more was the weapons trade carried on
by the Boston captains. Yankee skippers had no qualms about giving
guns and ammunition in exchange for furs. Those weapons were
sometimes turned on the Russians, as when Sitka was attacked in
1802 by Tlingit Indians armed with British and American firearms.

When Governor Baranov complained to the Americans, he got nothing but derisive laughter in return. As he put it, the Bostonians "before our eyes shamelessly trade powder, lead, pistols, and muskets."[5]

American ships cut deep into Russian profits and put weapons into hostile native hands. But even Baranov was forced to admit that those same ships were essential for the very survival of Russian America. From the time of Shelikhov's first plans for permanent settlements on the coast, it was plain that the Russians would face severe food shortages. No colony on the far north coast could feed itself. All sorts of supplies—everything from grain to vodka—had to be brought aboard ship from the Siberian mainland port of Okhotsk. Faced with chronic shortages, Baranov relied on American ships for grain and other foodstuffs. After surveying the entire provisions problem, Count Nikolai Rezanov told Baranov: "The shortage of foodstuffs causes diseases, starvation, and death among the people. Okhotsk is not able to supply America with the necessary quantity of foodstuffs; consequently, it is necessary to extend our commercial operations to find new sources of supply." Rezanov thought those new sources might include Spanish California, Japan, Hawaii, and the Philippines. But Boston remained the most reliable. "The grain shipped from there will at all times cost less than half as much as the grain from Okhotsk."[6] Despite the hazards of a two-ocean voyage, Yankee ships plied the Russian grain trade until 1839.

Competition from shrewd Americans, weapons in the hands of unfriendly local people, and the grim prospect of short rations all haunted Baranov and his poorly paid employees. To these was added a final problem. The domestic fur market in Russia was substantial but could never promise the kind of bumper profits realized in China. Yet Russian trade to China was severely restricted. Canton, the one port open to European fur merchants, was shut to the Russians. Their only access to the Chinese market came through the isolated frontier post at Kyakhta on the border between Siberia and present-day Mongolia. Furs sold there fetched much lower prices than at Canton, and even those profits were diminished by high transportation costs. The Russian-American Company needed a way to enter the China market through Canton. By 1800 both Baranov and the board of directors were beginning to think that informal ties to American merchants might solve most of the company's problems.

Early in his administration at New Archangel, or Sitka, Governor Baranov had tried to make such agreements with several American captains.[7] These short-term arrangements met immediate needs but did nothing to resolve underlying problems. With close ties to the imperial government, the Russian-American Company decided to use diplomacy as a means to solve its problems. In July 1806 Levett Harris, the first American consul in St. Petersburg, held a series of talks with Prince Adam Czartoryski, acting minister of foreign affairs. During these conversations the Russian minister observed that the United States could acquire "a branch [of maritime trade] which hitherto had not engaged" the country's attention. As Harris noted, the minister "alluded to the trade of the Northwest coast of America." When Harris pointed out that American ships already had a healthy share of the trade, Czartoryski suggested a way to make that interest even larger. Speaking for both the government and the company, he suggested that a system be developed using American ships to supply provisions for the Russian colony. Those same ships could also carry the company's furs to China. Harris was impressed by these arguments and promised to pass them on to Secretary of State Madison.[8]

This initial diplomatic opening came to nothing. Neither Jefferson nor Madison seemed much inclined to help an obscure Russian company a continent away. American indifference was the least of the company's troubles. Indian attacks, rapid price changes, and the loss of one million seal pelts due to spoilage between 1805 and 1810 all cost the investors dearly. In early May 1808 the company again appealed to the imperial government for relief. Its petition recounted the now familiar litany of problems. American competitors, the weapons trade, food shortages, and an uncertain China market all made for a bleak future in Russian America. Two years earlier neither the company nor the government had been able to offer specific solutions, other than some vague hope of American cooperation. Now the directors had a plan, a scheme that would eventually involve Astor and his western design. The company sought three things. It demanded that the United States force its citizens to stop the weapons trade, that all dealings with non-Russians be transacted only at the port on Kodiac Island, and that the imperial government pursue a formal commercial treaty with the Americans.[9]

When Foreign Minister Rumiantsev met with Levett Harris at the end of May, the company's complaints and proposals were presented to the American diplomat. As before, Harris was a sympathetic listener. "Having a personal acquaintance with the Governor and some of the principal directors of the Russian-American Company established here," Harris later wrote to Madison, "I took an opportunity to converse with them upon the nature and extent of the grievances of which they complained." Harris was convinced that a commercial treaty between the two nations might resolve the company's troubles while enhancing American profits.[10]

Later that summer the imperial government prepared to send its first official representative to the new American republic. That agent was Andrei Dashkov, soon to be consul general at Philadelphia and chargé d'affaires to the American Congress. Dashkov was experienced and imaginative, the sort of diplomat who could be counted on to seize opportunities not clearly spelled out in formal instructions. The range and complexity of Dashkov's mission became apparent in August 1808. The Russian-American Company named him "Honorable Correspondent" in the United States. He was ordered to show "special care and attention to the trade between its settlements on the northwestern part of America and the citizens of the said North American states." Just how the government wanted Dashkov to behave became clear in instructions sent at the end of August. The Russian diplomat was to explain St. Petersburg's complaints and problems, all the while pressing for a commercial treaty. Dashkov was to conceal from President Madison "the importance which it [the proposed treaty] holds for the commercial interests of the American Company." Dashkov would tell the president only that the convention would benefit nations, not private companies.[11]

When Dashkov arrived in Philadelphia the deception deepened. The Russian diplomat proposed that the first article of the treaty contain language "to forbid and not allow their subjects to furnish military goods to an enemy of the one of them at war." Once the treaty was ratified, the imperial government would declare war on the native people of the Northwest coast and would invoke article one of the convention. The United States would then be obligated to restrain any trading of firearms by American ships.[12]

But none of these cunning moves would have brought Dashkov and Astor together. In early September 1808, just before leaving for Philadelphia, Dashkov got final directions from the Russian-American Company. The firm's directors knew about the proposed treaty but they also recognized that diplomacy moved at its own slow pace. The company needed faster action. Dashkov was ordered to locate an American merchant who could deliver provisions on a regular schedule to Russian America. But the concern wanted no ordinary entrepreneur with some Northwest coast experience. Dashkov was to negotiate with someone who had solid credentials and contacts in Canton. To aid Dashkov in these dealings, the company sent him a list of the goods it most desired from a prospective American supplier.[13]

Dashkov did not arrive in Philadelphia until late summer 1809. After establishing his credentials with the American government, he began to press the Russian case of a treaty. By August he was convinced that open diplomacy with the Americans would yield no results. It was then that Dashkov suggested deceptive language in a commercial treaty. That proposal was a measure of Dashkov's frustration. American officials seemed uninterested in Russian problems. Abandoning diplomacy, Dashkov decided to follow the Russian-American Company's suggestion and find a private merchant able to fulfill company needs.

How Dashkov met John Astor remains something of a mystery. When Washington Irving wrote his version in the 1830s, he spun out an improbable tale in which the federal government, confronted with Russian complaints, turned to Astor for advice. Irving claimed that this plea suggested to Astor the possibility of including Russian America in his grand design. At least once Astor told a very different story. Writing to Thomas Jefferson in 1812, Astor insisted that he approached Dashkov about the chances for mutual ventures in the North Pacific and the China trade.[14]

The most likely sequence of events is described in a November 1809 letter from Dashkov to Alexander Baranov. During the fall of 1809 Astor was deeply involved in two complex maneuvers, both touching on his western venture. In August he was in Montreal discussing the possible purchase of the Michilimackinac Company, negotiations that included the unspoken chance of a joint venture with the North West Company beyond the Rockies. At the same time, Astor was planning his first voyage in the coastal fur trade. His ship *Enterprise*, under Captain John Ebbets, was in the New York harbor taking on cargo. Sometime during September Dashkov heard about the sailing of the *Enterprise* and decided that Astor was just the man the Russians needed.

The conversations between Astor and Dashkov changed the course of Astoria's history. Dashkov explained Russian problems and needs, suggesting "a direct and permanent trade with our settlements." When he asked Astor about his western plans, the merchant confided that the Pacific Fur Company intended to establish a colony on the north bank of the Columbia River. Astor consistently told the Russians that his post was planned for the north bank of the Columbia. Astoria was, of course, built on the south bank. Astor may have purposely misled the Russians as part of his notion of a joint Russian and American presence that would squeeze out the Canadians. Warming to the geopolitical benefits of cooperation between the two companies, Astor suggested that if the Russians moved south while American traders moved north, the British would be eliminated as a power in the Northwest. Dashkov was taken aback by such a daring observation and gave only the vaguest of replies. But the Russian was impressed with Astor's "capital, spirit of enterprise, and business acumen."

Finding that Astor was "well disposed" toward a Russian venture, so much so that it seemed to Dashkov "as if he had had this same thought before," the Russian fashioned with Astor a proposal for cooperation between the Pacific Fur Company and the Russian-American Company. Their plan called for both companies to sign a three-year agreement. The pact made Astor the sole supplier of all goods to Russian America. He would be required to send at least two or three ships each year. Payment for these goods could be in cash, furs, or bills of exchange. Astor's ships would then be chartered by the Russian company to transport furs to Canton. Astor promised that the Russian furs would be sold to the Chinese by his commercial agent, thus concealing their true origin. Dashkov believed that a deal with Astor would achieve the goals of both company and state far quicker than any tedious negotiations with American diplomats. He was convinced that once other American merchants learned of Astor's monopoly of provision for the Russian settlements, all incentive for northern voyages would vanish. The dangerous weapons trade would promptly collapse. The settlements would be fed, furs would be sold in Canton at good prices, and Russians might feel more secure in Alaskan waters.[15]

Any plan as ambitious and far-reaching as this needed approval from both the Russian-American Company and the imperial government. But Astor and Dashkov were unwilling to wait for so lengthy a process to take its course. Sometime in October 1809 they decided to change the sailing plans for Captain Ebbets and the *Enterprise*, to include a long stay at Sitka. If this voyage was successful, it would provide practical experience for future journeys from both New York and Astoria. This meant a flurry of work for everyone from Astor and Ebbets to the *Enterprise* crew and dockhands. New supplies had to be found, some Indian trade items unloaded, and cargo manifests rewritten. The *Enterprise* had originally been loaded with a cargo suitable for the maritime fur trade. Using the list of desired goods first given to Dashkov by the Russian-American Company, Astor and Ebbets were able to reload the ship with items more suited to the needs of the Russians at Sitka. Notes from Cap-

tain Ebbets reveal the sorts of things destined for the Russian colony.
The *Enterprise* cargo hold was crammed with everything from
twenty dozen junk bottles and countless strings of blue beads to
barrels of molasses and bolts of canvas cloth. Dashkov's original list
suggested one thousand gallons each of rum and brandy. Perhaps
because he had made earlier voyages to Alaska, Ebbets knew better.
Baranov and his men were prodigious drinkers. Ebbets suggested
doubling the amounts, adding that "the liquors must be as strong as
Agua Fortis if possible."[16]

Having the right cargo for Russian needs was essential for this
first venture and subsequent success. Because Ebbets was to be
Astor's initial contact with Baranov, the captain's detailed instructions occupied much of Astor's attention. During the first week of
November, with the loading of the *Enterprise* nearly complete, Astor
drafted two sets of orders for Ebbets. One set, enclosed in Astor's
November 4 letter to Dashkov, presented in straightforward terms
how Ebbets was to deal with the Russian company. The captain was
told to sail for the Russian settlements without delay, trade at the
best and fairest terms, and then take on Russian furs for Canton.
Ebbets was granted full authority to make a binding contract with
Baranov.[17] These bland instructions were meant for Dashkov's eyes.
A rather different set went directly to Ebbets. Astor and Dashkov
had agreed that if necessary the *Enterprise* could deliver its cargo at
Okhotsk on the Siberian mainland. What Astor feared was that
Russian officials might order the *Enterprise* and future ships to sail
throughout the North Pacific as something of a private navy for the
company. The Russian part of Astor's western plan was important,
but it could not be allowed to dominate the entire venture. Ebbets
was privately told that he was not obligated to go to more than one
post in addition to the call at Sitka.[18]

Changes in the cargo manifest and detailed instructions for Ebbets took much of Astor's time. During the busy first week of November, Astor made room for an important letter to Baranov. Good
relations with the company's governor were essential, not just for
this voyage but for Astoria's future. Astor gave a brief summary of

his dealings with Dashkov and the subsequent changes in the *Enterprise*'s lading. "Nothing would be more gratifying to me," wrote Astor, "than to be in a small degree useful in assisting in the *establishing a trade* on such a footing *between us* as would secure stability and success to a trade, the importance of which is as yet only known to yourself." Knowing that details of the arrangement between Astor and the Russian-American Company were to be spelled out in a letter from Dashkov to Baranov, Astor saw no need to repeat those items. But he did want to reassure the governor about the weapons trade. Here Astor and Dashkov were in complete agreement. If American ships were denied a place in the lucrative provisioning business because Astor had a monopoly, far fewer Yankee ships would trouble Alaskan waters.[19]

By the end of November all was ready and the *Enterprise* sailed for the far Northwest. Astor was confident that this was just the beginning of a rewarding commercial relationship. And since talks with the Canadians had hit a snag, here was an opportunity to have powerful allies in the West. For his part, Dashkov was equally optimistic. "I cannot tell you," he exclaimed to Astor, "how much I wish to see the trade of furs in Canton only in the hands of both you and Mr. Baranov." Dashkov worried only that the Boston competition might prove harder to stop than Astor thought. If the Bostonians could be swept from northern waters, "then the business should become very fair."[20]

From the time he had first plotted a western course, Astor had realized that Astoria would be hostage to the shifting winds of international diplomacy. He had seen just that throughout the difficult negotiations with the North West Company. Now the twists of national policy—Russian and American—threatened to sever Astor's Russian connection. Andrei Dashkov knew that his St. Petersburg masters expected more than a hastily drawn agreement with one American merchant. The imperial court wanted a treaty with the United States and counted on Dashkov to deliver it. But he found the negotiating more difficult than expected. Writing to Rumiantsev soon after concluding talks with Astor, Dashkov complained that with Congress not in session, little could be done. And as he had reported before, American constitutional provisions made a presidential order restricting the gun trade wholly out of the question. Despite these problems, Dashkov promised to press the Russian suit with Secretary of State Robert Smith.[21] If Dashkov proved successful and a treaty was forthcoming, there would be little need for Astor's services. What the New Yorker had promised would become national policy, with no special place for him. The future of Astoria's northern view now depended on a diplomatic failure.

Dashkov began what would eventually become seven meetings with Secretary Smith by sending him copies of correspondence between the two governments dating to 1806. Smith immediately recognized that what the Russian was after was "a subject of a very delicate character." The conferences, lasting from January to March 1810, had an unchanging agenda. Dashkov repeated his belief that an American president could find some way to restrain trade in weapons along the Northwest coast. Surely no head of state was so weak that he could not stop his own citizens from endangering the lives of others, no matter how great the distance. Smith's answer was always, "This is manifestly an error." The position of the State Department was that American traders were violating no federal statutes and were liable only to specific Russian regulations. Since the United States had neither sovereign nor tributary relations with the coastal Indians, no laws were being broken by selling them guns. Smith insisted that the president had no authority to prohibit American citizens from trading with those Indians. If such provisions were ever made, they would have to come from Congress. And, repeated Smith, nothing could be done "without the usual basis of mutual stipulations."[22]

Early in their talks, the question of boundaries and land claims emerged to trouble the diplomats. The Russian-American Company had always assumed that its hunting expeditions gave the company rights down the coast as far as California. Although Dashkov could not give the secretary a precise definition of Russian claims, it was plain that the emperor and his ministers paid little heed to the discoveries of Captain Robert Gray and Lewis and Clark. The secretary of state had a curious response to all this. In 1810 the Madison administration showed little interest in advancing American claims to the Northwest. But Smith must have known about Astor's western plans. Worrying over Russian claims far to the south of the Columbia, the secretary insisted that Russian influence be kept north of the river, since the lands south of the Columbia "will enter into the plan of Indian trade likely to be embraced by our citizens." Perhaps Gallatin had let Smith in on some of Astor's proposals. Whatever the case, it was the border question that eventually stopped the Smith-Dashkov talks.[23]

These complex negotiations had not escaped Astor's notice. Although no Astor-Dashkov correspondence for this period survives, a letter to Gallatin reveals Astor's concern. Astor knew that though Dashkov's meetings with Smith were over, the secretary had not ended the Russian negotiations for good. In early May 1810 Smith had sent the first in a long series of dispatches to John Quincy Adams, then American ambassador to the imperial court. Adams was told to begin informal talks with the Russians, talks that might produce the sort of commercial treaty the Russian-American Company had long desired. Small wonder that Astor implored Gallatin to learn if the United States was contemplating any change in its policy toward Russia.[24]

Astor did not need cabinet-room intelligence to tell him that his Russian plans stood in real danger. If Adams's meetings produced a treaty, Astor had no deal. Now there was a new complication. Astor had depended on Dashkov for both information and direction. But in the spring of 1810 Andrei Dashkov suddenly became only the second most important Russian official in the United States. His new superior, and the first official Russian ambassador to the American Republic, was Count Fedor Pahlen. In his instructions from Emperor Alexander I, Pahlen was specifically directed to "bring the most serious attention of the [United States] government . . . to the disastrous consequences which such a commerce [the weapons trade] has produced, and . . . request it to forestall similar excesses and to prevent the recurrance of a similar disorder."[25]

The new ambassador took up his duties in late June 1810. Like Dashkov, Pahlen soon found that American officials were not particularly interested in the problems of one Russian trading company. An angry Pahlen wrote that he was "more and more convinced that the government of the United States has just as little desire as it has power to put an end to this illegal commerce."[26] But not all Americans were unsympathetic. Sometime toward the end of June or early July Pahlen met one Adrian Benjamin Bentzon. This was no accidental encounter. Bentzon was a former Danish diplomat with an American wife. Mrs. Bentzon was none other than Magdalen Astor, John's eldest daughter. Just when Adrian Bentzon went to work for his father-in-law is not clear, but he soon became a valued agent for Astor.

Once Astor heard that Pahlen was in Washington, he dispatched Bentzon to the Federal City. Bentzon saw to it that he and the new ambassador became fast friends. Pahlen found Bentzon an easy listener, and the Russian soon poured out his bitterness over American indifference to the firearms trade. The diplomat told Bentzon he thought it "nearly beneath the dignity of Russia to make further sollicitations." Bentzon evidently gave Pahlen a quick lecture on American political and constitutional practice, pointing out the limitations of executive authority. When the ambassador asked what could be done, Bentzon was ready. "Following the clue," he later wrote to Astor, "I opened to him your plan." That plan had its origin in the 1809 agreement with Dashkov. But now there were new refinements and additions, products of the fact that Astor's ship *Tonquin* was soon to sail and Wilson Price Hunt about to set off across the continent. Through Bentzon, Astor made the now familiar offer. He would supply provisions to Russian America, carry furs to Canton, and work to halt the gun trade. But now Astor had two new demands, one explicit and the other unspoken but unmistakable. High import duties and specific exclusions had long kept Astor and other fur merchants out of the domestic fur market in Russia. Astor wanted permission to bring into Russia each year two thousand black bear, badger, and polecat skins duty free. This exception would be for Astor alone; no other trader could benefit from it. The second, implied demand required the Russians at least to slow down their diplomatic moves toward a treaty with the United States. Astor wanted his arrangement with the Russian-American Company to take the place of any official convention. Bentzon apparently had with him a detailed written proposal to go along with his verbal presentation. Pahlen was plainly impressed, entering into the discussion "with great readiness." The ambassador promised every assistance he could muster and suggested that the quickest way for Astor to get results was to send Bentzon to St. Petersburg for direct negotiations.[27]

Astor must have been delighted with Bentzon's report. With work going forward on his Missouri and Columbia river expeditions, Astor did not want to lose his Russian chance. The problem now was to organize an unofficial diplomatic mission to St. Petersburg without running afoul of either the State Department or the American ambassador, John Quincy Adams. Gallatin was essential in all this, but Bentzon cautioned against telling him too much too soon. The treasury secretary was planning to be in New York by July 10. Bentzon urged Astor to reveal no plans until they could test Gallatin's willingness to aid such a covert undertaking.[28]

No record survives of Astor, Gallatin, and Bentzon's meeting in New York. But it is plain that Astor decided his friend could be trusted to hear full details of Bentzon's proposed journey. What Astor wanted from Gallatin was a letter from President Madison to Ambassador Adams giving Bentzon's trip at least the appearance of official business. Astor also hoped the letter might tell Adams to help the American Fur Company get a privileged share of the Russian domestic fur market. Early in September 1810 Astor wrote Gallatin asking for just that sort of assistance. It was a very private letter, since the request was bound to bring charges of meddling from the State Department. Astor wanted special status for Bentzon at the very time that Secretary Robert Smith and Ambassador Adams were still working toward a formal Russian treaty. Astor and Gallatin knew this and asked that Madison's letter for Bentzon not be routed through the Department of State.[29]

Just how much Madison knew about Astor's western plans has always been unclear. There can be no doubt that in September 1810 the president learned a great deal about Astor's Russian strategy. Either Gallatin or Astor must have fully explained to the president that what the Pacific Fur Company wanted was a full-fledged working relationship with the Russian-American Company. As before, Astor wanted federal "approbation" for these moves. Gallatin may have thought the plans promising; Madison was not impressed. "Whatever personal confidence may be due to him [Astor] or public advantage promised by his projected arrangement with the Russian Fur Company, there is an obvious difficulty in furnishing the official patronage which he wishes, whether the arrangement be regarded as of a public or of a private affair." Madison insisted that what Astor desired could be gotten only by treaty or favoritism, neither of which was forthcoming. The president had evidently also been told about Astor's interest in getting a share of the Russian home fur market. That smacked of monopoly, something Madison could not countenance. In all, the president would promise no more than "an instruction to Mr. Adams to promote the opening of the Russian market *generally* to the articles which are now excluded, and which may be exported from the United States." Madison did promise to keep all this from the secretary of state, but it was hardly the response Astor had sought.[30]

With the *Tonquin* at sea and Wilson Price Hunt's overlanders already in St. Louis, it was more important than ever that Bentzon press Astor's proposals at St. Petersburg. If the government would not give Bentzon the kind of semiofficial standing needed for the mission, perhaps something could be done more quietly. Once again Astor turned to Gallatin for help. In December 1810 Astor heard that plans were under way for the frigate *John Adams* to carry an American diplomat, George W. Erving, to Denmark. Why not slip Bentzon and his wife on board? At a time when tensions in the Atlantic were mounting, Bentzon could have no safer passage than on a vessel carrying diplomatic agents. Astor bluntly asked Gallatin to find a way to get the Bentzons on board without attracting too much attention. The secretary had no doubt that he could make the necessary arrangements. What worried him was the appearance of favoritism. Yet, as Gallatin noted on the margin of Astor's letter, if passage was denied, Bentzon would not go and the whole Russian gambit would fail.[31]

Whatever his doubts, Gallatin passed the transportation request on to Madison. Once again the State Department was kept in the dark. Since the *John Adams* was scheduled to sail in early spring of 1811, some decision was needed quickly. Madison's response to all this has not survived, but when Astor wrote to Gallatin in mid-January 1811 it was clear that the names of Adrian and Magdalen Bentzon had been added to the *John Adams* passenger list. All these undercover moves had their comic consequences. Accommodations on the *John Adams* were anything but spacious. George Erving had been assigned the only spare cabin. When the Bentzons arrived for the March sailing, Erving was pushed out. The aggrieved diplomat spent his nights trying to sleep on a lumpy sofa. Adrian Bentzon was an officious character, and Erving reported that he offended everyone on board by claiming that his Russian journey was an official mission "*deeply interesting* to the United States."[32]

With the thorny transportation question settled, Astor and Bentzon met in New York at the end of January 1811 to plot their Russian strategy. They knew they could count on Pahlen to pave the way with officials at the foreign ministry. Pahlen had already written to Foreign Minister Rumiantsev declaring that Astor's company could "carry out the views of our court efficaciously without needing the intervention of the government of the United States." With Bentzon, Astor now reviewed the proposals to be offered to the Russian-American Company. He recognized that the greatest advantages to the Russians were in regularly scheduled supply shipments and the sale of furs at Canton. Astor gave Bentzon two different supply schedules, suggesting that the Russians could select the one best suited to their needs. Even though these arrangements were sure to bring Astor some profit, he wanted Bentzon to press for Russian acceptance of two additional demands. The first was economic: Astor wanted duty-free access to the Russian domestic fur market. This demand was closely linked to a second, geopolitical request. Bentzon was to get the Russians to agree to joint action against Anglo-Canadian activities in the Northwest. Having abandoned any hope of a venture with the Nor'westers, Astor wanted Russian allies "in order to effectually check the Canadian North West company." Astor granted Bentzon full power of attorney in the coming negotiations.[33]

Adrian Bentzon reached St. Petersburg in late summer of 1811. For once the winds of diplomacy were blowing in Astor's direction. So long as Adams and Rumiantsev continued to discuss a possible Russian-American treaty, there would be little official interest in Astor's proposals. The official negotiations had been proceeding slowly but with a reasonable prospect for success. President Madison had approved a preliminary treaty draft—a draft containing an article dealing with the weapons trade on the Northwest coast. But in early August, just as Bentzon arrived in St. Petersburg, the talks broke off. Adams was convinced that war between Britain and the United States was imminent. He decided that the "extraordinary uncertainty of the present state of political affairs" ruled out further discussions. If the Russians wanted their Northwest problems resolved, they would have to turn to Astor.[34]

Once settled in the Russian capital, Bentzon prepared his presentation for the company's chief director, Michael Buldakov, and others on the board. Initial discussions took place in September 1811. Although no record of them is extant, what has survived is the company's detailed response to the Astor proposals. Two of Astor's requests were immediately rejected. Early in conversations with Pahlen, Bentzon and Astor had suggested that the two firms agree on a boundary marking their trapping territories. Such a line would, of course, exclude the North West Company from the region. The Russian concern refused to be drawn into such a scheme, arguing that boundary decisions could be made only by national governments. Bentzon met equally strong resistance when he brought up Astor's interest in selling furs in Russia. The company's directors responded that tariff and duty decisions were outside their jurisdiction. But if the imperial government did decide to grant Astor's request, the company wanted American furs to enter at only one Russian port, with all business in the hands of their own employees.

Despite these difficulties, there was much about Astor's offer that was attractive. Regular food supplies for the Alaskan settlements, increased profits from fur sales at Canton, and the resolution of the firearms problem were all important goals now within reach for the company. Buldakov and the other directors did have some worries about the day-to-day workings of an agreement. If payment for American provisions was made in bills of exchange, on whose financial house would they be drawn and in what currency? The Russians wanted bills to be payable in St. Petersburg and made in state bank notes. And what about the prices paid for Russian furs? Would fixed prices, set months before, yield the expected profits? All these doubts were finally overridden by the chance to settle once and for all the gun trade. If Astor could shut down the weapons peddlers, the company was ready to start formal negotiations. As reported to Rumiantsev, "When it pleases your Excellency that both companies confirm their mutual interests and profits according to these articles, equally and generally, the directorate of the company can settle on a special treaty with Mr. Bentzon and submit it for your approbation."[35]

By mid-October 1811 the imperial government had decided to give its permission for the two companies to reach an accord. But its permission had two important conditions. There were to be no talks on the boundary issue, that being a matter for diplomats rather than private merchants. The Russian-American Company was also commanded not to discuss "the designation of permission to import furs into Russia on account of this American company, which also belongs to the consideration of the government."[36]

With this order in hand, Bentzon and Buldakov began to draft what Astor's agent termed "a convention of good understanding and commerce between the Russian and American companies." There was little disagreement on questions of provisioning, trading at

Canton, and ending the weapons trade. But all discussion came to
an abrupt halt when Bentzon raised the matter of Astor and the
Russian home fur market. The company's officials had been warned
away from the issue just a few days before. When they reminded
Bentzon of that directive and the fact that the question was not really
a part of the Northwest's troubles that had brought the two firms
together, Bentzon astounded them with his reply. He asserted that
such permission was "the principal motive that led the American
company to seek ties with the Russian company." Whether this was a
negotiating ploy or something that reflected talks with Astor in New
York is not known. Whatever priority Astor assigned the request,
Bentzon quickly discovered that pressing it put business at a dead
stop. Buldakov was furious at this turn of events. He insisted that
Astor never intended to reach an agreement with the company.
Instead, he thought that Bentzon had been sent to find illicit means
to bring furs into Russia without paying proper duties. The Russian-
American Company wanted nothing more to do with a company
pursuing illegal goals by means of deception.[37]

What should have been a simple commercial negotiation was now
at a standstill. With official talks with Adams going nowhere, Rumiantsev had pinned his hopes on Astor. Now everything seemed in
danger just because one American businessman wanted an advantage denied to all others. In early November 1811 Rumiantsev
began to circularize other members of the government, asking for
their advice and suggestions. The first reply came from Minister of
Finance Dmitrii Gur'ev. He had carefully reviewed all Astor's correspondence and had concluded that what the Pacific Fur Company
offered was not very important after all. The minister had taken the
time to evaluate Bentzon's claim that bringing in a limited number
of furs duty free each year would not endanger the Russian economy. Gur'ev agreed that the economic consequences would be mini-
mal. But speaking with the voice of a true bureaucrat, he opposed
permission because it would amount to violating a long-standing
rule. Osipp Kozodavlev, internal affairs minister, took a much more
pragmatic view than his colleague in the finance ministry. He be-

lieved that injecting fur trade problems into the official talks with Ambassador Adams could only endanger growing ties between the two nations. Kozodavlev supported a quick resolution even if it involved bending some time-honored rules.[38]

In the midst of all this fact-gathering and official head-scratching, the Russian-American Company issued its annual shareholders report. The report summarized talks with Bentzon, noting that the discussions were at a stop until the imperial court decided which course to take. "What decision our government will take in this matter," concluded the directors, "is still unknown." Russian stockholders now knew what had caused the delay. American friends of Astoria got much the same information. Astor had always viewed Jefferson as an unofficial partner in the Pacific Fur Company. When Bentzon informed Astor about the troubles in St. Petersburg, Astor passed the news on to Monticello. Although not giving Jefferson all the details, Astor did reveal the tangle over exporting American furs to Russia. Despite these difficulties, he was sure that Bentzon would smooth things out. Ever confident, Astor confided to Jefferson, "I think we shall do very well as far as respects that part of our business." In the meantime Jefferson was urged to consider "the contemplated arrangement with the Russians as Privet."[39]

It was not until the middle of February 1812 that the Russian government finally decided what to do about Astor's plan. Writing to Bentzon, Rumiantsev said that the emperor strongly desired cooperation between the two fur companies. However, Astor was not going to be granted any special concessions in the domestic fur market. Rumiantsev told Bentzon to settle as best he could with the Russian-American Company "if this will answer your mutual interests." Clearly exasperated with all the bickering and delays, Rumiantsev wanted to hear no more on the subject. "The intervention of the government is in no way necessary for this."[40]

Both Bentzon and Buldakov evidently got the message. Astor's man quickly dropped the fur importation demand, and the Russian director seemed less worried about means of payment for American goods. From February to early May 1812 the talks went on at a slow pace. Finally, on May 2 Bentzon and representatives of the Russian-American Company signed a tentative agreement. The two companies promised not to hunt or trade on the territory of the other. But the document scrupulously avoided defining those territories or setting boundaries. Firmer language could be found in the article dealing with selling firearms. This was the issue that had originally brought the two companies together. It was no surprise that the provisions here were unambiguous. Both parties agreed not to sell weapons to Indians "in all areas occupied now or in the future by the two companies, or in their vicinity." For all this firm resolve, the agreement held no method to punish those who violated the provision. Astor expected that his profits would come from the sale of foodstuffs to the Russian settlements. The Russians agreed to buy goods from Astor alone, with prices to be fixed both by the Russian manager at Sitka and by Astor. This purchase monopoly would be honored unless Astor's ships were delayed by accident or American prices were considered exorbitant by the field manager. These transactions were to be paid for either by bills of exchange payable in St. Petersburg or by furs at Sitka. The Russians had not forgotten Astor's promise to carry their furs to Canton whenever needed.[41] All that was required now was Astor's signature.

When Astor got his copy of the contract at the end of 1812, the war that was to doom Astoria was already seven months old. Whatever his fears for the post on the Columbia and trade with the Russians, Astor signed the agreement. Perhaps he thought his new partners might be of some value in keeping Astoria alive. On December 20, 1812, Astor approved his Russian connection. Astoria had less than a year left under the American flag. But none of that was known in New York. As Andrei Dashkov had once told Astor, "The business should become very fair."[42]

4

To Astoria by Sea

JOHN ASTOR NEVER set down the precise date that marked Astoria as a full-fledged western enterprise. Perhaps it was in early March 1810 when he and some of his Canadian partners signed an initial agreement creating the Pacific Fur Company. Or it may have been some months earlier when Astor had patiently explained to Albert Gallatin just how his maritime and overland parties would rendezvous on the Columbia. Then again a more fitting date may have been sometime in 1809 when Astor had hired Wilson Price Hunt as his chief field agent. Whatever Astoria's proper birthdate, by spring 1810 all was in place to launch the first American venture in the West since Lewis and Clark. Astoria's future now depended on strong men and sturdy ships.

Astoria was at last something more than requests for official approbation. That Astoria was rapidly becoming a substantial fact of western life had not escaped the Montreal Nor'westers. In late January 1810 the Canadians knew spring would see Astor's land and sea expeditions heading for the Columbia. What had been polite warnings to London in earlier letters now took on an air of urgency. "We are well informed that an expedition for the purpose of making establishments on the Columbia river and the Northwest coast, is

now in contemplation to sail from New York early next spring."
Would the home government allow such a clear invasion of territories long claimed by Britain? The Nor'westers wanted prompt official action, perhaps pressure on the East India Company to relax its
monopolistic grip on the China trade. Only then could the Montreal
traders defeat Astoria.[1]

Defeat was the last thing on Astor's mind in the early spring of
1810. In March he and his Canadian partners, Alexander McKay,
Duncan McDougall, and Donald Mackenzie met in New York to sign
the Pacific Fur Company's provisional agreement. At the same time
Wilson Price Hunt was busy in Washington meeting with Madison
and Gallatin. In one of the few extant letters written by Hunt, Astor's
agent noted that his talks centered on a suitable candidate for territorial governor now that Meriwether Lewis was dead. Perhaps
Hunt also let both officials know how far Astoria had progressed.[2]

Astoria now needed clerks and engagés. Despite all the nationalism in Astor's claims about hiring young Americans for his company,
Astoria required the skill and sinewy strength of Canadians. For
generations the settlement of Lachine, outside Montreal, had been
the place to recruit such men. The voyageurs of Lachine were bred
to the trade, ready to risk their lives paddling the great *canots de
maître* that could carry a three-ton payload through the Great Lakes
to Fort William. Like St. Louis and Westport on the Oregon Trail,
Lachine was the jumping-off place for the western fur trade. Men,
supplies, and canoes—all could be had at Lachine's taverns and
warehouses.

Early in May, Hunt, Mackenzie, and McKay set up shop at Lachine. The Canadian partners knew how to spread the word. The
Pacific Fur Company was touted as a powerful, well-financed concern every bit as prestigious as the North West Company. Alexander
Ross, one of the first clerks hired for Astoria, recalled that everyone
from experienced voyageurs to stay-at-home barbers and draymen
soon heard about the "gilded prospectus of the new company."
Astor's recruiters were quickly overwhelmed by "crowds of bluster-
ing voyageurs of all grades and qualities."[3] A bemused spectator to

all this described the eager applicants as "wonder-stricken believers" who flocked "from all quarters to share in the wonderful riches of the Far West." There were in fact far more prospective Astorians than places for them. Although Hunt was Astor's chief agent, he had no experience in either fur trade recruiting or expedition outfitting. With the list of eager candidates growing daily, Donald Mackenzie was given the task of selecting those with the best qualifications.[4]

Those not engaged by the new company went off in more than an angry huff. The unlucky applicants began to spread unpleasant rumors (out of spite, Ross believed) about the Astorian venture. Tavern gossip soon had it that the Pacific Fur Company was desperately short of funds; its employees would end up abandoned in the West with empty pockets and blasted fortunes. But the rumor-mongers were others besides the disgruntled and the rejected. In May the Montreal Nor'westers had finally decided to refuse any offer of a joint venture with Astor. His company was now the opposition, to be fought as the Nor'westers had battled the Hudson's Bay Company. Wherever voyageurs and traders gathered and the talk turned to Astor, men from the North West Company tried their best to "throw all the cold water of the St. Lawrence on the project."[5]

Despite these troubles, Mackenzie was able to begin hiring reliable men. That effort suddenly ground to a halt when Hunt and Mackenzie became embroiled in a nasty argument. The two men had been at swords' points from the first. Mackenzie had no use for the St. Louis merchant, a man he saw as inexperienced and unfit for any frontier adventure. For his part, Hunt evidently resented Mackenzie's boisterous, often colorful Nor'wester ways. Now the two clashed on an important issue. How many Canadians should be engaged for the two expeditions? Astor knew that some Canadians were essential, but he had instructed Hunt to keep the number as small as possible. Mackenzie held the opposite view. He believed that the fortunes of the company depended on French-Canadian skill and endurance. Mackenzie had no use for the southwesters, the American hunters and traders of Mackinac and St. Louis. There is no evidence to suggest who intervened to settle the wrangling. What

Gabriel Franchère. From Franchère, *Journal of a Voyage on the North West Coast* (1854). Collection of the author.

is clear is that an uneasy compromise was struck between Hunt and Mackenzie. The company would hire twenty-five or thirty Canadians. Some would travel with Hunt while the rest were to board the *Tonquin*. Hunt would enlarge his overland expedition by engaging Americans at Mackinac and St. Louis. The squabble was settled, but the rift between Hunt and Mackenzie deepened.[6]

With so many eager prospects Mackenzie had no difficulty engaging voyageurs. Soon the Pacific Fur Company's ledger held the names of men like Pierre Picotte, Louis La Liberté, and Jean Baptiste Delorme. Others soon followed, like the brothers Ignace and Bazile Lapensée and the blacksmith Augustus Roussel. Little is known about these Astorians, but one, Jean Baptiste Perrault, did leave behind a sketchy memoir revealing something more about recruiting at Lachine. Perrault had been a Nor'wester, but hard times in the trade had forced him to move to St. François des Abenakis. There he and his wife lived in near poverty, scraping to make ends meet by keeping a small country school. In May he heard that Alexander McKay was hiring for a "Colombine expedition." Perrault hurried to Montreal, met McKay, and was promptly engaged as a clerk. His engagement was for five years at eighty pounds per year. With his extensive Great Lakes experience, Perrault was assigned to the overland expedition. By the end of May voyageur hiring was complete. Mackenzie and McKay had engaged fourteen Canadians for the *Tonquin's* voyage. At the same time they had signed another fourteen for the overland journey. To get the overlanders through the Great Lakes, Joseph Robilliard had been signed as a guide.[7]

Astoria needed more than tough canoeists. Daily business affairs had to be transacted and recorded by diligent clerks. In the fur trade world, clerking was no menial occupation. Clerks were responsible young men who assumed that with hard work and some luck they might become partners in the company. Two of Astoria's clerks recorded their recollections of recruiting at Lachine. Gabriel Franchère was the son of a Montreal merchant. Stranded in the family countinghouse, Franchère dreamed of adventure and fortune in the West. Sometime during the winter of 1809–10 a friend told him about Astor's proposed expedition. When Astor's partners came to Montreal, Franchère hurried to enlist as a clerk. As he explained it, "The novelty of the voyage led me to seek employment in the new association."[8] Meeting with Alexander McKay on May 20, Franchère quickly signed his five-year engagement.

Franchère wanted adventure and escape from mercantile boredom. Alexander Ross's motives had more to do with financial survival. Ross was an immigrant Scot, a down-on-his-luck schoolmaster who needed a job and a fresh start. His chance came in May 1810 when his friend and countryman Alexander McKay invited Ross to Montreal. Once there he signed on as a clerk to the *Tonquin* party.

Alexander Ross. From Ross, *The Fur Hunters of the Far West* (1855).
Collection of the author.

The Pacific Fur Company needed more than two clerks. Others
were soon hired, including Donald McGillis, Ovide de Montigny,
and François Pillet. Although Russel Farnham was an American from
Massachusetts, he too was recruited at Montreal. And there were
two new Stuarts. David Stuart, perhaps an ex-Nor'wester, was offered a partnership in the company. His young nephew Robert, who

had been a clerk with the North West Company, was destined to become an Astorian junior partner.

Montreal and Lachine provided more than Astoria's manpower. Warehouses along the St. Lawrence were filled with the sorts of expedition supplies and trade goods needed for Hunt's overlanders. As an experienced senior partner, Alexander McKay took charge of outfitting Hunt's men. Although he assumed that the *Tonquin* would carry the bulkiest trade goods, the overlanders needed merchandise of all kinds. In the weeks before Hunt and Mackenzie left, McKay scoured the supply houses looking for everything from cooking kettles and provision bags to vermilion and point blankets. He paid special attention to medical needs, buying calomel, mercury for treating venereal diseases, and that all-purpose remedy Turlington's balsam salve. And like Lewis and Clark, McKay bought portable soup, paying $35.38 for twelve containers of what most explorers found unpalatable. McKay's drafts submitted to Astor amounted to fifteen hundred dollars "on account of articles furnished by A McKay for an Expedition to the Columbia River across the Country."[9]

With all recruiting and provisioning complete, it was time to divide the Astorians into the *Tonquin* and the overland parties. Fitted out with voyageurs and supplies, Hunt and Mackenzie left Lachine in a *canot de maître* on July 2. Several days later Alexander McKay took a crew of eight expert paddlers and headed to New York by way of Lake Champlain and the Hudson River. Two weeks later Alexander Ross, Robert Stuart, and more voyageurs went by land to New York. It was not until July 26 that Franchère and the remaining Astorians left Lachine. The young clerk found the moment of departure harder than he had expected. As he admitted in his diary, "For the first time I found myself obliged to part from all that I held dearest in the world."[10]

Franchère and his crew took the St. Lawrence to the Richelieu River portage and on to Lake Champlain. By the first of August they were at Lansingburg on the Hudson. In high spirits they headed toward New York. Franchère recalled that their songs and shouts while passing Troy and Albany made onlookers believe the fur men were "a canoeful of Indians." Late on the night of August 3 Franchère's canoe reached its destination. The next day the Canadians paddled around the harbor to their lodgings on Long Island. Once again the spectacle of voyageurs and a bark canoe drew much attention. "We sang," wrote Franchère, "and the sight of a birch-bark canoe attracted crowds of people to the quays."[11]

* * *

Long before the Canadians arrived, Astor had been busy preparing his maritime venture to the Columbia. He could already draw on experience gained in readying the *Enterprise* for a similar voyage. Astor's first task was to find a ship suitable for the journey. New York was the home port for many solid ships, but even the most ardent proponent of that city's commerce knew that the best ships and crews in the Northwest and China trades sailed from Boston. Throughout the summer of 1810 Astor searched for just the right vessel. Sometime during that search the ship *Tonquin* drew Astor's attention. Known as a fast sailer and described by her designer as "beautifully modelled" and a "first-rate ship," the *Tonquin* seemed the very vessel Astor had in mind. On August 23, no more than two weeks before she sailed for the Columbia, the final registration papers were made out to Astor. For $37,860 he bought a fine ship with a terrible destiny.[12]

The *Tonquin* was indeed a sweet ship. Her designer and first master was Captain Edmund Fanning, one of the first Americans to ply the China and Pacific trades. After several Pacific sailings, Fanning determined to construct a ship designed specifically for those routes. On the first day of March 1807 the *Tonquin*'s keel was laid at the New York shipyard of Adam and Noah Brown. Shipwrights working under Fanning's "superintendence and inspiration" completed the vessel by the end of May. The first certificate of registration describes her as ninety-four feet long, twenty-five feet wide, and twelve feet deep. Her burden was 269 tons. The *Tonquin*'s hull was pierced for twenty-two guns, but she never carried more than ten,

The *Tonquin*. From Edmund Fanning, *Voyages to the South Seas* (1838). Collection of the author.

the remaining ports filled with dummy cannon. The *Tonquin*'s speed was evident on her maiden voyage. After leaving New York on May 26, 1807, Fanning headed for Canton. The vessel made the entire China circuit in ten months, no record but surely some handy sailing. In later years the *Tonquin* made a second Pacific journey before being sold to Astor.[13]

While Astor was scouting for a ship, he was also hunting for a reliable captain. With John Ebbets away on the *Enterprise*, Astor needed a master with proven skill, initiative, and courage. The sailor Astor finally settled on was Jonathan Thorn, a United States Navy lieutenant on temporary leave from official service. Thorn had had a successful, even noteworthy, naval career. Born in Schenectady in 1779, Thorn had joined the navy in 1800 as a midshipman. When Thomas Jefferson sent naval forces to the Mediterranean in 1801, Thorn found himself far from home. During actions off Tripoli he served with distinction and was promoted to acting lieutenant. At the end of 1805 Thorn returned to the United States. In the following summer he was named first commandant of the New York Navy Yard. Perhaps it was here that he first caught John Astor's eye. A promotion to full lieutenant came soon after Thorn assumed his New York command.[14]

Thorn's years at sea had made him value order and obedience to authority. He expected prompt compliance with his every command. Gabriel Franchère, who had more time than he wished to observe Thorn at close quarters, summed him up in the following fashion: "A precise and rigid man, naturally hot-tempered, expecting instant obedience at the slightest sign, considering only his duty and caring nothing else for the discontented mutterings of his crew, asking advice of no man and following to the letter the instructions that he had received from Mr. Astor—such, approximately, was the man who had been appointed to command our ship."[15]

A naval career with so promising a beginning now ground nearly to a halt in the New York Navy Yard. Promotions in the peacetime navy were few. The chance for Thorn to command a ship was even more remote. By the fall of 1809 he must have been convinced that time away from the navy was essential. Going on half-pay status while taking a commercial command proved attractive for many younger officers. On October 20 Thorn petitioned the secretary of the navy for a two-year leave to attend to personal business. It has often been argued that this request was prompted by Astor. However, nothing in Thorn's letter points to the New York merchant. Navy Secretary Paul Hamilton did not act quickly on Thorn's plea. In fact, it was not until May 18, 1810, that the unhappy officer was granted his leave. Once again there is no surviving evidence to suggest that Astor had any hand in getting Thorn his half-pay status.[16] Sometime between May and August 1810 Thorn did become the *Tonquin*'s new master. With the amount of work needed to prepare for the Columbian voyage, Thorn must have been in Astor's employ well before August.[17]

Although the *Tonquin* had made two very successful Pacific voyages, there was much to be done before she could again put to sea. The vessel had been idle for nearly seven months and required a good overhaul. Equally important, the *Tonquin* had to be loaded with a salable cargo and manned by a good crew. No detailed cargo manifests for the *Tonquin* have been found, but it is possible to reconstruct her lading by examining the list of goods delivered to David Stuart at Astoria in July 1811. Stuart was then on his way to establish the Pacific Fur Company's first interior trading post. He obtained his trade goods directly from the stores left by the *Tonquin*. Like so many other ships in the maritime fur trade, the *Tonquin* carried everything from colored cloth and tobacco to gunflints and a wide variety of hardware. Her cargo cost Astor $54,263.37. Although Stuart's "Invoice of Sundry Merchandise" does not show it, the vessel also had on board nearly a ton of gunpowder.[18]

The *Tonquin*'s cargo hold carried something more than barrels of provisions and bales of trade goods. Stowed away were the timbers and frames for a small sailing vessel, which would be assembled at Astoria and used in the coastal trade. Just how Astor came on such an idea is not known, but at least one other fur trade skipper, Captain James Colnett, had tried a similar plan.[19] As it turned out, the *Dolly* (named after Astor's daughter Dorothea) proved far too unseaworthy for the coastal trade. She was eventually relegated to shuttling up and down the Columbia bringing supplies to Astoria.

No matter how good the ship or skillful the captain, success for the *Tonquin*'s voyage depended on an experienced crew. Throughout August, Thorn and his first officer, J. C. Fox, worked to fill the ship's complement. William P. Mumford signed as second officer while Peter Anderson came to the *Tonquin* as her boatswain. Henry Weeks joined the crew as the ship's carpenter and Stephen Weeks, perhaps his brother, was hired as armorer. Two free blacks also sailed with the *Tonquin*. Francis Robertson served as steward; Thomas Williams spent his days in the galley. Any ship under sail needed the skills of a sailmaker; Aaron Slaight held that place. Egbert Vandehoop was the ship's tailor. The *Tonquin* needed able-bodied seamen to handle her sails and lines. Like most sailing vessels, the *Tonquin* had a young crew. Edward Ames and Peter Verstille were seventeen; Adam Fictor and Elisha Gibbs were nineteen. Most of the sailors were in their twenties. At thirty-eight, John Martin was the crew's old man. The youngest member of the *Tonquin*'s crew was

James C. Thorn, the sixteen-year-old brother of the captain. James Thorn, along with Robert Hill, were the ship's boys.[20]

The *Tonquin* also had on board four "mechanics" destined for duty at Astoria. These men had maritime skills but were not listed as part of the *Tonquin*'s complement. The ship's carpenter, Johann Koaster, was hired to supervise construction at Astoria. George Bell was signed as cooper, a skill much in demand at every frontier post. Someone was needed to assemble the *Dolly*. That task fell to Job Aitken, a Scots rigger and caulker. Augustus Roussel, a blacksmith engaged at Lachine, filled out the list of Astoria's artisans.[21]

While Thorn and his officers were busy with the *Tonquin*, Astor looked after some last-minute details. Several clerks had been hired at Montreal but more were needed. One of those new additions was James Lewis of New York. Enlisting a new clerk may have reminded Astor that his Canadians were running up bills at boardinghouses in Brooklyn and on Long Island. Robert Stuart and most of the clerks were lodged on Long Island. Throughout August, Astor regularly paid bills from $60 to $70 for these men. The senior partners—David Stuart, Duncan McDougall, and Alexander McKay—who were to go on the *Tonquin* stayed closer to Astor, at Mrs. Saidler's rooming house. For what must have been handsome rooms, the company paid $394.50.[22]

Cargo manifests, bills payable, and ship's papers were the necessary routine before putting to sea. Astor knew about these transactions, but there were other preparations unknown to him. Once in New York, Alexander McKay and David Stuart began to worry about their possible capture by a British warship. In the summer of 1810 tensions between the United States and Britain were running high. Ships of the Royal Navy were regularly stopping American merchantmen and often impressing sailors into service for the crown. How would British subjects in the employ of a New York company fare if found aboard an American ship? McKay and Stuart feared that should war erupt between the two nations, Canadian Astorians would be at great risk. Sometime during August the two traders decided to take their concerns to the British ambassador,

Francis James Jackson, who was then in New York on official business. Astor was to know none of this. At the meeting with Jackson, McKay and Stuart explained the nature of their impending voyage and the chance that an Anglo-American war would jeopardize both them and their enterprise. As Franchère heard it later, the diplomat allowed that they "were going on a very hazardous enterprise." Accepting the commercial nature of the venture, Jackson promised "that in case of war [the Canadians] should be respected as British subjects and traders." McKay and Stuart were evidently pleased with this and let the other Canadians know that they were reasonably secure.[23]

Astor did not know about the meeting with Jackson until sometime later. In fact, he was led to believe that his Canadian partners and employees were headed not for British officials but for American ones. Astor also could not but worry that the citizenship of his men put both them and their venture in danger. Sometime during August he decided to require at least the engagés to become naturalized American citizens. The voyageurs agreed and promised to take the required oaths before sailing. As late as February 1813 Astor still believed that his Canadians were legally Americans. But he was quite wrong, and had he known about the secret meeting with Jackson he might have worried even more about Astoria's future.[24]

Having taken so much care with the *Tonquin*, Astor made one last move to insure her safe departure. Rumors in New York had it that British naval vessels from Halifax were just off the coast waiting to pounce on American merchant ships. Astor had even convinced himself that the North West Company had had a hand in stationing these ships as a means to block his Pacific plans. Recalling the events for Washington Irving, Astor claimed that he went to visit Commodore John Rogers, then senior naval officer in New York. Astor asked Rogers to provide an escort for the *Tonquin* past any British vessels. When Rogers questioned the propriety of such action, he was told by "a high official source" that the government had a "deep interest" in the voyage. According to Astor, the commodore promptly ordered the U.S.S. *Constitution*, then in the New York harbor, to convey the *Tonquin* into the Atlantic. This story has the ring of truth, but the only evidence to support it comes in Irving's *Astoria*.[25] A thorough search of the records of the secretary of the navy, of Commodore Rogers, and of the *Constitution*'s captain, Isaac Hull, reveals no mention of either Astor or the *Tonquin*.

By the first week of September 1810 nearly all preparations were complete. The *Tonquin*'s cargo was loaded, her crew signed, and passengers put on notice to ready themselves for departure. With so much riding on this voyage, Astor wanted both Thorn and the Canadians to have a clear understanding of what was expected from them. For that reason Astor drafted two letters, one for Thorn and the other for the partners. Astor knew that the tensions of a long voyage might explode to the injury of all. His letter to Thorn was filled with admonitions about "good humour and harmony on board." Perhaps already sensing the possibility of trouble between Thorn and the Canadians, Astor called on the captain to exercise "your particular good management." But nothing worried Astor more than the prospect of violence directed against his ship by coastal Indians. He knew the risks and, as it turned out, had a better grasp of the dangers than the overconfident Thorn. "I must recommend you," Astor instructed his captain, "to be particularly careful on the coast, and not to rely too much on the friendly disposition of the natives." He claimed that "all accidents which has as yet happened there arose from too much confidence in the Indians." Astor's history was inaccurate but his concern was well founded.[26]

Astor had similar words of advice for his partners. Again alluding to possible tensions with Thorn, Astor pleaded with the Canadians to "cultivate harmony and unanimity." Not knowing much about Thorn's strict attention to the rituals of command, Astor suggested that "all differences of opinions on points connected with the objects and interests of the voyage should be discussed by the whole, and decided by a majority of votes." But the *Tonquin* was no republic, and neither her master nor her passengers cared for reasoned debate. Indian affairs at Astoria were also on Astor's mind. Without good relations with the native people, Astoria would be a fruitless as well as a dangerous enterprise. "If you find them kind as I hope you will," Astor wrote, "be so to them. If otherwise, act with caution and forebearance, and convince them that you come as friends."[27]

* * *

On the morning of September 6 partners, clerks, and voyageurs gathered at the wharf to board the *Tonquin*. Alexander Ross never forgot the scene that greeted him when he got to the dock. "All was bustle and confusion on deck, and every place in the ship was in such a topsy-turvy state, with what sailors call live and dead lumber, that scarcely anyone knew how or where he was to be stowed."[28] Like other ships of the day, the *Tonquin* was not built for the passenger trade. Now she was expected to carry twenty-nine extra men. The partners certainly assumed they would enjoy accommodations befitting their rank. The clerks and canoeists also saw themselves as a cut above the sailors. When Ross, Franchère, and the others were assigned to a cramped, poorly ventilated space behind the fo'c'sle, a violent argument erupted. McKay charged that Thorn and his officers had ignored Astor's orders by putting company employees in such uncomfortable quarters. Thorn's reaction to this was quick and wholly predictable. McKay had challenged the power of a captain, one especially jealous of his own authority. The *Tonquin* was Thorn's first command, and he was not about to share the quarterdeck with anyone. In the first of what would be many threats of violence, the irate captain warned he would shoot any man—trader or sailor— who disobeyed his orders. As tempers flared, David Stuart stepped in to calm the waters. The storming and shouting subsided as the Canadians went off to string their hammocks in what Franchère described as a "dark, unventilated, unwholesome place." This row was over, but it was just "the first specimen . . . of the captain's disposition, and it laid the foundation of a rankling hatred between the partners and himself which ended only with the voyage."[29]

At midday on September 6 the *Tonquin* dropped her lines and headed out into the New York harbor. Although the voyage had started with a windy argument, the winds the ship really needed suddenly failed. The vessel spent the rest of the day tacking and drifting off Staten Island. The following day proved no better. Again the *Tonquin* wallowed in swells, anchored near the Sandy Hook light.[30]

On the eighth the wind freshened and the *Tonquin* crossed the bar, dropped her pilot, and sailed into the open sea. With the long-awaited voyage finally under way, Franchère found himself possessed by gloomy thoughts. "I found myself at sea for the first time and looking anxiously at the land that I might never see again." The clerk admitted that he "indulged in some serious thoughts about the nature of the voyage that we were embarking upon." What he had imagined would be the beginning of a novel adventure now seemed to promise only a "troublesome voyage." The reverie was snapped when the *Tonquin*'s lookout spied a large ship bearing down from the southwest. This vessel signaled, and Thorn reefed topsails to slow progress. When the ship came alongside, she was identified as the *Constitution*. For most of the rest of the day the two ships sailed in company. Both Ross and Franchère recorded the rendezvous, specifically identifying the escort as Old Ironsides. The Astorians and their chroniclers have all pointed to the incident as further proof of Astor's influence in government. On September 8, 1810, there were three naval vessels in the New York harbor, including the *Constitution*. A careful examination of the deck logs of those ships indicates that none left anchor on that day. The log of the *Constitution* makes no mention of escorting any ship beyond Sandy Hook. Astoria has many mysteries, and this remains one of the most perplexing. Franchère and Ross, both reliable observers, surely saw something. The identity of the phantom escort remains unknown.[31]

The *Tonquin*'s putting out to sea did not go unnoticed. John Philip Morier, British charge d'affaires in Washington, included her departure in his regular report to Viscount Wellesley. Morier knew about the *Tonquin*'s venture as well as the overland expedition. What drew his special concern was the chance that there might be trouble between the Astorians and British traders. "It has been impossible," he wrote, "for me to be informed whether any collision with our traders, established by priority on that coast, has been foreseen by the managers of the American Company." That concern was lost on official London, and the *Tonquin*'s voyage quickly slipped from notice.[32]

Sailing the Atlantic at last, the *Tonquin* made steady progress in brisk winds. Her seasick passengers fared less well. Overcrowding remained a serious problem. Clerks and voyageurs were so tightly packed into their narrow cabin that they often could not string their hammocks. But there were diversions and new sights. At a loss how to fill their days, the Canadians went fishing. Their first catch, flying fish, obliged the sailors by landing on deck without benefit of hook or line. Dolphins proved a more difficult quarry. Franchère and his companions did manage to catch two, and the young Canadian pronounced them "delicious eating."[33]

By the first week of October the *Tonquin* had caught the trade winds and was sailing south-southwest. On October 5 lookouts sighted the Cape Verde Islands. Ships often stopped at the islands to replenish dwindling water supplies. With heat and humidity so high as to be oppressive, crew and passengers certainly expected Thorn to put in for a brief visit. But the captain was worried about more than the level of his water casks. He was convinced that British cruisers were lurking nearby, ready to strike any unsuspecting vessel. No matter how thirsty the *Tonquin*, Thorn was not about to jeopardize his first command. With temperatures soaring, the captain's decision was unpopular. When the winds failed and the ship lay dead in a flat calm, all aboard suffered.[34]

Grumbling about short rations and slow sailing suddenly ended on October 16. On a day punctuated by violent thunderstorms, lookouts spotted an unidentified ship bearing on a course that would soon intercept the *Tonquin*'s own. Morning light the next day showed the unmarked vessel to be a large brig mounting twenty guns. In strong winds the ships ran neck and neck throughout the day. Toward evening the *Tonquin* gained the wind's leading edge and outdistanced her partner. But the Astorians had not seen the last of her. On the morning of the eighteenth she appeared again, once more flying no identifying flag or pennant. Thorn was now convinced that his ship was in real danger. He ordered all hands on deck, and both crew and passengers "pretended to be preparing for action." With decks cleared and guns run out, the *Tonquin* might appear formidable to any enemy. But it was a freshening wind, not the ship's guns, that saved the Astorians from a dangerous encounter.[35]

These were isolated moments of drama in what was settling down to be a long, often tedious voyage. Shipboard routine was broken toward the end of October when the *Tonquin* crossed the equator. Those "polywogs" who had never crossed the line were commanded to appear before King Neptune and his court. "Following the old custom of the sea, the crew baptized those who had not already crossed the line."[36] But these high spirits could not hide the growing tensions between Thorn and his passengers. Franchère's early fears that this would prove a "troublesome voyage" were coming true. Thorn detested his Canadian passengers, describing them as a "lubberly" lot. Looking to the clerks, he branded them "rank pretenders" who had never been west of Mackinac. The captain especially resented Ross and Franchère, thinking that their journals were secret records denouncing him to Astor. Thorn labeled Ross "as foolish a pedant as ever lived." The engagés bore the brunt of Thorn's wrath. Voyageur songs and stories infuriated the captain. Even the French-Canadian patois got under his skin. When the Canadians complained about their diet, Thorn exploded. "These are the fine fellows who made such a boast that they could 'eat dogs.'"[37] Thorn finally banished the partners from the captain's side (the starboard side) of the quarterdeck. The clerks were not permitted on the quarterdeck at all. As for the rest of the Astorians, Ross recalled that they were "ruled with a rod of iron."[38]

All these misunderstandings and petty tyrannies came to a head when the *Tonquin* reached the Falkland Islands. The Falklands had long been a water and provision call for ships in the South Atlantic. By the end of November the *Tonquin*'s company was on short water rations, each man allowed no more than three half-pints a day. When the Falklands were sighted at dusk on December 3, all aboard dreamed of thirsts slaked at last. The following morning some of that good cheer was dampened when the men got a clear look at the desolate Falklands landscape. Contrary winds and threatening weather kept the *Tonquin* from sending her crew ashore until December 6. Putting in at Port Egmont on Saunders Island, the ship found good anchorage. For the next few days both crew and passengers busied themselves replenishing water barrels and hunting island game.[39]

By the morning of December 11 all work was complete and the *Tonquin* was ready to stand out to sea. Eight or nine men, including Ross, Franchère, Farnham, McDougall, and David Stuart, were still on the island. While they lingered on shore, Thorn grew increasingly angry. By noon he had had enough. After sending signals for an immediate departure—signals evidently not seen on the island—the *Tonquin* was readied for sea. About 2 P.M. one of those on shore saw the *Tonquin* weigh anchor and begin to leave Port Egmont. "We knew too well," wrote Ross, "the callous and headstrong passions of the wayward Captain to hesitate a moment in determining what to do." Some ran down to the beach to prepare a longboat while others shouted and fired guns to summon McDougall and Stuart. It was more than a half hour before the unlucky company could put to sea in what Ross described as a "trumpery little boat scarcely capable of holding half our number." With the *Tonquin* some three miles out and the wind and tide running against the men, all seemed lost.

While the Astorians were bending their backs in pursuit of the ship, there was high drama on the *Tonquin's* quarterdeck. Once the men had turned up missing, a furious argument erupted between Thorn and Robert Stuart. When Stuart's pleadings proved fruitless, he turned to direct action. Drawing two pistols from his coat, the Canadian threatened to kill Thorn unless the ship put about and picked up the longboat and its nearly exhausted crew. "You are a dead man this instant" was what Stuart was reputed to have told the astonished captain. Confronted by a man Thorn knew was as good as his word, the captain ordered the course change. High seas and shifting winds made a rendezvous with the longboat difficult, and it was not until dark that the rescue was complete.[40]

No single incident did more to poison relations between Thorn and the Astorians than this. The Astorians found their near-marooning proof that the captain was a heartless martinet determined to exercise his authority no matter the human cost. But Thorn saw the incident in a very different light. Writing later to Astor, he apologized for the rescue. Thorn argued that the whole enterprise would have been better off without such untrustworthy employees. "They seem to have no idea of the value of property," he exclaimed, "nor any apparent regard for your interest, although interwoven with their own." The *Tonquin* now carried two hostile camps, neither speaking to the other. Ross caught the mood on board. "The partners on the quarter now made it a point to speak nothing but the Scotch dialect, while the Canadians on the forecastle spoke French—neither of which did the Captain understand; and as both groups frequently passed hours together, cracking their jokes and chanting their outlandish songs, the Commander seemed much annoyed on these occasions, pacing the deck in great agitation."[41]

Despite storms both personal and atmospheric, the *Tonquin* made good progress. At the end of December 1810 she doubled Cape Horn and entered the Pacific. Blustery weather during January made for swift sailing. The *Tonquin's* destination was the Hawaiian Islands. From the time of their European discovery by Captain James Cook in 1778, the islands had been recognized by maritime fur traders as an ideal place to obtain provisions, water, and other comforts. In 1786 two English vessels, commanded by Captains George Dixon and Nathaniel Portlock, had spent twenty days in the islands. The following year six ships had called to trade. Hawaii soon became an important part of the China trade. The Hawaiians were astute bargainers, ready to exchange island produce for European metal goods. The experience of John Boit, the young skipper of the American sloop *Union*, was typical. For nails, iron hoops, and assorted hardware Boit filled his vessel with vegetables and fruit. Pigs and hogs, the royal monopoly of King Kamehameha, were available only for guns and ammunition.[42] The islands offered more than provisions. Young Hawaiians ready for adventure and profit could be hired as skilled sailors. By the 1790s island natives were signing on for voyages to Nootka Sound and China. When the *Tonquin* reached the islands in 1811, Kamehameha and his people were already part of an international trade system that stretched from Bristol and Boston to Alaska and China. Long before pale tourists filled her beaches, Hawaii was the commercial crossroads of the Pacific. Whatever the weary traveler needed—food, affection, or a berth on a new ship—could be had beneath the shadow of Mauna Loa.[43]

On February 11 the *Tonquin*'s lookout sighted the top of a snow-capped mountain. Second Officer Mumford, who had been to the islands before, quickly identified the peak as Mauna Loa on the island of Hawaii. Perhaps taking direction from Mumford, Thorn steered toward Kealakekua Bay on the west side of Hawaii. As the *Tonquin* neared the island she was surrounded by canoes filled with local merchants eager to sell vegetables and coconuts. The following day the *Tonquin* dropped anchor in Kealakekua Bay. Once again Hawaiian vendors swarmed around the ship, offering everything from bananas and yams to cabbages and poultry. Amid all the buying and selling, Franchère took the time to note an exotic landscape so different from Montreal and the St. Lawrence. The shore appeared a "fine sight," and the mountains were of "a prodigious height." Lush greenery, white beaches, and blue water all dazzled someone more accustomed to long, gray Canadian winters.[44]

All day on February 13, trading for much-needed provisions continued. "The islanders called on us," Franchère wrote, "coming in great numbers about the ship and offering us, as they had done the day before, fruit, vegetables, and a few pigs, in exchange for which we gave them beads, bits of iron hoops, needles, white cotton cloth and so on." The brisk trade brought sailors and Hawaiians into direct contact, and the results surprised no one except perhaps Thorn. Sailors cooped up in the narrow, damp confines of the

Tonquin were suddenly confronted with what must have seemed a paradise. Plentiful food and easy liaisons with island women were temptations that few could resist. As taro and breadfruit changed hands for hardware and cloth, several crewmen slipped over the side and headed for shore. When Thorn discovered their absence he was furious. This unscheduled liberty call flew in the face of his authority. In his mind the seamen were deserters. Alexander Ross captured Thorn's rage in his diary. "Storming and stamping on deck, the captain called up all hands; he swore, he threatened, and abused the whole ships company, making, if possible, things worse." Intent on returning the pleasure-seekers to the *Tonquin*, Thorn employed several Hawaiians to track them down and turn them over to him.[45]

In the middle of this trading Astor's partners made an unsettling discovery. Most of the provisions they desired could be purchased at Kealakekua Bay. But one important commodity was unavailable. The partners planned to provide Astoria with a large swine herd. Hogs would join poultry, sheep, and goats to supply the post's needs. Lewis and Clark had fared miserably on "pore elk" at Fort Clatsop. The Astorians were determined to do better. That determination ran up against the royal monopoly for the sale of pigs and hogs. Kamehameha knew the European taste for pork and had decided to keep that lucrative trade for himself.[46]

Not about to be thwarted in their search for ham and bacon, the Astorians asked one of the Kealakekua Bay headmen to send a canoe north up the coast to Kailua Bay, home of the island's governor. The governor of Hawaii was an Englishman named John Young, certainly one of the most extraordinary characters in the Astoria adventure. On February 15 the Kealakekua messengers returned carrying a letter from Young. He invited the Astorians to sail northwest to Oahu, there to meet Kamehameha. Young was certain that, for the proper price, the adventurers could have all the pork the *Tonquin* could carry.[47]

On the following day Thorn set a course for Honolulu. Coasting along Hawaii's western edge, the *Tonquin* got as far as Kailua Bay before the wind died and the ship was becalmed. Thorn, McKay, and McDougall decided that it would be proper to make a call on Governor Young. John Young had arrived at his position as royal governor through an amazing sequence of events. In 1790 Young had come to the islands as boatswain on the American ship *Eleanora*. Both the *Eleanora* and her sister ship *Fair American* were involved in episodes of considerable violence that cost many American and Hawaiian lives. Because Young was on shore at the time Hawaiians captured the *Fair American*, Kamehameha detained him lest he warn those on the *Eleanora*. The sailor was eventually persuaded to enter the King's service. Young was given a royal title, lands, and wives. Despite limited formal education, he ably served as governor of Hawaii until his death in 1835.[48]

The governor patiently explained the royal monopoly on pork. Kamehameha, so reported Young, "wished to keep all the profits of this trade for himself." When the partners asked why fresh water seemed so difficult to get, Young recounted the unhappy consequences of a drought that had lasted three years. But water and hogs could be had at Honolulu. As canny a trader as his sovereign, Young offered four fat pigs as just a sample of what could be obtained from the hand of Kamehameha. Grateful for both pork and information, the Astorians paid with coffee, chocolate, tea, and several gallons of wine.[49]

After leaving Kailua Bay, the *Tonquin* sailed northwest toward Oahu. The ship's destination was Honolulu and the royal court. On February 21 the Astorians sighted Oahu and dropped anchor in Waikiki Bay. As soon as the ship came to anchor, her crew was greeted by an unusual welcoming party. By 1800 Honolulu had a truly cosmopolitan population. Spaniards, Yankees, Chinese, and Englishmen all lived around the royal court serving the needs of the crown. The *Tonquin* was greeted by three of those imperial consultants. Isaac Davis and a sailor named Wadsworth were Americans, Davis the only survivor of the attack on the *Fair American*. The third man in the canoe was Francisco de Paula Marin, known locally as Manini. Impressed with his language skills, the Astorians promptly hired him as their interpreter.

No sooner had this been accomplished than a second, more elaborately decorated canoe came alongside the *Tonquin*. This canoe carried Kamehameha's prime minister and leading advisor. Kalanimoku was a man of considerable diplomatic skill and experience, a politician whose nickname "William Pitt" only hinted at his real power. Both Kamehameha and Kalanimoku sought foreign trade and western technology. Like other vessels, the *Tonquin* was formally greeted and reminded that business would be successful only if transactions conformed to Hawaiian rules. The prime minister invited Thorn and the partners to visit the royal court. Much of that afternoon was spent ferrying parties to shore for a meeting with the king. Franchère described Kamehameha, now entering the prime years of his power, as "well built, above average height, robust and inclined to be corpulent." The clerk added, "He seemed to me to be between 50 and 60 years old." Befitting his station, the king dressed in formal European attire and sported an impressive sword. Kamehameha had visited many sailing ships, but he inspected each as if he were on deck for the first time. Followed at a respectful distance by the rest of his entourage, the king made a careful inspection of the *Tonquin*. Perhaps he did it more to judge what to ask for his royal hogs than to see some new piece of western technology. But there was one gadget that did attract his attention. The *Tonquin* had been outfitted with a water still, something the king found amazing and, given the recent drought, quite useful. But neither the king nor the Astorians were there for scientific chatter. Ushering the king below to Thorn's cabin, the partners began to discuss provisions. Several glasses of wine were provided to make commerce run quicker. None of this was new to Kamehameha and he was not about to be rushed. At six in the evening, after several hours of talk, the king signaled that business was done for the day. Perhaps tomorrow a bargain could be struck.[50]

The following morning Kamehameha returned. This time he was ready to do business. Unlike ordinary Hawaiians, the king was not interested in exchanging provisions for hardware. He already owned several pieces of artillery and was busy adding to his treasury

with an eye toward buying a warship. Knowing that English ship-
yards wanted hard cash, the king called for payment in Spanish or
Mexican silver coin. While the crown was making deals for imperial
pork, less aristocratic merchants continued to surround the *Tonquin*.
As before, there were the usual food items. This time, however, rum
in gourds was also offered. A thirsty crew made quick work of the
drink, and in the process several sailors became rowdy. Always
watchful in matters of discipline, Thorn ordered that only First
Officer Fox be allowed to carry on trade.[51]

Buying and loading supplies continued for the next few days. By
February 28 the *Tonquin* had full water casks and a storeroom bulg-
ing with yams, taro, and assorted vegetables. The ship's deck resem-
bled a farmyard with one hundred squealing pigs, several goats,
poultry, and two sheep. Two canoe-loads of sugarcane had also been
purchased to feed the pigs. There were additions to the crew as well,
additions that sparked yet another argument between Thorn and
the partners. The Canadians, impressed with Hawaiian nautical
skills, wanted to engage thirty or forty men for work along the
Columbia and on the company's vessels. Thorn refused, insisting
that there was no room on board for so many additional men. In the
end there was a compromise. The captain signed twelve Hawaiians
for service on the *Tonquin*. A second lot of twelve were engaged for
labor at Astoria. These Hawaiian Astorians contracted to work for
the company for three years and to be paid in goods valued at one
hundred silver dollars at the end of their term.[52]

With provisions stowed and extra men on board, the partners
must have thought that their Hawaiian interlude was very successful. At least some of Astor's agents told Kamehameha to expect
three or four ships from the Pacific Fur Company each year. Captain
Thorn saw these island days in a very different light. Writing to
Astor before leaving Oahu, Thorn painted a picture of Canadians
dressed in red coats and plaid kilts, passing out tots of rum and
telling the islanders they were "the great *eares* [lords] of the Northwest." Thorn was equally bitter when he heard that Franchère and
the other clerks had gone to see the place where Captain Cook had

been killed. Each of the tourists, Thorn reported, came away with "a piece of the rock or tree that was touched by the shot" that ended Cook's life. Journals kept by Ross and Franchère contained valuable notes on Hawaiian life, comments gathered by observation and by conversation with islanders. These journals also came in for a share of Thorn's sarcasm. The captain branded them "ridiculously contemptible."[53]

On the first of March 1811 the *Tonquin* weighed anchor and set a course for the Columbia River. As the ship headed into the North Pacific, the weather turned wet and cold. Bone-chilling days, combined with decks cluttered with pigs and goats, made shipboard life unpleasant. One foul day followed another until the Astorians were convinced that it was time to break out the cold-weather gear. Once again there was an argument with the irascible Thorn. When some of the Canadians threatened to seize and distribute warm clothing no matter what the captain thought, shouting became something more deadly. Thorn went for his pistol, and at least some of the partners followed suit. Once again, as in the Falklands imbroglio, cooler heads prevailed and the guns were put away.[54]

Throughout the rest of March the Astorians suffered as high winds and drenching rains slowed the *Tonquin*'s northward progress. In one especially violent storm, waves broke over the ship and swept many of the pigs and goats overboard. It was not until March 22 that the *Tonquin* reached the mouth of the Columbia. Few places along the Northwest coast were so dangerous. Here river currents mixed with ocean tides to create a swirl of waters deadly to ships both then and now. Hidden beneath the surface was a series of sandbars ready to snag any vessel lucky enough to survive the treacherous passage.[55]

Despite poor visibility, Thorn was convinced that his ship was opposite the Columbia. Three miles off the entrance, all on board could see towering waves breaking over the river bar. Thorn's immediate problem was to locate a safe channel through the whirlpool currents and over the bar. Churning waters dense with sand made visual soundings nearly impossible. Determined to find a channel no matter the price, the captain ordered First Officer John Fox to take a longboat and crew into the river. As afternoon winds kicked waves ever higher, Fox prepared for his hazardous mission. His inexperienced crew consisted of the Lapensée brothers, both Lachine draymen; Joseph Nadeau, a Montreal barber; and John Martin, the only seaman in the lot. When Fox complained that the reconnaissance was sure to cost lives, Thorn retorted, "Mr. Fox, if you are afraid of water, you should have remained in Boston." The company's partners quickly took up Fox's cause, urging the captain to wait until the weather moderated. Thorn saw this as another infringement on his authority and "swore that a combination was formed to frustrate his designs." All the Canadians could do for Fox was give him a bedsheet, since the longboat lacked a proper sail. Alexander Ross recalled that a tearful Fox turned to the Canadians and said, "My uncle was drowned here not many years ago, and now I am going to lay my bones with his." As the boat lowered away, Fox shouted, "Farewell my friends, we will perhaps meet again in the next world." The officer's prediction proved tragically accurate. In high seas and fading light the boat vanished from sight when no more than one hundred yards away. Just before disappearing, the boat was seen spinning in the twisting winds and currents. The Columbia bar had claimed more victims. No trace was ever found of either the longboat or its doomed crew.[56]

The *Tonquin* spent the next day beating back and forth at the Columbia's entrance searching for any sign of the missing men. The search proved fruitless, and at the end of the day the ship headed into deeper waters. Everyone on board had "long faces, even the captain looking worried."[57] At dawn on the following morning the *Tonquin* was anchored north of Cape Disappointment. Once again Thorn decided to send a boat to probe the Columbia passage. This time Second Officer Mumford was selected. Taking the ship's remaining boat, Mumford spent the morning cautiously edging toward the river mouth. The officer and his crew counted themselves lucky when they returned to the *Tonquin* at noon. While Thorn's thoughts were centered on getting his ship over the bar, the partners still held some hope that Fox might be found. Alexander McKay and David Stuart volunteered to lead a shore party to carry out a search. A boat was launched, but high seas and a rocky coast forced its return.

Thorn was not to be denied his Columbia passage. With a freshening northwest wind at her back, the *Tonquin* maneuvered very close to the river bar. Once there the captain ordered the rigger, Job Aitkin, to take the pinnace to sound the channel. This time there was an experienced crew on board—Stephen Weeks, the armorer; John Coles, a sailmaker (a crew member listed by Franchère but not on the official crew complement filed in New York); and Harry and Peter, two Hawaiians. Led by the pinnace, the *Tonquin* moved toward the bar and its vicious currents. When the water depth reached less than four fathoms, Thorn signaled for Aitkin's men to return. The pinnace's crew saw the signal but the force of the ebbing tide carried them into the river "with incredible speed and we soon lost sight of them."[58]

The *Tonquin* now stood in danger of grounding on the bar. Once stuck, she would be pounded to pieces by wind and waves. In fading light, with his sounding boat lost, Thorn had little choice but to hazard a run. Second Officer Mumford was sent aloft to keep as good a watch as possible. Water depths beneath the *Tonquin*'s keel kept dropping until the ship had no more than two and one-half fathoms. With waves breaking over her stern, the ship ground over one sandbar after another. "She struck again and again," Ross remembered, "and, regardless of her helm, was tossed and whirled in every direction, and became completely unmanageable." As darkness closed in and the wind failed, the *Tonquin* lost all seaway. A shout from the rigging warned that the ship was drifting toward the rocks. Two anchors were thrown over to slow that drift, but the current relentlessly dragged the ship toward what seemed certain destruction. What saved the *Tonquin* was the coming of the ocean tide, a current that gave the ship more water and some forward motion. It was near midnight when the ship and her exhausted crew finally found shelter in Baker Bay.[59]

Baker Bay had long been a rendezvous for ships and Indians in the maritime fur trade. When Chinook Indians living in villages on the north side of the Columbia saw the *Tonquin* in the bay on March 25, they assumed that commerce was about to begin. Bringing their canoes alongside, the Indians called for trade. But the Astorians had other things in mind. By signs they explained to the Chinooks that some of their crew were missing. At the same time, Thorn and some of the partners went ashore to search the north side of the Columbia. That hunt proved successful, and later in the day Thorn returned with Stephen Weeks. The armorer recounted his terrifying adventure, reporting that Aitkin and Coles were drowned but that the two Hawaiians were in the woods clinging to life. Search parties were sent to find them, but at dark they returned empty-handed.[60]

The search for the Hawaiians resumed the following day. At last they were found. Only one had survived the river ordeal. Franchère summed up the whole passage nightmare. "The loss of eight of us within two days was deeply felt and we especially regretted the death of the Lapensée brothers and Joseph Nadeau. These young lads had been entrusted by their parents to the particular care of Mr. McKay on his departure from Montreal. Mr. Fox and Mr. Aitkin were two fine men; the loss of the former was a great blow for the company as having already made one voyage to this coast he could render especially valuable services. Besides, in the course of such a long voyage, among men who see one another every day, live in the same quarters, share the same dangers, ties form which make such a sudden and unforseen separation doubly painful."[61]

Those eloquent words were all the burial service Fox, Aitkin, and the rest ever got. The Hawaiians insisted on performing traditional rites for their lost countryman. These words and rituals marked the end of the *Tonquin*'s Columbian journey. Franchère's "troublesome voyage" to the Northwest was over. Far to the east an equally troublesome voyage, that of Wilson Price Hunt and his overlanders, was still in the making.

The Overland Passage:
Montreal
to the Arikara Villages

IN THE YEARS immediately after Lewis and Clark returned from the Western Sea, no party of American explorers crossed the continent to the Pacific. A handful of trappers, including Lewis and Clark veterans George Drouillard and John Colter, did follow beaver signs west of the Missouri. And sometime in 1810 the redoubtable Andrew Henry built the first American trading post across the Continental Divide, on Henry's Fork of the Snake River. These forays were daring adventures and they laid the foundation for the golden age of western trapping in the 1820s. But individual exploits and short-lived trading houses did not amount to a sustained American presence in the West. A substantial commercial expedition was yet to follow in the tracks of Jefferson's westering captains.

That was about to change. On July 2, 1810, Wilson Price Hunt, Donald Mackenzie, and fourteen engagés left Lachine for a voyage through the Great Lakes, down the Mississippi, and on to St. Louis. The trade flotillas of the North West Company usually left Lachine for Fort William in early May. With so many canoes already gone, the Astorians may have found it difficult to hire a suitable craft. Hunt and Mackenzie needed the biggest *canot du maître* they could find. What they got was a Montreal canoe something over thirty-six feet long with a six-foot beam. This canoe could carry three tons of goods with an additional ton left over for provisions and crew. Each Montreal canoe had an *avant* stationed in the bow to spot unexpected hazards. A *gouvernail* stood in the stern, steering the canoe with a large nine-foot paddle. Neither Hunt nor his clerk took the time to record the names of the *avant* and *gouvernail*. Although those posts were important, the real direction of the canoe was in the hands of an experienced guide. That position in the Astorian canoe went to Joseph Robilliard.[1]

The route from Lachine to Mackinac was an old and familiar one. Experienced hands like Robilliard and Jean Baptiste Perrault knew each portage, *décharge*, and rapid by name and reputation. Starting the voyage at the head of the churning Lachine rapids, Robilliard pointed the Astorian canoe past the North West Company's old, grey stone warehouse and into the Ottawa River. Voyageur tradition dictated that after some sixteen miles of travel the party would stop at the church of Ste. Anne. There French Canadians made a final confession before challenging the white water. Most guides planned the first day's paddling to end at a camp on the Lake of Two Mountains. On leaving that camp, the Astorians faced a long series of rapids and portages. The first of those came at the Long Sault, a twelve-mile series of rapids in three sets. Hunt and Mackenzie reached the Long Sault on July 8.[2] The Astorians ran these rapids under Robilliard's watchful eye. Generations of experience had taught that each rapid had to be run at top speed to give the keelless canoe proper steerage. The Long Sault was just the place for Robilliard to test the skills of his *avant*, *gouvernail*, and the paddlers *au milieu*.

From the Ottawa, the Astorians pressed west on the Mattawa River. The Mattawa presented no great challenge to the crew. The river was a forty-mile stretch of rocky shores, sharp cliffs, and many portages. By now voyageur songs like "A la Claire Fontaine" and "En Roulant ma Boule" were familiar to Hunt. There was even more singing when the canoe stopped at Rapide des Perches at Pimisi Lake. Here the voyageurs could throw away their setting poles (*perches*), knowing that there would be no more upstream rapids. The Mattawa ended at Trout Lake, and here the Astorians had to portage to Lake Nipissing. Robilliard surely knew that the shallow Nipissing could turn viciously choppy in a high wind.

Paddling around Nipissing's south shore, the Astorians came to the French River. Most fur trade canoes got to the French in late May. High water meant only two portages. The Astorians may not have been so lucky. Lower water in mid-July might have made for slower going. After threading their way through the Voyageur's Channel at the end of the French, the Astorians were in the open water of Georgian Bay on Lake Huron. Robilliard kept the canoe close to shore to shield it from sudden storms. As a newcomer to the region, Hunt may have been shown *La Cloche*, a prominent bell-shaped rock. If struck smartly, *La Cloche* would ring with a dull but resonant tone. On July 25, just before reaching Mackinac, Hunt paid Robilliard $83.33 for his services. The journey to Mackinac had taken less than four weeks, surely no record but a respectable rate.[3]

When the Astorians reached the Straits of Mackinac at the end of July 1810, the island and its mainland fort had lost its place as the gateway to the western fur trade. Throughout most of the eighteenth century, Mackinac had served as the provisioning point for convoys of canoes heading west to Lake Superior and south to Lake Michigan and the Illinois country. Mackinac then was a wild, roistering place where every voyageur showed off his best L'Assomption sash and told tales of courage and fortitude. But with the rise of the Athabasca trade and changes in fur trade transportation routes, Mackinac was eclipsed by Fort William on Lake Superior. The island and the mainland still had strategic importance, as both British and American troops would discover in the War of 1812, but Mackinac's fur trade glory days were slipping away.

Despite a decline in its fortunes, Mackinac could still boast the presence of many experienced traders, both Canadian and American. But as Hunt was soon to discover, there were plenty of men Alexander Ross called "disorderly Canadians already ruined in mind and body."[4] Hunt and Mackenzie had to avoid the broken down and disabled while not offending those not selected for the enterprise. Recruiting was made all the more difficult by the agreement Hunt and Mackenzie had made months before at Montreal. Mackenzie had wanted to hire as many Canadians as possible, believing them best suited for the arduous overland journey. Since the Astorian plan called for a route that followed the Lewis and Clark track—a passage mostly by water—Mackenzie's position made good sense. But Hunt had rejected the advice. He was under orders from Astor to make the expedition as American as possible. Eventually Hunt and Mackenzie had reached a grudging agreement. Some Canadians would be engaged at Lachine, whereas Americans would be added at Mackinac and St. Louis.

There were some Americans at Mackinac, mostly men working in the Great Lakes, or "southwestern," fur trade. They listened to Hunt's offer and firmly rejected it. Ramsay Crooks, who arrived at Mackinac sometime in early August, was probably the source for Irving's apt description of those frustrating days. "If offers were made to any," wrote Irving, "they were listened to with a shake of the head. Should any one seem inclined to enlist, there were officious idlers and busy bodies, of that class who are ever ready to dissuade others from any enterprise in which they themselves have no concern. Those would pull him by the sleeve, take him on one side, and murmur in his ear, or suggest difficulties."[5] Tavern gossip at Montreal had hurt the Pacific Fur Company, and now Mackinac inns and grogshops buzzed with tales about what would befall any prospective Astorian. Traders were warned against joining an enterprise with so uncertain a future. Men who had never been beyond St. Louis talked knowingly about the hazards of western travel. With each telling, the Indians became fiercer, the rivers swifter, and the mountains higher.

In desperation Hunt decided to alter the proposed terms of engagement. He had originally sought a five-year term. With no takers, the term was reduced to three years. At last one man agreed to join the company. He may have been François Landry. His name appears on July 31 in the company ledger, the first among the

names of those who finally enlisted at Mackinac. But Landry was a
Canadian, and his nationality was not lost on Hunt. Thinking to
sweeten the pot, Astor's agent accepted the demand that he advance
wages to each man. That lured a few more men, including Jean
Baptiste Breaux, François Marcial, and Jean Baptiste Ouvre. But the
advances were quickly spent, and Hunt was faced with more demands. Guillaume Le Roux and Jean Baptiste Prevost came to Hunt
on August 3 asking for money. They wanted to pay off engagements
made before the Astorians arrived. The next day the voyageur Jean
Baptiste Pillon came begging money so he could pay debts and join
the company. But no Canadian was so bold as Joseph Perrault.
Sometime in early August he had been involved in a barroom brawl.
For his part he had incurred an $11.25 fine and had also been
ordered to pay a Mackinac cooper $8.50 to repair a smashed table.
Hunt must have wanted this man very much, since the Canadian
was advanced the money to satisfy the court.[6]

With the days slipping away, Hunt and Mackenzie were still far
short of their recruiting goal. More worrisome, no Americans had
yet signed. Perhaps it was Mackenzie who suggested a clever ruse to
lure more men to the company roster. Voyageurs loved to parade at
Mackinac or Fort William showing off a bright sash, fancy garters, or
a colorful cap. But no piece of finery was more prized than a plume.
Stuck at a jaunty angle in a cap, the plume signified that its owner
was one of the elite *hommes du nord*. The *mangeurs de lard*, those who
paddled the freight canoes no farther than Mackinac or Fort William, wore no plumes.[7] The Astoria partners now decided to award
all their engagés with fancy feathers. The message was simple and
powerful. Astorians were true men of the North and could wear that
badge with pride. John Reed, Hunt's newly hired clerk, filled his
account book with the names of men eager to join the company and
display their reward. Despite all these efforts, only one American
joined. William Cannon, an ex-soldier, first appears in the company's records on August 6 as a hunter and hired man.[8]

As busy as Hunt and the other partners were, recruiting was not
the only Mackinac pursuit. Alexander McKay had provided some

trade goods for the party, but more were needed. Late in July the Astorians began to purchase a wide variety of supplies from the Montreal merchants George Gillespie and Toussaint Pothier. Hunt knew from his experience as a St. Louis merchant that trade goods were often hard to come by. Prudence suggested buying items at Mackinac rather than trusting to luck in St. Louis. Warehouses at Mackinac were always well supplied. The Astorians sought three kinds of merchandise from Gillespie and Pothier. Items for the Indian trade headed the list. The partners certainly knew that cloth, beads, and tobacco would be their passport across the continent. Hunt purchased everything from three-point trade blankets and scarlet cloth to hawks' bells and brightly colored garters. Vermilion paint, fancy hair pipes, knives, and a large assortment of beads all went into Astoria's inventory.

But Hunt needed more than trade goods. His own men had to be supplied, both for the voyage to St. Louis and for the transcontinental journey. Getting all hands to St. Louis demanded the purchase of a second boat. Hunt obtained a Mackinac boat with ten oars and a sail. Provisions were not forgotten. The Astorians ate typical voyageur fare, and Hunt laid on fresh stocks of corn, peas, beef, and the ever present cooking grease. Tobacco and alcohol also had their place. The expedition had its own needs. Hunt bought shirts, caps, trousers, and suspenders. These were not given to employees but could be purchased from John Reed's "company store" with the price deducted from annual wages. Finally, perhaps a more experienced frontiersman reminded Hunt that tools were as essential for survival as guns. Drawknives, saws, and hammers were added to the outfit. Whatever the future, the Astorians were heading to St. Louis with full kits.[9]

In the midst of all the recruiting and provisioning were two unexpected events—one a departure and the other an arrival. As an experienced trader and clerk, Jean Baptiste Perrault was one of the most valuable employees signed at Lachine. When the Astorians had set out for Mackinac, Perrault's wife had just given birth. It was only financial exigency that forced Perrault to join the company. By the time he reached Mackinac, the clerk was already "thinking and imagining all sorts of things constantly" about his family. Perrault later admitted that worries about his family kept him in such "a state of anxiety" that he "could no longer render account" of himself. This depression did not escape the partners, and at a noon meal one of them told the Canadian: "Perrault, you seem to me sorrowful. You are doubtless worrying about your family. Necessity has compelled you to separate from them, but at your descretion we will give you your Release." Hunt and Mackenzie did more than let their clerk out of his engagement. The partners arranged a place for him with a Lake Superior trader, Otis Denum. To fill the clerk's post, Hunt hired John Reed.[10]

On August 12, just as the Astorians were ready to leave for Green Bay and the Fox-Wisconsin portage to the Mississippi, an unusual party arrived at Mackinac. Aaron Greeley had recently been appointed the surveyor of the territory of Michigan. One of his tasks was to record and map lands at Mackinac. When Greeley had left Detroit at the end of July, his birchbark canoe carried a peculiar passenger. Thomas Nuttall was an extraordinary botanical explorer. A man of energy and eccentricity, Nuttall was just beginning what would prove to be one of the most productive careers in nineteenth-century American science.

Born in England in 1786, Nuttall left school at fourteen to apprentice in his uncle's Liverpool printshop. But being a printer's devil held no fascination for him. Like so many of his contemporaries, Nuttall was drawn to natural history. Long walks in the countryside with his friend John Windsor made him a self-taught botanist. In 1808 Nuttall left England to begin scientific exploration in North America. He did so with neither sufficient funds nor the promise of support once in the new world. It was obvious that Nuttall should head to Philadelphia. Home of the American Philosophical Society, Charles Willson Peale's museum, and the University of Pennsylvania, the city was at the heart of American science. Nuttall soon met the most prominent botanists, including William Bartram, Bernard McMahon, and Dr. Benjamin Smith Barton. Bar-

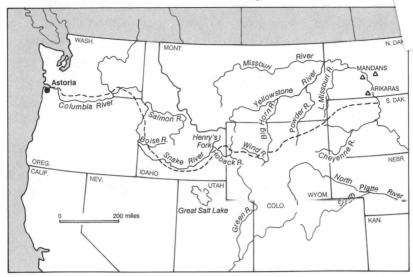

Wilson Price Hunt's overland party route

ton, professor of materia medica, natural history, and botany at the University of Pennsylvania, became Nuttall's patron.

In 1810 Barton was struggling to prepare and organize the large number of botanic samples collected by the Lewis and Clark expedition. He had expected to have the services of Frederick Pursh as a trained assistant, but Pursh's departure for England left Barton in the lurch. Nuttall was the obvious replacement. Instead of setting him to work on the specimens, Barton decided to send his new assistant on a western expedition. Nuttall was to gather samples throughout the Great Lakes and the western plains—all this with little equipment and no previous frontier experience. Little wonder that French boatmen on the Missouri called him "le fou." Barton did ask Albert Gallatin for help in planning the venture, but not even so knowledgeable a geographer as the secretary of the treasury could rescue so confused a scheme.[11]

Nuttall left Philadelphia in early April. Headed for Pittsburgh by stagecoach, the botanist soon discovered that one of his traveling companions knew a great deal about the upper Missouri and the great plains. Nuttall's coachmate was none other than Manuel Lisa,

trader, explorer, promoter, and driving force behind the St. Louis
Missouri Fur Company. Lisa fired Nuttall's imagination with stories
about the river and its plants, animals, and native peoples. By the
time the botanist got to Mackinac he was intent on seeing the West
beyond St. Louis.[12]

Astoria's records do not reveal why Hunt decided to include
Nuttall in the party. Since Hunt later brought John Bradbury, another botanist, into the undertaking, perhaps Hunt sensed that the
expedition might produce important scientific results. Astor himself
was not oblivious to such consequences. He had told both Jefferson
and Gallatin that he would gladly share any bits and pieces of
natural history and ethnology gathered by his employees. Whatever
the reasons, when the Astorians left Mackinac about mid-August,
Nuttall was in the convoy.[13]

The Astorians now followed the old French traders' route from
Mackinac through Lake Michigan. In the path of Nicolet they en-
tered Green Bay, and like Marquette and Jolliet they followed the
Fox-Wisconsin waterway to the Mississippi. By August 24 the As-
torians were at Prairie du Chien, the junction of the Mississippi and
Wisconsin rivers. From there it was a quick ten-day paddle to St.
Louis. Along the way the indefatigable Nuttall added to his store of
specimens. At the Dubuque lead mines he scooped up fossils from
limestone tailings. By the time the Astorians reached St. Louis,
Nuttall could boast a collection of some 220 plant species.[14]

* * *

St. Louis in 1810 was no provincial outpost in the American West.
The city had a post office, churches, a thriving business district, and
a notable newspaper. More important, St. Louis had become the
unofficial capital of a rising American empire. The fur trade gave St.
Louis that claim, but it was the presence of General William Clark
and other federal officials that lent the city legitimacy in its western
claims. The city was the jumping-off place for any wilderness adventure. Whether the destination was Santa Fe or the Columbia River,
all western roads began in St. Louis.

The Astorians were in St. Louis by September 3. Although Alexander Ross later wrote that the arrival caused considerable stir, the event seemingly escaped the notice of the *Missouri Gazette*'s vigilant editor, Joseph Charless. William Clark, always eager to know about parties heading west, was evidently also in the dark about the Astorians. Writing to Secretary of War William Eustis, Clark reported that Hunt and Mackenzie had arrived but admitted that he was "not fully in possession of the Objects of this expedition."[15]

In the days to come, both Charless and Clark would learn more about the Astorians and their plans. Hunt, Mackenzie, and Crooks had much to do. Just as at Lachine and Mackinac, recruiting was the priority. Although the partners now had some thirty employees, they believed that more were needed. As always, Hunt sought additional Americans. Within a few days of their arrival the partners were swamped with "visitors of all grades, anxious to enlist in the new company." Faced with so many eager recruits, Hunt and Mackenzie were confident that they could quickly fill the company's ranks. Their confidence soon evaporated when they took a close look at the applicants. As Ross noted later, "The motley crowd that presented itself could boast of but few vigorous and efficient hands, being generally little better, if not decidedly worse, than those lounging about the streets of Mackinac, a medley of French Creoles, old and worn-out Canadians, Spanish renegades, with a mixture of Indians and Indian half-breeds, enervated by indolence, debauchery and a warm climate."[16]

Alexander Ross was not without his prejudices, but his appraisal of recruiting troubles was reasonably accurate. By mid-September only a handful of French Canadians had engaged. The services of men like Michel Carriere, Louis St. Michael, and Alexis Le Compte were valuable, but Hunt still wanted to see Yankee names on the list.[17] And it was those Americans who proved most elusive and troublesome. When recruits like Robert Whitehead, Harry Caulk, and Samuel Harrington came forward, Hunt must have welcomed them. But these prospective Astorians demanded a high price. They required better fare—coffee, tea, and a steady supply of alcohol—

than that offered to Canadian employees. Hunt seemed ready to meet these requests, only to find that the Canadians were on the verge of making the same demands. Never a skillful manager of men, Hunt then decided that all Astorians—Yankees and Canadians alike—should share the same spartan diet. That edict prompted the predictable reaction. The Americans quit in high dudgeon, taking their advances with them. Again the Astorians became the object of rumor-mongering. Every tavern along the riverfront now echoed with the sarcastic jibes and taunts of the ex-Astorians. Men thinking of joining the company were "warned against the parsimonious conduct of the new enterprise." The tale tellers were effective, and recruiting ground to a halt.[18]

At this point Ramsay Crooks came to the rescue. Crooks had been associated with Joseph Miller in the Missouri River Indian trade. Before becoming a trader, Miller had been an army officer. Unhappy with the army's decision not to grant him an extended furlough, he had resigned his commission. Described by Irving as "well educated and well informed," Miller joined the Pacific Fur Company as a junior partner. Miller had been included in the partners' list on the final company agreement (June 23, 1810) but did not formally join the expedition until late September 1810. Miller's prestige was enough to erase the memories of Hunt's commissary bungling and the rumors it had spawned. By early October the Astorians had engaged nine Canadians and at least four American hunters.[19]

Because Hunt had been in the general-merchandise business before joining Astor, the task of finding additional supplies fell to him. By now the Astorian overland party had grown to nearly forty-five men with the strong possibility that others would be added as the expedition traveled the Missouri. An undertaking this size needed substantial provisions and a bountiful supply of trade goods. The purchases made at Montreal and Mackinac were plainly insufficient. To fill his requirements, Hunt turned to merchant friends in St. Louis, St. Charles, and Ste. Genevieve. His most reliable suppliers were Major James Morrison, Forgus Moorhead, and John G.

Comegys. Morrison, a St. Charles retail merchant, sold the Astorians everything from saddle tacks and gunpowder to lard and some two hundred gallons of whiskey. Forgus Moorhead, a St. Louis merchandiser, provided Hunt with some of the most essential expedition goods. From Moorhead came foodstuffs, including 980 pounds of biscuits, 50 bushels of corn, and 6 barrels of flour. He also sold the traders an assortment of tools, including axes, hoes, lanterns, and a canoe adze. Knowing that ailments of all sorts were bound to afflict the party, Hunt asked Moorhead to provide medicines ranging from sweet oil and paragoric to opium. No one could ignore venereal complaints, and Moorhead wisely included the essential mercury ointment. Early in October the Astorians took delivery of an important weapons shipment from a St. Louis gunsmith, John Smith. That order included rifles, muskets, bayonets, and lead, and to make sure that the river tribes were sufficiently impressed with the Pacific Fur Company, Hunt ordered a howitzer.[20]

Although Morrison, Moorhead, and Smith got the bulk of Astoria's orders, other St. Louis businesspeople benefited from the expedition's presence. John G. Comegys operated a general store in Ste. Genevieve. The store was a branch of C. and J. G. Comegys, a Baltimore firm. Many of the company's engagés and hunters bought small items—thread, socks, red flannel, and sugar—from Comegys. A number of St. Louis seamstresses took orders for the company. Hunt bought six flannel shirts from Madame Benito and paid 75¢ for shirts and a capeau from Madame Honore. Mackenzie also patronized Madame Honore, spending $9.00 for shirts. Madame Robidoux, a prosperous city baker, sold Hunt fifty-four loaves of bread, charging the reasonable price of $4.72.[21]

Of all the St. Louis merchants who enjoyed Astoria's patronage, no other had a closer relationship with the company than James Aird. Aird was a Scots trader who had lived at Prairie du Chien since 1800. He regularly did business between Mackinac, St. Louis, and the upper Mississippi. In September 1806 Lewis and Clark had met Aird on the Missouri near the mouth of the Vermilion River.[22] Aird's connection to the Astorians came through Ramsay Crooks. As a young man, Crooks may have clerked for Aird and perhaps had been with him in 1805 when the trader had met Zebulon Pike on the Mississippi.[23] Aird never enjoyed any large Astoria provision contracts. He did no more than occasionally supply the company with potatoes and beef. Far more important, sometime before October Aird and the Astorians decided to join forces for at least the Missouri River leg of the transcontinental journey. Aird traveled with the Astorians in the fall of 1810 as far as Fort Osage and may have gone all the way to the Nodaway winter camp. Part of the Aird-Astoria agreement was that he and the partners would share the services and expenses of William Rogers, a trader and interpreter among the Oto and Missouri Indians.[24]

When Astor had begun to plan his overland enterprise in 1808, he had assumed that his traders would follow the Lewis and Clark track up the Missouri, across the mountains, and on to the Columbia. Published accounts of the expedition gave little hint of the difficulties in that northern Rockies route. When Hunt got to St. Louis, he had no reason to doubt that the Lewis and Clark trail was the best highway across the continent. It was a route that Hunt had known about since 1806. He clearly knew about the course of the Missouri, the nature of the Great Falls on that river, and the passage to Pacific waters. His image of that passage was an interesting mix of pre-expedition notions and more accurate information brought back by the captains. Like most geographers before Lewis and Clark, Hunt still believed that only a short distance separated the heads of rivers flowing east and west. But after hearing about expedition experiences, he recognized that "the dividing is a mountain on which there is snow all the year." That the Astorians were heading west by this path soon became common knowledge. William Clark noted as much when he wrote that Hunt's party was "preparing to proceed up the Missouri, and prosue my trail to the Columbia."[25]

Even before returning to St. Louis in 1806, Lewis and Clark knew that there were quicker and safer routes to the Pacific. By 1810, knowledge of those passages had been enhanced by the fur trade explorations of men like John Colter and George Drouillard. Once in St. Louis, Hunt could not have escaped hearing about such new ways west. Because almost all of Hunt's letters have been lost, it is difficult to know how much contact he had with Clark. Hunt's 1806 letter does indicate that he was very interested in western geography and travel routes. For Clark's part he always sought out anyone either coming or going west. Part of Hunt's 1811 overland route found its place on Clark's master map. Since Hunt altered his plans once in St. Louis, it is possible that conversations with Clark were at the heart of such changes. Clark's exploration of the Yellowstone in the late summer of 1806 had convinced him that the river was an important western trail. Writing in that year, Clark characterized the Yellowstone as "a large and navagable river with but fiew obstructions quite to the rocky Mountains." Lewis agreed, describing the Yellowstone as a "delightful river" teeming with beaver.[26] Most important, both explorers believed that the Yellowstone could take a traveler to the eastern slopes of the Rockies more quickly than any other southern route. And southern routes were increasingly important. Open conflict between Blackfeet warriors and American trappers, coupled with the constant threats from both the Teton Sioux and Arikaras, made northern trails even more chancy. Clark might have been the first to tell Hunt about these hazards and the possibility of an attractive Yellowstone detour.

But government officials like Clark were not the only ones in the city with valuable information. St. Louis was the great clearinghouse for both pelts and western lore. Western geography—the courses of rivers and the shape of the land—was a topic eagerly discussed in every tavern. Trapper lore was in the air, and the Astorians would have been hard pressed to avoid it. Of all the traders now living around St. Louis, no other had seen more of the West than John Colter. First with Lewis and Clark and later with the Missouri Fur Company, Colter trapped and explored from the Three Forks of the Missouri to the farthest reaches of the Yellowstone country. During the winter of 1807–8 he made one of the grandest tours of the

Rocky Mountains ever attempted. In the middle of winter he trekked alone across the Bighorn Mountains, through the Wind River valley, over the Teton range, and eventually back to Manuel's Fort on the Yellowstone. Colter returned to the St. Louis region in the spring of 1810, married, and settled along the Missouri above La Charette. It was there that Hunt met him in March 1811.[27] Colter's ideas about western geography were well known, and the Astorians had probably been acquainted with them many months before that meeting. Like Clark, Colter was convinced that a more southern course was the surest way to the Pacific. In an interview published in the *Louisiana Gazette*, Colter maintained that "at the head of Gallatin fork, and of the Grosse Corne [Bighorn River] of the Yellowstone . . . it is found less difficult to cross [the Rocky Mountains] than the Allegheny Mountains." Colter thought that both the Bighorn and the Gallatin would provide access to passes like Union and Teton, over which, so he claimed, "a loaded wagon would find no obstruction in passing."[28]

Information from Clark and Colter had its effect on the Astorians. Sometime before making the final push up the Missouri in March 1811, Hunt changed his plans. The notion of simply following Lewis and Clark's northern track was abandoned. Hunt selected instead the course along the Yellowstone. Since both Clark and Colter believed a route westward on the Yellowstone to the Bighorn would surely lead to a "Southern Pass," Hunt may have added the Bighorn to his plan.[29]

No other St. Louis citizens watched Astoria's comings and goings more carefully than those connected with the Missouri Fur Company. Although never as much a threat to Astor as the North West Company, the Missouri concern had both impressive connections and energetic employees. The company had been founded during the winter of 1808–9. Its directors amounted to a blue book of the St. Louis elite—Pierre Chouteau, Pierre Menard, William Morrison, and the most dominant director, Manuel Lisa. Official St. Louis was represented by William Clark and Meriwether Lewis's brother Reuben. Andrew Henry, just beginning a distinguished fur trade and exploration career, served as the company's field captain. The firm could count among its trappers men like Colter, Drouillard, and a third Lewis and Clark veteran, John Potts. An enterprise endowed with such talent seemed sure to succeed. Joseph Charless certainly thought so. His newspaper announced that the company had "every prospect of becoming a force of incalculable advantage, not only to the individuals engaged in the enterprise, but the community at large."[30]

But the fates and furies were never kind to the Missouri Fur Company. After an initial success in delivering the Mandan chief Sheheke to his home village, the company's fortunes plummeted. The directors, all jealous for personal profit, squabbled endlessly. Lisa, certainly the company's driving force, managed to alienate most of the rest of the board. In the field the firm fared no better. By the time the Astorians reached St. Louis, the company had suffered grievous injury at the hands of the Blackfeet, costing the lives of eight trappers, including the redoubtable Drouillard. On the Missouri the company's post at Cedar Island was burned, with the loss of furs valued between twelve and fifteen thousand dollars. A depressed international fur market added to the bleak outlook for the Missouri company.[31]

Despite these reverses, Lisa and the Missouri Fur Company could not be counted out as a force to reckon with. When the Astorians arrived, the company was both alarmed and ready to do battle. Thanks to Jefferson's July 1808 letter to Lewis, fur merchants in St. Louis knew about Astor's western plans well before the Pacific Fur Company's boats had tied up on the levee. Lisa and his partners saw many reasons to worry about the Astorians. Both companies would surely compete for the services of skilled boatmen and experienced hunters, who were always in short supply. The Missouri River labor market was not the only place the firms collided. High-quality trade goods were always scarce. The on-again-off-again nature of federal embargo legislation made it difficult to obtain many European items.

If the two concerns were rivals in St. Louis, they would be even more bitter enemies on the trapping grounds. Astor had every intention of engrossing the entire western trade from the Missouri to the Pacific. He knew that such a drive would encounter stiff opposition from the Missouri Company. Lisa and his partners already had posts on the Missouri and at the junction of the Yellowstone and Bighorn rivers. The Pacific Fur Company dreamed of China and Alaska, but as far as Lisa was concerned the Astorians were every bit a Missouri River operation as his own. Although Lisa's thoughts about expansion beyond the Great Divide are unclear, two of the company's ablest traders—Reuben Lewis and Andrew Henry—certainly entertained such hopes. Henry's 1810 crossing of the Divide to build a post on the fork of the Snake River named for him suggests his approach. Reuben Lewis had even more specific plans, plans that directly involved both firms. Writing to his brother Meriwether from Three Forks in April 1810, Reuben suggested that if Astor's concern got going, it might be wise for the Missouri Fur Company to buy an interest in the venture. Despite recent disasters, he was sure that a fortune could be made trapping west of the Divide. "My principal hopes," he wrote, "are now from the Collumbia." Reports reaching Three Forks told of vast beaver colonies on the upper branches of the Columbia. Lewis was not about to see all those pelts bear the Astor mark.[32]

Anyone even on the fringes of the St. Louis fur business knew that the two companies were rivals. In the fall of 1810 the struggle was an uneven one. The Missouri Fur Company had suffered heavy losses and was unable to send a relief expedition upriver to support Andrew Henry's trappers. When the company's directors met on September 10, they knew that the firm had its back to the wall. The company's surviving letter book does not reveal much about what must have been three days of tough talk and hard choices. On September 12 the company decided to send an expedition as soon as possible to aid Henry's men. Nowhere in the record is there any mention of Hunt, Mackenzie, Crooks, and the Astoria adventure. In fact, on the same day that the company finally decided to send a party upriver, William Clark wrote the secretary of war asking for information about the Pacific Fur Company. It seems unlikely that Clark and Lisa knew nothing about the plans for Astoria. With its fortunes at a low point, perhaps the company's strongest response was a group to reinforce Henry and forestall competition from Astoria.[33]

Lisa and other members of the Missouri Fur Company had sound business reasons for keeping a close eye on the Astorians. One newcomer to St. Louis also watched with keen interest. Like Thomas Nuttall, John Bradbury was a self-taught English botanist intent on exploring the American West. That both scientists should eventually become attached to the Astorians is one of the fascinating coincidences that dot the story of Astor's venture.

Bradbury was born in England in 1768 and by the time he was in his early twenties he had published studies on local plants and insects. Those researches caught the eye of Sir Joseph Banks, who proposed Bradbury for membership in the prestigious Linnean Society. In 1809 Bradbury was selected to travel to North America to gather plant samples for the Liverpool Botanic Garden. Armed with a letter of introduction from William Roscoe, one of the garden's founders, he visited Jefferson at Monticello in August 1809. Jefferson was sufficiently impressed with Bradbury to write Meriwether Lewis urging cooperation with his efforts. Jefferson also urged Bradbury to make St. Louis his base rather than disease-ridden New Orleans. By late December 1809 Bradbury was in St. Louis. When the Astorians arrived in the following September, Bradbury and Nuttall became fast friends. Just how Hunt and Mackenzie decided to take a second naturalist along is not known. However it came to be, Bradbury would accompany Hunt in March 1811, joining Nuttall in local excursions until that final departure date.[34]

* * *

By early October 1810 most of the important St. Louis preparations were complete. Provisions had been secured and Crooks had purchased two boats—a keelboat and a Schenectady barge—to fill out Astoria's navy.[35] But the time taken to accomplish all these tasks

made any passage far up the Missouri impossible. The Astorians
were forced to readjust their schedule. Hunt decided that instead of
wintering with the Mandans, the company would build winter quarters on the Nodaway River some five hundred miles above St. Louis.
In the following year the overlanders would make their crossing and
join the *Tonquin* on the Columbia. It was not until October 21 that
the Astorians finally pulled out of St. Louis. This late in the season a
river trip was hard going, since low water exposed sandbars and
mud flats. Sweating boatmen barely had time to be grateful that
sawyers, those hidden logs that could rip the bottom from any boat,
would be less a hazard in low water. For the next ten days the
Astorians pulled, poled, and paddled up the muddy river. Only
occasionally was there enough wind to hoist sails and rest from the
backbreaking labor. Like Lewis and Clark and dozens of other river
travelers, they passed familiar landmarks. Tavern Rock with its
Indian pictographs was a river milepost known to many.

First stop for the Astorians was Fort Osage. The post had been
built in the fall of 1808 by William Clark and Captain Eli Clemson.
Clemson then became Osage's first commanding officer. Fort Osage
not only was an important western post but also provided river
travelers with needed provisions and services. The Astorians
reached Fort Osage on October 30. Hunt quickly made good use of
the post's store operated by George C. Sibley, buying ten kegs of
gunpowder for $224.00. The following day was an especially busy
one for the expedition. Knowing they were to winter on the Missouri, most men in the party hurried to Sibley's store to buy buffalo
robes. The going price was three to four dollars, and by the end of
the day twenty-one robes had changed hands. While men such as
Michel Carriere and Antoine Papin bargained with Sibley for the
warmest robe, Astoria's partners were doing some last-minute recruiting. The Pacific Fur Company had plenty of boatmen; what it
lacked were woodsmen and hunters. Because the ledger kept by the
clerk John Reed does not always contain precise information about
where each man engaged, it is difficult to know who joined at Fort
Osage. Among those who probably became Astorians at Osage were

Daniel Laurison and David, John, and Thomas McNair. It is possible that Jean Baptiste Gardapie, a hunter, also enlisted at Fort Osage. Perhaps the most interesting recruit was Caleb Greenwood. Greenwood was at the beginning of a long, eventful career as a fur trader and Oregon Trail guide. Laurison and Greenwood were among those hunters who refused to continue beyond the Nodaway camp. When the Missouri Fur Company sent out one of its last expeditions in 1812, Greenwood and Laurison were again at Fort Osage and promptly signed with Lisa.[36]

Hunt and Mackenzie had no intention of staying long at Osage. If Alexander Ross is to be believed, Mackenzie was already grumbling at the slow pace. Mackenzie claimed that if the Astorians had followed his advice, they would have wintered on the Columbia! It was an idle, uninformed boast, but the sentiment again revealed the rift between Hunt and Mackenzie. The Astorians left Fort Osage on November 1. Beyond the post the Missouri became a river of twists, turns, and false channels. Cold nights and a browning landscape must have reminded the expedition members that winter was soon upon them. After two weeks of upriver struggle the Astorians reached the mouth of the Nodaway on November 16.[37]

The Astorians made their winter camp at the base of bluffs near the mouth of the Nodaway in present-day Andrew County, Missouri. This first post of the Pacific Fur Company was nothing more than a cluster of huts and a crude storehouse.[38] No Astorian diarist kept records for that winter. Reed's ledger provides only the barest outline of life at Nodaway. Once the camp was complete, the daily routine was a simple one. Hunting, cooking, and chopping wood gave shape to each day. John Reed kept track of those days, perhaps remarking on the falling temperatures to Hunt when he came to spend a dollar for a red woolen cap. Other customers with winter thoughts bought tobacco, caps, and warm capotes. Nearly everyone at Nodaway purchased breech flaps, hoping to keep at least some more exposed parts of the body warm and dry. Hunt and Reed kept busy entering long lists of invoices dating back to the days at Mackinac.[39]

In December the Nodaway routine was broken by two events, one an unexpected death and the other an unannounced arrival. Joseph Perrault was one of those voyageurs engaged at Mackinac. Perrault possessed a violent past, and Hunt had had to pay for his fine and damages incurred in a Mackinac tavern brawl before the Canadian joined the company. Sometime in December Perrault died. Nothing is known about the circumstances of his death, and both Ross and Irving are silent on the episode. On December 30 there was an auction of Perrault's goods. Those items suggest how slim an estate a voyageur might amass. Pipes, a tobacco pouch, ragged trousers, tattered calico shirts, and worn stockings were among the simple goods put under the hammer. The proceedings yielded $137.00, which was added to Perrault's wages and brought the estate to $199.50. Before the journey was over, there would be other deaths and other estates to tote up and parcel out.[40]

Sometime during the same month a new partner joined the expedition. Courageous to a fault and often unpredictable, Robert McClellan was an enigma to those who knew him and a mystery to historians. Born about 1770 in Mercersburg, Pennsylvania, McClellan got his first lessons in frontier survival helping his brother guide packtrains over the mountains to Pittsburgh. When the Ohio country was convulsed by Indian wars in the 1780s, McClellan joined William Wells's scout company. His feats of daring became legendary, attracting the attention and friendship of the young William Clark. In 1799 McClellan went to the West beyond Ohio. First in New Orleans and later at St. Louis and on the upper rivers, he sought fortune and adventure as an Indian trader. James Aird was at one time his partner before Crooks and McClellan joined forces. McClellan was a man of mercurial passion. The foremost object of his anger and distrust was Manuel Lisa. Both Crooks and McClellan were convinced that Lisa had instigated the Teton Sioux's attack on them in 1809. As things fell out, Hunt and the other partners would have their hands full keeping McClellan from killing Lisa.[41]

Just how McClellan was drawn into the Astorian enterprise is not clear from surviving evidence. Washington Irving believed that Hunt had extended the invitation to him. Crooks and Aird may have had a hand in the business as well. Sometime in the fall of 1810 McClellan left his trading house two hundred miles above the Nodaway and made his way to the Astorians' camp. Arriving in December, he was offered two and a half shares in the Pacific Fur Company. If he resented the fact that Crooks had a larger interest, there is no record of it. What is plain is that McClellan saw the journey as yet another chance for profit and adventure. Writing to his brother William, he cast the trek as a fresh start both personal and financial. "If I possessed anything more except my gun at present, I would throw it into the river, or give it away, as I intend to begin the world anew tomorrow."[42]

Someone else about to begin the world anew was John Day. This Virginian first appears in Reed's ledger on December 21 when he bought tobacco, a cotton handkerchief, a knife, and a tomahawk from the company store. Day was in his early forties when he joined the Astorians. He already had a considerable reputation as a woodsman and hunter. Day's future held suffering, insanity, and a place in the geographic naming of a western river.[43]

Wilson Price Hunt had not planned on wintering over at Nodaway. His intention had been to return to St. Louis as soon as possible. Perhaps it was the need to see things settled at Nodaway that kept him from setting out downriver until January 1811. Sometime in that month Hunt and eight men marched from Nodaway to Fort Osage. A shortage of horses at the post may have been the reason six of the Astorians returned to Nodaway while Hunt and two others rode on to St. Louis. Hunt and his men made good time and by the end of January they were back in the city.[44]

Hunt may have thought his wait in St. Louis would be uneventful. He should have known better. The months since Hunt had first gone up the Missouri had given Lisa and the company's other directors time to ponder their future. Something had to be done both to resupply Andrew Henry and to oppose the Astorians. Plans for such a voyage had been made in September 1810 but had not gotten beyond the talking stage. Now the Missouri Fur Company decided to act. Since Hunt was still determined to hire more skilled woodsmen, the two companies again locked horns on the St. Louis labor market. Lisa had no equal in his recruiting abilities and Hunt soon found him "a keen and subtle competitor." Although there is no contemporary record of those engaged by Hunt, it appears from John Bradbury's account that the company signed an additional dozen men.[45]

Lisa and Hunt had their bitterest clash when the Astorian sought a skilled Sioux interpreter. Every river trader knew that the Teton Sioux had a choke-hold on the upper Missouri. These Sioux bands were determined to monopolize river traffic, holding sway over Arikara village farmers while benefiting from tolls extracted from every keelboat and pirogue up from St. Louis. Meriwether Lewis paid tribute to the power of the Teton Sioux when he wrote that they would always be a barrier to river trade "until some effectual measures be taken to render them pacific."[46] Hunt had to run that Teton gauntlet. Having an experienced interpreter was essential for survival.

The man Hunt sought to engage was Pierre Dorion, Jr., son of Lewis and Clark's Sioux interpreter Old Dorion. Young Pierre, married to a plucky Iowa Indian woman named Marie L'Ayvoise, had served Lewis and Clark when they had counciled with the Yankton Sioux in August 1804. The younger Dorion had considerable trade experience and had worked at one time for the Missouri Fur Company at its Mandan post. He must have seemed an ideal choice to Hunt. Since Lisa was also outfitting his expedition, Dorion became the object of intense competition. Lisa wanted him not only to help his party but also to weaken the Astorians. Without an able interpreter, Hunt and his men might never get beyond the Sioux's blockade. Dorion was inclined to join the Astorians, partly as revenge on Lisa. In 1809 Dorion had run up a considerable liquor bill at the Missouri Fur Company's Fort Mandan. Irving was later told that the bill was "a matter of furious dispute, the mere mention of which was sufficient to put him [Dorion] in a passion." After considerable negotiation, Dorion agreed to engage at three hundred dollars per year with a two-hundred-dollar advance.[47] If Hunt thought that getting Dorion's mark ended the contest with Lisa, he was sadly mistaken.

Hunt's busy days in St. Louis were suddenly interrupted in early March. Just as he was making final preparations for the river journey, Hunt was greeted by five disgruntled hunters fresh from Nodaway. No contemporary account gives their names, but they were probably Caleb Greenwood, Daniel Laurison, Harry Caulk, John Trask, and one of the McNairs. The story they told must have worried Hunt. Without giving many details, the hunters insisted that they had been mistreated by Mackenzie and the other partners. When Hunt tried to soothe their ruffled feelings they went off in a huff. Eventually Hunt was able to persuade two of the hunters to remain in his employ. The others made the tavern circuit, spreading rumors about abusive partners and a doomed enterprise.[48]

The confusion with the hunters and the possibility of tension at Nodaway took a toll on Hunt's nerves. Ross described him as a man "perfectly worn out with anxiety."[49] And a letter addressed to him from Astor could not have lessened his concern. The letter, probably dated sometime in November 1810, has not survived. However, Hunt later revealed its contents to Alexander Ross. In the fall of 1810 several things were clear to Astor. There was no longer any hope of a joint venture with the North West Company. Changes in federal legislation now made it illegal for British subjects to trade on American soil. Since Astor believed that most of his Canadian employees had taken American citizenship at New York, he was concerned only with the command of the overland expedition. Throughout the days at Lachine, Hunt and Mackenzie had informally shared command. This had been a practical matter and not Astor's policy. Now he wanted it made plain that Hunt was in sole charge. With several arguments already marring their relationship, Hunt and Mackenzie seemed sure to be driven further apart by this ill-timed letter.[50]

With so many troubles and distractions, it was not until March 12

that Hunt, Bradbury, Nuttall, and sixteen men were ready to set out
for Nodaway. Hoping to get a last-minute mail delivery, the two
botanists stayed in St. Louis and promised to meet Hunt the next
day at St. Charles. That delay allowed Bradbury and Nuttall to
defeat yet another Lisa ploy aimed at thwarting the Astorians. Intent on keeping Dorion from Hunt's service, Lisa revived the 1809
alcohol debt. Lisa had always been adept at using the law, and now
he had a warrant sworn out for Dorion's arrest. It was not the first
time Lisa had tried that tactic. In 1806, interested in the Santa Fe
trade and fearful that Pike's expedition might damage his chances,
Lisa had tried to have Pike's interpreter, Vasquez, arrested on the
same kind of debt warrant. Still in St. Louis, Bradbury and Nuttall
got wind of the stratagem and hurried to St. Charles to warn Hunt.
The scientists left St. Louis in the predawn hours on March 13, and
by noon Dorion was hiding deep in the woods outside St. Charles.
Had Lisa's frustration been reduced to paper, the record would have
been scorched indeed.[51]

Early on the morning of the fourteenth Hunt's entourage left St.
Charles. Settling into the cadence of upstream paddling, the voy-
ageurs filled the air with rhythmic songs. Some ways up from St.
Charles the pirogues pulled alongshore to pick up Pierre Dorion.
When it was discovered that his wife, Marie, was missing, Hunt sent
one of the Canadians to find her. A family quarrel had split the
Dorions and it was not until the following day that Marie finally
rejoined the expedition.[52]

The Astorians crossed paths with the West's fabled past when they
reached the village of La Charette. There Hunt and Bradbury met
and talked with the elderly Daniel Boone, who had settled in the
neighborhood some years before. Now in his seventies, the great
Kentucky frontiersman had lived to see waves of traders and farmers sweep over the Blue Ridge to the threshold of the Great Plains.
Boone represented a West already receding into memory. His upriver neighbor John Colter had just come from the farther West.
Bradbury asked after him and had the young son of a settler named
John Sullens send word for Colter. The trapper came to the As-

torians' camp the next day. Colter had recently married and had
sworn off the western trapping life, believing that his luck had run
out. Despite that, he did travel some miles with Hunt. Bradbury
noted that Colter had a "strong inclination" to join the expedition
but that his new wife kept him back. If Hunt and Colter talked about
anything, it was the best route across the mountains. Colter surely
would have recommended the Yellowstone-Bighorn passage to Pacific waters, confirming advice Hunt had already heard in St.
Louis.[53]

Once the voyageurs were past La Charette, signs of white settlement nearly vanished. Thick rushes along the banks kept Bradbury
and Nuttall from much exploring. Days of constant rain made travel
unpleasant. By March 21 the party was at Côte sans Dessein, the last
white settlement on the river. While the rest made camp, Dorion
hiked to the village to visit friends. What he learned put all the
Astorians on guard. A large war party of Iowas, Sauks, Sioux, and
Potawatomis was nearby. These Indians were at war with the Osages. Having heard that an Osage boy was in the village, the warriors
were bent on taking his scalp. Since the Astorians had a considerable
supply of trade goods to protect, they began to post extra watches
and to sleep with weapons at the ready. These were rare moments of
excitement in what was rapidly becoming a wet, dreary voyage.
Endless rain dampened even the most ebullient voyageur spirit.
That same rain soaked bread already poorly baked and turned it so
mouldy that it had to be thrown away. Mired in rain, mud, and rising
river currents, Hunt's boats made slow progress.[54]

Had he known about the turn of events in St. Louis, Hunt would
have cursed the weather and fought the river. Manuel Lisa once told
William Clark, "[I] put into my operations great activity; I go a great
distance while some are considering whether they will start today or
tomorrow."[55] It was just that sort of resolve that brought the Missouri Fur Company's directors together on March 25. Lisa believed
that the 1811 trading season would decide western destiny for years
to come. If the Astorians made successful commercial arrangements
up the Missouri and in the Yellowstone country at a time when the

Missouri Company was weak, the whole West would eventually be-
long to Astor. The little checks and turns Lisa had employed against
Hunt had failed. The only course left was to speed up the Missouri,
overtake the Astorians, and make sure the river peoples stayed clear
of the Pacific Fur Company's influence. Lisa's bitterest enemies,
Crooks and McClellan, later believed that Lisa also had in mind
instigating Indian violence against the Astorians.

Despite his company's meager treasury, Lisa began to outfit the
expedition. The directors plainly expected little from the voyage,
since only Lisa, Clark, and Pierre Menard put up money to buy trade
goods. Working with short funds, Lisa had to scrape to find twenty
men to row and pole a keelboat. The craft for the venture was a
twenty-ton barge described by one of her passengers as "the best
that ever ascended this river." Considering the company's finances,
this might have been a generous appraisal. The boat carried a swivel
gun at her bow, and two brass blunderbusses pointed out of cabin
windows. Lisa knew from experience that goods carried in a keelboat were an open invitation for river tribes to exact high tolls. To
prevent this, Lisa's boat had a cleverly designed false cabin, which
allowed trade items to be hidden from prying eyes.[56]

Lisa kept no chronicle of his push upriver to catch Hunt. That
duty fell to Henry Marie Brackenridge, son of the prominent novel-
ist and lawyer Hugh Henry Brackenridge. The younger Brackenridge had gone west to St. Louis for travel and adventure. His
important essays, first published in the *Louisiana Gazette*, later appeared as *Views of Louisiana*. Brackenridge had made Lisa's acquaintance and in late March joined the party as a sometime hunter.

All these hurried preparations were unknown to Hunt as he
plodded against the Missouri current. Tangles of rushes and bram-
bles along the river flats kept Bradbury and Nuttall from much
botanizing. And the torrential rains continued. The expedition
found travel even slower as the river, swollen with spring rains, rose
dramatically. The company's hunters found plenty of game, but not
even a full larder could soften the long hours of rowing, hauling,
and poling.[57]

No matter how feverish his efforts, it was not until April 2 that Lisa was finally able to leave St. Louis. If he entertained any notions about openly confronting the Astorians, he kept them to himself. When Brackenridge inquired about the need for such speed, he was brusquely told that a larger convoy stood a better chance against the Sioux. Joseph Charless got a slightly different story for his newspaper. He heard that Lisa and Hunt planned to join forces to challenge both the Blackfeet and the British traders on both sides of the Great Divide. Lisa's engagés heard nothing except the order to "strain every nerve." Among those on board was the Lewis and Clark veteran Toussaint Charbonneau. As Pierre Dorion took his wife, Marie, so Charbonneau had along another member of Jefferson's Corps of Western Discovery, Sacagawea. Brackenridge described her as "a good creature, of a mild and gentle disposition, greatly attached to the whites, whose manners and dress she tries to imitate."[58]

While Lisa's men rowed for all their worth, Hunt still moved slowly. High water and hidden logjams kept the daily pace in low numbers. The miles counted each day increased in early April when the river suddenly dropped nearly four feet overnight. Low water slowed the current and made travel easier. At midmorning on April 8 Hunt and his men spotted Fort Osage. Lookouts at the post saw the boats about the same time and hoisted a flag in greeting. That greeting was made official when Hunt got to the fort about noon. Troops from the garrison formed ranks and fired a volley. Lieutenant John Brownson, commanding while Captain Eli Clemson was absent, was there to welcome Astor's agent. Hunt was probably surprised to see Ramsay Crooks and ten men from Nodaway. These Astorians had come down to Osage some days before to await Hunt's arrival.

While Hunt and Crooks spent the next day and a half catching up on news and company affairs, Bradbury was busy with ethnographic studies. His guide was Dr. John Murray, post surgeon's mate. Murray had recently resigned from the army but was staying on until his resignation became final. Bradbury had heard about Murray and carried a letter of introduction addressed to the physician. Murray had spent considerable time studying the Osage language and culture. His vocabulary of 180 Osage words and phrases was eventually included in Bradbury's published account of the expedition. After the two spent a day exchanging information, Murray suggested that they go down to a place outside the fort where some two hundred Osages were camped. Bradbury quickly agreed and was taken to the lodge of a headman named Waubuschon. Once inside, Murray and Bradbury were treated to Osage cakes made from pounded persim- ╱ mons. While making their way through this fare, and probably puckering all the time, the scientists were greeted by several young Osage women who had just come into the lodge. Murray, the young women, and Waubuschon's wife were soon engaged in joking banter that, so Bradbury was told, was "of the most obscene nature." The naturalist did not stay to see if talk might lead to action. But he did take considerable pains to observe the Osage custom of predawn keening for the dead. Wrapping a blanket around himself and covering his head with a black handkerchief, Bradbury slipped into the woods to watch a warrior cry his vigil for the dead.[59]

Heavy rains on the morning of April 10 did not stop Hunt and Crooks from heading up to the Nodaway camp. The difficult task of sorting out men, supplies, and boats was temporarily interrupted by a domestic quarrel between the Dorions. Marie had made friends in the Osage village and wanted to remain among them. The Astorians stood by as Pierre beat his wife and bundled her into one of the boats. That storm past, the party rowed upriver. In the following days the weather cleared, and enough wind rose to hoist sails.[60] Back downriver Lisa and his men reached Côte sans Dessein on April 11. "We enquired with eagerness after the party of Mr. Hunt," wrote Brackenridge. "We were informed that he had passed this place 21 days ago." This meant that Lisa had gained only two days on Hunt, a pace that had to pick up if he was to catch the Astorians. Lisa began to do just that. Three days later, at the junction of the Mine and Missouri rivers, he learned that the gap had been narrowed by another two days. If the weather held fair and his voyageurs did not flag, Lisa now had some chance to catch Hunt before entering Sioux country.[61]

On April 17 Hunt, Crooks, and the St. Louis Astorians reached Nodaway camp. The next three days were spent checking equipment and breaking camp. If Hunt and Mackenzie exchanged any harsh words about Astor's letter putting Hunt in sole command, such an argument was not noted by Bradbury, Ross, or Irving. Instead all seemed hopeful as John Reed sold tobacco, cloth, knives, and pipes to men ready to challenge the upper river and the distant mountains.[62] By the morning of April 21 the Astorians were ready to leave winter quarters. The expedition now numbered some sixty men, one woman, and the Dorions' two children, all traveling in four boats. That first day out from Nodaway offered fair winds, allowing the Astorians to set sails and breeze along the Missouri.[63] They would need every ounce of speed. On the same day, Lisa's crew camped just below Fort Osage. Their daily exertions had paid off. They were now only ten or twelve days behind Hunt. Lisa knew he was closing the gap. Every Astorian dawdle or brush with bad weather brought a meeting that much closer.[64]

Over the next week the great Missouri River keelboat race took on a seesaw quality. Fair winds early in the week pushed the Astorians much closer to their next milepost, the Platte River. Shifting winds always bedeviled river travelers, and after two days of quick pace, the winds hauled around and forced a full day's halt.[65] Uncooperative winds would not have stopped Lisa. By April 27 his boat had passed Fort Osage, making hard for the Platte. At midmorning on the same day Lisa encountered a group of traders coming down from Sioux country. They had been doing business among the bands and reported that those Indians seemed "peaceably inclined." The traders had met Hunt some five days earlier around the Little Nemaha. They reported Hunt's bout with contrary winds and the Astorians' generally slow progress. These rivermen estimated that the two parties would meet at the Platte or not far above. For the exhausted boatmen it was welcome news.[66]

Missouri River boatmen and traders had long considered the

Platte a plains equator—the real beginning of the Upper Missouri country. On April 28 the Astorians crossed the line, had breakfast at the mouth of the Platte, and headed to camp upriver at Papillion Creek. Knowing that good timber would soon become scarce, the more experienced of the Astorians probably suggested camping at Papillion for a day or two to lay in an extra supply of oars and poles. As this work went forward, Ramsay Crooks approached Hunt about a change in plans. Crooks had done some business with the Otos and wanted to visit them to collect beaver pelts due him. He proposed journeying to the Oto village and then heading up to the Omaha town to rendezvous with the Astorians. Itching to explore the plains world beyond the river's margins, Bradbury sought to join Crooks on this side trip. Hunt gave his assent, and Crooks and his naturalist companion set to making preparations for the trip.[67]

The Astorians always seemed to attract bad luck. That unpredictable genie struck again just as Crooks, Bradbury, and two Canadians were ready to leave for the Otos. Among the expedition hunters were two brothers, Samuel and William Harrington. Samuel, the more experienced hunter, had joined in the fall of 1810, whereas William had been hired when Hunt was ready to leave St. Louis in March 1811. What Hunt did not know was that the Harringtons' doting mother had ordered William to go upriver and bring Samuel home before he went to the mountains. Hunt was "extremely exasperated" when he heard that the Harringtons were ready to leave. He needed their skills both as hunters and as marksmen in any encounter with the Sioux. No amount of persuasion could counter Mrs. Harrington's command, and the brothers soon turned their backs on the enterprise and headed off downriver.[68]

The first week of May saw the main party of Astorians working its way upriver to the Omaha town of Tonwantonga, near present-day Homer, Nebraska. At the same time Crooks and Bradbury were headed to the Oto village. Both groups met trouble and disappointment. When Crooks and Bradbury got to the village on the Platte River they found it deserted except for the trader William Rogers. Rogers was the interpreter whose wages were being shared by Aird and the Pacific Fur Company. While Bradbury took time to explore the Otos' lodges, Crooks asked Rogers to find horses for the overland journey to the Omahas. Two days later the interpreter returned with the unpleasant news that no horses were available. Now Crooks and Bradbury would have to walk to the Omahas. Plainly disgusted, they set out on May 7. They would not arrive until May 11.[69]

Crooks and Bradbury had seen signs of a war party. Hunt's men saw more than the signs. Well after dark on May 7 eleven Sioux warriors slipped into the Astorians' camp. At a signal the Indians, shouting and waving tomahawks, ran through the tents. But the attack misfired and the warriors were quickly surrounded and subdued. They had misjudged the camp's numbers, and now fearing for their lives, their leader shouted, "My children, do not hurt the white people." The greater danger was that the Astorians might take out their fury on the prisoners. Many in the camp wanted to kill the Sioux but Hunt refused, insisting that they be released. It was a wise decision, since killing even a few warriors would have insured violence later.[70] Back downriver, Lisa continued his steady gain on the Astorians. On May 5 he met the Harringtons. Talking with them made it plain that Hunt was only a few days ahead. With any good luck Lisa might catch him within the week.[71]

Hunt and his party got to the Omaha village on May 10. The next day Crooks and Bradbury arrived. Since the days of their cunning chief Blackbird, the Omahas had been a power on the river. They had done business with the Spanish and French and now were busy in the growing trade with the Americans. Despite a devastating smallpox epidemic in 1802, the Omahas had retained considerable influence. Hunt surely hoped that through Aird the Pacific Fur Company might also count the Omahas as trading partners.

The Astorians spent almost a week among these Indians. For Bradbury it was a time to explore the Omahas' lodges and observe the Indians' daily rituals. Both Bradbury and Nuttall roamed the hills and meadows outside Tonwantonga collecting plant specimens. That pursuit got Bradbury his Omaha name—Wakendaga, mean-

ing physician, or one who heals with plants. The expedition's boatmen engaged in less scientific pursuits. John Reed's ledger shows a
run on supplies of vermilion and calico. Long away from the plea-
sures of the opposite sex, men like Joseph St. Amant and François
Robert sought that comfort among the villagers.[72] Omaha women,
like their Arikara and Mandan sisters, used their contact with the
traders as a means to enhance their own material status.

For Hunt and the partners the days with the Omahas were filled
with business affairs and diplomacy. Astor never expected any of his
employees to act as official agents of American policy, but both he
and they knew that the Pacific Fur Company did enjoy some kind of
special status. That position was not lost on the Omahas. On May 13
two headmen, Big Elk and White Cow, brought Hunt a tribal dispute. Both men were seeking federal approval as principal chief.
They wanted Hunt to recommend one or the other to that red-
headed chief—William Clark—in St. Louis. Hunt did what he could
to sidestep this issue, but he could not avoid the troubling news that
arrived the next day. That intelligence was carried by three Yankton
Sioux warriors fresh from upcountry. They reported that the Tetons
were determined to stop the company's boats somewhere above the
Niobrara River. Hunt had heard this warning before, but now it
carried extra weight. His immediate concern was to make sure the
unsettling news was kept from company employees. He wanted no
more defections, something sure to happen if word leaked of an
impending attack. That night, with all preparations made for departure the next morning, Hunt wrote a long letter to Astor describing
the voyage thus far. It must have been a time to calculate the coming
dangers. Until then, the challenge had come from the river and the
unpredictable weather. Now the hazards would wear a human
face.[73]

Leaving the Omaha village early on May 15, the Astorians caught
brisk winds and made rapid progress. For the next five days steady
winds pushed the company's boats past familiar river landmarks like
Floyd's Bluff and Elk Point.[74] That same good weather smiled on
Lisa's straining crew. By May 19 they were at the Omaha village,

where traders told Lisa that Hunt was only four days gone. Lisa now decided to send one of his men and a Ponca guide overland to intercept Hunt at the Ponca village on the Niobrara. Writing to Hunt, he asked the Astorian to remain with the Poncas until both parties could join forces. Lisa knew about the Sioux blockade and reminded Hunt that a combined force might mean a better chance for survival.[75]

The Astorians' run of quick sailing ran out in a stretch of river between the James and the Niobrara. Strong head winds and rising water levels put a near stop to river travel. On May 22, the second day of very slow going, the expedition met two trappers fresh from the mountains. Meeting traders heading for St. Louis was nothing new for the Astorians, but Benjamin Jones and Alexander Carson were something special. The men had spent two years trapping around the Three Forks of the Missouri. Offered a place in the expedition, both men readily accepted. Hunt plainly saw them as valuable both for their frontier skills and for their geographic information.[76]

By May 24 the Astorians reached the Ponca village just below the mouth of the Niobrara River. No sooner had the expedition pulled up to the lodges than Lisa's emissaries arrived. After reading Lisa's letter and holding a hurried meeting with the other partners, Hunt set in motion a clever strategy designed to gain a few days on his competitor. He told Lisa's men that the Astorians would wait for the Missouri Company party. Hunt had no intention of waiting. In fact, he hoped that his misleading story would slow Lisa down. And Hunt planned to push the deception one step further. He decided to tell the Tetons that Lisa was their trader and that the Astorians had few goods to offer.[77] Such a scheme must have drawn appreciative looks from men like Crooks and McClellan, bent on doing Lisa every possible bad turn.

Hunt was ready to leave the Poncas on May 26 and to put as many miles between his party and Lisa's as possible. But that departure was suddenly delayed by the arrival of three more mountain men. Edward Robinson, John Hoback, and Jacob Reznor were no ordinary Missouri River trappers. They had been members of Andrew Henry's 1809 western expedition. That expedition had taken Henry and his men from Three Forks and the upper Yellowstone to the Snake River over Bannock Pass. After leaving Henry, the three trappers had crossed the Teton Range into Jackson Hole. Leaving the valley by way of Togwotee Pass, the men had headed southwest along the Wind River. By the time they reached Hunt, they had seen much of the mountain West virtually unknown to even the best-informed trader or explorer. But now it seemed that Robinson and his fellows were turning their backs on the mountains. That determination must not have run very deep, since it took little to persuade them to join the Astorians.

Hunt initially hired Robinson, Hoback, and Reznor to beef up the company's firepower for the inevitable showdown with the Tetons. But it soon became plain that these mountain men had more to offer than quick eyes and sure rifles. Their geographic experience, when added to that of Carson and Jones, was an Astorian treasure. On learning that Hunt's party was preparing to follow a northern trail, the trappers offered a more southerly passage. Robinson and his companions argued that both the original Lewis and Clark route and a Yellowstone march would expose the Astorians to unnecessary danger from Indians. They suggested what seemed a more direct and less hazardous highway across the mountains. Hunt was told that his party should go no farther up the Missouri than the Arikara villages on the Grand River. Once there, the company might purchase horses for the overland trek. The trappers proposed a journey that would run southwest through present-day South Dakota and Wyoming to meet the Wind River at modern-day Shoshoni, Wyoming. The traders were sure that from that point Hunt, "by following up Wind River, and crossing a single mountain ridge, . . . would come upon the headwaters of the Columbia."[78]

Hunt's newest Astorians had an accurate picture of much of the route they advocated. They certainly understood the role of the Wind River valley, although they may have confused Togwotee and Union passes. What the trappers did not fully grasp was the demanding nature of the Snake River plain. But to Hunt's mind the traders made a persuasive case, and experienced travelers like Carson and Jones recorded no objections. Once the quality of the trappers' information was grasped, it became what Bradbury called "a subject of anxious inquiry." That inquiry was evidently settled by the evening of May 26. The Astorians were now committed to an overland voyage on trails unmarked and perhaps not fully comprehended.[79]

Armed with new information and a clever strategy to delay Lisa, Hunt pressed upriver into Teton Sioux country. On May 27 Lisa pulled his keelboat up at the Ponca village fully expecting to share a berth with the Astorian navy. To Lisa's chagrin and amazement, the Astorians were nowhere to be found. After questioning two Canadians, probably Hunt deserters, Lisa was convinced that he knew Hunt's game. "It is the intention of Hunt," so Brackenridge heard it, "to pass the Sioux, who may wish to detain him, by telling them that their trader is coming on with goods for them." Lisa was more than ever determined to catch Hunt and defeat his plan. Brackenridge admitted that Hunt probably thought Lisa would try the same ploy should the Missouri Company outdistance the Astorians. Whatever the crosscurrents of deception, Lisa now pushed his men harder than ever.[80]

The confrontation with the Sioux came sooner than either Hunt or Lisa had expected. On the morning of May 31 the Astorians were on a stretch of the Missouri below present-day Fort Thompson, South Dakota. Here the river was a narrow channel twisting through islands and sandbars. High bluffs on either bank increased the risk of ambush. Early in the day two Indians were spotted on bluffs along the northeast side of the river. These Indians shouted to the traders so often that Hunt finally decided to halt for breakfast and talk with them. While the rest of the expedition clustered around mess fires, Hunt and Dorion went to parley. The news they brought back was unsettling. Some 280 lodges of Yanktons, Brules, and Miniconjous were a short distance from the river. Word of the Astorians had long preceded the expedition. Hunt was told that the Indians had been in place for eleven days "with a decided intention" to waylay the party. Hunt guessed that the camp held some six hundred warriors, with more expected every day.[81]

Hunt and Dorion's talk with the Indians produced more than an estimate of Sioux numbers and intentions. The Astorians also heard about the motives for what seemed an inevitably violent encounter. The traders were told that the Sioux bands would "suffer no one to trade with the Ricaras, Mandans, and Minaterees, being at war with those nations." But the Sioux decision to stop the Astorians was no simple military blockade. Economics was at the heart of the matter. The Teton bands occupied a middleman position in northern plains trade. Arikara farmers provided foodstuffs vital for the growing Sioux population. The Tetons needed to control the flow of trade goods moving upriver lest they lose their position in an intricate exchange system. St. Louis traders and official explorers knew from bitter experience that the Sioux were determined to protect their role, with considerable force if necessary.

As the Astorians inched their way up the narrow river channel, more warriors could be seen coming to the bank. Using a spyglass, Hunt saw that these were armed and painted warriors, not idle curiosity seekers. Hoping to buy time, the Astorians pulled their boats up on the opposite shore. Canadian engagés, fearless in white water, were predictably jumpy as rifles, pistols, and knives were checked and checked yet again. Hoping to avoid bloodshed, Hunt ordered the keelboat's swivel gun and two small howitzers to be charged with powder only. Those pieces were fired and then, as a precaution, reloaded with shot. That harmless artillery barrage had its desired effect. The warriors gathered at the river's edge now began to mill about in seeming confusion. A number of them held up buffalo robes and waved them from side to side, a recognized signal for talk and council. Dorion was the first to see the sign and shouted for all to hold fire. At that moment the Sioux made their intentions plain. Some fourteen headmen made their way to the shore, arranged themselves in a semicircle, and kindled a fire. The message seemed simple. The Sioux were ready to talk; what about the Astorians?

Hunt and the partners now faced a difficult situation. The expedition certainly had sufficient firepower to make the Indians pay dearly for any attack. But like Lewis and Clark, who had encountered the Tetons in 1804, the Astorians knew that violence could defeat the entire venture. The Pacific Fur Company needed an open Missouri, not one shut against all future voyages. Calling together Crooks, McClellan, Mackenzie, and Bradbury, Hunt held a hurried meeting. Diplomacy, no matter how unpredictable, seemed the only acceptable course. That settled, Hunt, Dorion, and several of the partners headed across the river to begin the council.

The protocol of plains diplomacy may have been new to Hunt and Bradbury, but it was familiar ritual to Pierre Dorion. Once the Astorians filled in the circle, a single chief stood and began the traditional pipe rite. With the ceremony complete, Hunt rose and spoke, his words translated by Dorion. Hunt tried to explain the nature of the Astorians' expedition. The object of their voyage, he asserted, was not to trade. Spinning out a fanciful tale, Hunt insisted that several of his "brothers" had gone to "the great salt lake in the west." Separated for nearly a year, the brothers east and west were now "crying" to see one another. "We would rather die," Hunt insisted, "than not go to them, and would kill every man that should oppose our passage." For someone new to plains diplomacy, Hunt seemed to find just the right balance between force, bluster, and symbolic compromise. Guns alone could not force the Tetons' passage. It would take gifts and soothing words. Hunt did not neglect either. Assuring the chiefs of the expedition's "pacific intentions," Hunt set out fifteen carottes of tobacco and an equal number of bags of corn.

No Sioux chief could have missed how well Hunt played the game. Now it was their turn. With Dorion again interpreting, one of the headmen repeated Sioux concerns about trade with the village peoples. Hunt must have been both surprised and relieved to hear that the chiefs had seemingly accepted his story about brothers pining for reunion. Perhaps more telling was a shrewd calculation of the casualties that would surely result from any battle with the expedition. And the news that there was another boat downriver laden with goods just for them must have helped the Sioux make up their minds to let the Astorians pass. This had been a high-stakes game, with both the immediate survival and future development of Astor's plans hanging in the balance. Wilson Price Hunt, business-man turned frontiersman, had acquitted himself well in this first real piece of danger. William Clark, who had had his own tense days with the Tetons, would have been impressed.

With so many Indians along the Missouri below the Big Bend, Manuel Lisa was not going to escape his own encounter with the Sioux. And he would have to face the Indians alone. For all their struggle and sweat, Lisa and his men had lost the race—lost it by one day. At dawn on June 1 the Missouri Company's party was snapped awake by shots coming from some miles downriver. Lisa was con-vinced that an attack was imminent, and he promptly mustered his forces for what was to come. Some time later several warriors came to the bank opposite Lisa's camp. After firing their guns, they waved an American flag—not necessarily a sign of peaceful intent. Not one for waiting for someone else to make the first move, Lisa took a small but well-armed party to meet the Indians. Toussaint Charbonneau did not have the language skills for this interpreting assignment, and Lisa had to rely on signs for his conference.

Guessing that Hunt had probably told the Sioux that the Missouri Company boat carried their trader, Lisa brazenly admitted that he was the merchant. Not even hinting at the rich store of trade goods hidden in his keelboat, Lisa told the Indians that he and his com-pany had suffered terrible reverses. Pelts had been burned, posts had been abandoned, and his "young men, who had passed two years before to go to the head of the Missouri," had been "attacked and distressed by the Indians of those parts." Playing hard luck to the hilt, Lisa described himself as "poor and much to be pitied." But no matter his poverty, he claimed he was not about to abandon his Sioux friends. If they allowed him to pass, he would return in three months to rebuild the burned-out trading post at Cedar Island. Lisa put out his obligatory stock of presents and waited for a response.

Like Hunt, he must have been surprised when he saw signs that made it plain his crew and boat could pass untouched.[82]

The Astorians might have thought that they had escaped the Teton empire. But confrontations with the Sioux seldom ended so cleanly. Making their way above the Big Bend on June 2, the expedition members were visited by two more Sioux chiefs. These men had come to Hunt complaining about his stingy gift policy. From a fleet so large they had expected more. This was one request too many, and Hunt met the demand with uncharacteristic anger. "He had given all he intended and would give no more—that he was much displeased by their importunity and if they or any of their nation again followed us with similar demands, he would consider them as enemies, and treat them as such." Hunt's sharp words did not sit well, and the Sioux headmen took to their horses, riding off "seemingly in a rage."[83]

That nasty exchange set the Astorians on edge and for the rest of the day all eyes scanned the river bluffs for more unwelcome visitors. It would have been more prudent for Hunt to have assigned extra eyes to watch the narrow channel. Here the Missouri snaked its way between islands, over sandbar shallows, and around tight bends. The unwary boatman might easily find himself on a deadend surrounded by more sand than water. Late in the afternoon the Astorians took the wrong channel and soon discovered that their boats were cut off from the river's main stem. At that moment a war party of some hundred men clustered around the grounded keelboat. With no time to prepare for action, all seemed lost. But the crisis vanished as quickly as it had appeared. The warriors were Mandans, Hidatsas, and Arikaras bent on raiding the Sioux. Amid greetings and expressions of friendship, Astorians and Indians settled into an evening of singing, dancing, and feasting. Lewis and Clark had had moments like that—moments of shared pleasure and delight that bound together plains people old and new. For the Astorians, there would be few such times.[84]

Manuel Lisa lost his race to join Hunt before either man met the Sioux. But there were still the Arikara villages to deal with. Although Lewis and Clark had enjoyed good relations with the Arikaras, recent travelers upriver had been much less fortunate. In 1807 a Lewis and Clark veteran, Ensign Nathaniel Pryor, had encountered considerable resistance when he had sought to take the Mandan chief Sheheke home past the Arikara villages. The Arikaras did not take kindly to the notion that they might be bypassed in the trade with villages higher up the Missouri. The Grand River towns were a military and political presence not to be taken lightly. Hunt refused his Arikara visitors firearms but was quick to offer each warrior powder, shot, and knives.

As Hunt busied himself delivering these gifts, an Indian appeared to report that a boat was coming upriver. There could have been no doubt in Hunt's mind that it belonged to Lisa. Dropping further gift distributing, Hunt moved his boats and his Indian guests another five or six miles upriver. It was a move probably suggested by Crooks and McClellan. These Astorians feared that if Lisa talked directly to the Arikaras, he might be able to turn them against the expedition. As Bradbury could not help noticing, Crooks and his companions were "extremely apprehensive of treachery on the part of Lisa, whom they suspected had an intention of quitting us shortly, being now no longer in fear of the Sioux, with an intention of doing us an injury with the Arikaras." Once the two parties met, Bradbury and Brackenridge greeted each other warmly. Other expedition members only exchanged sullen glances, and it took all of Hunt's influence to keep Crooks and company from openly confronting Lisa. Hunt restrained his men, but he himself had suspicions aplenty about Lisa. Lisa appeared friendly enough, but Hunt was sure that his rival was "anxiously desirous that the expedition should fail."[85]

The two parties now traveled in company but kept their distance. The tension finally exploded on the afternoon of June 5. After coming to camp, Lisa invited Pierre Dorion to his boat. Over a friendly glass of whiskey Lisa tried once again to lure the interpreter away from the Astorians. When sweet words and a plentiful supply of liquor failed, Lisa fell back on Dorion's old alcohol debt. He may even have mentioned the warrant sworn out in St. Louis for Dorion's arrest. All this sparked the predictable burst of angry words. His fury only momentarily vented, Dorion stalked back to his tent.

A few minutes later the ruckus took on a new, threatening face. Lisa took this inopportune time to show up at the Astorians' camp, asking to borrow a boat towline. Dorion caught sight of him, flew out of his tent, and punched Lisa. Bradbury witnessed the assault and saw Lisa burst into "the most violent rage." Recovering from Dorion's blow, Lisa shouted, "Where is my knife?" While Lisa ran back to get his weapon, Dorion armed himself with two pistols. By now a considerable crowd had gathered to watch the spectacle. Both Crooks and McClellan were there. They not only urged Dorion on but wanted to join him. It was all Hunt could do to keep them out of the impending duel. When Lisa returned, armed only with a knife, Hunt became directly involved. He told Lisa to get a gun so that the combat might be on equal terms. Bradbury and Brackenridge had been silently watching all the commotion. Now they were horrified at the prospect of such bloodshed and furious that Hunt would condone it. Both men walked with Lisa back to his camp, pleading with him to swallow his pride and abandon the duel. Whether it was those arguments or his own good sense, Lisa finally cooled off enough to remain in camp. Violence had been averted, but bad feelings now ran higher than ever. None of this boded well for the coming visit with the Arikaras.[86]

For the next three days both parties kept their distance as each made its way upriver. By June 9 the extended convoy was past the Cheyenne River and within a day or two of reaching the Arikaras. In a rare moment of cooperation, Hunt and Lisa decided to send a joint embassy to the Arikaras to announce their arrival. The traders were also ordered to check on the number of horses the Indians might be willing to trade. Led by Robert McClellan, the party quickly found that overland travel was slower than expected. Fair winds made for fast sailing and it was soon evident that McClellan and his men could not reach the Arikaras before the main party.[87]

When Lewis and Clark had visited the Arikaras in October 1804, they had found the village farmers living in three towns. Sawa-haini, a village of some sixty earth lodges, at that time was situated on Ashley Island in the Missouri. That settlement had been abandoned sometime after 1806, and its inhabitants now lived in the two remaining villages a short distance upriver. The first of these was Rhtarahe. Just across Cottonwood Creek was Waho-erha. Arikara villagers were prosperous farmers and astute traders. Their corn and bean crops and horse herds attracted Sioux and Cheyennes eager to exchange their goods for the Arikaras' produce. Imperious Tetons may have thought they were the lords of the Missouri. But Arikara headmen like Grey Eyes and Le Gauche believed they had just as good a claim.[88]

It was not until June 12 that the Astorians reached the Arikara villages. Drenched by a severe overnight thunderstorm, the travelers must not have been an inspiring sight. Past Ashley Island, Hunt and his men came upon a canoe carrying two Arikara chiefs and their French interpreter. The Arikaras were Le Gauche, a civil chief, and Big Man, a war chief. Their interpreter was Joseph Garreau, a French trader who had lived among the Arikaras for more than twenty years. The Astorians already knew that their arrival had sparked considerable debate within the villages. When the expedition had met some villagers two days before, they had learned that once the joint Mandan-Hidatsa-Arikara war party had returned to the Grand River towns there had been open argument about what course of action to take toward the Astorians. The Hidatsas, closely tied to North West Company traders, had once cold-shouldered Lewis and Clark. These Indians proposed an attack on the expedition. Mandans, usually friendly to St. Louis merchants, agreed to join in the raid. Hunt understood that only the Arikaras' reluctance to participate in the assault had prevented bloodshed.[89]

This confusion of threats and possible violence now came home with great force. Speaking through Garreau, the two chiefs announced that the Arikaras had decided not to permit the party to pass unless a boatload of presents was left to pay river passage. The request was a common one, made perhaps more as a start to bargaining than as a final demand. Hunt may have sensed that as he launched into a long speech explaining the expedition's plans. Most important, he broached the subject of trading for horses. The Arikaras' herds were reserved for Sioux and Cheyenne customers, and getting them would pose a real challenge.

With this initial meeting with the Arikaras concluded, the Astorians reached the villages at midmorning. They pulled their boats up on a bank opposite the earth lodges and laid out soaked trade goods to dry. It soon became plain that not all the Arikara chiefs were bent on delaying the expedition. Carefully looking over the displayed items, an unnamed chief declared that he was ready to council at any time. At least some of the Indians were ready to talk. The same could not be said for the Astorians and Manuel Lisa. Of all the Astorians, Robert McClellan harbored the deepest resentment against Lisa. McClellan was wholly persuaded that if Lisa got to the Arikaras first, he would persuade them to trade no horses. The embittered McClellan repeatedly threatened to shoot Lisa if he made his way across the river ahead of the Astorians.

By noon, tempers had cooled enough to allow a joint party from the two companies to head for Le Gauche's lodge. Still worried about his safety, Lisa crossed the Missouri in a separate boat. Entering the lodge, Lisa and the Astorians were joined by some twenty chiefs and elders. When Dorion leaned over and told Bradbury that more Indians were yet to come, the interpreter touched on one of the essential features of Arikara politics. Waves of epidemic disease had dramatically reduced the natives' numbers. Survivors crowded into refuge villages. As the veteran trader Jean Baptiste Tabeau put it, village politics was an intense struggle among "captains without companies." When Tabeau tried to call a conference with the Arikaras and invited forty-two chiefs, he was harshly reprimanded for forgetting so many others.[90] Le Gauche, plainly worried that so few Arikaras had come to the gathering, asked an elderly man who served as town crier to call the tardy ones.

The conference began in earnest when Le Gauche performed the required pipe ritual. Pointing a sacred pipe in the cardinal directions, he invoked spirit powers to purify thoughts and bless the proceedings. The ceremony completed, Le Gauche made a carefully worded speech. Claiming poverty had long been an accepted river tactic. Traders were supposed to show their concern for future customers by providing substantial gifts. Le Gauche mouthed the obligatory words and declared his happiness that the boatmen had come to trade. In what must have been a turn of events that could only worry the Astorians, Lisa made the first reply. He told the Arikaras he was ready to trade so long as the price for beaver pelts and buffalo robes was not too high. What he had to say about the Astorians surprised everyone, but perhaps Crooks and McClellan most of all. Lisa claimed that Hunt and the Astorians were his friends and insisted that his company would join them in repulsing any attack. It was hardly what Hunt had expected Lisa to say. Perhaps the words accurately reflected Lisa's decision to abandon any Far Western dreams and concentrate on the middle Missouri trade. Whatever the motive, Hunt must have been relieved. Crooks and McClellan were probably not satisfied and were doubtless determined to watch Lisa closely.

Hunt's speech followed the pattern set at the Sioux gathering. He repeated the now familiar lines. He and his men were searching for long-lost brothers dwelling "at the western great salt lake." Their quest required horses for the overland journey and Hunt hoped the Arikaras would be generous in trade. Although Hunt sought to distinguish his mission from Lisa's, actions taken by the two blurred any differences. In the presence of the Arikaras both Hunt and Lisa rolled out bundles of gifts. Amid the bolts of cloth, cakes of vermilion, and strings of beads Hunt must have looked every bit the trader.

When Lewis and Clark had dealt with the Arikaras they had learned two lessons. Replies to official requests came slowly and were often contradictory. The Arikaras' answers to trading questions could come quicker but they too sometimes reflected that political climate of "captains without companies." Le Gauche now listened attentively to Lisa's and Hunt's speeches as Garreau translated them.

Responding quickly, Le Gauche reported that the Arikaras were pleased to see boats up from St. Louis. The chief declared that trade with Lisa was a welcome prospect but that more time was needed to set prices. Le Gauche thought that an exchange rate of thirty loads of powder and ball for each buffalo robe was about right. These were high prices, but at least Lisa had some hope that negotiation might bring them down. When Le Gauche turned to Hunt the atmosphere suddenly changed. The Arikara was "certain they could not spare the number of horses" the Astorians sought. In fact, Le Gauche thought that the villagers should sell Hunt no horses. Le Gauche's motives for taking this position are obscure. He may well have been reluctant to deplete herds on the eve of the arrival of Cheyenne traders. Perhaps the chief thought that giving the Astorians horses might anger the Tetons. The Teton-Arikara relationship was always an uneasy one, rapidly alternating between war and trade. The chief also may have thought that tough talk might mean better prices in the coming days.

In the unpredictable world of Arikara politics, no one chief or elder spoke for all the villages or even for all the inhabitants of a single town. Le Gauche was surely influential, but his was not the only Indian voice to be heard. When Lewis and Clark had revisited the Grand River villages in August 1806, they had met an Arikara chief named Grey Eyes, who had just acquired considerable influence at Sawa-haini. Grey Eyes was a shrewd diplomat, something Lewis and Clark soon learned. In 1823 he would lead Arikara warriors against American forces in the ill-fated Leavenworth campaign, an action that would cost him his life. Grey Eyes now wore the peace medal originally given to the principal chief Kakawissassa. If Le Gauche wanted to trade with the Astorians, Grey Eyes saw no reason to delay such exchanges. He told the gathering that the villagers could easily spare the horses Hunt required. Besides, he reminded them, the Arikaras could always get more horses by trade or raid. Whether it was the force of his arguments or his growing prestige, Grey Eyes won the day for the Astorians. Trade would begin once the price was set. In the meantime the headmen would detail some warriors to guard trade goods from any pilfering. To seal the bargain, the Arikaras invited Hunt and his companions to a rich feast of corn and buffalo fat.[91]

The Astorians remained with the Arikaras until mid-July. For an expedition bent on crossing the mountains and reaching the Pacific before winter, it was a dangerous delay. Seasoned mountain men like Alexander Carson and Edward Robinson surely knew the hazards of so late a start. The long delay was caused by unexpected difficulties in trading for enough horses to transport the Astorians and their goods. The overland party now numbered sixty-five people. Hunters, partners, engagés, Marie Dorion, and the Dorions' two children all had to be provided with horses. Counting the necessary number of remounts, Hunt probably required 150 horses. This was a very substantial demand, one that would surely strain the Arikaras' herds. The Astorians wanted these horses at a very difficult time for the Indians. Food supplies, stored in deep, cone-shaped caches, had been spoiled by seeping water. That food shortage might be alleviated by the prompt arrival of Cheyennes bringing dried meat in exchange for horses. The Arikaras knew that if they gave Hunt as many mounts as he wanted, the Cheyenne trade might go begging.

To his dismay Hunt found that the horse dealing went poorly. After a burst of quick trading, the business slowed and then stopped. Each horse destined for the expedition had its tail bobbed as a mark of ownership. When Hunt counted those bobbed-tailed ponies on June 16, he found not many more than thirty. The Arikaras made it plain that this was their limit. Worry about the Cheyenne trade and rumors that a Sioux war party was in the neighborhood put a clamp on all further business. In desperation Hunt turned to Manuel Lisa. Hunt proposed buying additional horses from the Missouri Company's Mandan post. Lisa was offered a large supply of trade goods, the expedition's boats, and its two howitzers for the animals. Lisa agreed, one more sign that he had forsaken his far western designs. On June 18, Crooks, Bradbury, and several others headed for the Mandans carrying bills of exchange written by Lisa to Reuben Lewis. Lewis, then in charge at the Mandan trading house, was cordial but could provide no more than fifty horses. When Hunt made his final horse count at the end of June he could tally only eighty-two, some not in especially good condition. This number was sufficient to carry the partners, the clerk John Reed, the Dorions, and packs of merchandise. The rest of the Astorians seemed destined to walk to the Pacific.[92]

While Hunt was busy trying to fill out the company's remuda, ordinary employees were following their own trading interests. Those pursuits centered on exchanging trade goods for sexual favors. European men traveling the Missouri had long known that village women were available for liaisons so long as the proper price was paid. To traders and explorers from Montreal and St. Louis, all this looked like common prostitution. As Bradbury observed, "In this species of liberality no nation can be exceeded by the Arikaras, who flocked down every evening with their wives, sisters, and daughters, each anxious to meet with a market for them."[93]

For the Arikara women who enthusiastically sought the blue beads and hide scrapers offered for intimate encounters, those affairs had a wholly different meaning. Having sex with strangers was based on well-recognized sanctions in village life. The Arikaras were eager to obtain manufactured goods, and offering favors to traders meant having those desirable objects. Every outsider knew that the Arikaras did not sell cheap sex. As Bradbury noted, "I observed several instances wherein the squaw was consulted by her husband as to the *quantum sufficit*." But sex was more than the acquisition of valued goods. It was also a mark of plains hospitality. Perhaps most important, the Arikaras and their neighbors understood sex as a means of transferring spiritual power from one person to another. Whites had power that could be gained through sexual intercourse. As Meriwether Lewis put it, "The Indians believed these traders were the most powerful persons in the nation." Having sex with Antoine Plante or Joseph Landry meant snatching some of that spiritual power for the Arikaras.[94]

The Astorians had been with the Arikaras no more than a day when John Reed began to sell the prized blue beads and the scrapers. Reed's company store charged 50¢ for each scraper and $1.50 for several strings of beads. The full pages of Reed's ledger testify to a very active trade. Business was so brisk that one chief paused to inquire of Brackenridge whether or not the white men had any women in their world. When Brackenridge assured the chief that there were indeed white women, the Indian wondered aloud, "Then why is it that your people are so fond of our women, one might suppose they had never seen any before."[95]

* * *

By July 17 Hunt knew that he had to set out overland no matter the size of his horse train. As hunters and engagés hurried to buy last-minute supplies of tobacco and clay pipes, Hunt set himself to write Astor one final letter before heading west. That report has not survived, but Astor's summary of it in a March 1812 letter to Jefferson suggests what Hunt had to say. He reminded Astor that the expedition was not going to follow the Lewis and Clark track. Instead, the party would bend its course along the Grand River, "this being recommended as nearer and easier to the south branch of the Columbia [Snake] than the route taken by Lewis." Astor told Jefferson that Hunt had a hundred horses. That wishful thinking was the same number that Bradbury reported to Joseph Charless for an account of the expedition's progress printed in the August 8, 1811, issue of the *Louisiana Gazette*. No doubt Hunt knew the true number but hoped that somehow it might grow. His letter to Astor betrayed no lack of confidence. Astor assured Jefferson that all reports from the upper Missouri were filled with "fair and encouraging" words promising "ultimate success." Hunt and his companions were soon to learn that confidence and resolve needed more than paper expression. The overland voyage would test resolve and press endurance to the limit.[96]

6

From the Arikara Villages to Astoria

A YEAR BEFORE coming to the Arikara villages Wilson Price Hunt had talked vaguely about "some idea of going across the country by the Missouri."[1] Now his thoughts were both settled and precise. Influenced by trapper lore as well as information from William Clark, Hunt planned to strike southwesterly across the plains to find a pass over the Great Divide—a pass far from Blackfoot warriors and their troublesome Canadian allies. Once over the Divide, Hunt would shape his course along rivers sure to join the Columbia. Along the trail he might plot sites for future company posts. And in July 1811 all of that seemed within reach. The Astorians had a carefully laid travel strategy based on the best available geographic experience. More than that, Hunt had the men, equipment, and horses required for such a hazardous voyage. Delays, setbacks, rumors, and confusions all had bedeviled the Astorian enterprise. If ever Hunt and his men needed good fortune, it was now.

If July 18, 1811, was like other Dakota midsummer days, it dawned hot and got hotter. Early that morning voyageurs and hunters became packers and drivers setting to work on the Astorians' horse train. With only eighty-two animals in the company corral, it was soon plain that most of the party would walk their way west. Mounts were set aside for the partners and for Marie Dorion and her two children. Much of the morning was taken up adjusting packsaddles and checking cinches. With all the hustle that attended any enterprise so large, the overlanders may not have left the Arikaras until near noon.

Guided by Robinson and the other mountain men, Hunt's expedition headed southwest from the Arikaras to Rampart River, a small stream that ran to the Missouri below the Indian villages. From the Rampart, or Oak Creek as it is known today, the Astorians pointed their horses toward Grand River. By the time the expedition made its first camp on the south bank of the Grand, several lessons had been learned. The most painful was that moccasins wore out quickly on rough, rocky ground. Voyageurs who had engaged for white-water paddling must have grumbled as they nursed sore feet. Antoine Plante did more than grouse. He went to John Reed's "company store" and spent twenty-five cents of his future wages for two pairs of new moccasins. Keeping track of men, merchandise, and horses that first day had been difficult enough. Organizing a system to feed and bed down men and animals was even more trying. Lewis and Clark had been able to fall back on military routine with its messes and camp cooks. Voyageur traditions were somewhat less formal. That first night there must have been considerable confusion as men tried on their own to sort themselves into parties for cooking, eating, and picketing. Hunt was determined not to repeat such fumbling, and the next day he assigned men to messes and parceled out camp kettles to each.[2]

Over the next several days the Astorians continued their westward track along the Grand. On July 21 the party crossed to the right, or north, bank of the river. Prairie grass sometimes knee-high provided good grazing for the horses. But that same lush grass slowed the expedition's progress. In this first week of travel Hunt's party made about nine miles a day, a respectable pace but not fast enough to avoid snow in distant passes. Not only were the Astorians moving slowly, but also some members of the caravan now fell ill. Voyageurs hardened to long hours of paddling were not prepared for the demands of tramping over broken prairie ground. Bruised and footsore, several of the Canadians were near exhaustion. But no one was sicker than Ramsay Crooks. For all his adventuring, Crooks had never enjoyed robust health. Now he was so ill that he could not stay in the saddle. A litter was hastily assembled for him. By the time the Astorians reached Firesteel Creek in today's Corson County, South Dakota, Hunt knew it was time to make camp for an extended rest. Crooks and the other disabled needed attention. More than that, the expedition desperately required more horses.[3]

Settling in to the Firesteel camp, Hunt first turned his attention to the sick. Once tents were pitched beneath the cottonwoods that fringed the creek, other Astorians lined up to buy replacement moccasins from Reed's supply. Caring for the sick and generally refitting were important duties, but Hunt knew the future of the expedition depended on getting additional horses. Talks with the Arikaras had led him to believe that Cheyenne traders were nearby, making their way to the Missouri. These Indians were bound to have horses for trade. Hunt decided to send Benjamin Jones, John Day, and several other hunters to scout the Cheyennes. That quest proved successful. On July 26 Jones and his companions found the Indians. Once they were sure the Cheyennes were interested in doing business, the hunters hurried back to the Firesteel to alert Hunt.[4]

Hearing the good news from Jones, Hunt decided to make for the Cheyennes' camp as quickly as possible. The location of that camp cannot be exactly pinpointed today, but it was in an open prairie near a stream. Hunt was plainly impressed by the large, handsome teepees as well as the orderly ways of the camp. For their part, the Indians welcomed the explorer as just another northern plains trader. The Cheyennes had had some contact with whites, usually along the Missouri. In 1806 several chiefs had held a brief meeting with Lewis and Clark at the Arikaras' villages. As was so often the case on the plains, trade bridged the cultural divide, and both Hunt and the Indians quickly set to horse dealing. Neither Hunt's diary nor Reed's ledger reveals the rate Astorians had to pay for the horses. When the Cheyennes traded with the Arikaras, they always sought guns and ammunition as well as foodstuffs. It is doubtful whether Hunt had extra weapons, powder, and lead to sell. The Cheyennes may have had to settle for cloth, beads, knives, and hide scrapers. Whatever the exchange schedule, Hunt managed to get thirty-six good horses. He proudly noted in his diary that these were bought "at a much better price than at the Arikaras village."[5]

Hunt's good relations with the Cheyennes went so far as a tentative agreement to include these Indians in future fur trade ventures. When the Cheyennes had met Lewis and Clark, they had asked for instructions in beaver trapping, a request renewed to Hunt. But this sunny version of affairs between the Astorians and the Cheyennes was not the only account current in the northern plains world. When Manuel Lisa went back to St. Louis in the fall of 1811 he carried a different tale. As Charles Gratiot heard it, Hunt had been waylaid by the Cheyennes. The Indians "would not let him pass until he had traded with them." Saying nothing about fresh horses, Lisa insisted that the Astorians had been forced to give up valuable merchandise in return for twenty packs of unwanted beaver pelts. Gratiot swallowed the story and passed it on as fact to an anxious Astor. Even more worrisome was Gratiot's news from informed St. Louis sources that Hunt's delays at the Arikaras' villages would cost him dearly. "It was to be apprehended," Gratiot explained, "he [Hunt] would experience many difficulties before he could cross the mountains and would be exposed to winter on the roads before he could reach the place of his destination."[6]

With the new horses to fill out the expedition's stock, it was possible to assign two men to each mount. The Astorians spent much of August 4 and 5 shifting loads and rearranging baggage. By the sixth they were back on the trail, still following the Grand River. On those days out of the Firesteel camp, it was plain what a difference the Cheyennes' horses made. The expedition was now averaging some twenty miles a day. The pace might have been even quicker had it not been for dramatic changes in the terrain. More rocky and broken ground, shorter grass, and less water all signaled the end of the prairie. Here the explorers could sense the beginnings of a mountain world. At the same time Hunt had his first experience with a large buffalo herd. At camp on the seventh, the Astorians found themselves in the midst of a great bison congregation. Hunt captured the moment in a brief but memorable description. "They are all about us. As it was the rutting season, they made a frightful noise like the sound of distant thunder; the males tearing the ground with their hoofs and horns."[7]

By August 11 the Astorians were finding the going much more taxing. Struggling over sharp hills known today as the Slim Buttes (Harding County, South Dakota), Hunt complained, "The road was irksome because of the steepness and the great number of stones." Hard climbs and the fact that the expedition was drifting more north than west dictated a course change. On August 12 the Astorians slanted away from the north fork of the Grand, crossed the south fork, and headed for the Little Missouri River. Crossing the Little Missouri at the South Dakota–Montana border on August 13, Hunt and his men could see the Powder River Range looming on the western horizon. Those mountains worried Hunt. They seemed, so he thought, to "bar our route."[8]

The Powder River Range proved to be the Astorians' first real overland challenge. Robinson and the other mountain men were out buffalo hunting, so the path had to be found by Hunt and others. Just how they expected to thread their way through these mountains remains unclear. What is plain is that the Astorians were about to become hopelessly tangled in the southern foothills of the Powder River Mountains. On August 15, after camping the night before on Boxelder Creek south of present-day Mill Iron, Montana, the Astorians began to push over the Powder ridges. Although these were but foothills, they were demanding enough for men accustomed more to fast water than to steep rises and deep ravines. By the sixteenth, Hunt laconically termed the country "extremely rugged." The next day was even more exhausting as the expedition toiled over the northern end of the Missouri Buttes, a set of razorback ridges with elevations between 3,500 and 3,700 feet. Bighorn sheep, seen scampering over the jagged rocks, seemed to mock the Astorians' sweat and struggle.[9]

Since the fifteenth the expedition had been angling southwest through present-day Crook County, Wyoming. Hunt had kept his men moving at as quick a pace as possible. Now those exertions were beginning to take their toll. By August 18 it was clear that the explorers had to escape these mountains or risk becoming wholly lost and exhausted. Dwindling stores of food and water made the decision even more urgent. Hunt decided to turn southwest, away from the mountains. Once off the western slopes, the expedition found itself on the northeastern end of Thunder Basin. The basin was a great bowl of grass bounded on the east by the Bear Lodge Mountains and on the west by the Bighorns. Watered by scores of creeks and seasonal streams, the basin was rich in buffalo and other game.

Away from the mountains, the Astorians quickly made camp to celebrate their escape. While messes eagerly divided up eight freshly killed buffalo, Hunt and Donald Mackenzie climbed a nearby hill to survey their situation. What they saw was not especially encouraging. The travel plan proposed by Robinson and his fellows called for the Astorians to ride west by southwest until they struck the Wind River. What Hunt and Mackenzie saw far to the west cast real doubt on the wisdom of such a course. Looming on the western horizon were the Bighorn Mountains. Snow had already dusted those mountains, and the peak Hunt called Mt. Big Horn—today's Cloud Peak—was fully wrapped in snow. The Astorians might have fat times on the buffalo ranges of Thunder Basin, but the Bighorns promised trouble.[10]

The prospect of passage through the Bighorns surely worried Hunt. But for the moment the Astorians enjoyed the bounties of Thunder Basin. Fresh game spiced with gooseberries, currants, and chokecherries made the daily trek less burdensome. But a close look at those chokecherries showed that other guests, perhaps four-footed ones, had enjoyed them as well. The expedition now had its first "bear scare" as rumors of "white," or grizzly, bears flew up and down the packtrain. Only half in jest Hunt wrote, "With the slightest breeze moving in the bushes, one felt in spite of oneself a shiver of dread." Guarding their ways, the Astorians were by August 20 at a camp on Prairie Creek east of Weston, Wyoming. At the partners' mess that night Hunt must have taken pleasure in adding up the daily mileages. Since leaving the mountains the expedition had averaged twenty-five to thirty miles each day. Not even a hard freeze that night—one so stiff it put ice in the buckets to the thickness of a dollar—chilled Hunt's determination to be on with the journey.[11]

In the grass ocean of Thunder Basin no traveler was ever quite alone. On August 22, as the Astorians neared the Little Powder River, they fell into a trail used by Crow traders. That trace led from Absaroka homelands to the Mandan villages on the Missouri. Each year Crow merchants rode to the great trade festival held in and around the Mandans' earth lodges. Like the Cheyennes, the Crows were intent on getting guns and other trade goods in exchange for horses and dried meat. Thinking the Crows' route a good one, the Astorians followed it southwest through northern Campbell County, Wyoming. What Hunt expected to be a good trading path soon turned into a rough crossing. Here the basin was scored by a series of washboard hills and dry washes. The twisting trail was made harder by sudden heat. With little water and no shade, all suffered. Donald Mackenzie's dog, always alongside, died of heat exhaustion during that sweltering day. Parched throats and burning eyes were constant companions. Hunt admitted that some of his men "were on the verge of losing courage."[12]

This blazing *jornada* lasted until August 25, when the expedition finally got to Clear Creek, a tributary of the Powder River. Fresh water and sizzling slabs of buffalo meat filled empty bellies and bolstered faltering resolve. For the next two days the Astorians moved slowly, gathering strength for the coming battle with the Bighorns. By August 28 the expedition was near present-day Buffalo, Wyoming. Knowing that they were nearing the end of Thunder Basin and good bison hunting, the partners decided to make camp for two days to prepare meat for the coming mountain assault.

Company hunters were soon bringing in meat to be cut and quickly fire-dried. By August 29 Hunt was convinced that provisions were sufficient to carry the expedition across the Bighorns.[13]

Heading southwest from their camp, the Astorians followed a rough trail that cut across the headwaters of the north and middle forks of Crazy Woman Creek. On August 29 hunters reported fresh signs of Indians. For explorers laboring over steep and rocky ground the news was unwelcome. Nonetheless, many of the engagés hurried to John Reed seeking blue beads, handkerchiefs, and other trade goods. Hunt might have feared a fight; his men were probably more ready for a frolic. Indian sign became Indian presence the next day when two Crows showed up at the Astorians' camp. Their arrival signaled the beginning of serious trouble between Hunt and a remarkable character named Edward Rose. Rose had joined the Astorians at the Arikara villages. His background and extraordinary personal history would soon set him at odds with the entire Astorian enterprise.[14]

There was little hint of impending trouble when a great parade of Crows came to the Astorians' camp on August 31. Men, women, and children—all mounted on fine horses—made a spectacular entrance. Dressed and bedecked to the nines, the Crows put on a grand show of plains Indian finery. The Crows' welcome put Hunt at ease and soon the Astorians were headed to pay a visit to the Indians' camp. Escorted by chiefs and warriors, Hunt and the partners made their way to a large teepee. The remaining travelers were shown a convenient place to settle alongside the Crow encampment. Perhaps using Edward Rose as an interpreter, Hunt explained his journey to the Crow chiefs and gave them gifts of cloth, powder, bullets, and knives. The presents were graciously accepted and the next day Astorians and Crows busily engaged in trade. The Astorians offered beads, cloth, and knives for buffalo robes. More important, the expedition was able to exchange some worn-out horses for fresh ones. By the evening of September 1 Hunt could count 121 horses, mostly good animals, in the company herd.[15]

In the midst of this good-natured swapping, Hunt began to hear rumors about Rose. The trapper had been engaged because he was an experienced mountain man. Hunt apparently knew little about his background. Rose was the child of a white trader and a woman of Cherokee and African ancestry. He grew up in Kentucky and in his teens went to New Orleans on a riverboat. By 1806 he was in St. Louis looking for work. Hired the next year by Manuel Lisa, Rose went west with the Missouri Fur Company's Bighorn River expedition. There Rose had his first contacts with the Crows. After a falling out with Lisa, he went to live with his Crow friends, never intending a permanent residence there. In 1809 Andrew Henry found him among the Arikaras. After another sojourn among the Crows, Rose was again at the Arikara villages on the Grand River in 1811. Hunt once described Edward Rose as "a very bad fellow full of daring." Perhaps it would have been fairer to have marked him as a man who lived by his wits, always ready to grab the main chance.[16]

Rumor in camp had it that Rose's main chance would come when the Astorians reached Crow country. As Hunt heard it in whispers from others, Rose "planned to desert us, . . . taking with him as many of our men as he could seduce, and steal our horses." The expedition's leader vowed to watch Rose closely in the days to come. Robert McClellan, always an advocate of direct action, wanted to end the affair quickly by shooting Rose. On September 2, with the Astorians traveling south along the eastern foothills of the Bighorns, a second band of Crows suddenly appeared. Hunt took their arrival as an opportunity to confront Rose. Hunt had decided that it would be wiser to bribe the trapper than force his outright expulsion from the party. Pointing to the newly arrived Crows, Hunt suggested that Rose join them. As an incentive, Hunt promised half a year's wages, a horse, three beaver traps, and some trade goods. Just what scheme Rose had in mind remains unclear, but with Hunt determined to watch his every move, Rose decided to clear out before the bargain got less attractive.[17]

Rose's departure may have eased some fears about mutiny, but it did nothing to smooth what was quickly becoming a treacherous mountain passage. The Astorians' problem was a simple one. They had to find a pass over the crest of the Bighorns and a suitable path that trended southwesterly to the Wind River. Mountain passes, routes to navigable rivers—these were issues fundamental to all western exploration. The solution for the Astorians was both complex and dangerous. By September 3 the expedition was laboring to escape "precipices" in elevations of seven and eight thousand feet. Stumbling horses and men gasping for breath slowed progress to an agonizing crawl. When Edward Rose suddenly reappeared on September 4, Hunt must have thought his troubles had just compounded. But Rose brought salvation, not discord. Throughout the history of western exploration, Indians often provided crucial geographic information that spelled the difference between success or failure, survival or death. The Crow chief whose band Rose had joined realized that the Astorians had strayed off the main trading path. Rose was now at Hunt's camp with accurate travel directions. The next day the Astorians struck that path, found a pass over the main divide of the Bighorns, and came down on the west side of the range just east of present-day Ten Sleep, Wyoming.[18]

For the next two days the Astorians traveled west-southwest through modern-day Washakie County, Wyoming. In the level ground along Nowood Creek, Hunt and his men found abundant grass and berries and plenty of fresh game. And the Astorians were not making the passage alone. On September 6 the expedition was joined by some Shoshoni and Flathead Indians. These Indians not only made good company but also offered some additional travel information. The Astorians still needed to make their rendezvous with the Wind River. Rising to the west were the snow-covered Owl Creek Mountains, yet another barrier between the explorers and the river. Information from the Indians suggested following present-day Bridger Creek south to its junction with Badwater Creek. That stream would lead the expedition directly west to the Wind River at present-day Shoshoni, Wyoming. Hunt had learned the value of Indian geography and he shaped the expedition's course to what he heard from native sources. By September 9 the Astorians were camped on the Wind River. One mountain journey was complete. More beckoned.[19]

Working with information supplied by Robinson and other trappers, Hunt now charted a course roughly northwest along the Wind River. From September 10 to 15 the Astorians enjoyed relatively easy going along the Wind. Thick sagebrush, sometimes as high as saddle pommels, was preferable to the broken country of the Bighorns. That same sagebrush made fragrant fires each night as the expedition ate grayling fresh from the river. Passing near present-day Crowheart and Burris, Wyoming, the Astorians could not help noticing that the river was beginning to narrow and the mountains crowd in from each side. An ever-tightening twist to the trail made progress slower by the hour. By September 14 the expedition was near modern Dubois, Wyoming. Here it was plain that the Astorians had to head west to find a pass over the Continental Divide. Robinson, Hoback, and Reznor knew something about passes in the region. They had used Togwotee Pass, north of Dubois, in their journey east. There was a second route over the Divide, Union Pass, directly west of Dubois. With two important passes so closely situated, the trappers may have confused one for the other. It is equally possible that the trappers thought Union Pass was identical to Togwotee.

On September 15 the Astorians turned due west, picked up an Indian trail, and started to cross the Great Divide. That Indian trace slanted southwest over Union Pass. Sometime during the day, Robinson or one of his companions paused to point out three jagged peaks to the west. The Grand Tetons were, so the trappers claimed, on the banks of a river that ran directly to the Columbia. Hunt was sufficiently impressed by the landmark character of the Tetons that he dubbed them the "Pilot Knobs," a name less earthy than the English translation of the original French appellation.[20] On the sixteenth the party crossed the summit at Union Pass. Scattered patches of snow reminded everyone of their late start from the Missouri and what might happen if a sudden storm trapped the travelers.

Coming down the west side of the Divide, Hunt again employed Indian geographical data to confirm his position. At some point he had been told that once off the pass, the expedition would run upon the Spanish, or Green, River. Camped that night on the banks of the Green, Hunt recorded that Indians believed the river flowed west to the elusive Gulf of California. Because the Green actually ran more south than west, the Astorians followed it for only a day. Like later mountain men of Green River Rendezvous fame, the Astorians noted that the river "seemed to abound in beaver and otter." Hunt was quite certain that this whole region, sheltered between the Wind River Mountains and the Salt Range and Commissary Ridge, would make ideal trapping grounds.[21]

Once the Green struck almost due south, the Astorians left it to pursue a slanting northeast path through the Gros Ventre Range. On one of the region's innumerable Beaver Creeks, Hunt called a halt. Information from both trappers and Indians suggested that the Mad, or Snake, River—Hunt's illusory path to the Columbia—was just over the next set of mountains. Now was the time to dry strips of bison sufficient to last to "the shores of the Columbia and of the rivers where we hoped to procure some fish." Hunters out to scout game soon encountered several Shoshoni Indians. When Hunt, Mackenzie, McClellan, and two others went to meet the Shoshonis, a wild eight-mile chase ensued. Two of the younger Indians, mounted on slower horses, were eventually caught. Hunt admitted that these two were at first "very disquieted." After calming their fears, he convinced them to lead the overlanders to the Shoshoni camp. Although some natives, especially those who had never seen whites, were quite frightened, others eagerly welcomed the travelers and promptly provided food all around. Knowing that the Indians had plentiful supplies of dried buffalo, Hunt purchased a large share for the expedition. To encourage the Shoshonis to take part in the company's trade system, Astor's men bought a few beaver pelts with the promise to take more in the future.[22]

Picking up a trail that headed southwest toward present-day Bondurant, Wyoming, the Astorians followed the Hoback River into the canyon of the same name. Sometimes the route left the river, forcing the Astorians to climb steep hillsides. One heavily laden packhorse lost its footing and tumbled head over tail into a deep ravine. Amazingly, the animal emerged from the mishap none the worse for the fall. The Hoback current was so swift that whenever a ford was required, great caution was necessary to avoid being swept away. Thinking the expedition was near a branch of the Columbia that would lead to the Pacific, Hunt decided to detach two small trapping parties. Sent in pairs, Alexander Carson, Louis St. Michael, Pierre Detaye, and Pierre Delaunay expected to hunt the waters just east and west of the Divide. Had Hunt known how very far and how hard was the road to Astoria, he might have thought again about the fate of these men.[23]

By September 27 the Astorians were at the confluence of the Snake and Hoback rivers near present-day Hoback Junction, Wyoming. Throughout the long weeks of the overland crossing Hunt had been guided by advice and direction from Robinson and his mountaineer friends. Now on the banks of a river the trappers called the Mad—a river Hunt would only later realize was Lewis's, or the Snake, River—some doubts about the quality of that advice from the trappers began to creep into Hunt's mind. For the first time he admitted that the expedition should have followed the Wind River trail northwest to cross the mountains at Togwotee Pass. Hunt and his trapper guides now believed that such a route would have taken them directly to the headwaters of the Snake. Short provisions earlier in the journey and a general uncertainty had forced a swing south to cross the Continental Divide at Union Pass.[24]

But the long detour caused by the Union Pass route was not at the heart of Hunt's unease. Hunt noted, "This was the place where we had been led to hope that we might pursue our journey by water." Thus he organized a search for suitable canoe-building materials. Voyageurs accustomed to canoes made from light but durable birchbark soon found the quest disappointing. The banks of the Snake offered only knotty and wind-shaken cottonwoods. Not discouraged, Hunt ordered camp moved lower downriver, thinking that trees in that neighborhood might be better. By the end of the day on September 29, not a single good canoe log had been found. Some of the Canadians thought that boats could be patched together with what was at hand. But such was not a pleasant prospect.[25]

Hunt must have watched glumly as the Canadians set to chopping one splintering cottonwood after another. Two things were now becoming painfully clear to him. Good canoes could not be built from the available trees. Even if a few boats were cobbled together, Hunt now worried that the Snake's current made the river unnavigable. Perhaps it would be possible to continue overland to Henry's Fort and there find another branch of the Columbia. Because Robinson and the other mountain men were not quite sure where they were and how to get to their old post, Hunt sent Reed, Day, and Dorion to scout a path south into the Grand Canyon of the Snake. Reed's party was told to march for at least four days. They were back in two. The report they carried was anything but encouraging. After being forced to abandon their horses in rocky, steep terrain, Reed's men had tried for more than an hour to scramble over and around the boulder-strewn riverbank. Nearly exhausted, the explorers had returned to the Astorians' camp. As Reed explained, the river was choked with rapids. Its banks were virtually impassable. And any attempt to cross on the highlands south of the Snake also was doomed to failure.[26]

Reed's evaluation of the river and the southern overland routes confirmed Hunt's worst fears. Information from several Shoshonis sealed the case. The Astorians would have to find a northern route to Henry's Fort. On October 3, against lowering skies that drenched the travelers with sleet and cold rain, the expedition pointed itself northwest toward Teton Pass. Just how Hunt had learned about this pass and the trail to Henry's Fort remains unclear. The former Missouri Fur Company trappers may have known something about it. But it is more likely that the Astorians were following the advice of several Shoshonis now acting as the expedition's guides.

Throughout the days of October 4 and 5 the Astorians followed a well-beaten Indian trail over Teton Pass. Snow at the summit foreshadowed winter's closing in. By October 6 the expedition had arrived in the flatlands near present-day Victor, Idaho. Camped on the banks of the Teton River, the Astorians could rest for a moment before trying to find Henry's Fort. That post lay some forty miles northwest. Hunt's Shoshoni guides and the trappers were confident they could find the way. Two days of travel in chilly weather and occasional snow showers brought the explorers to the fort on October 9.[27] Little remained of this first American trading post west of the Great Divide. But the place meant more than the sum of its scattered stones, decaying buildings, and fireplace holes. Here was an apparently known point in a confusing maze of jagged mountains and unpredictable rivers.

During the next few days at Henry's Fort, Hunt began to plot his next moves. He still was certain that a branch of the Columbia could be found that might take the party to the Columbia by boat. Hunt believed that Henry's Fork, the north fork of the Snake, was that river path. He did not know that the stream he would call Canoe River was still the dreaded Snake. Sure that he had come upon the clear path to the Pacific, Hunt set his Canadians to building canoes. The cottonwoods, willows, and aspens surrounding the abandoned post proved suitable for boatbuilding, and the voyageurs were soon busy framing the Astorian flotilla.[28]

From Montreal to the Rockies the overland Astorians had been beset by one nasty surprise and unexpected accident after another. Rumors, confusions, and intrigues both real and imagined were everywhere. On October 9, as the canoe builders wielded their axes and drawknives, Joseph Miller showed up at Hunt's tent with unpleasant news. Miller, as a partner in the Pacific Fur Company, held two and a half shares in the enterprise. Now he wanted out of both the overland trek and the company. Hunt had decided to fashion another detached fur party consisting of Robinson, Hoback, Reznor, and Martin Cass, but Miller was not to be in that group. Now Miller wanted to join the venture. Although he avoided the subject in his diary, Hunt was evidently shocked by Miller's impetuous decision. Ramsay Crooks may have been the one who told Irving that Hunt tried to "dissuade him [Miller] from this sudden resolution; representing to him its rashness, and the hardships and perils to which it would expose him." But Miller had made up his mind and told Hunt so quite forcefully. Later that day formal papers were drawn and Miller relinquished his shares in the company.[29]

Miller's abrupt departure may have troubled Hunt, but he needed to put the incident behind him and concentrate on preparations for the long-planned paddle to the Pacific. With canoe building progressing quickly, Hunt decided to leave his large horse herd in the hands of the Shoshonis. There would be, so he thought, no need for those animals in the coming days. Virtually every student of the expedition has faulted Hunt for his decision to trust the venture's future to frail canoes and an uncharted river. Edgeley Todd's comments are typical. He wrote that by "abandoning their horses and setting forth in canoes, the party committed the most serious mistake of the journey."[30] There can be no doubt that leaving the horses at Henry's Fort put the Astorians on a collision course with suffering and death. But the decision must be understood in the context of Hunt's geographic notions about the West.

From the beginning of the journey, Hunt had believed that there were practical water routes west of the Divide that could provide quick and safe access to the Columbia. From his earliest conversations with Meriwether Lewis in 1806 to his later contacts with William Clark and John Colter, Hunt believed all evidence pointed to the existence of such rivers. Trapper lore only reinforced what Hunt already believed. He knew that his Canoe River was unexplored. But in his foreshortened view of the West, that river simply had to flow into the Columbia. Using the best available information, Hunt took his chances. Had he known that the Mad and the Canoe were one and the same river—the Snake—he might have been more wary. But in the end, Astor's fur empire needed water routes, and Hunt was bent on finding such a path to the Pacific.

By October 19 saddles and tack had been cached, horses put in the Indians' hands, and the fifteen canoes loaded and balanced. Moving swiftly with the current, the canoes made some thirty miles on the Snake. On the following cold and snowy days the progress was equally fast. If Hunt and his party thought that their Canoe

River might be their promised highway to the Columbia, they were about to learn otherwise. The Snake's current was fast enough, but the river's course was increasingly broken by one treacherous set of rapids after another. On October 20 two canoes were suddenly swamped in white water, and though the crews escaped, valuable goods and provisions were lost.[31] The following day the Astorians confronted the twisting, churning Idaho Falls. Hunt described the river as "confined between two perpendicular mountains, which, throughout nearly half a mile, allow it, in some places, only 60 feet of width and sometimes less." Hunt knew that running such a course would only court disaster. The canoes were guided through the narrows by lines from the shore. Despite considerable care, another canoe capsized and more goods were lost. The sudden demand for tobacco from Reed's dwindling supply suggests that all hands needed smokes and chews after so demanding a day.[32]

Once past Idaho Falls, the Snake again smoothed out, allowing the explorers to make unchecked progress. October 23 saw the Astorians count seventy-five river miles past beaver lodges, flocks of ducks, and banks fringed with willow and cottonwoods. This stretch of the river often attracted Shoshonis eager to catch whatever fish might be had. Indian fishers worked the river margins with flax-fiber nets. The sudden presence of grizzled strangers terrified the Shoshonis and they fled whenever the Astorians came into view. At one point, at the confluence of the Snake and Raft rivers (near present-day Heglar, Idaho), Hunt went ashore hoping to meet with some of the natives. He wanted whatever geographical information they might have to offer. Although one Shoshoni was willing to trade some fish and dried meat for knives, "his fear was so great that I [Hunt] could not persuade him to indicate by signs the route I ought to take."[33]

Had the Shoshoni been less frightened, he might have warned Hunt about the vicious rapids and deep gorges yet to come. And by strange coincidence, on the same day that Hunt was able to learn nothing about the way ahead, editor Joseph Charless offered his St. Louis readers a grim prediction of trouble. "It is the general opin-

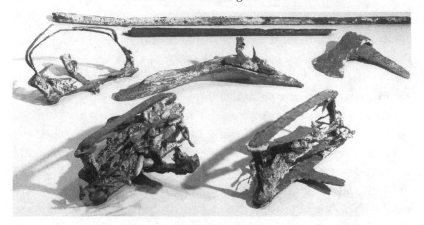

Trade goods recovered from Crooks's canoe. Courtesy of the
Idaho State Historical Society.

ion," announced the *Louisiana Gazette*, "that he [Hunt] will encounter great difficulties before he reaches the Columbia, if it be possible
for him to succeed in this attempt this fall." Those "great difficulties"
now hit the Astorians with awesome fury. Once past the present-day
Minidoka Reservoir, at the entrance to a narrow canyon, Ramsay
Crooks's canoe upset. Goods and men went tumbling into the churning waters. Any hope of saving the bales of merchandise was immediately abandoned as Crooks and his men desperately struggled to
escape the powerful current. When the exhausted and battered men
were finally onshore, a count was made. One was found missing.
The engagé Antoine Clappine, who had been with the expedition
since its earliest days on the St. Lawrence, had fallen victim to the
Snake. Hunt's Canoe River, named with more hope than sure
knowledge, now seemed to promise only hazard and death.[34]

From a base camp on the south side of the Snake, Hunt decided to
rest the expedition while he took a small party to scout what lay
ahead. Hunt hoped that it might be possible to line his canoes down
the north side of the river. What the reconnaissance uncovered
made for an unpleasant report. Not more than ten miles from the
base camp, the Snake gave its greatest show of pounding violence.
Here was the Devil's Scuttle Hole, or Caldron Linn. Robert Stuart

saw this nightmarish spot in August 1812 and caught some of its terror in his journal. "At the Caldron Linn the whole body of the River is confined between 2 ledges of Rock somewhat less than 40 feet apart and Here indeed its terrific appearance beggars all description—Hecate's caldron was never half so agitated when vomiting even the most diabolical spells, as is this Linn in a low stage of the water and its bearing in idea such a proximity or resemblance to that or something more infernal, I think well authorizes it to retain the name it has, more particularly as the tout ensemble of these 30 miles has been baptized the Devils Scuttle Hole."[35] The precise location of Caldron Linn remains something of a mystery. The best guess places the whirlpool at the foot of Dry Creek Falls, near present Murtaugh, Idaho.

Hunt's advance party saw more than one stretch of vicious river. For thirty-five miles, down as far as Twin Falls, the river was broken by dozens of rapids and falls. The Snake had cut a deep canyon with walls so steep that in only two places could men on the bank reach the river. With provisions running short, Hunt took his scouts back to camp, knowing that difficult decisions lay ahead.[36]

The last days of October found the Astorians huddled around campfires, eating short rations, and stymied by one of the West's most treacherous rivers. Hunt's probe of the north bank had found no suitable places to launch canoes once past Caldron Linn. But an informal search of the south shore seemed to indicate that the canyon walls were less steep and that canoes could be put in with minimum risk. Hunt decided to press ahead and bring the expedition's boats along that south bank. Four of the sturdiest canoes manned by sixteen of the best Canadian voyageurs were selected for the mission. At the same time John Reed and three other men were sent overland to find Indians willing to trade for food and horses. Reed was also ordered to examine the Snake past Twin Falls. Hunt admitted that the expedition was at a crucial pass. With food for no more than five days, the party needed to move ahead and resupply. Those who remained at the base camp hurriedly bought supplies from what was left in the company's stocks, everything from tobacco

Caldron Linn. Courtesy of the Idaho State Historical Society.

and knives to shirts and blankets. Hunt's only purchase during those days was a cake of soap. Perhaps he thought a good scrub might refresh his spirits. Not knowing about these grim prospects and dampened spirits, Astor wrote his St. Louis correspondent, Charles Gratiot, that he was "very anxious about Mr. Hunt and his party."[37]

The fur trade world, so long dominated by French-Canadian customs, always celebrated All Saints' Day as a special holiday. At Astoria, Duncan McDougall called off daily work assignments to let all at the post enjoy the occasion. But the day was not marked by any festivities at Wilson Price Hunt's rude camp along the Snake. Voyageurs who had tried to launch canoes past Caldron Linn straggled back to camp with nothing but bad news. The rapids were so fierce that when one canoe was run through with lines, it was lost along with more provisions. Reed's scouts were equally dispirited. Their progress had been blocked by rock barriers that came down to the water's edge. These unwelcome reports now required dramatic action. The expedition's nearly empty larders and the unmistakable onset of winter meant that Hunt and his expedition had to find some way to escape the Snake River trap.[38]

In his diary Hunt laconically wrote, "We altered our plans." Those alterations amounted to a virtual breakup of the overland expedition. Each one of the partners would take a party by land, hoping to find Indians willing to trade for horses and food. Donald Mackenzie would march four men north in hopes of finding the Columbia. At the same time Robert McClellan and three others were detailed to follow the Snake in an easterly direction. Ramsay Crooks and a party of five men were assigned the most difficult task. Crooks was to blaze an overland trail back to Henry's Fort, "where they hoped to find the horses they had left there, and to return with them to the main body."[39] Once these parties were on their way, Hunt would still be left with a sizable contingent. Unwilling to abandon the notion that some route might be found along the Snake, Hunt once again sent John Reed to scout the river's course. On November 2, drenched by yet another chill rain, the various divisions of the expedition parted ways. To find a better location for the base camp,

Hunt took his group back upriver to the present-day site of Lake Walcott.[40]

Settling at the place where the expedition had been on October 27, Hunt must have made one more appraisal of his situation. The probes led by Mackenzie, Crooks, McClellan, and Reed faced uncertain futures. All around him were faces pinched by cold and hunger. Hunters brought in eight beavers, but that did little to replenish the expedition's stocks. On November 4 the Astorians got another dose of bitter medicine. A weary Ramsay Crooks rejoined the main party. His mission to Henry's Fort had been thwarted by threatening weather, difficult terrain, and a serious miscalculation about the round-trip distance. Nothing could be done now but wait for Reed's scouting report. The Snake was no place to winter. It was either advance or starve.[41]

The report came on November 6. Two of Reed's men carried the disheartening news. Their reconnaissance simply confirmed previous information. The Snake was not navigable. Any passage would have to be by land. Hunt and Crooks measured their supplies against the impending winter and decided to risk such a march. The Astorians would be divided into two parties, Hunt leading the larger (some twenty-two people) on the north bank while Crooks took a second group along the opposite side. Throughout the day, as Hunt and Crooks laid their plans, other Astorians struggled to catch a few river fish. As if to emphasize the perils of winter on the Snake River, the day's haul was a single fish.

Once the decision to advance was made, the expedition roused itself to make preparations for the journey. The bulkiest trade goods were cached. Provisions were Hunt's first concern, and he carefully doled out five and a quarter pounds of meat to each traveler. The expedition could still count forty pounds of corn, twenty pounds of grease, and a few remaining bullion tablets. On these slim rations the Astorians were prepared to challenge some of the West's most demanding terrain.

November 9, another day of cold rains, found Hunt and Crooks leading their parallel parties along the Snake. Throughout that day and the next the explorers kept to the high banks above the river. The slopes were so steep that going to the river for drinking water proved impossible. Parched throats had to make do with puddles of rainwater collected from holes and rock hollows. It was not until November 11 that the footsore travelers stumbled on a heavily used horse trail leading to the river. Once on that path, Hunt encountered two Shoshonis. One of the Indians had a knife, reportedly traded from one of the Astorian parties. Eager for trade and route directions, Hunt followed the Shoshonis to their camp near present-day Hagerman, Idaho. The Astorians' reception was something less than a warm welcome. Although these Indians surely had heard of such pale strangers and although some members of the band probably had traded with Crooks's party, most had not seen whites. At Hunt's approach, the Shoshoni women "fled so precipitately that they had not time to take with them such of their children as could not walk." Hunt found those infants cowering under heaps of straw. Indian men were equally terror-stricken, and Hunt thought they treated him as if he were a "ferocious animal." The Shoshonis mastered their fear long enough to sell Hunt a small supply of dried fish. One of the Indians was sufficiently curious about the strangers to accompany them back to the Snake. Later that day some fifty Shoshonis paid a call at the Astorians' camp. Relations between the explorers and the Indians proved "very civil and extremely obliging" and Hunt decided to stay an extra day.[42]

By November 13 Hunt's party was at camp near King Hill, Idaho. They had continued their track along the Snake, angling north by northwest. The following day the expedition came upon yet another Shoshoni camp. Perhaps by now, news of Hunt, Crooks, and their parties had traveled far ahead of the Astorians. For whatever reason, Shoshonis along the river no longer fled at the sight of the expedition. Though willing to trade for fish, most Shoshonis proved reluctant to barter horses no matter what the offer. At length, on November 17, Hunt was finally able to persuade one Indian to part with his horse. Now at least some of the expedition's baggage might be shifted from backpacks to a hastily made packsaddle.[43]

On November 19, still following the Snake, the Astorians gathered from the Indians a bit of information that suggested a route change. The Indians urged leaving the river and heading north across a sagebrush plain to join the Boise River. This detour cut a good number of miles from the Snake River passage, but few in the party stopped to count the shorter track. Instead, the explorers were now in the midst of a dry passage. Some of the Canadians were reduced to drinking their own urine. All the travelers must have been relieved when they finally reached the Boise on November 21. Large numbers of Indians were camped along the river margins, and from them the Astorians bought fish and dogs. But Hunt sought information on routes. From observation and "the few words" he could understand, Hunt learned that the distance to the Columbia was still "very considerable." And when he pressed for directions to "the big river" no Indian seemed to know the way.[44]

Lacking any more-reliable information, Hunt and his party set off again on November 24. Falling temperatures and snow squalls conspired with broken ground to make the next three days especially hard ones. The Astorians forded three rivers—the Boise, the Payette, and the Weiser—in rapid succession. By November 27 the explorers were reduced to killing their horse for food. "I ate it reluctantly," confessed Hunt, "because of my fondness for the poor beast." Now following the Weiser River and some of its tributaries, the expedition was able to shorten its Snake River route. As always there was a shortage of food and of travel information. November 28 found the exhausted Astorians at the upper reach of Mann Creek in present-day Washington County, Idaho. There Hunt found a scattering of Shoshonis. The Indians had just killed two horses and had fresh meat. But all efforts to trade failed. The Indians would part with neither food nor live horses. Hunt did better in his quest for geographic data. From these Shoshonis he learned that Crooks's party had passed by some days before and that Crooks still had his pet dog. Hunt noted, "[This] greatly assured me as I concluded that he had not suffered too much from lack of food."

Fearing that Hunt might stay too long with them and devour

their meager provisions, the Shoshonis gave the Astorians some self-serving travel directions. The Indians insisted that after nine days of travel Hunt would be on the Columbia. Hunt was not quite sure where he was, but he was certain that such advice was aimed only at getting rid of unwelcome guests. After leaving the Shoshonis, the Astorians spent two difficult days struggling back to the Snake. Snow and steep trails made progress slow and Hunt later recalled, "We climbed mountains so high that I would never have believed our horses could have gotten over them."[45]

By the end of November the expedition was back at the Snake, near its confluence with the Powder River. Hunt was still convinced that the banks of the Snake would provide the best path to the Columbia. But following that path now proved increasingly difficult. Heavy snows cut visibility and made travel almost impossible. Precariously low food supplies added to the burden of daily survival. By December 5 the Astorians were near present-day Oxbow Dam (Homestead, Oregon), on the southern edge of the Seven Devils Range. Snowstorms that day were intense, and it was plain that the travelers had to escape to lower elevations. Guided by the sounds of the river, Hunt and his party slid down the banks to reach the Snake. Snow higher up had become rain at river level. Eating horsemeat while huddled together to fend off a drenching, chill rain, all must have wondered when the eternal Snake passage would end.[46]

There seemed little choice but to press north along the river. The Astorians were pursuing just that course on December 6 when Hunt caught sight of Crooks and his party on the opposite side of the river. Hunt had imagined that Crooks was well ahead, perhaps even on the Columbia. That he and his bedraggled men were here could only mean trouble. Hunt quickly ordered a skin boat made from horsehide. Soon after, Crooks and François Le Clairc made their way across the Snake to talk with Hunt. Crooks was a terrible sight. "Poor man!" exclaimed Hunt. "He was well-nigh spent from fatigue and want." The news brought by Crooks and Le Clairc about the way ahead was even more disturbing. Crooks's party had traveled at least three days farther north along the river. What they had found, in the place today called Hells Canyon, was a river gorge some fifty-five hundred feet deep. They could only conclude that "it was impossible for men in their condition to proceed." Reed and Mackenzie's party, stronger and better equipped, had gone ahead to find the Columbia. McClellan's route was less clear to Crooks. Evidently the impetuous ex-soldier had headed northwest to find the Flatheads or some other friendly tribe.

That night some painful decisions had to be made. Hunt's own words provide the best record of those difficult hours. "I had to provide for the needs of more than twenty starving people and, in addition, give my utmost aid to Crooks and his party. Notwithstanding all the discouraging reports to me concerning the region below here, I would have continued my journey on the mountains if it had not been, as I already knew from experience, that the depth of the snow would make the undertaking impracticable. It was necessary therefore, to my great regret, to retrace my steps, hoping to encounter in the meantime some Indians on one of the three small rivers [Weiser, Payette, Boise] above the mountains." Hunt expected that once he found such Indians he could buy horses "to feed us until we should reach the Big River [Columbia] which I flattered myself to accomplish this winter." Hunt knew that the retreat would be a demanding one and that Crooks might not be able to march the whole course. Hunt decided to leave Crooks behind in the care of John Day and J. B. Dubreuil.[47]

From December 7 to 16 the Astorians stumbled through a kind of mountain nightmare. They plodded over rocky ground and were numbed by cold and hunger. Crooks's men suffered the most. One of that party, Jean Baptiste Prevost, was drowned when his canoe capsized in the turbulent waters of the Snake. Hunt's fears for Mackenzie and Reed mounted when Shoshonis told him that any venture through Hells Canyon was simply impossible. When the surviving Astorians finally made it back to the Weiser River, Hunt bitterly confided to his diary, "Thus, for twenty days we had uselessly tired ourselves in seeking a route along the lower part of the river."[48]

The overlanders had never enjoyed good fortune. Confusing

geography, bad weather, unfortunate decisions, and just plain bad luck had dogged the expedition since its departure from the Arikaras. Camped among some Shoshonis on the Weiser River, Hunt was forced to reevaluate his entire approach to finding the Columbia. From the beginning the Snake had appeared to be the only practical means to reach the "Big River." Now both the experience of the expedition and reliable information from Indians made it plain that the Snake promised only suffering and death. Hunt spent December 18 and 19 struggling to make sense of geographic data gleaned from the Shoshonis. The Astorians understood that Indians called the Sciatogas—perhaps the Cayuses at the confluence of the Columbia and the Snake—could furnish horses for the rest of the journey. But how to reach those Indians now that the Snake was a barred route? Some Shoshonis thought that the expedition might make a quick passage through present-day Washington to the Sciatogas, whereas others predicted a difficult trek of two or three weeks. All agreed that the trail to the Columbia was clearly marked but that at this time of year it was bound to be choked with snow sometimes waist-high. Clearly the Astorians needed a guide to direct them along the path. When Hunt sought such a guide and promised everything from firearms to a horse for payment, he was told that any who ventured the route would surely freeze. When some Shoshonis counseled Hunt to stay at their village until spring, he retorted, "To remain at this place [would be] still worse after having travelled for so long a time and at such great expense." Angered by such advice and hoping to shame at least one Indian into joining the expedition, Hunt charged that the Shoshonis were lying about the country ahead. The gambit evidently worked because at least one Shoshoni agreed to conduct the Astorians as far as the Sciatogas.[49]

On December 21 Hunt felt his expedition was ready to resume travel. Two other Shoshonis had joined the party, now giving the Astorians three Indian guides. Once back at the Snake, Hunt found more of Crooks's original party. Shouted across the river came news that no one had seen either Crooks or the men detailed to care for him. Crooks's men were so weak that three of them—J. B. Turcotte,

A. La Chapelle, and François Landry—asked to stay with the Shoshonis. Hunt agreed, hoping that once they regained their strength they might be able to help the ailing Crooks.[50]

The day before Christmas 1811 Hunt took stock of his tattered company. "My party," he wrote, "now consisted of thirty-two whites, a woman more than eight months pregnant, her two children, and three Indians. We had only five wretched horses for our food during the passage of the mountains." For the remainder of December the expedition made its slow way west, crossing the Powder River and seeing in the distance the Blue Mountains of Oregon. By the end of the month the travelers were in the Grande Ronde Valley. There, near present-day North Powder, Oregon, Marie Dorion gave birth to a child. The Astorians had not halted to celebrate December 25, nor did they slacken their pace for this seasonal infant.[51] Astorians on opposite sides of the continent marked the holiday in ways quite remote from Hunt's painful exertions. At Fort Astoria Duncan McDougall called a stop to routine post duties and ordered an extra grog ration for all. A world away in New York, the day before Christmas found John Astor worrying about Hunt's expedition. Writing to Charles Gratiot, he asked "Is there any further account of our friend Mr. Hunt and his party?"[52]

Had Hunt been able to answer Astor, he might have told his employer that in the first week of the new year the expedition's fortunes began to change for the better. After a brief rest on January 1 to celebrate the voyageurs' traditional new year, the Astorians shaped their course to the Grande Ronde River. For the next six days the party followed a route that roughly parallels today's Interstate 84 through eastern Oregon. January 6 brought a break in the clouds and snow. The sun made its first appearance in many weeks. Not even the death of the Dorions' infant seemed to dampen rising spirits. Hunt's Shoshoni guides were certain that the Umatilla River and the Columbia were close at hand.[53]

Although the expedition would not reach Astoria until mid-February, January 8 marked a memorable milestone in what had become an endless journey. On that day, near present-day Pendleton, Oregon, the Astorians stumbled into a large encampment of Cayuse and Tushepaw Indians. Hunt guessed that these Indians had more than two thousand horses. Surely there would be some available for both food and transportation. The famished Astorians found a ready welcome with these Indians. Once again western explorers had been saved by native generosity. Hunt put it best. "I cannot sufficiently express my gratitude to Providence for having let us reach here; because we all were extremely fatigued and enfeebled."[54]

For six days the Astorians enjoyed the full range of native hospitality. There was time to rest, eat, and trade. Hunt bought eight horses and two colts. Two of the animals went to stewpots, whereas two others were offered as payment to the Shoshoni guides. For the travelers, who had known weeks of privation, the temptation to overeat was hard to resist. Hunt soon discovered that some of his men were sick from too much horsemeat. Others suffered severe gastric distress brought on by eating unfamiliar roots. Amid all this there was one strange and unsettling note. Michael Carriere, a voyageur engaged at St. Louis, vanished from the company. He had last been seen riding along with a Shoshoni. A careful search turned up no trace of Carriere, and it must have seemed as if the earth had opened to swallow yet another Astorian.[55]

By January 15 the rejuvenated adventurers were back on the trail, reaching toward day's end a Cayuse Indian camp on the Umatilla River. These Indians told Hunt about the Walla Walla River and the general location of the Columbia. From his knowledge of the Lewis and Clark route, Hunt now knew his location with considerable accuracy. Geographic information from William Clark had been of little use to Hunt in his journey through what is now Wyoming, southern Idaho, and eastern Oregon. But now, nearing the Columbia, Hunt evidently consulted a copy of a Clark map showing that river and some of its tributaries. After hearing about the Walla Walla River from Indian sources, Hunt wrote, "I suppose according to Clark's map, that it [the Walla Walla] is the small river whose confluence with the Columbia he [Clark] places near beds of shell fish." Clark's sketch map also confirmed something that Hunt may have suspected for some time. "From what I have learned," he explained, "the Canoe River [the Snake] is the Kemoenoum of Lewis." Had Hunt known the character of the Snake some months before, the history of the expedition might have been substantially different.[56]

Heavy mid-January rains flooded the Umatilla and slowed the expedition's progress. On January 18 Hunt's company was still not on the Columbia. Indians did reassure him that Celilo Falls on the "Big River" was no more than six days' journey away. For Donald Mackenzie, Robert McClellan, John Reed, and eight voyageurs, the crossing was complete on the eighteenth. That detachment had succeeded in struggling up the Snake to the Columbia. Hunger, thirst, and exhaustion were constant companions, but the party had survived. They were less certain about Hunt's fate. Their report to McDougall suggested that Hunt's larger party would surely face hard going.[57]

Partners and employees at Astoria set aside January 19 to celebrate the arrival of Mackenzie and the others. Had they known that two days later Hunt's expedition would finally reach the Columbia, they might have extended the festivities. For Hunt it was a moment of both relief and joy almost beyond words. Since those days at Montreal, the Columbia had been "for so long the goal of our desires." Hunt's journal holds few passages of such intense emotion as that written when the Umatilla trail finally led to the great River of the West. "We had travelled 1751 miles, we had endured all the hardships imaginable, With difficulty I expressed the joy at sight of this river."[58]

When Lewis and Clark had reached the Pacific in November 1805, there had been as much weary anti-climax as exhiliration. On the morning of February 15, 1812, Hunt's expedition left Cathlamet Bay in rain and fog. Paddling six canoes, the explorers reached Astoria in early afternoon. "It was a very real pleasure for travellers harrassed by fatigue to rest in quiet and be surrounded by friends after so long a journey in the midst of savages of whom it is always prudent to be wary."[59]

In the midst of this happy reunion John Reed's account book was a reminder that the Astorians' crossing had not been planned as a heroic adventure. The journey was to be part of a commercial venture. Fort Astoria and the ways to get there represented profit and empire, not romantic westering. Reed knew as much when he began to cast up accounts on February 18. His first duty was to the dead. The estates of Jean Baptiste Prevost, Antoine Clappine, and Michael Carriere filled his pages with their meager store of possessions. The clerk then fell to listing those "items long since lost." A knife, an axe, some now forgotten trade goods—these were the markers left by the second American crossing of the continent.[60]

Some days later and a continent away, John Astor was still trying to square his own new year's balance sheet. Writing again to Charles Gratiot, he confidently declared, "I hope to get some accounts in about 2 or 3 months by way of Canton of our friends." Ten months later Astor was still waiting. Now he wrote again, this time six months after the outbreak of war, inquiring of Gratiot whether he had any news from the western country. After so long, Astor admitted that he was "more and more anxious about our friend Hunt." Had Astor known about Hunt's troubled journey, he might have been even more anxious for Astoria's future.[61]

7

Life at Fort Astoria

WHEN WILSON PRICE HUNT'S exhausted overlanders straggled into Fort Astoria on February 15, 1812, they found an impressive fur trade establishment. From its site near what is now Smith Point, Oregon, Astoria overlooked the Columbia and commanded the entrance to a river that Astor confidently predicted would be the key to the entire Northwest. Astoria was never quite the "town" touted by many American diplomats and politicians. But almost a year after the site was cleared and the post established, Astoria did amount to something more than a makeshift trading house. Astor had told his employees to build a great commercial entrepôt on the Columbia, and the Astorians had set about doing just that. By 1812 Astoria boasted a large trading store, a substantial dwelling house, a blacksmith shop, and a storage shed. A second house was planned, as was more storage and cooking space. These buildings were enclosed by a stout palisade making Astoria ninety feet square. At the front corners were bastions mounting cannons. Outside the post were well-tended gardens. No visitor could miss the herds of unruly goats and hogs. In the days after his arrival, Hunt must have heard stories about how the site had been chosen as well as about the struggles to clear land and build the post. And perhaps he also caught snatches of what Alexander Ross called the "feuds and petty grievances" that lay behind life at Fort Astoria.[1]

Near the end of March 1811 the *Tonquin* rode quietly at anchor in Baker Bay. The nightmare crossing of the Columbia bar behind them, the Astorians now faced the challenge of building a post, making trade arrangements, and securing their future in an uncertain land. Hogs, sheep, and goats—Astoria's complement of livestock—all demanded immediate attention. The animals' continued presence on the *Tonquin* gave the ship a certain air that neither Captain Jonathan Thorn nor the company's partners found especially attractive. Beginning on March 27, the livestock were put in the ship's boats and landed along the north shore of the Columbia. Although no diarist of the company recorded the scene, loading surly hogs and cranky goats into small boats must have had all the makings of comic opera. Perhaps Hawaiians like Edward Cox and James Kimoo, who later took charge of the animals, lent whatever skills they had to the enterprise. Despite those efforts, several hogs escaped into the woods to breed what would become a large and troublesome pack of wild pigs.[2]

Astoria's livestock were not the only passengers to disembark from the *Tonquin*. The Astorians were eager to leave a ship that all disliked and a captain that most loathed. By the first of April nearly all the company's men were onshore at Baker Bay. Some employees were washing clothes while others were cutting firewood and filling water casks. Looking at the dense, hardwood timber that covered both sides of the river, the partners broke open packs of axeheads and ordered handles to be cut and shaped.[3]

Herding swine, washing dirty trousers, and making axe handles were necessary pursuits, but far more important for the future of Astoria was finding a suitable location for the post. That process began on March 27 when Thorn, Alexander McKay, David Stuart, and several others hired a Clatsop headman, Daitshowan, to guide them on an upriver reconnaissance. When the *Tonquin* had first entered the Columbia, she had been surrounded by Clatsops and their Chinook neighbors, all experienced merchants in the maritime

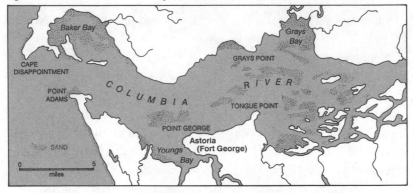

Astoria and the mouth of the Columbia

fur trade. One of those was Daitshowan, a headman from the nearby village of Neahkeluk on Point Adams. He now directed the Astorians up the Columbia, pointing out prominent landmarks while Thorn took soundings of the channel. This first probe proved disappointing. Daitshowan took the party as far as the Cowlitz River. No location appeared suitable, and with spirits dampened by heavy showers, the would-be explorers made their way back to the *Tonquin*.[4]

Despite more rain and lowering clouds on April 5, the partners were determined to press their search. They were already being hurried by Thorn, who was eager to begin his coastal trading voyage. By now Duncan McDougall and his fellows had abandoned hope of establishing a site up the Columbia. Something had to be found within the river estuary. Toward afternoon McDougall, David Stuart, Daitshowan, and four of the company's men took a small boat to the south shore of the Columbia. That expedition was not without incident. On April 7, after searching the shores around modern-day Astoria, Oregon, the party headed back to Baker Bay. Swift tidal currents and sudden winds capsized the boat, and the entire crew had to be rescued by the Chinook chief Comcomly. It was not until the evening of April 8 that the weary explorers got back to their temporary camp.[5]

What the Astorians found when they got back to Baker Bay made it more necessary than before to find a place for the trading establishment. Relations between Thorn and the Astorians had always been stormy. Thorn was now intent on leaving the Columbia as soon as possible. Late in the afternoon on April 5, after McDougall and the others had gone, Thorn had given orders to unload all trade goods and camp equipment at Baker Bay. The captain had gone so far as to begin building a shed for his unwanted cargo. When the partners learned what he had done, they were furious. The bay was not suited for a trading post, and even more infuriating, they had not been consulted about such a decision. Late on the night of April 8, McDougall, McKay, and the two Stuarts held a hurried meeting. No location up the Columbia was suitable and all sites on the north shore were ruled out. Their cursory survey of the south shore had turned up one possible post location. Smith Point, then called Point George, was selected because it provided direct access to the river and had water deep enough to allow the *Tonquin* room to maneuver quite close to shore. Pressured by Thorn and pressed for time, Astor's men had chosen a site that would pose a real test for the company's muscle and determination.[6]

The Astorians planned to build their post east of the entrance to Youngs Bay. Astoria would be situated between Point George to the west and Tongue Point to the east. Alexander Ross recalled the view from Astoria in those early days. To the north stretched the broad Columbia estuary. At low tide the Upper Sand Bank was exposed, making plain just how hazardous Astoria's anchorage really was. Looking upriver, Ross and his companions could see Tongue Point. Beyond that were the Swan Bay mudflats. Astoria's western prospect revealed the hard sandbanks that made the Columbia bar a sailor's terror. Squinting to see past Point Adams, Ross could make out "the breakers on the bar, rolling in wild confusion." Behind Astoria to the south, the land rose sharply in a series of steep hillsides and deep ravines. All told, Ross and the many travelers who visited the place in later years found the view "a varied and interesting scene."[7]

The men working at Astoria would have little time to appreciate the scenery. Instead, their efforts were bent to clearing ground for buildings and gardens. Ross's sharp pen quickly characterized Astoria's demanding location. "The place selected for the emporium of the West might challenge the whole continent to produce a spot of equal extent presenting more difficulties to the settler." The site was covered by a dense forest of Douglas fir, hemlock, and red alder. Some of the trees were well over one hundred feet tall with huge trunks. The ground was matted with underbrush, twisted under and around rocks and boulders. Fallen timber and decaying stumps added to the hazards. With his usual romantic flourish, Ross put the best face on the land. "The impervious and magnificent forest," so wrote the ex-schoolmaster, "darkened the landscape as far as the eye could reach."[8]

Squally weather kept the Astorians from sending the first work party to the building site until April 12. Once the clouds lifted, Gabriel Franchère exclaimed, "The weather was magnificent and all Nature smiled." Sixteen men, including Franchère, Ross, several Canadian voyageurs, and a number of Hawaiians, boarded a longboat for the journey to the south shore. Although the workers were "armed with all the necessary implements for clearing land, building houses, etc.," a close look would have revealed just how inadequate their tools were for the task. The advance party carried light trade axes. Heavier felling axes and whipsaws were still stowed in the *Tonquin*'s hold. Unaware how demanding the effort would be, Franchère wrote in his journal upon landing, "The forest looked like pleasant groves and the leaves like flowers."[9]

In the following days his initial optimism vanished. Trees, fallen logs, and twisted undergrowth resisted all hacking and hewing. Most of the Astorian pioneers had never faced such a task and had only the barest acquaintance with the business end of an axe. Working with more enthusiasm than skill, the inexperienced woodsmen stacked their guns and set to the task. The first duty was to fell some of the towering firs and alders. Ross admitted that no one in the group knew the first thing about bringing down a tree. At last the Astorians decided to divide into four work parties. Each gang would select a large tree, build a small scaffold some eight or ten feet above the ground, and begin to hack away at the trunk. Axe handles of differing lengths and no sense of chopping rhythm made for uneven progress at best. Joined to all this was the ever present fear of attack by Indians. Throughout the first days at Astoria a number of sight-seeing Clatsops came to watch the strangers. Their presence worried the Astorians, and there were frequent halts in the axe work as every rustle and shadow had to be investigated.

By April 15 some of the trees were ready to fall. As hard as the chopping was, even more difficult was the task of bringing each tree down safely. When a trunk appeared to be almost cut through, all the laborers would gather to discuss just where the tree might fall. Since the trees were close to one another, such predictions were often wide of the mark. Simply getting the tree to drop was hard enough. Trees that were apparently cut through defied gravity and refused to come down. Ross recalled the ensuing spectacle as a daring lumberjack would leap to the scaffold, take a few whacks with his axe, and then beat a hasty retreat. Because the forest was so dense, trees fully cut would often catch on others. "Sometimes," Ross remembered, "a number of them would hang together, keeping us in awful suspense, and giving us double labor to extricate the one from the other."[10]

Four days of unrelenting work had earned the Astorians blistered hands, strained backs, and frayed tempers. Little wonder that when the *Tonquin* dropped anchor at Astoria on the afternoon of April 15, all hands gave three cheers and fired welcoming volleys from their guns. McDougall and the partners may have appreciated the welcome. They were surely unhappy at the slow progress in clearing the land for the post. McDougall blamed poor tools and a serious underestimate of the difficulty of the task. Men working at the site had a less-charitable view of the affair. According to Ross, the problems were health, food, and climate, all compounded by inadequate leadership. High humidity in days of rain and fog had been hard on the Hawaiians. The food—mostly roots and boiled fish—was unappetizing to European and Hawaiian tastes and prompted many complaints. To these grumblings Ross added two of his own. He was angry that Astor had not provided the expedition with a trained medical officer. Heavy work and the hazards of using black powder to blast out stumps were bound to cause serious injuries. But the real focus of Ross's fury was Duncan McDougall. He was convinced that McDougall was an incompetent bungler with neither organizational nor commercial talents. Ross labelled him "a man more interested in personal comfort than the health of his hardworking employees."[11]

Despite this bickering, the partners were determined to press ahead. By April 19 enough land had been cleared to begin preparations for a large company store and warehouse. The ship's carpenter, Johann Koaster, took charge of constructing Astoria's first structure. His hammer-and-saw assistants included a clerk, William W. Matthews, and two voyageurs, Michel Laframboise and Joseph Lapierre. After digging a sawpit, this gang began to cut and square timber for the store's frame. All this sawing drew a crowd of Indian spectators. Chinooks, Clatsops, and Wahkiakums had seen the bearded strangers do peculiar things, but they had not witnessed such sweating and straining since Lewis and Clark's men had built Fort Clatsop on the nearby Netul River. While most Astorians continued the slow battle against tangled brush and trees that hung fire like a poorly primed gun, the carpenters roughed out a frame, twenty-five by sixty feet, to fit over a deep root cellar and a stone foundation.[12]

Thick sap clogged saws, and the lack of files to sharpen the teeth hampered work, but by the end of April more ground had been cleared and Koaster could report good progress on the store. Work came to a sudden halt on April 30 when an Indian from the Cascades came to Astoria with disturbing news. He reported having seen a party of some thirty men building houses near The Dalles. McDougall was soon convinced that the builders were employees of the North West Company and were bent on limiting the activities of the Pacific Fur Company. When the *Tonquin* had left New York in September 1810, negotiations between Astor and the Nor'westers had failed. McDougall and the other partners surely expected some opposition from the North West Company. But now it had come

Fort Astoria, 1812. From Franchère, *Journal of a Voyage on the North West Coast* (1854). Collection of the author.

much sooner than anyone had thought possible. Uncertain about the full extent of the Nor'westers' penetration, McDougall decided to send a party upriver to check the report. Alexander McKay, Robert Stuart, Ross, Franchère, Ovide Montigny, and two voyageurs were joined by a Clatsop headman, Coalpo, for the journey. Leaving Astoria on May 2, the detail got as far as the Cascades. By the time they returned to the post on May 15, they were sure the story about Nor'westers was just a rumor. But it was a troubling tale, one that reminded the Astorians they were not the only traders looking for empire in the Northwest.[13]

* * *

The alarm was a sudden interruption in what was becoming a predictable pattern of daily life at Astoria. Like the days spent at every outpost of empire, whether commercial or military, Astoria's days were filled with the routines of cooking, cleaning, and hard work. For Astorians like the blacksmith Augustus Roussel, the Hawaiian hogherder James Kimoo, and the voyageur Paul Denis Jérémie, the Pacific Fur Company represented not so much the epic struggle for western domain as hot, smoky work at the smithy, daily chasing after hogs, and for Jérémie, a growing obsession with escape from the Columbia. Astoria might have symbolized the beginnings of empire for the likes of Astor, Jefferson, and Gallatin. Men at the post thought it was about backbreaking work, the reek of fish, and a monotonous diet.

Although John Astor intended to measure Astoria's success in terms of pelts counted, pressed, and sold, his distant employees had a different calculus. For them food and shelter, along with some security, spelled progress. When Lewis and Clark had wintered at nearby Fort Clatsop, their major complaint had been a meager, boring diet. Dried fish and "pore elk" had made those explorers homesick for the corn and buffalo they had enjoyed on the Dakota plains at Fort Mandan. Because the Astorians planned to occupy their post for more than one winter, they gave careful thought to diet and provisions. Fruits and vegetables purchased in Hawaii were soon gone, and by mid-May 1811 partners and laborers alike were compelled to give attention to tomorrow's meal.

The diet at Astoria drew from two separate sources. The company's men expected that a substantial portion of their food would come from hunting and from trade with native neighbors. Since none of the Astorians were experienced hunters, virtually all fresh game and fish passed through Indian hands. Once the *Tonquin's* supplies were exhausted, the Astorians began to look to the bounties of the Columbia for provisions. That meant a trade in fish, mostly salmon and sturgeon. Although there were wild strawberries and raspberries to add color and variety, Astorians had to accept a daily regimen of salmon, either fresh or smoked. McDougall recorded the first purchases of salmon from Indian traders in early June. By the middle of the month native vendors were visiting Astoria almost daily with as many as seventy or eighty fresh salmon. Some of those fish were eaten at once, whereas others were fire-dried and salted. So much fish was purchased that by the end of July, salt supplies were running dangerously low. Salmon caught in the July run tended to be very oily. Although the Hawaiians relished these rich fish, the Europeans' digestive systems revolted and only gradually grew accustomed to the fare.[14]

Fish was the Astoria staple as it was for all who lived along the Columbia. Those at the fort expected that the region might also hold some wild game. Lewis and Clark had thought the same. Both Jefferson's captains and the Astorians found deer and elk populations slim and prices high. In the fall of 1811 Astorians were exchanging a two-and-a-half-point blanket, a knife, a half pound of tobacco, and a quantity of powder and shot for one deer. This was venison that most found lean and dry. Even after the arrival of an Iroquois hunter and former Nor'wester, Ignace Shonowane, in October 1811, fresh game was scarce in Astoria's stewpots.[15]

Like its counterparts the Hudson's Bay Company and the North West Company, Astoria had extensive gardens. When the *Tonquin* had left New York, several bushels of seed potatoes had been carefully wrapped to protect against dampness and the salt spray. The Astorians had also brought along turnip, radish, corn, and cucumber seeds. Astor did not envision the sort of agricultural economy that would eventually come to the Columbia, but his establishment did follow the pattern of other large posts. That meant substantial kitchen gardens and the men to work them.

In mid-April, while most Astorians were struggling with dull axes against towering firs, four Hawaiians were ordered to begin the post's garden. For the rest of the month and into May the gardeners sowed Indian corn and planted potato eyes. They also put in turnips, cucumbers, and radishes. Rape, a leafy plant useful for animal forage and for its oil-bearing seeds, also found a place in Astoria's garden. Knowing that the hogs and goats might soon invade their plot, the Hawaiians spent the first week of July fencing the ground.[16]

Heavy rains, poor drainage, and inadequate sunlight gave rise to worries about the future of this first crop. Nevertheless, by early August the Hawaiians reported that the turnips and potatoes looked promising. Unsure about fall weather and concerned lest the harvest be destroyed by an early frost, the Astorians decided to begin digging out the crop in September. Turnips proved the best yield. They not only turned out in abundant numbers but also, as Franchère noted, were "of extraordinary size." Though not quite of state-fair proportions, one Astorian turnip measured thirty-three inches around and weighed some fifteen pounds. A second turnip harvest came in mid-November. Quite pleased with all this, the gardeners decided to transplant six turnips to see if they would survive the coming winter. There is no record of the result of this experiment, but turnips remained a staple at Astoria until the post was finally abandoned. The potato harvest was equally rewarding. Twelve seed potatoes had survived the sea crossing to be planted at the post. These seeds yielded ninety new potatoes. Rather than put them in the kitchen baskets, the gardeners decided to use them as seeds for the next year's planting. By the fall of 1813 potatoes had joined turnips as an Astorian standard. The disappointing crops were corn, radishes, and cucumbers. The corn failed completely for lack of sun, and only one cucumber reached harvest. Radishes, usually a hardy plant, did poorly in Astoria's soil and simply went to seed without producing any bulbs. Rape leaves and stalks provided valuable live-stock forage, but no fence could keep out mice, who ate all the oily seeds.[17]

Encouraged by their initial successes, Astoria's farmers developed a garden rhythm for the following years. The cycle began in mid-March when workers headed for the plots to clear away winter debris. The grounds were tilled and fences mended. Planting began in April and lasted well into May. Summer months were filled with weeding, all done with a watchful eye on the burgeoning pig popu-lation. Harvesting turnips and potatoes started in October and lasted until mid-November. Although Astoria's gardens were never as extensive as those laid out years later at the Hudson's Bay Com-pany's Fort Vancouver, the Hawaiians did make their patches yield valuable produce.[18]

Fish from the Columbia and vegetables from the post's garden provided the bulk of food at Astoria. Like other trading settlements, Astoria had a livestock herd. When the *Tonquin* had made its way from Hawaii in February 1811, the ship's deck and gangways had been crowded with pigs, sheep, goats, and crates of chickens. Most of the chickens were lost in a storm before reaching the Columbia, but at least sixty pigs, several goats, and two sheep made the passage. Despite their presence, they never provided the post with substantial provisions. The goats enjoyed their own shed and paid their way with small amounts of milk. The sheep, mentioned in McDougall's official journal in the spring of 1811, vanish from the record and may not have survived. Those animals probably gave truth to the farmer's adage: "There are live sheep and dead sheep. Blink your eyes and you will miss the sick sheep." The pigs were a nuisance. Their numbers grew rapidly as they ate rape leaves and foraged at will. By the fall of 1812 the hog population, "which had multiplied tremendously," was causing serious trouble. Rooting through gardens and tearing up paths, the pigs had become unwelcome neighbors. And the Astorians evidently had no special taste for pork. As much as they disliked dried fish and lean venison, the company's men rarely ate pork. By the 1820s, when Astoria was in the hands of the North West Company, men at the post routinely shot the pigs and left the animals to rot. As reported by the visiting Hudson's Bay Company field governor, George Simpson, the traders "shot the poor little Grunters at 12 paces."[19]

All who lived along the Columbia, whether Chinook, Yankee, Scot, or Hawaiian, found that the seasons of the salmon controlled each day's food. Diets at Astoria were as seasonal as those at any Indian village. After a year at the post, Astorians began to understand those salmon cycles and to prepare for them. In many ways Astoria's food year began in July with the midsummer salmon run. The Columbia was choked with fish swimming upstream. Indian fishermen from the bar to The Dalles caught the salmon, taking some for food but more for drying in preparation for trade with neighboring tribes. The Astorians bought many of those salmon, finding them oily and rich. A second salmon run took place in the fall. Now the dog, or chum, salmon became available. These fish were leaner and drier than those in the July run. Their flat taste led the Astorians to call them "the fish of seven layers," since after cleaning and cooking them, one could find "little substance."[20]

By November Astoria was often on short rations. Because they were still unfamiliar with the seasonal food cycles, the partners found it necessary on November 25, 1811, to put all hands on two meals a day. At Christmas 1811, employees were given small measures of carefully hoarded bread, butter, and cheese. These were rare holiday treats, which, as Franchère recorded, "delighted" the men, who "had lived for nearly two months on fish dried by fire, which was very poor food."[21] In February some of the monotony of dried salmon was broken by the arrival of Indians bringing a unique fish from the Northwest coast. The eulachon, or candlefish, was first described by Lewis and Clark in February 1806. These plump, fatty fish began their spawning run in early spring and were much sought by native fishers. The Astorians, weary of their dried fish diet, were delighted with the eulachon. As Franchère said, "It was a welcome change which we badly needed, for our provisions were poor in quality and limited in quantity."[22] Astoria's lean times were late winter and early spring. Indian traders were at winter villages and days of torrential rain kept all hunters indoors.

Astoria's mess hall promised little variety. Boring meals, unexpected shortages, and dietary ailments such as scurvy marked the first food year at the post. In 1812 two important steps were taken to alleviate some of the provisioning problems. In early October Franchère took the schooner *Dolly* on a twenty-day shopping expedition up the Columbia. Carrying a wide variety of trade goods, he was able to purchase large quantities of geese, ducks, and smoked salmon. Anticipating shortages, the Astorians cut their trading patterns to fit the tight times to come.[23]

At least part of the reason for Astoria's dull menus and sometimes bare larders during 1811 can be traced to inadequate stocks left behind by the *Tonquin*. The ship's subsequent destruction robbed the post of any possible resupply from her stores. Astor intended that several ships would call at the Columbia each year. When the *Beaver* finally reached Astoria in early May 1812, she carried substantial amounts of provisions for the post. The ship's invoices listed foodstuffs from rice to molasses. Something more than a year later, when an inventory of Astoria's food supplies was made in preparation for the sale of the post to the North West Company, it was plain that the Astorians were eating well. The inventory revealed large amounts of beef, potatoes, coffee, sugar, and the predictable stocks of salmon and sturgeon. Rice, biscuits, and a healthy supply of flour put the scarcities of 1811 in the almost forgotten past.[24]

Of all the lines in Duncan McDougall's journal of Astoria, no other is more common than the phrase reporting that all men were busy at their various trades.[25] Work ordered the ways of this community. It was what ultimately gave shape to life at Astoria. Whether with pen, saw, hoe, or trap, each man filled most days with labor. But labor was not simply task-oriented work. In the hierarchy of fur trade society—a world of partners, clerks, tradesmen, and laborers—each job represented a social place in the post's community. The arguments and tensions that Alexander Ross called "feuds and petty grievances" were about more than just hard work and sometimes meager food. They reflected all the strains that one can find in any small community. And Astoria was just that—a small community filled with Scots, French Canadians, Yankees, Hawaiians, and Indians.

Fur trade diaries constantly refer to those living at a particular post as "our people" or "our family." Those words were not so much an expression of biological kinship as a statement about the nature of trading post society. Partners and clerks imagined a place like Astoria as home for a large, extended family. Andrew Graham, writing from the Hudson's Bay Company's York Fort in the 1760s, put such social organization into sharp focus. "This Fort is governed by a Chief Factor, who has under him a proper number of officers, and from forty to fifty servants of different trades and callings."[26] Perhaps ordinary laborers did not share their leaders' paternalistic vision, but there can be little doubt that those at the top of the fur trade social ladder enjoyed imagining themselves as baronial heads of great estates. The Pacific Fur Company was largely patterned after the North West Company. Men like Alexander McKay, Duncan McDougall, and Wilson Price Hunt were wintering partners and factors. In Hunt's absence, McDougall was chief factor at Astoria. Since Hunt ended up spending very little time at the post and since the unexpected death of McKay robbed the company of an experienced trader, McDougall dominated policy making. Astoria's partners were officers, judges, and social arbiters. They led expeditions, decided where new posts would be located and who would operate them, and negotiated with native neighbors. In Astoria's world, partners exercised minds, not muscles. Sensitive to the nuances of social place and power, Astoria's partners were always mentioned by name in McDougall's official journal. They were properly "mistered" and given all the respect due the most influential Nor'west nabob.

Immediately beneath the partners at Astoria were the clerks. Gabriel Franchère, Alexander Ross, and Ross Cox—three Astorians who wrote extended accounts of their western experiences—were typical of the dozen or so "young gentlemen" who served as the company's clerks. Fur trade clerks did many things to fill a workday. There were ledgers to keep, packs of furs to mark, and papers to copy. Their pen-and-paper tasks would have been the same had the clerks worked at Astoria or in Astor's New York office. Western clerks had additional duties. Like Ross or John Clarke, some headed small posts and conducted important trading affairs. Clerks occasionally led expeditions to search out new Indian customers. Clerks were not expected to engage in manual labor. They were, after all, junior officers of the company. But at Astoria, especially in the first months at the post, clerks found themselves pressed into service along with ordinary laborers. Ross and Franchère put in their licks cutting down trees while William Matthews joined Koaster's carpenter crew. Clerks expected promotion and profit. In that, Astoria's clerks proved an unhappy lot. James Lewis died in the explosion of the *Tonquin*, Ross later joined the North West Company and never advanced beyond a clerkship, and Matthews spent his later years working for the American Fur Company in Montreal. Ross Cox returned to Ireland and became a clerk in the headquarters office of the Dublin Metropolitan Police. On the other hand, Franchère and his fellow clerk Alfred Seton did much better. Franchère continued to work for Astor as an important fur agent, and Seton became a prominent New York insurance executive.

By their own admission, clerks had plenty of free time. Boredom was the great enemy. Fur trade clerks visited neighbors at rival posts, made music, kept diaries, wrote letters, and above all read avidly. Almost all western posts boasted substantial libraries. Daniel Harmon explained, "As to Books I am very well supplied, therefore I hope and expect to pass the Summer without experiencing much what the French call ennui." When Harmon was at a post with no library he complained, "I now begin to feel the want of Books."[27]

Although there is no record of books carried to Astoria in the *Tonquin*, by late November 1812 Franchère could report that he and another clerk, Benjamin Clapp, were enjoying the post's "good library."[28] Those books had come on the *Beaver*. When that vessel had left New York in October 1811, several large cartons of books, magazines, and newspapers had been stowed in the cargo hold. A list of those books contained in the *Beaver*'s shipping manifest suggests the variety of literature available at Astoria. High on the list were books of poetry by Robert Burns, George Crabbe, and Peter Pindar. Walter Scott's historical romances also had their place. Perhaps fitting what Astor thought were the national interests of men bearing names like McKay, McDougall, and Stuart were copies of Sir John Carr's *A Tour through Scotland* and Jane Porter's ever popular *The Scottish Chiefs*. Porter's historical novel *Thaddeus of Warsaw* was also slipped in. Biography was represented by a four-volume life of Napoleon and a one-volume study of William Pitt. For Astorians not ready to tackle such heavyweights, there was S. W. Ryley's *The Itinerant; or, Memoirs of an Actor*. Light fiction came in the shape of *Tales of Real Life* and *Tales of Fashionable Life*. Astor's longtime friend and business partner Alexander Henry the elder had just published his *Travels and Adventures in Canada*, and a copy of that lively book was sent to Astoria. Prospective explorers at the post could also read Alexander von Humboldt's *Political Essay on the Kingdom of New Spain*, perhaps seeing the new English translation just published in

New York by the printer I. Riley. Certainly the most intriguing book
note on the *Beaver*'s list is "Clark on long voyages." A book buyer in
the fall of 1811 could have purchased the first of what would be
several apocryphal Lewis and Clark accounts. The Astorians may
have seen the hasty fabrication called *The Travels of Capts. Lewis and
Clark*, printed in Philadelphia by Hubbard Lester. The book contained Thomas Jefferson's 1806 Message to Congress, Clark's letter
from St. Louis, pieces of Sargeant Patrick Gass's recently published
journal, and smatterings of travel accounts by Jonathan Carver and
Alexander Mackenzie. Newspapers and magazines like the *Port Fo-
lio*, the *American Register*, and the *Edinburgh Review* were packed for
the Northwest. Astoria's library was rounded out with Joshua Mon-
tefiore's *The American Trader's Compendium*, Muller's *Elements of Fortification*, and Nicholas Dufief's home-study course in the Spanish language. Travel, adventure, poetry, biography, and the practical arts—
any reader in Astoria struggling to overcome the rainy greyness
of afternoons on the Northwest coast had much to choose from.[29]

Like every frontier community, Astoria had its full complement
of skilled craftsmen, including a blacksmith, a cooper, a carpenter,
and a tailor—the post's "mechanics." In the eyes of the company
there was no other tradesman more valuable than the blacksmith.
Working at his smithy, he was responsible for everything from the
repair of guns and traps to the manufacture of barrel hoops and
building hardware. Indians regularly brought bar iron for smiths to
pound into arrow points. Astoria's blacksmith was Augustus Roussel. Engaged at Lachine, he was the highest paid of all the mechanics. Roussel eventually spent at least ten years shaping hot
metal, first for the Pacific Fur Company and later for the Nor'westers. As late as 1821, Donald Mackenzie reported, "Roussille knocks
away upon his anvil."[30] Two of Roussel's most reliable customers
were the cooper, George Bell, and the carpenter, Johann Koaster. In
an age that stored everything in barrels, Bell was a craftsman much
in demand. He had been recruited in New York, had come to Astoria
on the *Tonquin*, and was listed as a company employee as late as
1813. Bell was plainly a valued servant, since his wages, $240 a year,

were the second highest of those of all the mechanics. Astoria's carpenter, Johann Koaster, had also been a passenger on the *Tonquin*. Koaster, described by Franchère as a "Russian," remains something of a mystery. He was plainly a very busy man at Astoria, constructing several substantial buildings and overseeing a large gang of assistants. For some reason, Koaster was never named in either the Ross or Cox diaries and he appears as only "the carpenter" in the post's official journal. He was not listed among the company's employees when a roster was compiled in 1813. Even more shadowy is Astoria's tailor. McDougall frequently noted that the tailor was busy stitching and mending. But nowhere in Astoria's surviving record is he named. The *Tonquin*'s tailor was Egbert Vanderhoop, but this man was evidently not a company employee and probably died in the blast that destroyed his ship.

One rung down on the fur trade social ladder were the hunters. These men were typically French Canadians or Mohawk Iroquois from the Caughnawaga, Oka, and Saint Regis reserves. Although the Astorians relied principally on local Indian hunters, the post had three hunters on the company's payroll. Pierre Dorion, Jr., had been part of Hunt's overland party and served until his untimely death in 1814. Regis Bruguier, a free trapper, arrived at Astoria from the Okanogan country in October 1811. Arriving at the same time was Ignace Shonowane, an Iroquois hunter. The Shonowane family lived at Astoria until early April 1814, when they joined a canoe brigade returning to Montreal.[31]

In the Astorian world of work, the hardest physical labor was reserved for the French-Canadian engagés. Men like Joseph St. Amant, Jean Baptiste Belleau, and Antoine Papin provided the energy and muscle to build Astoria and turn the company a profit. Everything at Astoria and its outlying posts required hard work. There was land to clear, timber to haul, and firewood to cut. Charcoal pits needed constant tending, as did gardens and livestock. Thousands of salmon required drying and salting. The fur press demanded strong backs. Astoria moved by brute force, and that power was paid only modest wages. The 1813 employee roll of the

Pacific Fur Company shows a voyageur earning between $150 and $200 a year.[32]

Although laborers at Astoria and its auxiliary posts worked hard, not every observer thought highly of them. When Alexander Henry the younger came to Astoria in 1813, he cast a sharp eye on them and was not impressed. Like many Nor'westers, Henry was convinced that there was a real difference between the hardy, courageous, and obedient French Canadians who worked in the northern fur trade and the "insolent and intriguing fellows" who were employed in the southern trade from Mackinac to St. Louis. Henry insisted that the southern traders, driven by greed, changed employers each year and had loyalty to no one but themselves. The southerners hired by Wilson Price Hunt came in for a furious broadside by Henry. He labeled them "undisciplined, impertinent, ill-behaved vagabonds, devoid of that sense of subordination which our business requires."[33] For men who had braved the terrors of the Snake River and the rigors of work along the Columbia, Henry's judgment seems unduly harsh. And as it turned out, Astoria's most celebrated desertion involved French Canadians of the very sort Henry praised.

The workers who Henry claimed did "nothing more than they concieve they are bound to do by their agreement" surely had their share of mishaps, accidents, and injuries. Every occupation had its hazards. Blasting tree stumps with black powder caused several injuries and, according to Ross, cost one man his hand. Even the simple task of chopping wood had its dangers, as Joseph St. Amant discovered when an axe slipped and cut his foot.[34] The blacksmith, Augustus Roussel, was the victim of a spectacular accident. Repairing a double-barreled gun, he did not notice that it was loaded. The weapon suddenly fired, and he was gravely wounded in the right thigh. Although the shot and wadding were removed and the wound eventually healed, the smith spent several painful weeks hobbling about on crutches.[35] Not every illness and injury was life threatening. Day by day, the strains, sores, and bruises took their toll. In May 1811 McDougall wrote that at least four men were unable to work each day. Since Astoria's work force at that point was not many more than twenty men, the sick call was substantial. The numbers of the ill and injured continued to rise as everything from dysentery and scurvy to broken bones and sprained backs put Astorians off the job.[36]

Heavy drinking and fighting also took a toll. Every voyageur expected a daily grog ration and perhaps a bit more. The extra round often sparked violence. When a number of Astorians set to drinking with John Mumford, former second officer of the *Tonquin*, they all became quite intoxicated. Mumford and some of the Hawaiians soon fell to fighting. In the wild scuffle Mumford severely cut one of the islanders with a sharp bone. Edgy tempers sometimes flared when men were assigned long, lonely duty at the charcoal pits. In one such fray, an unnamed Astorian was so badly injured that he could not work for some time. Even after Astoria became the North West Company's Fort George, the troubles continued. When Alexander Ross asked the voyageur Benjamin Duchesne to help raise the flag on Sunday morning, the engagé exploded in anger and slashed Ross across the face with a knife. Echoing the resentment of many at the post, Duchesne complained that he never had "a spare moment on week days" even to darn his stockings.[37]

Complaints were rife at Astoria. The clerk William Matthews wrote McDougall a bitter letter charging that the sick were getting insufficient food. Mumford, the ship's officer, often quarreled with the partners about the command of the schooner *Dolly*.[38] But no Astorian carried his grudges and complaints further than Paul Denis Jérémie did. Perhaps taken in by what Ross called "the flattering hopes and golden prospects" offered by Astor's company, Jérémie had engaged and had taken passage on the *Tonquin*. If Jérémie had expected adventure and wealth, he got neither at Astoria. The post's journal reveals him herding pigs one day and helping raise a chimney on another. By late June 1811 the Canadian was so unhappy with his lot that he asked permission to leave the post once the *Tonquin* returned. Angered by this request, McDougall reprimanded the engagé and sent him back to work.[39]

The resentful Jérémie was not to be thwarted. For much of July 1811 he carefully planned an overland escape from Astoria. Each day he gathered small stocks of food, tobacco, wine, and ammunition, hiding them outside the fort. As the month drew to a close Jérémie must have been on the brink of desertion. His plans failed at the last moment when on July 26 his cache was discovered. Furious at the news, the partners sent Jérémie, under guard, into the woods to carry all the goods back to the post. That done, he was then closely questioned by McDougall. It was plain from his answers not only that was he as determined as ever to escape but also that his plans were widely known among the other engagés. After forcing Jérémie to sign a statement explaining his discontent and promising not to spread rumors about the company, the unhappy Canadian was clapped into irons. Those who had known about his design were also punished. Astorian custom dictated that liquor be handed around three times each day. Determined to let all the laborers know just who held real power, the partners cut the ration to twice each day.[40]

A few days in irons and a signature on paper were not enough to stop Jérémie. Seeking help in his escape, he turned to the Belleau brothers, Jean Baptiste and Antoine. Their reasons for discontent are not clear, but by early November the brothers had thrown in with Jérémie. On November 8 Jérémie and the Belleaux got permission to leave the post on a short hunting excursion. Taking several guns, some ammunition, and a small Indian canoe, the voyageurs were soon gone. When they did not reappear by November 10, McDougall realized that Jérémie had made good on his often repeated threat to desert. Determined to stop him, the post's officers sent out an armed party led by Franchère and Matthews. For the rest of November, Astoria's constables scoured the Columbia from Tongue Point to the Cascades. At last the deserters were found being held prisoner at an Indian village on the Willamette River opposite Sauvie Island. After considerable negotiation with the village's chief, Franchère was able to ransom Jérémie and his confederates, paying eight blankets, an old pistol, and some trade goods for their release. By the end of November the unfortunate trio was at Astoria awaiting an uncertain future.[41]

For Paul Jérémie the adventure was not over. Attempted escapes and successful recaptures only intensified his determination to leave a company and a country he hated. He finally got his chance in December 1813. After the sale of Astoria and the arrival of the HMS *Racoon*, many former Pacific Fur Company men either joined the Nor'westers or returned east. Jérémie shook off Astoria's dust in a singular way. He importuned the *Racoon*'s captain to take him on as an assistant clerk. When the ship stood out to sea at the end of December, Paul Jérémie was finally free of Astoria.[42]

But the Astorians were not quite free of him. Once the *Racoon* returned to England, Jérémie was closely examined by admiralty authorities. Just what the disgruntled ex-Astorian told his questioners is not plain, but Jérémie's travels were not yet over. In November 1818 the USS *Ontario*, carrying Special Agent J. B. Prevost, put in at Lima, Peru, before heading for Astoria. Paul Jérémie was there. Prevost met him and recorded more of Jérémie's tales. The Canadian now claimed that he had been one of the company's clerks and had been the only one stalwart enough to resist the sale of the post. For his loyalty, so he told Prevost, he had been kidnapped and forced to sail for England. Jérémie also filled the diplomat's ear with wild stories about the possibilities of trade with "a million Chenooks." After Lima the Jérémie trail grows cold, and the unhappiest Astorian drops from sight. Other company men traveled farther to get home, but none tried harder to escape Astoria's empire.[43]

The troubles of toil at Astoria were eased by a regular round of holidays. Except when all hands were hurrying to prepare canoes and goods for outlying company posts, Sunday was considered a day set apart to scrub clothes, mend socks, and escape the demands of the daily routine. Astorians also celebrated a whole calendar of holidays, both national and religious. Although most Astorians were not United States citizens, an American flag flew over the post. The Fourth of July was properly observed at Astoria with salutes of gunfire, a flag raising, and extra grog for all. Astoria also took note of its own birthday. April 12, the date on which the first work party had begun clearing ground for the post, was set aside to make merry and toast the company, its founder, partners, clerks, and all its loyal servants.[44]

Fur trade society paid special attention to religious holidays. Scots Presbyterians and Canadian Catholics marked All Saints' Day, Christmas, and Easter with equal veneration. Despite a dwindling larder, Astoria honored All Saints' Day in 1811 by putting out the best bread and meat available. Christmas often found the fort's supplies even scarcer. But as Franchère wrote, "We treated our men to the best the post could offer." Easter signaled the season of better supplies. Now the partners could be freer with extra shares of liquor, flour, and molasses.[45]

But no other holiday got more attention than New Year's Day. Fur trade tradition made the day a time for feasting, drinking, dancing, and general carousing. Nearly every diary kept by a trader records the festivities of the day. Alexander Mackenzie's men, resting at Fort Fork before their epic march to the Pacific, greeted the first day of 1793 with shooting and an all-day feast. Lewis and Clark's Corps of Discovery, spending the winter at Fort Mandan, heralded 1805 with a two-day party complete with dancing, music, and a procession to a nearby Indian village.[46] The Astorians certainly upheld the tradition. New Year's was always a time to throw a memorable party. The advent of 1812 was no exception. At dawn a drummer beat a smart roll to assemble all employees to watch the hoisting of the colors. After three rounds of gunfire and a ceremonial discharge of the fort's three cannons, everyone got down to enjoying a special ration of grog, cheese, bread, and butter. At sunset the flag was lowered to the accompaniment of more artillery rounds. Music and dancing filled the night, and the festivities did not wind down until nearly three o'clock in the morning. No reveler could have asked for more.[47]

The first of January was not Astoria's only New Year's celebration. In late October 1812 the Hawaiians at Astoria announced that this was the beginning of their new year. October 27 was promptly set aside for that purpose, a reminder of the substantial Hawaiian presence at Astoria.[48] Men like Joseph Powrowie, James Kimoo, and

Dick Paou were as much Astorians as were the Canadians they worked alongside. The first eleven Hawaiians to work at the post had come on the *Tonquin*. They were joined in 1812 by a second party of twelve or thirteen islanders. When the company drafted its list of employees in 1813, there were twenty-four "Sandwich Islanders" on the roll. Those men worked at all Astoria's tasks. They tended pigs, weeded gardens, went hunting, and accompanied traders to distant posts. Although Hawaiians worked along with other Astorians, the islanders lived apart from the Canadians. When a new house was built, tradesmen occupied one side of the sleeping hall and Hawaiians used the opposite end. Seeking adventure beyond the islands, these young men found hard work, short rations, and an inhospitable climate. The Hawaiians suffered more than most Astorians from the long damp seasons of the Northwest. In a typical entry, McDougall noted that on one November day nearly all the Hawaiians were unable to work because of illnesses caused by the cold, wet weather. Little wonder that by 1814 many of them "wished much to see their homes."[49]

* * *

Reflecting on the slow turn of soggy days at Fort Clatsop, Meriwether Lewis had written, "Every thing moves on in the same old way."[50] Astoria's life moved at a quicker pace in part because the post had almost daily visits from Indians. Clatsops, Chinooks, Wahkiakums, and Cathlamets all came to talk, trade, and just stare at those they called "Pah-shish'-e-ooks," the cloth men. Fort Clatsop had been off the beaten track on the Netul River. Astoria commanded an important place on the Columbia River highway. Lewis and Clark had kept their native neighbors at arm's length; the Astorians were eager for trade with and information from the Indians.

These Indians, long accustomed to dealings with ships in the maritime fur trade, must have found Astoria something of a novelty. Here was a year-round, beached "ship" filled with cloth men and their goods. By mid-May 1811 large numbers of Indians were coming to the post each day. Some showed up simply to see the new tourist attraction, as they had when Lewis and Clark had built Fort Clatsop. But increasingly Astoria's neighbors came to trade. As food supplies left by the *Tonquin* ran out, post officers encouraged a provisioning business by the Indians. The river folk, all experienced merchants, were quick to see the value of the Astorian marketplace. During the yearly salmon runs, Chinook and Clatsop traders brought large numbers of fish. A typical shipment destined for Astoria might be between forty to seventy salmon.[51] Increasingly dependent on Indian traders, the Astorians soon found them to be astute bargainers. Duncan McDougall would have promptly agreed with William Clark's assessment of the Chinooks as "tite dealers" who "Stickle for a very little, never close a bargin except they think they have the advantage." Just how "tite" those dealers were became plain when the post's clerks began to add up the cost of each salmon and sturgeon. Five salmon commanded two yards of cotton cloth, with occasional additions of brass buttons, knives, files, and beads.[52]

Astorians confronted not only sharp Chinook traders but also the Chinooks' cherished cultural patterns about eating salmon. The first salmon ceremony was an age-old ritual undertaken by river peoples to mark the beginning of the salmon runs. When the first salmon was caught, the lucky fisherman sent messengers to alert all neighboring villages. The first fish was treated with great care, its mouth filled with clean sand and its body brushed with moss. Attention paid to the salmon would insure that its kin would continue to come to the river. Neighbors and friends now gathered at the fisherman's house to decide how the fish would be cooked. If the decision was to boil it, the fish was carefully broken into pieces by hand. The heart was promptly burned and the eyes swallowed to guarantee good fortune. Roasting the first salmon (and subsequent ones as well) demanded a different set of procedures. The fish was slit lengthwise down the back with a mussel-shell knife. Great care was taken not to cut the salmon crosswise. Once the backbone, heart, and intestines were removed and burned, the fish was roasted. As before, everything edible had to be consumed before sundown.[53]

The Astorians encountered these salmon rituals almost at once.

In early June 1811 Duncan McDougall noted that his Indian neighbors had plenty of salmon but seemed unwilling to bring them for trade. The few fish that were offered for sale had to be gutted and cooked by native people. At first McDougall feared that this was a concerted strategy to starve the Astorians. On investigation, he learned something about the first salmon ceremony. Men at the post were plainly relieved that their food supply was not in danger, but they were quick to brand the Indians' practice as "superstitious belief." But if the Astorians wanted those salmon, the Chinooks made it clear they would have to accept native rituals. Once the Astorians agreed not to cut the fish crosswise, a busy trade grew up.[54]

The daily provisioning trade centered on fish, but Fort Astoria was also a ready market for fresh game and hides. Although the salmon runs brought fish aplenty, the region around the post was not especially well supplied with deer and elk. Only rarely did Indian hunters bring in an animal for sale. When five native woodsmen offered what they claimed was a fine male elk, the partners readily paid twelve strings of beads and two clasp knives for the meat. On stretching out the hide, the Astorians found the elk to be a less-desirable female. Much to his chagrin, McDougall admitted that this was not the first time Astorians had been fooled by the Chinooks' cunning. A week and a half later, he paid sixteen strings of beads and a quantity of tobacco for another elk. Perhaps this time he was more careful, although his journal is silent on the quality of the meat.[55]

The Pacific Fur Company never intended Astoria to be its principal trading site. Astoria was envisioned as an administrative field headquarters. The fort was meant to provision distant satellite posts and to store pelts for shipment to market. But because of its location on what had become an important part of the maritime fur trade, Astoria got its share of pelts. When clerks inventoried what had been traded between April 1811 and the end of May 1812, the count revealed that some 3,500 pelts had passed from Indian to company hands. The skins ranged from 1,750 large beaver and 61 large sea otter pelts to 15 squirrels and 1 red fox.[56]

More than any other person, the Chinook-proper chief Comcomly made Astoria's fur trade a success. The chief had a keen sense of the power that could be exerted by controlling access to the trade. Even someone as disenchanted as Paul Jérémie recognized the chief's abilities, calling him a "shrude one-eyed old man and great warrior." The Astorians discovered just how skillful a politician Comcomly was when a trading party led by Robert Stuart and Alexander Ross headed north from the post into present-day coastal Washington. The partners had been wondering why so few Chehalis and Quinault traders were coming in with pelts. At several coastal villages Stuart and Ross found the reason. Here were piles of furs waiting to be picked up by Comcomly's people. Plainly the Chinooks were acting as middlemen. Ross noted the Quinaults' reaction when they were told about the prices the furs might fetch without Comcomly's carrying charges. "They put their hands on their mouths in astonishment and strongly urged us to return again, saying they would never trade with the one-eyed chief."[57]

Despite this promise, it was clear that "foreign Indians" were not coming to Astoria. Comcomly had spread carefully crafted rumors suggesting that native people who set foot inside the post did so at risk to their lives. All trade with the cloth men had to go through him. The partners did their best to dispel such tales but they proved hard to scotch. If the company wanted pelts from the lower Columbia and the north coast, it would have to deal with Comcomly. Late in June 1811 the chief was given a large, unspecified gift symbolizing Astoria's recognition of his role as a vital trade broker. This was no bribe but a plain statement of Comcomly's place in the river world. Soon after, regular parties of Indians began to troop through Astoria's main gate bearing all sorts of furs. By skill and perseverance Comcomly had bent the company to his will. If he had his way, Astoria would not be the only empire on the Columbia.[58]

John Astor's men were never official, credential-carrying American diplomats, but an American flag flew over the post and the Pacific Fur Company intended to advance federal influence west of the Great Divide. Although Astor never spelled out in precise detail the company's diplomatic mission, it is plain that the Astorians were to pursue two distinct goals. The company's posts were in the Northwest to lay American claim to the region. Astor clearly understood this imperial goal. Writing a confidential memorandum for Navy Secretary William Jones, Astor argued that his company could "place the monopoly of the fur trade of the world in the hands of this country, and at no remote period extend its dominion over a most interesting part of the opposite coast of the North American continent." And of course Astor believed this would eventually "open communications of no small moment with Japan and the East Coast of Asia."[59]

Other than extending the trading network outward from the Columbia, the Astorians would have little opportunity to pursue such ambitious diplomacy, at least until the War of 1812 came to the Northwest. Until that time the partners busied themselves with Astor's second diplomatic objective: the need to "reconsile" the Indians.[60] Astor sought reconciliation both to pursue profit in the trade and to eliminate any British competition. Astoria's partners tended to emphasize good trade relations with their native neighbors, believing that those relations were the foundation for any struggle against Canadian opponents. Contacts with Comcomly, Daitshowan, and Coalpo appeared to insure a steady flow of furs and provisions. But the Columbian world of trade and politics was never quite so simple. Personal, family, and village rivalries filled the air. Though McDougall and the other Astorians understood little about those tensions, they did assume that such animosities could be resolved easily. The Astorians got their first chance to play the diplomacy game in mid-May 1811. The Clatsops and their Tillamook neighbors to the south had always been uneasy rivals. The location of the Clatsops' villages gave those people an advantage in the fur trade that geography denied the Tillamooks. On May 16 the headman Daitshowan visited McDougall, asking him to travel to the Clatsops' village at Point Adams. The chief factor was given to understand that there were mounting tensions between Clatsops and Tillamooks. The Astorian evidently thought he could mediate any dispute. Perhaps Daitshowan had a different agenda. The headman may well have sought out McDougall as an ally to bolster the Clatsops' position.

By afternoon McDougall was at Neahkeluk, a substantial settlement of eight large wood houses surrounded by a palisade. If the Astorian thought he could play the go-between, he was soon disappointed. No Tillamooks were at the village to present their side of the argument. Instead, the Clatsops filled McDougall's ear with complaints about their troublesome neighbors. When he urged the Clatsops to seek a peaceful solution, the Indians agreed but hurried to remind their guest that the Tillamooks were the villains in the piece.[61]

The Astorians may have imagined that they were on the verge of witnessing a full-scale Clatsop-Tillamook war, which in truth was highly unlikely. Plainly dissatisfied with the results of his mission to Neahkeluk, McDougall decided to consult with Comcomly. The Chinook headman had considerable influence on the north side of the Columbia, but his power did not extend to the Clatsops and the Tillamooks. Accustomed to thinking about politics and diplomacy in terms of sovereign authority, the Astorians easily made Comcomly a kind of river emperor. It was a status the Chinook soon came to enjoy and play to the hilt. On May 17 McDougall joined forces with Alexander McKay for a journey to Comcomly's village on Baker Bay. McDougall's journal is silent on the course of those discussions except to say that when the Astorians returned to the post the following day they carried assurances from the Chinook headman that all Indians along the river wanted peace with each other and the cloth men. Uncertain about the true nature of the Clatsop-Tillamook affair and equally unsure about the intentions of Indians living near the post, the Astorians may have taken some comfort in Comcomly's promises. If they did, they were soon disappointed.[62]

Eager to use their good offices to settle disputes among the natives, the Astorians found that their diplomacy was increasingly directed to resolving troubles between themselves and their native neighbors. Worries about sudden attack were a constant part of life at Astoria. When the post was abuilding in the spring of 1811, every axeman kept a gun close at hand. Although there is no compelling evidence that any Indians ever planned such a foolhardy venture, Astorians were convinced that such an assault was imminent. Their fears surfaced in early July when the Astorians got word of possible violence between Comcomly's people and some visiting lower Chehalis folk who had been making sport at a ball-and-racket game. The artist Paul Kane, who traveled in the region during the 1840s, was a spectator at this lacrosse-style play, which sometimes involved a hundred men on each team. Kane wrote, "The play is kept up with great noise and excitement." The game had high stakes, both in bets and personal honor. Injuries were common, and in the rough-and-tumble of this particular match Comcomly's son Gassagas gravely injured a Chehalis chief. Should the man die, there would surely be revenge killings. Seeing this possibility, the Astorians reasoned that such troubles would keep the Indians preoccupied, with little time left over to think about a raid on the post's warehouse. Persistent rumors had led the Astorians to think that an attack might come in the fall once the *Tonquin* had completed her coasting voyage and had left for Canton. The sporting fray and those rumors now induced the partners to press ahead with plans to ring the post with a stout log palisade.[63]

Astoria's laborers were kept busy cutting and setting palisade pickets during the rest of July. At the end of the month their work took on a sudden urgency. Wickaninnish, or Nootka, Indians from the west coast of Vancouver Island were fishing at Baker Bay. In what was probably another example of rumor-mongering, Comcomly told the Astorians that these northern Indians were plotting an attack. When an Indian friendly with Robert Stuart told the same story, all were convinced that the long-expected assault was upon them. Taking the news at face value, the partners ordered all hands to hurry the palisade and to construct two elevated bastions. By the last day of July, picketing was complete, cannons had been set in the court square, and swivel guns were placed in the hastily built towers.

All these military preparations clearly worried Comcomly. He may well have thought that his rumor campaign, intended to keep trade in his hands, had backfired. The headman wanted Astoria as a private trade monopoly. Should the post become an armed, belligerent camp ready to fire on any Indian, Comcomly's advantage might be lost. If the Chinook was worried, so were the Astorians. They wanted a strong defense, but not at the price of alienating Comcomly or other trading partners. When the chief openly complained about Astoria's warlike face, he was brushed off with a polite lie. The partners assured him that all the pickets were temporary and that further work was really meant to enlarge the blacksmith shop.[64]

Throughout August 1811 Astoria took on more and more the appearance of a garrison. The bastions were completed, and Koaster's carpenters built and hung a heavy gate. Weapons drills became an everyday part of Astoria's routine.[65] Although Comcomly resented these preparations, Chinooks and Clatsops continued to bring stocks of fish and fur for trade. Making ready for war had to share time with making a profit. The uncertainties of these late summer days increased toward the end of August. On the nineteenth Comcomly sent a strange message to Astoria. He claimed to have contracted a nasty sore throat and wanted both McDougall and Robert Stuart to pay a house call at his village. Although somewhat suspicious, the two partners initially agreed to make the journey. At the last moment they were stopped by a warning from Daitshowan's sister. The Clatsop woman insisted that Comcomly's sore throat was no more than a clever ruse to capture Astorian hostages. Whether her caution was justified or was yet another bit of sniping between Clatsops and Chinooks remains unclear. But McDougall and Stuart believed the advice and told Comcomly to seek doctoring elsewhere. The confusion heightened tensions and made the partners hasten defensive measures at Astoria.[66]

Several days later there was yet another troubling incident. Astorians had long suspected Comcomly of spreading stories about the dangers posed by trading at the post. When a small group of Clatsop and Nootka Indians appeared to trade pelts and sturgeon, the Astorians asked the Nootkas why they rarely came to do business in person. The Astorians knew the Nootkas routinely used Comcomly as a middleman. Nootka traders revealed that they had been told by the Chinooks that the cloth men were hostile toward northern Indians because of alleged cases of violence between native people and shipboard traders. Angered by what they heard, the Astorians branded the Chinooks' tale a baseless lie and insisted that business with the Nootkas would always be welcome.[67] In this swirl of rumor, threat, and contradiction the Astorians could do no more than tighten defenses and keep weapons at the ready. Only the coming of fall and the movement of native people to winter villages could relieve the tension. Men at the post had no reason to think that the spring of 1812 would bring anything other than renewed alarms and confusions.

Not all relations between Indians and Astorians were so official or so fraught with tension. Long before the Pacific Fur Company came to the Columbia River, Chinook women had used sexual relations to seal business agreements. These women were often the principal village merchants and frequently owned trade canoes. Sexual liaisons were an accepted part of Columbian commerce. Lewis and Clark discovered that some women struck more or less permanent arrangements with various ship captains, even going so far as to have names like "J. Bowmon" tattooed on their arms.[68]

By the time the *Tonquin* unloaded her passengers, venereal diseases were also a part of the Columbian world. Syphilis and gonorrhea had come with the maritime fur trade. Although not yet of epidemic scale, the ailments were unmistakably present. Astoria's surviving accounts contain only a few scattered references to sexual relations before 1814. In 1813 Duncan McDougall admitted that venereal complaints were commonplace. What especially concerned him was the lack of proper medication for the diseases. David Thompson had left some quicksilver at Astoria, and that had been used in place of the more effective mercury. But by early 1812 even that supply of ointment was exhausted. If the post's journal is to be trusted, one group of Astorians was hard hit by the "French pox." As

early as July 1811 McDougall found that several of the Hawaiians
had venereal diseases. One of those men, Thomas Tuanna, had an
especially virulent case. Whereas most of the infected recovered
after a time, Tuanna's case worsened. In late November 1812 his
condition was so precarious that the Astorians decided to undertake
a remarkable medical experiment. Tuanna was now suffering from
chills and may have appeared near death. Hoping to halt the chills
and elevate his body temperature, the Astorians killed a horse,
gutted the carcass, and placed the Hawaiian inside the still warm
animal. No record remains to reveal the outcome of this heroic
measure. When Alexander Henry the younger listed Hawaiians
present at Astoria in 1814, Tuanna did not appear on the list. He
may have finally succumbed to his infection or it is possible that he
was among those islanders who returned home after the sale of
Astoria.[69]

Henry's journal, beginning in 1813, provides a fuller account
both of sexual adventures at Astoria and of their more unfortunate
consequences. In February 1814 the Nor'wester predicted that by
spring at least half the men at the post would have various stages of
venereal diseases. "This foul malady," complained Henry, "is so
prevalent among our people and the women of this quarter that it
may seriously affect our commerce." Henry was always critical of the
Pacific Fur Company's personnel policies, but nothing angered him
more than the Astorians' evidently open willingness to have women
overnight. He noted that Chinook women were often sleep-over
guests. Henry charged them with "bartering their favors with the
men," something neither the Indians nor their customers would
deny. Exasperated by all this, Henry finally issued orders barring
women from sleeping in the company's buildings. As an added
incentive to keep Astorians away from such visitors, Henry proposed deducting from yearly wages time lost because of venereal
complaints. When a canoeful of Chinook women showed up at the
post to ply their trade, the Nor'westers drove them off with threats
of imprisonment.[70]

The many Indians who regularly paid calls at Fort Astoria came for every reason from curiosity to business. Unlike Lewis and Clark's Fort Clatsop, Astoria welcomed Indians as necessary trading partners. Ordinary river folk as well as headmen like Comcomly, Kamaquiah, Coalpo, and Daitshowan found Astoria a convenient place to socialize, sell goods, or have the blacksmith, Roussel, repair a broken tool or gun. All these gatheı ings produced remarkably little friction. McDougall's journal records no serious incidents of violence or injury between company employees and native visitors.

But one aspect of the Indians' behavior sparked constant trouble. Fur trade captains as well as explorers knew that unguarded goods, everything from belaying pins to guns, might soon vanish into native hands. Virtually every European who spent any time along the Northwest coast complained about theft and the seemingly unrepentant thieves. From the Indians' perspective, this unabashed pilfering wore a very different, noncriminal face. Astoria's neighbors took axes, files, cloth, and loose hardware for two reasons. First, the Chinookans believed that those who had large numbers of axes or other valuable goods should be willing to share with those having only a few. What the furious partners saw as theft, Indians viewed as a sensible redistribution of surplus goods. But there was a second, more subtle explanation for the natives' behavior. From The Dalles down to the sea, Indians saw themselves as the lords of the river. They expected that outsiders, especially the cloth men, would pay them proper respect and tribute. Taking European goods was a way to force those strangers to pay attention to the real masters of the Columbia.[71]

Such explanations were well beyond the cultural horizons of those living at Astoria. For them it was theft, pure and sometimes not so simple. During days of hard work grubbing out a clearing and framing Astoria's first buildings, company men found axes disappearing at an alarming rate. Infuriated by this, the partners grabbed the next Chinook caught with an axe and clamped him into irons for the night. During the night the Chinook slipped his bonds, not only escaping from Astoria but making off with the irons as well. Angered and perhaps not a little chagrined, the Astorians demanded that Comcomly present himself at the post for some serious talk about the escapade. The chief appeared and promised to take action against the escapee, but the Astorians had good reason to doubt his pious declaration.[72]

The Astorians found a more cooperative police partner in the Chinook headman Kamaquiah. He proved helpful in recovering three stolen axes that had been traded upriver. But not even Kamaquiah's vigilance could stop the continuing disappearance of Astoria's property. When one suspected thief was seen making away with some goods, company men rushed to his canoe and stove it in. Despite this prompt action, the Chinook escaped with his prize. Although some Indians showed remarkable dexterity in setting themselves free, the Astorians finally settled on a sentence of overnight in handcuffs for any native caught with company goods. The cuffs and their characteristic snapping sound added a new word to the Chinook trade jargon. With a wonderful sense of onomatopoeia, Indians called them "Click-a-min."[73]

That new word for the trade jargon is a reminder of the difficulty the Astorians had communicating with nearby Indians. The Chinooks' trade jargon had been developed by river people as a means to do business with outsiders. Maritime fur traders all learned to make use of this simple but effective language. Despite their isolation, at least some of Lewis and Clark's men appear to have mastered some jargon phrases. Although Astoria's records are strangely silent on the matter, some of the clerks and partners must have become fluent in the tongue. Doing business along the Columbia required it and the Astorians would not have been slow to pick up important words and sentences.

* * *

Life at Astoria soon settled in to a familiar routine of daily work, broken only occasionally by unexpected events. Two surprises came in June and July 1811. On June 14 Kamaquiah came to Astoria with an odd piece of news. He explained that there were two Indians from "very far in the interior" then at a Cathalamet village. The Chinook headman told a long, involved story about the strangers and their journey, but no one at the post could fully understand his explanation. It was plain only that these Indians were carrying a message from some white traders and were intent on delivering it to the "fort men."[74]

When the two travelers arrived at Astoria the next day, questions about them were everywhere. Who were they, where were they from, and might they be carrying a note from Wilson Price Hunt? The appearance of the strangers fueled such speculation. Dressed in plains-style buckskin leggings and long hunting shirts, the two stood in sharp contrast to both the post's traders and the nearby Chinooks. At first glance the pair seemed to be husband and wife. But closer inspection showed that both were women. The most talkative of the pair was Ko-come-ne-pe-ca, described by Alexander Ross as a "very shrewd and intelligent Indian." David Thompson, who got to know the Indians in the following month, learned that Ko-come-ne-pe-ca had experienced a powerful dream, "declared her sex changed, that she was now a Man, dressed and armed herself as such, and also took a young woman to Wife."[75]

The Astorians were less interested in Ko-come-ne-pe-ca's gender and spirit vision than in the information she and her friend might have. What they were carrying was a letter dated April 5, 1811, from Finan McDonald, a trader with the North West Company, at Spokane House, addressed to John Stuart at a place called Fort Estekatadene. McDougall opened the letter and read it but did not reveal its contents to either his own journal or any of the Astorians standing around. Because the travelers spoke only Cree, McDougall hurried to get the translating services of clerk François Pillet. Through him more of the tale came clear. The pair indeed had been sent by Nor'westers at Spokane House. Somewhere on the upper Columbia they had become lost, followed the Columbia, and eventually heard about Astoria. The travelers assumed that the letter was for the Astorians and were eager to deliver it.[76]

Whatever the contents of McDonald's letter, its very existence proved that the North West Company now had a post close enough to challenge Astoria's expansion. In the days that followed, Ko-come-ne-pe-ca and her partner had long conversations through Pillet with McDougall and other company officers. The Indians provided detailed information about the Spokane–Okanogan–upper Columbia region. To illustrate their points, they drew several sketch maps of the country. It was now plain that the Pacific Fur Company had to establish one or more trading houses east and north of Astoria. From the Indians' information, the best place appeared to be somewhere along the Okanogan River among the Sinkaietk Indians in present-day central Washington. David Stuart and Alexander Ross were detailed to prepare such an expedition scheduled to leave Astoria in late July.[77]

Preparations for the journey were abruptly halted on July 15. Most hands at the post had been busy throughout the day preparing canoes and packing trade goods for the Stuart-Ross expedition. Early in the afternoon all work stopped when a canoe came around Tongue Point and headed for the wharf at Astoria. All eyes strained to see the markings of the flag that flew from the canoe's stern. Franchère and the clerks were sure that the canoe could not be from Hunt's overlanders. The identity of the strangers was revealed a moment later when the flag showed the Union Jack. Once the canoe was secured at the dock, "a relatively well-dressed man who seemed in command jumped ashore." Alexander Ross noted, "Approaching us without formality [he] told us his name was David Thompson and that he was a partner in the North West Company."[78] As clerks and workers clustered around, Thompson began to give a brief account of his westward journey.

At that point McDougall and both Stuarts arrived. Ross, typically critical of McDougall and all things Nor'wester, declared that the Astorians welcomed Thompson "like a brother." Ross bitterly recalled that in the following days Thompson "had access everywhere, saw and examined everything, and got whatever he asked for, as if he had been one of our selves." Whatever Ross's unhappiness, it must have been nothing compared with the confusion sparked by the message Thompson carried. When he had left Rainy Lake in late July 1810, there had been strong evidence that Astor and the North

West Company were about to agree on a joint Pacific venture. Now, at Astoria, Thompson showed McDougall and the other partners a July 1810 letter to William McGillivray laying out such plans. Thompson seemed certain that by now all the necessary arrangements had been made and that, at least here beyond the Great Divide, Nor'westers and Astorians were partners. As Franchère heard it, "The wintering partners [of the North West Company] thought it best to abandon the posts they had established west of the mountains rather than compete with us, on condition that we did not interfere with their trade east of the mountains." All of this appeared beyond question when Thompson handed McDougall a formal letter he had written earlier in the day. The letter congratulated the Astorians on their journey, summarized what Thompson understood to be the terms of the American-Canadian enterprise, and added, "I have only to hope that the respective parties at Montreal may finally settle the arrangements between the companies which in my opinion will be to our mutual interest."[79]

All this came as a great surprise to the Astorians. When they had left New York in September 1810 it had appeared certain that negotiations between Astor and the Canadians had failed. Now Astor's men were being assured that the coalition was fact. Although McDougall and the others must have known Thompson had outdated information, there was still a slim chance that the joint enterprise had indeed come to pass. Some clerks and laborers at Astoria also guessed that the friendly relations between Thompson and the partners came from a careful plan designed to get the Nor'wester to reveal his company's true intentions.[80] Whatever their reservations, the Astorians decided to accept Thompson's story, at least publicly. On July 16 McDougall and the Stuarts drafted a proper reply directed to Thompson. The letter expressed delight at the news of corporate cooperation in the Northwest. If McDougall had any lingering doubts, he was not about to let Thompson see them. Putting on a bold front, the Astorians assured Thompson that the joint venture would "inevitably secure to us every advantage that can possibly be drawn from the Business."[81] Despite their seeming acceptance of Thompson's story, the Astorians were not about to slow their drive to expand the company's trade sphere. Preparations continued for the Stuart-Ross journey and now there was some talk about a post at Spokane, whether the Canadians abandoned their trading house on that river or not.

David Thompson's role in all these events requires some comment. Alexander Ross once wrote that Thompson was McDougall's match when it came to sharp dealing, "duplicity, and diplomatic craft." The Nor'wester certainly believed that his company and Astor's were now working in tandem. Hence there was no reason for him to "race" across country to beat the Astorians to the Columbia. At the same time, his assertion that the Canadians had decided to abandon all their posts west of the Divide was a falsehood. In early July 1811 Thompson was at the confluence of the Snake and Columbia rivers, near present-day Pasco, Washington. After meeting with the Walula chief Yelleppit, the explorer wrote a revealing note and fixed it to a small pole. The text of the declaration suggests that the Nor'westers had not quite given up their dreams of Pacific empire, noting their intention "to erect a factory in this place for the commerce of the country around." Whatever Thompson's game was and whatever the Astorians made of it, "the country around" ought to have braced itself for a noisy trade war.[82]

Throughout the following week Astorians hurried to complete work on Stuart's Okanogan journey. Despite Thompson's frequent comments that the upper Columbia offered poor trade prospects, the Astorians pressed ahead. McDougall evidently distrusted Thompson's advice and decided to tell him that Stuart and Ross were heading south, perhaps somewhere along the Snake River. By July 22 all was ready. The plan called for Thompson and Stuart to travel together, at least as far as The Dalles. Stuart took along Ross, Pillet, Donald McLennan, three engagés, and two Hawaiians. Their canoes were heavily laden with twenty packs of trade goods.[83] As the travelers were ready to push off, McDougall handed Thompson a packet addressed to Astor. The bundle contained copies of the Astoria-Thompson correspondence, McGillivray's letter, and a note from the partners to Astor. In the note McDougall and the Stuarts expressed pleasure at the Astoria-Nor'wester combination, saying that Canadian "experience and local knowledge of the country this side of the Rocky Mountains will enable us the sooner to derive every possible advantage the country affords."[84] This curious letter ought not be taken at face value. It may have been a "plant," given to Thompson on the assumption that he would open the parcel and read all the documents. No matter what they wrote about cooperation with the North West Company, the Astorians were as determined as ever to expand their empire.

All the hurry of June and July tended to obscure a gathering tragedy. On June 1 the *Tonquin* left Astoria bound for Vancouver Island. The ship carried not only Captain Jonathan Thorn and his crew but also company partner Alexander McKay, clerk James Lewis, and voyageur Louis Brule. Unfavorable winds kept the *Tonquin* in the Columbia and it was not until June 5 that she crossed the bar and stood out to sea.[85] Thorn's orders called for him to shape his course along Vancouver Island and points north, stopping to trade at familiar rendezvous points. In late summer he would return to Astoria for a brief stop before sailing to Canton and the China market. From there the *Tonquin* would finally make her way back to New York.

Astorians busy with building their post and preparing trade arrangements did not expect to see the *Tonquin* for at least three months. In early July, McDougall heard, perhaps from Comcomly's Chinooks, confused rumors about an attack on the ship. The stories were so jumbled that the partners easily discounted them. It was a bit harder to ignore troubling tales when they surfaced again at the end of the month. Indians from Grays Harbor reported that there had been a surprise attack on the *Tonquin*. Because they could offer few details, these informants were brushed off. But the Astorians were not the only ones hearing unpleasant maritime news. Stephen Reynolds, foremast hand on the trading ship *New Hazard*, recorded in his private journal that on July 15 Indians at Nahwhitti (the northwest end of Vancouver Island) reported that a ship had been seized at Nootka. By August there were so many rumors about the fate of the *Tonquin* that they were impossible to deny. Clatsop head-man Coalpo told McDougall that "it was current among the Indians that the *Tonquin* had been destroyed by the natives along the coast." In his August 11 entry, McDougall now admitted that the ship might have come to grief. Although the Astorians did not have confirmation of the *Tonquin* disaster until the arrival of the *Beaver* in early May 1812, the partners now began to reshape their strategy to fit changed circumstances.[86]

The fate of the *Tonquin* has attracted considerable attention. The journal keepers at Astoria—Gabriel Franchère, Alexander Ross, and Ross Cox—all took time to record what they knew about the ship's final hours. Washington Irving devoted much space to the *Tonquin*, as did later writers. In more recent times there have been several efforts to locate the wreck, including an attempt in 1983 using sophisticated sub-bottom acoustic profile equipment from the Canadian Royal Roads Military College. All efforts to date have proven unsuccessful.[87] Although the remains of the *Tonquin* continue to be an elusive prize, the sequence of events during the ship's last days is now reasonably clear. In 1813 the *Tonquin*'s only survivor, the Indian interpreter Jack Ramsay (also known as Lamazu), came to Astoria and gave an eyewitness account of the ship's destruction. As Ramsay told it, after leaving the Columbia the *Tonquin* sailed north until coming to an anchorage in the Templar Channel at Clayoquot Sound on the west coast of Vancouver Island. Once at this trading station, the ship began business with a substantial number of native people. As a sign of friendship, McKay was invited to spend several days at a nearby village. At the same time Thorn, Lewis, and Ramsay were busy conducting shipboard trade. Confident of his own abilities, the captain did not rig the usual boarding nets commonly used in the maritime fur trade to prevent surprise attack. Thorn also proved an overbearing trader. When one chief complained about the prices his pelts were fetching, Thorn exploded in a characteristic rage and rubbed the headman's face in the furs.

Such an insult could not go unavenged, and the unnamed Indian prepared his revenge. One morning some days later he and some twenty others appeared alongside the *Tonquin* waving furs and calling to be allowed on board. Seeing no reason to deny their request, the crew helped the Indians reach the deck. When a second canoe filled with Indians arrived, Thorn grew worried. Those Indians were on deck before he could stop them. Unsure what was going on, the captain hurried to get McKay and Ramsay. They agreed that something dangerous was afoot and urged Thorn to weigh anchor as quickly as possible. From his station on the poop deck Thorn ordered hands to the capstan while others scrambled aloft to unfurl sails. At that moment the Indians drew knives, clubs, and hatchets from beneath furs and attacked the crew. McKay died first, his skull crushed by a war club. Thorn soon fell defending himself to the last with a small knife. Other members of the crew were soon killed. In the bloody confusion, Ramsay jumped overboard and was rescued by some Indian women. Others who sought to escape were not so lucky. At least four men, fleeing in a ship's boat, were pursued and finally killed. On the following day large numbers of Indians crowded on the *Tonquin* to celebrate their victory and divide the spoils. What the celebrants did not know was that at least one member of the crew was still alive. The *Tonquin*'s survivor now exacted his revenge, setting off the ship's large powder magazine. Ramsay told the Astorians that "arms, legs and heads were flying in all directions and this tribe of Indians lost nearly 200 of its people in this unfortunate affair."[88]

The unexpected loss of the *Tonquin* was just one more entry in Astoria's long chapter of accidents. Because the ship was destroyed in so dramatic a fashion, it is easy to overestimate the consequences of the event. The Astorians were now effectively isolated from maritime contact until the arrival of the *Beaver*. On the other hand, the overall strategy pursued by the Pacific Fur Company was not altered by the ship's demise. Astoria's course had been set long before the *Tonquin* blew apart. More than one blast of powder would be needed to change its direction.

* * *

Astoria celebrated the coming of 1812 with the usual flurry of gunfire and heavy drinking. Some three weeks later there was another reason to make merry. The first overlanders—Donald Mackenzie, Robert McClellan, John Reed, and eight voyageurs—arrived at the post. From them the Astorians had their first news about Hunt's travelers and their suffering on the Snake River. Everyone at Astoria could only wonder how many overlanders would survive to be greeted at the fort. A month later, on February 15, that question was answered. Hunt and his exhausted companions staggered through the main gate to be welcomed as if they had come back from the dead. At last all the partners and adventurers save Crooks and company were present or accounted for. Now the company could get on with the business of expanding Astoria's empire.[89]

That process had already been started by McDougall and the other partners at Astoria. In June 1811 Robert Stuart and the Clatsop headman Coalpo had gone north along the Washington coast to visit the Quinault Indians. The reconnaissance reported a fur-rich country and Indians ready to have a small trading post close to their villages. This northern prospect was matched by favorable returns from Fort Okanogan. Alexander Ross had done well and profits seemed assured. Such encouraging reports prompted McDougall to send a large party, led by Robert Stuart, for a brief look at the Willamette country. The short expedition, undertaken in December 1811, proved yet another success for the company. Stuart was sure the region was worth the firm's attention. Perhaps it even merited a small trading house. What the Astorians needed now was a comprehensive design that would build on these initial successes. With Hunt and Mackenzie at the post, such planning could move ahead.[90]

In early March 1812 Hunt and the other senior Astorians settled in to make those plans. The first order of business was to form a party to carry dispatches overland to St. Louis and on to Astor in New York. Astor's original design called for regular overland expresses much like those used by the North West Company. John Reed, now an experienced western traveler, was given command of the messenger service. With him would be three hunters—Benjamin Jones, André Valle, and François Le Clairc. These men would be joined by a surprise addition. Robert McClellan, mercurial as ever, had suddenly decided he wanted nothing more to do with the Pacific Fur Company. On March 1 he signed away his shares in the enterprise.[91] With the overland express arranged, the partners turned to the recovery of valuable trade goods cached by Hunt. Clerk Russel Farnham and a small party were detailed for that duty. Because the Willamette country seemed promising, Donald Mackenzie and William Matthews were ordered south to further test the trade waters. In their early March meeting the Astorians paid most attention to Okanogan and the country to the north around present-day Kamloops, British Columbia. Everything pointed to the region as a place of possibility for the company. Going into what the Nor'westers called New Caledonia would surely be challenging the Canadians, but it was plain that Hunt did not accept Thompson's tale of a union between Astor and the North West Company. Robert Stuart and several voyageurs were directed first to Okanogan and then north to the Thompson River and the Shuswap Indians. With Astoria fully established, leadership in place, and outposts set down in promising country, the Pacific Fur Company seemed ready to fulfill Astor's dreams.[92]

If the Astorians thought their stars had finally crossed them for the last time, they were quite mistaken. Bad luck nipped at the heels of nearly every Astorian enterprise. In late March 1812 the various parties set out up the Columbia. No group of traders, native or European, could expect to slip past The Dalles without paying tribute in goods or trouble or both. The Wishram and Wasco peoples who made The Dalles their home expected tolls to be paid for use of the Columbia highway. When the Astorians reached the Long Narrows in early April, there was serious trouble. Reed's shiny metal dispatch box, carrying correspondence for Astor, caught the eye of the Wishram Indians. In a confused melee, Reed was wounded by a hatchet blow, and at least two Indians were shot. The precious tin box was lost. With the reason for Reed's journey gone and Reed himself gravely wounded, Robert Stuart decided the entire party had to retreat. Going first to Okanogan, the bedraggled crew finally made it back to Astoria on May 11. There was only one bright spot in

the whole sorry affair. On their retreat they encountered Ramsay
Crooks and John Day, two more members of Hunt's party still trying
to make Astoria.[93]

When the entire group—both Stuarts, Crooks, McClellan, Reed,
and the voyageurs—reached Astoria, they found the ship *Beaver* in
the river. The vessel, under the command of Captain Cornelius
Sowle, had left New York in October 1811 bound for Astoria, the
Russian posts, and Canton. On board were seven new clerks and a
substantial supply of trade goods.[94] The fray at The Dalles and the
arrival of the *Beaver* prompted Hunt to convene a second partners'
meeting. This one, set for early June 1812, suggests that between
March and June Hunt had further refined his strategy for company
expansion. The partners would now prepare plans for more trading
houses scattered over a much bigger area. Astoria's empire was
about to grow even larger.

Sometime during the first days of June, Hunt and his associates
began to plot those grander schemes. First on the agenda was an
expanded list of trading stations. William Wallace and John Halsey
were directed south down the Willamette, where they would eventually build Wallace House near present-day Salem, Oregon. Perhaps sensing that David Thompson and the Nor'westers were more
than mildly interested in the Snake River country, the partners
detailed Donald Mackenzie and the recently arrived clerk Alfred
Seton to begin trading at the Snake-Columbia confluence around
present-day Pasco, Washington. Alexander Ross and Donald McGillis were sent back to Okanogan, a post that was already proving its
value. The Shuswaps country had also met the company's expectations, and David Stuart returned to that region. Trouble at The
Dalles notwithstanding, dispatches had to be delivered east. That
hazardous duty was assigned to Robert Stuart.

Just how much the Astorians knew about the growing presence of
the North West Company in the territories west of the Great Divide
is not plain. Hunt and McDougall certainly knew about the Spokane
post now headed by James McMillan. They may have had some
inkling about Finan McDonald's activities at Flathead and about the

The *Beaver*. Courtesy of the Mystic Seaport Museum, Mystic, Conn., Mary Anne Stets photo.

trading done by Nicholas Montour in the Kootenai country. They would soon discover that David Stuart was not alone on the Thompson River. Even partial knowledge of this opposition suggested a forceful response. The partners decided to challenge the Nor'westers at Spokane. Two new clerks, Ross Cox and John Clarke, were directed to build a post on the Spokane River as close as possible to the North West Company site. But Hunt had more in mind than just a one-to-one competition. Astoria's Fort Spokane would become a district headquarters for trade in what is now eastern Washington and Oregon, northern Idaho, and western Montana. Russel Farnham was directed toward the Flathead country, François Pillet headed to the Kootenai, and Donald McLennan marched up to the Coeur d'Alene. The Astorians were not about to relinquish one pelt to the Nor'westers.

The June meeting promised a spirited trade campaign. Confident that the field would soon be theirs, the partners concluded the gathering with a decision that ultimately weakened Astoria and hurried its demise. Captain Sowle and the *Beaver* were about to depart for the Russian settlements. Knowing the importance of the Russian-American Company for the future of the entire Astorian enterprise, Hunt decided to accompany Sowle and to meet directly with Baranov. The voyage would also give Hunt an opportunity to survey trade prospects all along the Northwest coast. Command of Astoria was handed back to Duncan McDougall as Hunt made ready for the sea voyage. Hunt intended to be gone only a short time. As it turned out, he would not return until late February 1814. Astoria's future was now entrusted to a man less committed financially and personally to Astor and his western dreams.[95]

Timing always eluded the Astorians. Ships and men seemed forever in harm's way. When Astoria's laborers began to set out goods and prepare packs on June 15, they could not know that Britain and the United States were but three days from war. The Pacific Fur Company had been born in a world of international negotiation and intrigue. John Astor had willingly entered that dangerous arena knowing that high stakes often turned on hands dealt by others. From Montreal and Washington to New York and St. Petersburg, Astor had courted the great powers. Those powers could be wooed but not controlled. Astoria's future was now subject to questions of war and peace far beyond Astor's ability to manage. The War of 1812 plunged Astoria into crisis and jeopardized American hopes of empire beyond the mountains.

8

Astoria at War

THE PACIFIC FUR COMPANY was always intended to be something more than an efficient means to trap animals and sell their skins to Chinese merchants. What Astor and his rivals sought went beyond bales of pelts listed in ledgers at New York, Montreal, or New Archangel. It was not so much the calculations of profit that shaped Astoria's last days as the calculus of national power. The prize was political and economic dominion beyond the mountains. Nor'westers put the connection between commerce and sovereignty in sharp focus when they wrote that it was "the peculiar nature of the Fur Trade to require a continual extension of its limits, into new Countries." Where the Canadians were elegant in their prose, Astor was characteristically blunt. Struggling to secure protection for Astoria, he lashed out at federal bureaucrats for their penny-pinching ways. "Good god," he raged, "what an objict is to be securd by Smale means." As he had said so many times, that "objict" was the chance for the new American republic to "extend its dominion over a most interesting part of the opposite coast of the North American continent, and perhaps open communications of no small moment with Japan and the East Coast of Asia." As the United States edged toward an Atlantic war with Britain, Astoria's dominion was put at risk. Having gone in search of empire, Astor found the game far more hazardous than he had ever imagined.[1]

Astoria was born in a shadowy world of whispers and intrigues. Some of those dangers were plain as soon as Astor proposed his plans. Writing to De Witt Clinton in 1808, he cautioned the politician to say nothing about the design. Were the Nor'westers to get wind of the scheme they would "take measures to oppose with more effect." Just what measures Astor feared most were given voice when he met with Jefferson and several cabinet officers in the spring of that year. As Astor recalled later, he explained that if the venture proved successful, "the north-west company might by means of aid from there government Destroy us."[2]

Once the Pacific Fur Company became more than a paper dream, Astor's fears of a combined North West Company–British government assault increased. Each bit of London coffeehouse gossip and Montreal countinghouse rumor was enough to set alarm bells ringing. In April 1811, while his men were busy clearing ground along the Columbia, Astor got a "confidential letter" from London filled with just such tales. His correspondent told him that the North West Company had chartered the armed ship *Prince*. The vessel was to sail from England in mid-March bound for Montreal. Once there, she would load a cargo of trade goods and men, all destined for the Columbia. Here, Astor now wrote to his Russian friend Andrei Dashkov, was the blow he had "long Since expected." That it had come so soon surprised Astor and he urged Dashkov to keep the intelligence to himself.[3]

Although no ship of the North West Company was readied for such a mission that year, Astor's fears were not groundless. The Canadian drive to win a Pacific empire went back to Mackenzie and his series of petitions in the 1790s. The dream of the Columbian Enterprise never died, and Astor's moves now sparked it back to life. The North West Company had long sought a monopoly charter for the western trade. Astor's plans renewed that interest. The real push for royal patronage had begun in 1809. Increasingly aware of American ambitions beyond the Rockies, the company sent London a brief note warning about such Yankee "pretensions." Rehearsing the claims of discovery made by Cook, Vancouver, and Mackenzie, the Nor'westers urged royal officials to oppose any American presence either on the coast or along the Columbia. How Whitehall was to stop ships from Boston or traders from St. Louis was a tactical detail not yet worked out.[4]

That vague protest was easily overlooked by a government wholly focused on both domestic troubles and European controversies. No longer satisfied with polite notes to functionaries only dimly aware of North America, the Canadians formulated a strategy to defeat Astor and any potential American successors. By now the Montreal associates knew about plans for the *Tonquin*'s voyage and perhaps had inklings about efforts to recruit experienced voyageurs. Putting their thoughts to paper in January 1810, the Nor'westers decided they needed two things from London. The company had to have a twenty-one-year trade monopoly for those parts of the West not already claimed by the Hudson's Bay Company. Far more important, the East India Company had to relent and grant the Montreal traders a license to export furs directly to Canton. Without these concessions and the promise of official support, no campaign could be waged against Astor's forces. These requests were hardly new. Their origins were in the petitions of Mackenzie and the ideas of Peter Pond. What was different now was a sense of urgency born from the challenge posed by Astor.[5]

The men of the Beaver Club entrusted their case to Nathaniel Atcheson, the firm's London agent. Atcheson, who moved easily in Whitehall and Westminster corridors of power, also represented a powerful commercial interest group known as the Committee of British North American Merchants. Members of the committee included owners of fur trade supply houses in London as well as prominent Canadian traders. Because timing was crucial—the Nor'westers had to know about possible support from the crown no later than April—Atcheson acted quickly. In March 1810, soon after getting instructions from Montreal, he arranged a meeting between members of the Committee of British North American Merchants and Secretary of State for War and Colonies Lord Liverpool. Among those attending was Simon McGillivray, a partner in the supply firm of McTavish, Fraser. What Liverpool undoubtedly heard were the now familiar arguments urging official support for the Columbian Enterprise. The threat from Astor was discussed and Liverpool was given all available details concerning possible ways to thwart the Americans. But the secretary's mind was perhaps drawn more to the exploits of Wellington's army and the Peninsula Campaign in Spain. The American Northwest must have paled in comparison. And besides, relations with the Americans were tense enough. Why risk an incident over so remote a country? The meeting closed with no promises, hardly an outcome to cheer either Atcheson or his Canadian employers.[6]

A London agent like Atcheson knew that if one door closed, others might still be opened. He now turned his attention to the foreign secretary, Marquis Wellesley. Writing to Wellesley, Atcheson reported that the latest Atlantic mail packet carried news of two American expeditions bound for the Pacific coast. Their goal was reportedly a permanent settlement on the Columbia and occupation of the entire region. Here was a plain violation of the "rights of discovery." Atcheson maintained that such an invasion could not be halted unless the Canadian traders obtained prompt and direct government support. Carefully skirting the North West Company's financial interest in the affair, Atcheson emphasized the imperial consequences of a western fur trade dominated by Americans. The agent argued that the trade secured vital alliances with the Indians. And playing on ever present fears of a revived French empire, Atcheson raised the specter of a Louisiana in Napoleon's hands. All of British North America would then be in grave danger. Pressing his case, Atcheson asked for an immediate interview.[7]

Despite all the urgency in Atcheson's petition, Wellesley and other crown officers remained unmoved. At the end of June an increasingly frustrated Atcheson wrote again to Wellesley urging some action before winter set in. The agent's persistence finally paid off, although in typically bureaucratic fashion. On June 29 the foreign secretary gathered copies of all the North West Company correspondence and bundled them off to John Philip Morier, secretary to the British Legation in Washington. Morier was ordered to study the papers and then gather additional material "whenever an opportunity may present itself." At the very time when Astor was pushing his plans with all possible energy, the Nor'westers were stymied by a government bent on collecting information for yet another report.[8]

During the summer and fall of 1810 the North West Company pursued a strangely contradictory policy toward Astoria. On one hand the wintering partners meeting at Fort William in mid-July were still under the impression that negotiations with Astor for a joint venture remained alive. Writing to William McGillivray, the winterers recognized the danger from Astor and despaired at London's inability to act. Not knowing that the arrangements with Astor had fallen through, the wintering men urged McGillivray to proceed with the agreement. That same partners' gathering detailed David Thompson to the Columbia, not to race the Astorians but certainly to protect the firm's western interests. And as Thompson's actions made plain, the winterers were ever wary of Astor no matter what deals had been cut in Montreal or New York.[9]

The Canadians' other hand remained steadfast in opposition to Astor. Although Morier's early October report to Wellesley was filled with reasonably accurate intelligence about both the *Tonquin* and Hunt's overlanders, the crown seemed as uninterested as ever in blunting the American advance. In early November, Simon McGillivray collected Wellesley's and Atcheson's papers for one more presentation to Lord Liverpool. There had been no official reply to either the initial April petition or Atcheson's June letter. Nor had any high-ranking minister expressed even the slightest interest in the issue. With a bluntness not usually found in letters addressed to members of the cabinet, McGillivray told the secretary that the Americans were already occupying the entire West. Even now, effective opposition might be impossible. No longer could a civilian force, even acting with crown approval, carry the day against Astor.

Out of desperation, McGillivray called on Liverpool to dispatch a naval vessel to the Columbia. The Royal Navy could harry away the American interlopers and finally claim the Columbia country for Britain. Sounding much like his New York rival, McGillivray declared "the object to be one of great importance, for it may and probably will involve the ultimate right of Possession of the whole Northwest coast of America." Having lost its Atlantic colonial empire, England could now, by delaying, also lose a western domain. The Nor'westers were ready to act in concert with London, but they alone could not stop Astor. Now was the time for decisive action.[10]

Although this intense lobbying produced few immediate results, it did yield a plentiful crop of rumors. Little wonder Astor was convinced that a ship was bound for the Columbia. He might have been even more apprehensive had he known how relentless the Nor'westers would prove in pursuit of their Pacific dreams. Despite the lack of any glimmer of official recognition, the Canadians continued to pepper London with pleas for action against the Americans. In May 1811 the Montreal partners drafted another in the ceaseless round of petitions. As before, the requests were for formal incorporation and a twenty-one-year trade monopoly. Royal officials were reminded once more that what the Canadians were doing was "an object of great National Importance."[11] But the sense of urgency that had filled earlier requests was gone. Perhaps it was because by the summer of 1811, the same season that saw Astoria come to life as a busy trading post, the men of the North West Company had finally decided to act alone.

In mid-July 1811 the wintering partners met at the annual Fort William rendezvous. The results of David Thompson's Astorian reconnaissance would not come to hand for quite some time, but the winterers were determined to press the Columbian Enterprise. After a detailed discussion of several routes to the Northwest, the partners concluded that the more familiar Saskatchewan River path remained the most reliable. More important, the Nor'westers decided to send a large party to the Columbia. If these traders could not attack Astoria in the name of the crown, they could at least begin to whittle away at the Pacific Fur Company's business base. John George McTavish was given command of a brigade some sixty strong. Orders called for McTavish to travel from Rocky Mountain House to Spokane and then on to the lower Columbia. But the North West Company's strategy called for more than a face-to-face trade war. The partners voted to attempt a purchase of some Hudson's Bay Company stock valued at fifteen thousand pounds. Pursuit of the China trade remained an important goal, and the concern's London agent was instructed to redouble efforts to obtain a trade license from the East India Company.[12] The men of the North West Company were not about to let the Columbia country slip away without a fight.

John Astor once wrote that had Astoria come of age in an era of peace he could have easily withstood the Canadian assault.[13] But Astor and his venture would not have that luxury. For all its Atlantic origins, the War of 1812 changed the face of western politics and economics for the next three decades. When the Twelfth Congress of the United States met in November 1811, war between Britain and the American states appeared likely. President Madison and congressional leaders now faced what seemed intractable problems. Present prosperity and future economic growth demanded free access for American agricultural products in European markets. Locked in war with France, Britain insisted on seizing neutral vessels bound for French ports. British Orders-in-Council not only endangered the American economy but were seen as an affront to national honor. The practice of impressing American sailors into the Royal Navy was another source of friction. The crown's Indian agents in the Great Lakes engaged Tecumseh in talks aimed at halting the American occupation of the Ohio country. Negotiations with Augustus Foster, the new British ambassador in Washington, failed to resolve any of these disputes. By the time Congress assembled, the voices of the War Hawks were loud for a second fight with the old colonial master.[14]

Throughout the winter and spring of 1812 Madison and those like Henry Clay and John C. Calhoun who supported war moved to

prepare for the coming conflict. Meetings of congressional commit-
tees were filled with talk about militia-recruiting and naval-building
programs. Commercial sanctions dating back to Jefferson's Embargo policy had failed to change British behavior. Madison himself
held that a prompt invasion of Canada might both force that desired
change and add important territory to the American nation. Bills
proposing increases in the strength of military and naval forces were
everywhere. Raising customs duties and floating loans were suggestions widely discussed as means to pay for such a state of prepared-
ness.

All this bellicose talk did not escape Astor's attention. Writing to
his St. Louis correspondent, Astor reported, "Pepol Speek here of
war but I think and hope we shall have peace." Although the drift
toward war plainly worried him, Astor had more on his mind in the
late winter and early spring than international tensions. Sometime
in February he got the first reports about the loss of the *Tonquin*. At
the end of March he was telling Gratiot about the ship's tragic fate.
By the end of May Astor was clearly burdened by mounting concerns, both personal and international. The loss of the *Tonquin* and
the lack of any word from the *Beaver* since her October 1811 sailing
had made him, so he told Gallatin, "poor for the present." But it was
the ever louder drumbeats of war that now occupied more of his
attention. With all hope of reconciliation between Britain and the
United States gone, Astor must have realized that his business concerns, and most particularly the Pacific Fur Company, were in great
danger. Writing to Gallatin barely three weeks before the declaration of war, Astor informed the secretary that New York was "full of
Speculation and conjecture as to the measure to be next adopted by
government. Some say war with england others with france and
england while some belive that all restrictions on commerce will be
taking off and that our merchant vessels will be permitted to arm."
Astor suggested that allowing cargo ships to be heavily armed would
serve national interests short of war.[15]

John Astor always liked to imagine that through personal influence he could control events on a national and even an international

scale. Friendships with men like Gallatin and Thomas Hart Benton did serve him well during a long and complex career. But events now were moving beyond the power of personal influence. Seeing no change in British policy, Madison delivered to Congress on June 1 a recommendation for war. Astor could only send a plaintive note to Gratiot begging for any news from the Northwest in general and Hunt in particular.[16] On June 18 Astor was simply a powerless bystander as Congress voted to declare war on Great Britain. The following day, still unaware of the formal beginning of hostilities, he decided to go to Washington. Just what Astor hoped to accomplish remains unclear, but perhaps he thought it better to be closer to the action. On the road between Baltimore and Washington Astor heard the dreaded news. It is plain that his first concern was for a shipment of goods in the Great Lakes, and Astor did what he could to warn his agents about the war before Canadian authorities could impound the cargo.[17]

By June 27 Astor was back in New York trying to cope with a war now nine days old. Putting the best face on what he knew were going to be troubled days, he contended, "Pepol here are more reasonable about the war measure than what I expected and altho many Disapprove of the manner and time it was Declared all agree that we have plenty of cause." Those brave words directed to Gallatin hardly concealed Astor's growing concern about the future of his entire Pacific venture. He admitted a year later, "As soon as war was declared I considered Columbia in danger if not lost." Determined to sustain Astoria—"wishing to save it as I wished to save my life"— Astor began to develop a complex set of schemes to preserve his cherished venture.[18]

Uppermost in his mind was the need to alert Hunt and the other Astoria partners about the war. Astor was certain the conflict would soon reach the Columbia, either by the North West Company's overland parties or by the guns of the Royal Navy. Thinking that the *Beaver* might soon be in Canton, he wrote a hurried note to Captain Sowle ordering him to sail for the river post at once. The *Beaver* was to provide Hunt whatever protection might be possible. As things fell out, Sowle and his ship did not reach Canton until the end of January 1813. The captain found Astor's letter but decided that a voyage to the Northwest coast might be too risky. The *Beaver* sat out the war, letting the Astorians fend for themselves.[19]

Astor was not about to rely on one letter or a single uncertain ship to secure Astoria in the coming storm. Whereas Boston merchants in the maritime fur trade eventually chartered the armed brig *Tamaahamaah* to protect their vessels, Astor decided on something far more dramatic and dangerous. Sometime in July 1812 he met with William J. Pigot and Richard Ebbets, two of his most trusted ship captains. What Astor and his skippers plotted proved to be the Pacific Fur Company's most daring exploit. Pigot and Ebbets were sent undercover to London, there to meet with Astor's principal English representative, Thomas H. Wilson. Astor's men carried drafts for twelve thousand pounds to buy a ship and cargo flying a neutral flag and bound for the Columbia. No rescue mission could be mounted from New York. Astor was gambling that his enterprise could be saved under the very noses of those intent on bringing it to ruin. What Astor set in motion was an extraordinary intrigue whose results would not be known for nearly two years.[20]

Astor saw the war as a threat to the very survival of his western empire. The Nor'westers viewed the conflict in quite a different light. War between the United States and Britain might force London to recognize the importance of the Columbia country. New York's curse became Montreal's oppportunity. On July 18, 1812, while the wintering partners were at the annual Fort William gathering, an express canoe brought news of the conflict. Colonel William McKay had a copy of Madison's proclamation, a document now eagerly read in the company's great hall. The wintering partners immediately set upon a forceful course of action. Donald McTavish and John McDonald of Garth were directed to sail for London at once. Their mission was to gain the protection of the Royal Navy for the company ship *Isaac Todd*. That vessel's destination was Astoria. At the same time John Stuart was ordered to hurry west with news of the war. His party would join that of John George McTavish. The company's grand strategy was for their land parties to rendezvous at Astoria with Royal Navy ships and the *Isaac Todd*. In the face of such overwhelming odds, the American post was sure to fall.[21]

By late summer 1812 Canadian plans for the conquest of Astoria were well under way. On August 18 Donald McTavish and John McDonald of Garth took passage on the *Isaac Todd* from Montreal to London in a Royal Navy convoy. McTavish carried with him a letter to agent Nathaniel Atcheson explaining all the elements in the Nor'westers' plan. "The progress already made by the American Party who have established themselves in the River rendered this determination on our part absolutely necessary for the defence of our only remaining Beaver Country and we know from dear bought experience the impossibility of contending from *this* side of the mountains with people who get their goods from so short a distance as the mouth of the Columbia is to the mountains." With the coming of war the Canadians insisted they had every reason "to expect on this occasion that government will come forward in a decided manner to let the World understand who are the proprietors of the country." Atcheson was instructed to press for a naval escort for the *Isaac Todd*. If the *Todd* proved unreliable for a Pacific voyage, Atcheson was to charter another ship, "of respectable strength" and carrying a letter of marque.[22] After years of petitions and talks the North West Company finally seemed ready to do battle with Astor.

* * *

For the next eight months—from September 1812 through April 1813—Astoria's future depended on decisions and events far from the Columbia. Hurried meetings, last-minute agreements, and clever deceptions in London, New York, and Washington held sway over Astoria's empire. In late September Astor's secret agents Pigot and Ebbets reached Britain. Landing along the Devonshire coast, they quickly made their way to London. Registration at the Alien Office evidently proved no difficulty, and the two were soon at the offices of Astor's commercial agent. Pigot and Ebbets held two meetings with Thomas H. Wilson, explaining Astor's plan. Wilson did not think it would be possible for any American ship to obtain a license for a voyage out of England and he rather doubted that a journey under neutral colors was possible either. However, he did suggest something more covert and certainly more dangerous. Wilson proposed hiring a fast ship with British registry and an English captain. Astor's agents could sail along in lesser capacities as supercargo and clerk. Wilson was certain that the crown would permit such a Pacific voyage if no mention was made of a port of call on the Columbia River. "It strikes us very forceably," Pigot explained to Astor, "that the voyage can be made as far as Canton much safer in a British vessel than any other particularly as she will have convoy as far as the coast of Brazil."[23]

Throughout the fall and winter of 1812–13 Astor's operatives moved quietly to arrange their secret voyage. The ship they set upon was the *Forester*, French built and with a reputation as a fast sailer. As important as her speed was her complement of eighteen guns. Pigot and Ebbets hired John Jennings as captain, making sure he understood their role in directing the voyage. Clearance papers for any ship, especially in wartime, could be an expensive proposition. Astor had provided twelve thousand pounds to finance the entire undertaking. Paying for the ship, cargo, crew, and master soon depleted those funds. By early February 1813 Pigot needed an additional three to four thousand pounds to cover expenses. Alluding to customhouse "fees," he explained that "the heavy expenses of the Port of London" put a real strain on available funds. War or not, money was found and bills were paid. The *Forester*'s lading and the citizenship of her crew remain something of a mystery. Since the ship's ostensible destination was Canton, a cargo hold filled with weapons for the defense of Astoria would have raised the eyebrows of even the most compliant customs officers. As the *Forester* ended up trading at Russian posts along the California and Alaska coasts, her cargo may have been trade goods of the sort commonly carried by ships in the maritime fur trade. Little is known about the *Forester*'s crew. Some of her sailors may have been Americans trapped in England by the war. Whatever the nationalities and loyalties of those before the mast, the men would prove an unruly and unpredictable lot.[24]

Astor's men were not the only ones in London planning a journey to the Columbia. The North West Company's hopes were pinned on the crown's prompt acceptance of the *Isaac Todd* plan. The *Todd* needed convoy protection across the Atlantic and armed escort to Astoria. In late fall 1812, once the ship had reached England, Nathaniel Atcheson initiated a vigorous campaign to win that support. At the end of September he sent the new foreign secretary, Viscount Castlereagh, a full set of North West Company correspondence, asking that the secretary move quickly on the firm's requests. Uncertain what reception the project would get, Atcheson also wrote the King-in-Council. After summarizing past efforts, the agent made it plain that war and the presence of the Americans on the Columbia called for swift action. Previous requests for a monopoly charter had been resisted by the crown's lawyers. The Nor'westers were willing to forgo the monopoly if the government would lend its protection to the *Isaac Todd*. The company's ship was currently loading arms and ammunition at Portsmouth in preparation for the Pacific voyage. The King-in-Council was asked to provide the necessary license for the export of such weapons.[25]

What followed was a flurry of correspondence between company men and various royal officials. All knew that Atlantic convoys would depart in March. If the Canadian plan to conquer Astoria was to have any hope of success, the *Isaac Todd* had to be in those March sailings. Atcheson now busied himself sending documents to Lord Bathurst, the influential president of the Board of Trade. At the same time he pressured Henry Goulburn, undersecretary for war and the colonies, to get a decision on the plan from Bathurst. When no decision seemed forthcoming, the Canadians sent another lengthy memorial to Bathurst. In a remarkably prescient observation, Atcheson predicted, "The territorial possession of the Countries bordering on the Columbia River, and finally the whole Northwest coast of the Continent of America, will depend upon the measures to be adopted by His Majesty's government on the present occasion." With Donald McTavish now in London, Atcheson pleaded with Bathurst for an immediate interview.[26]

By the end of November, with no sign that either Castlereagh or Bathurst was interested in the venture, Atcheson wrote a desperate note to Goulburn. The *Isaac Todd* was now loaded and plans for the spring convoys were well along. The Nor'westers had to know if their ship could find her place in the sailing schedule. And more important, would the Admiralty cut orders for an armed escort to sail with the *Todd* against Astoria? It may have been the influence of prominent merchants like Edward Ellice and Simon McGillivray that finally opened the Board of Trade's doors at Whitehall. At the end of December representatives of the North West Company, probably Atcheson, McTavish, and McGillivray, met with Bathurst. At the gathering Bathurst agreed to provide the protection of the Royal Navy across the Atlantic and on to the Columbia. One other issue also got an airing. From the 1790s the Canadians had been alarmed by Russian commercial expansion along the Northwest coast. Just how much the Canadians knew about Astor's dealings with the Russian-American Company is not clear, but the presence of the Russians in the region complicated matters. And the complications were doubled by the role of the Russians as mediators in the war. How should British forces, both official and private, deal with Russian traders along the coast? Bathurst agreed to make "some arrangement" with the Russian ambassador so that the Canadians could be "introduced to each other on a footing of reciprocal friendship, and good offices."[27]

Throughout February and into March 1813 preparations for the *Isaac Todd*'s voyage moved ahead quickly. The Admiralty drafted orders marked "Most Secret" for Captain James Hillyar and the HMS *Phoebe*. Hillyar was commanded to sail in convoy with the *Todd* across the Atlantic and around Cape Horn and to make a fast passage to the Columbia. Once on the Northwest coast, the flotilla would rendezvous with armed traders sent overland from Fort William. Hillyar's mission was just what Astor had always feared. "The principal object of the Service on which you [Hillyar] are employed is to protect and render every assistance in your power to the British traders from Canada and to destroy and if possible totally annihilate any settlements which the Americans may have formed on the Columbia River." Knowing that American trading ships on the coast might be easy prey, Hillyar was directed to pursue those targets as well.[28]

At the end of February, as both the *Phoebe* and the *Todd* prepared for sea, John McDonald of Garth and Donald McTavish traveled with Edward Ellice and Simon McGillivray to Portsmouth. At the last moment two unexpected events in port nearly scuttled the entire enterprise. When the North West Company's officials had come to England they had brought along a dozen voyageurs and four clerks. Bored by endless weeks of shore life, the French-Canadian engagés and Scots clerks spent time in taverns and alehouses. One evening, as Donald McTavish and his friends were at a Portsmouth hotel, a waiter approached their table with a message requesting McTavish and McDonald of Garth visit some of the Canadians. Worrying that the voyageurs had "made a little free with wine and women," McTavish hurried to the wharf. Finding the men quite drunk, McTavish hustled them into a ship's boat and headed for the *Isaac Todd*. The small boat had not gotten far when it was intercepted and boarded by a press gang intent on adding more Jack-tars to the Royal Navy. Despite vigorous protests from McTavish, the voyageurs and all clerks save one were bundled off to a recruiting barge. The next day, thanks to personal influence wielded by Edward Ellice, the unfortunate Canadians were set free.[29]

Troubles with rowdy Canadians and overzealous press gangs masked a more serious difficulty. The admiralty was intent on making this voyage a secret undertaking. Although the American navy was in pitiful straits and there was no evidence of an armed American presence in the Pacific, the danger from Yankee privateers was quite real. Despite strenuous efforts, news of the sailings became common knowledge in Portsmouth. Admiralty officials were furious. Had they known that Astor's agents were already in Portsmouth they would have been even more alarmed. Despite all this confusion, it would have paid Captain Hillyar and the Canadians to look closely at the ships riding in the harbor. One of those was the

Forester. William Pigot was on board as her supercargo while Richard Ebbets served as clerk. It is very likely that when the *Phoebe* and the *Isaac Todd* put to sea on March 25, the convoy included the *Forester*. Such would have been only the latest in the twists and turns marking the course of Astoria's empire.[30]

As Nor'westers and Astor's men waged their shadow war in London and Portsmouth, Astor himself pursued strategies in New York and Washington. Alexander Ross once charged that his employer did little to save Astoria. Had the trader seen Astor at work throughout 1813 he might have written otherwise. Astor had long been sure that it would take more than one plan to save his enterprise on the Columbia River. Recent reverses in the war, including the surrender of an American army at Detroit and a stunning defeat at the Battle of Queenston Heights, had convinced Astor that all his commercial ventures were at risk. With the Great Lakes in British hands and many Indians on the upper Mississippi and upper Missouri listening to Canadian advice, the Republic's western hopes seemed almost gone. At the end of December 1812 a worried Astor begged Gratiot for "any news from the upper Missouri." He freely admitted to being "more and more anxious for our friend Hunt." Writing years later to Thomas Hart Benton, Astor maintained that he had been "promised by the administration the protection of government and in fact more." Now, with so much at stake, Astor decided to press Washington to make good on those promises.[31]

Albert Gallatin had become Astor's most reliable and trusted friend in the government. His knowledge of finance and his interest in the western country made him the perfect ally. Sometime toward the end of 1812 Astor became convinced that the best way to save the Columbia post was to have an American naval vessel patrol along the Northwest coast. That ship might even go to the coast in convoy with a merchantman chartered by Astor. The problem was to persuade an already overburdened, undermanned navy to detach a ship for Pacific duty when the Atlantic and Great Lakes stations were pleading for guns and crews. Because Astor did not count Secretary of the Navy William Jones as a personal friend, he turned to Gallatin for a proper introduction. In early January 1813 Gallatin wrote Jones a brief note recommending Astor to the secretary's attention. "He will converse with you," explained Gallatin, "on the subject of his settlement at the mouth of the Columbia." Although Gallatin admitted that Astor's enterprise had been "heretofore unsupported by government," he felt certain that in the current circumstances the entire undertaking "may at this time claim attention and will probably be taken into consideration after you arrive here."[32]

Despite that carefully placed letter, it was not the Navy Department that Astor called on when he visited Washington at the end of January 1813. Instead, he determined to talk with Secretary of State James Monroe. Perhaps Gallatin suggested that Monroe had more influence than the newly appointed Jones. By now Astor had copies of correspondence from Astoria, including letters written by Duncan McDougall and David Thompson. More relevant to his Washington mission, there was a letter from London dated November 19, 1812. Written by an unidentified correspondent—perhaps Thomas H. Wilson or William Pigot—the letter detailed preparations for the *Isaac Todd*'s voyage and attempts by the North West Company to secure royal support. As of November, Astor's London agents believed that no agreement between the company and the crown had been reached, but the observer felt certain the Canadians would move against the Columbia with or without London's aid. Armed with this information, Astor was convinced that the Pacific Fur Company promised both personal profit and national power if only it could survive the war.

No notes from the Astor-Monroe meeting survive, but the discussion was summarized in a detailed letter Astor wrote the secretary of state shortly after the conference. Unsure just how much Monroe knew about the western country, the political significance of the fur trade, and the dangers posed by the North West Company, Astor patiently outlined the importance of the region and the Canadian threat to American interests. He confidently told Monroe that the North West Company was sure to gain some official help in the contest for the Columbian country. But Astor was there to do more

than educate a cabinet officer. He wanted to test government resolve. Would the Madison administration fulfill promises Astor was
convinced were made years before? "In this situation," as he deli-
cately put it, "it becomes very interesting to know some what of the
views of our government on this subject and whether the United
States have or will assert any claim to or any part of that country and
whether it will be deemed expedient for government to take possession of a country which will aford wealth and comfort to many and
to protect the establishment which has been made." All this polite
diplomatic language—written no doubt by one of Astor's employees—was just an opening to what the entrepreneur had in mind.
Astor suggested that a naval force with some forty or fifty troops be
sent to the Columbia. While the ship cruised coastal waters, the
soldiers could either occupy Astoria or build their own post nearby.
Astor now asked Monroe to bring all this to the president's attention.
"I am sure," he concluded, "the government will readily see the
importance of having possession and command of a River so extensive as the Columbia as well as the impression which such an enterprise would make in favor of the American nation."[33]

Few other businessmen in the early Republic had so thoroughly
mastered the art of personal politics as had John Astor. His politics
were not so much a matter of party and ideology as friendship and
influence. Toys for the Gallatin children, tea and china porcelain for
politicians' wives, and a dozen other favors were meant not as bribes
but as gifts to cement personal relationships. Having presented his
case to Monroe, Astor turned again to Gallatin. Astor was evidently
uncertain that the president would get the full story from the Department of State. Gallatin could make sure that all the proper eyes
and ears understood Astor's request. As Astor explained, "It now
appears quite necessary for me to act and my further opperation
must be guided more or less by the reply I may recieve from Mr.
Monroe." In mid-February, with no word from Monroe, Astor again
approached Gallatin. News from London via private sources indi-
cated that the *Isaac Todd* would sail sometime in the spring. Just as
the Canadians had so often pleaded for quick action, now Astor

urged Gallatin to press for some decision. And Gallatin did just that. At the bottom of Astor's letter, in Gallatin's crabbed scrawl, was a revealing notation. "Suppose a frigate to be sent to cruise off Canton or vicinity, to go by way of mouth of Columbia river and land there a company of marines, so as to embrace this opportunity of taking possession—submitted by A.G. to President."[34]

Astoria did not bulk large in the mind of a president increasingly preoccupied with a war growing more unpopular. Madison and others in his administration must have found it difficult to think seriously about the West at a time when the tide seemed to be running against American survival. Astor did not get his speedy reply. Knowing that the Canadians would soon be at sea, he turned his attention to a private voyage to the Columbia. Astor had always planned to send several ships each year to the Pacific. These vessels would ply the sea otter trade routes, calling at Astoria, the Russian settlements, and Canton before returning to New York. But sailing schedules were quickly rendered obsolete by war. The *Lark*, commanded by Captain Samuel H. Northrop, had been slated to sail in September 1812 but the threat of capture by the Royal Navy kept her in port. Now, in the spring of 1813, Astor desperately needed to put a ship to sea. The problem was to elude both British blockaders and American privateers. To do this Astor turned to Gallatin and the Russian diplomat Andrei Dashkov. As Astor explained in an oblique way to Gallatin, Dashkov was preparing a ship and cargo for the Northwest coast and the New Yorker planned to put a "friend" on board. Four days after writing to Gallatin, Astor decided that the secretary needed to know the entire *Lark* plot. Describing Dashkov's decision to send a vessel to the Northwest coast as a "circumstance of deep interest," Astor explained that he would provide the ship and crew, whereas the Russian diplomat would make sure the *Lark* had Russian sailing papers. Astor wanted Gallatin to obtain an American passport for the *Lark* should she encounter Yankee privateers. Thus the ship could pass both British and American barriers.[35] Having slipped past the Royal Navy Atlantic blockade, Captain Northrop was to make his way as quickly as possible to Astoria. Once there, he was directed to reinforce the post against attack and, if necessary, move both goods and furs to safety at New Archangel.[36]

When the *Lark* sailed on March 6 she carried not only Russian documents and an American passport but also an important letter from Astor to Wilson Price Hunt. In the spring of 1813 Astor knew little about Hunt's dealings, assuming only that by now he was in command at Astoria. Uppermost in Astor's mind was the need to prepare Astoria for any British assault, whether by land or by sea. "Were I on the spot," wrote a bellicose Astor, "and had management of Affairs, I would defy them all." But this saber rattling was tempered by an almost resigned observation that "everything depends on you and your friends about you." Irving may have dressed up the words to have Astor say that the loss of Astoria would be "like a dagger to my heart," but there is little doubt that Astor was moving heaven and earth to save what he once called "my darling project."[37]

Once the *Lark* put to sea, Astor turned his attention to Washington affairs. In February he admitted to Gallatin that just a few words from Monroe would "put me out of suspense." Writing a month later he began to betray clear signs of irritation. "I must confess," he bristled, "that I feel a disappointment in not having seen any reply to my letter to Mr. Monroe and did expect something by which to Shape my course relative to the Business but not even a hint or word." Astor by now knew most of the details about the sailing of the *Isaac Todd* and the *Phoebe*. In the face of this real threat to an American empire in the West, Astor saw a government mired in petty bickering and a war gone sour. Thinking that Monroe had not fully informed Madison about the Columbia country, Astor wrote again to the secretary of state in late March. He carefully rehearsed the course of events and pointed out their larger significance. Astor could on occasion exercise a fierce brand of sarcasm. Now he leveled a blast at the unsuspecting Monroe. "Altho my former Letter to you on this subject Seems to have escaped Notics or not to have merited a reply, I still think It is my Duty to mak this communication which I request you will have the goodness to make Known to the President." Despite the edge on Astor's words, there is no evidence that the secretary passed western news to an already harassed Madison.[38]

When the most recent London intelligence reached Astor at the end of March he may have wished he had used a sledgehammer on Monroe rather than a sharp needle. John Dorr, a prominent Boston merchant, had long served Astor as an agent for gathering commercial news from both New England and across the Atlantic. Despite the war, Dorr maintained reliable contacts in London. On March 30 Dorr sent Astor a full report on the North West Company's dealings in England. Although Dorr did not know the convoy's precise sailing date, he was certain the *Todd* had been ready at Portsmouth since January. Armed with both heavy guns and a letter of marque, the ship was a formidable threat. Dorr seconded Astor's contention that the best way to defeat the British was by sending a naval vessel to the Pacific. The Bostonian suggested the *Argus* (later the USS *Wasp*), a vessel then being readied for sea duty. Dorr was convinced that quick action by the American navy could "strangle" the Nor'westers and "save many questions after peace."[39]

Dorr's information and strong views clearly had a powerful effect on Astor. With the *Lark* at sea and responses from Monroe nowhere in sight, perhaps a direct appeal to the Navy Department might bear fruit. In early April someone in Astor's employ prepared a confidential report summarizing Dorr's intelligence and proposing direct naval action. The best maritime information had it that the *Todd* was a "very dull sailer." If an American ship ordered to the Columbia left from the East Coast in the spring, that ship might well reach Astoria ahead of any British expedition. As the memorandum argued, such an American ship not only could save Astoria but also could protect trading vessels working in the maritime fur trade.[40] Astor's course was now set. He would lobby Secretary Jones, using all available resources to have the navy save Astoria.

* * *

With all these eastern intrigues it is easy to lose track of Astoria and the coming of the war to the Columbia. The Astorians learned about the war some seven months after its declaration, but once the news came to the river, events moved in sudden and unpredictable ways. Sometime in late December 1812, Donald Mackenzie had decided to leave his wintering post on the Clearwater River near the border of present-day Washington and Idaho. A trip to Fort Spokane to visit his fellow Astorian John Clarke might break the boredom of the season. The traders evidently looked forward to celebrating Christmas and New Year's in good company. Festivities and good cheer were abruptly halted at the end of the month when Nor'wester John George McTavish and his overlanders pulled into Spokane. McTavish had just been told about the war by John Stuart. The Canadians had more than word of mouth to verify the hostilities. McTavish had in his baggage a copy of Madison's Declaration of War. That document was quickly handed around to stony-faced Astorians. Astor's Canadian employees had not been unaware of the threat of war. Some of those who had come out on the *Tonquin* had discussed the issue and their future both among themselves and with the British diplomat Francis James Jackson. But now, whatever their past worries, war was upon them. What really stunned Mackenzie and Clarke was news about the *Isaac Todd* and plans for a seaborne assault on Astoria. McTavish insisted that the British flotilla would be in the river by March or April. He confidently expected to see those ships when he arrived at Astoria come spring. And McTavish boasted that the Nor'westers had plenty of trade goods to wage economic war until Astoria fell. Shocked at this unexpected turn of events and disconcerted by McTavish's bold predictions of imminent victory, Mackenzie hurried back to his Clearwater post, cached goods, and prepared to carry the bad tidings of the season to Astoria.[41]

New Year's at Astoria had always been a rolicking time filled with eating, drinking, and sport. The celebration ringing in 1813 was no exception. Liquor and food abounded, and four days after the party there were still men not quite up to the daily work routine.[42] All that gaiety evaporated when Mackenzie arrived on the evening of January 16. The trader carried a copy of the Declaration of War, something read by McDougall and his clerks with great alarm. News of war between Britain and the American states changed everything at Astoria. For reasons that are not now clear McDougall recorded little about those crucial January days in his official journal. Gabriel Franchère was at the post, but even his account is thin and unrewarding. Alexander Ross, then at Okanogan, evidently based his comments on later correspondence with Donald Mackenzie. Although sources are skimpy, it seems that the senior partners— McDougall and Mackenzie—decided almost at once to abandon Astoria. They would argue later that Astoria, confronted by invasions from both land and sea, was undefendable. The abandonment plan called for traders at interior posts to rendezvous at Astoria in early spring. Once the entire company was present, perhaps sometime in July, all would make their way overland to St. Louis. McDougall and Mackenzie plainly believed that British naval forces were just two or three months away. They were also convinced that article sixteen of the Pacific Fur Company agreement gave them the power to dissolve the concern if within five years from 1810 the enterprise proved unprofitable.[43]

Once the decision to abandon the post was made, McDougall moved quickly to implement his policy. Franchère and the other clerks began a thorough inventory of post goods and provisions. Though that survey revealed foodstuffs ranging from brandy and gin to flour and rice, the quantities were not great. Mackenzie had brought twenty-two employees with him. Should the rest of the interior parties arrive in the next month, the post would be hard pressed to feed them. Trade goods were also in short supply. The storehouse held blankets, knives, pots, and cotton fabrics but not in sufficient amounts to carry on a profitable commerce in the coming season. Astoria's shelves had not been restocked since the *Beaver* had docked in May 1812. With war now declared, there seemed little hope of fresh supplies. The inventory report prompted immediate action. All trade with native neighbors, except for provisions, was suspended. Flour and ammunition were strictly rationed. To ease the burden on Astoria's larder, McDougall scheduled the Willamette trading party for an early departure. Most important, Donald Mackenzie made ready to travel east to Spokane and Okanogan with letters for John Clarke and David Stuart.[44] Unaware of their employer's struggles to save the enterprise, Astor's men looked to the spring and taking leave of the Columbia.

Delay and misfortune were Astoria's middle names. From their earliest beginnings, Astor's plans were buffeted by the winds of rumor, doubt, and confusion. Missed cues and bad timing snapped at every Astorian's heels. Mackenzie should have left the Columbia in February to notify Clarke and Stuart about abandonment. Instead, for unspecified reasons, he lingered at the fort until mid-March. Wet, cold February weather in the Columbia country did make for unpleasant travel, but the delay remains hard to explain. Mackenzie's express dallied at Astoria, guaranteeing delays that would make a summer departure almost impossible.[45] Had the Astorians known that the *Isaac Todd* had sailed from England only the week before, decisions might have been quite different.

* * *

It was wartime finance, not the troubles of western empire, that brought Astor to Philadelphia in early April 1813. A Congress once enthusiastic for war had failed to provide adequate funds for the struggle. Gallatin was forced to borrow massive sums to pay the bills of a coming summer campaign. Military reversals and a low interest rate drove loan subscribers away when the Treasury attempted to raise some sixteen million dollars. As Astor pointed out, the government's offer of 6 percent interest was hardly attractive. He was willing to loan two and a half million dollars but at a rate of 7.5 percent.[46]

These negotiations with Gallatin provided a way to renew the attempt at official backing for Astoria. While waiting in Philadelphia for Gallatin to arrive, Astor drafted an important letter to the State Department. He had just received from the department a note dated March 31. Although no copy of it has been found and its author remains unknown, Astor reported that the communication dealt with his "once Darling objict the Settlement at Columbia."

Whatever the news from Washington, Astor now believed he had assurances of some unspecified federal action to save Astoria. Now all that seemed to be required was to hurry that action. As he had so often argued, "If a sloop of war was now sent I belive we should be completely triumphant in that quarter of the world." Thinking that the USS *Hornet* might be a faster sailer than the USS *Wasp*, Astor suggested that vessel as a good candidate for Pacific duty. In previous correspondence he had carefully avoided any mention of the covert *Forester* project. Believing the administration was on the edge of authorizing a naval force bound for Astoria, he revealed some details about the Pigot-Ebbets mission. The message was plain. He had done his part to protect a valuable American asset. Now it was Washington's turn. "No Sacrefise," Astor insisted, "would be considered to great if government will only act quickly."[47]

The following day, April 5, Astor and Gallatin had their Philadelphia meeting. Although most of their talk focused on treasury loans and interest rates, the West was not neglected. The men agreed that speedy action was required for Astoria to be defended. One of the ships suggested as a possible choice for the assignment was the frigate USS *John Adams*. But the lighter USS *Hornet* could probably outsail the heavier *Adams*. On the other hand, the *Adams* was apparently available on shorter notice. Buoyed by the State Department's note and his discussions with Gallatin, Astor decided to begin lobbying Navy Secretary Jones at once.[48]

When William Jones had become the secretary of the navy in 1813, he had admitted that departmental affairs were in chaos. Writing later to Madison, he argued, "A radical change of system can alone remedy the evils."[49] But in the spring of 1813 such reform-minded housecleaning was far away. Astor knew that negotiating with the Navy Office would require both diplomatic skill and dogged perseverance. Astoria's cause needed someone to camp on Jones's doorstep. For that duty Astor turned to his son-in-law, Adrian Bentzon. Both Astor and Bentzon realized that the usual turmoil in naval affairs was made greater by feverish efforts to prepare ships and crews for the crucial Great Lakes campaigns. Despite what Bentzon blandly characterized as the "multiplied affairs" of the navy, Astor's agent appeared at Jones's office early on the morning of April 19. Nearly overwhelmed by a sea of paperwork, Jones probably did not welcome yet another interruption, especially on so unimportant a subject.

Whether a willing listener or not, the secretary became a captive audience as Bentzon launched into a lengthy discussion about the significance of the western country, the *Forester*'s secret mission, and Astor's willingness to arrange a merchant ship and cargo to sail in convoy with any American naval vessel. Although surviving naval records are silent on the matter, it is plain from correspondence between Jones, Bentzon, and Astor that sometime in April a decision was made to send a ship to the Columbia. That ship, the *Adams*, was commanded by Captain William M. Crane. Bentzon must have learned about the decision during his meeting with Jones, since he concluded the conversation by offering Astor's advice on what course of action should be pursued once the *Adams* reached her destination. The ship ought to carry twenty or thirty regulars and perhaps a light fieldpiece or two. Command of the landing party might best go to "some young officer who understands something of the art of an engineer." Bentzon knew how to push without being pushy. Later in the afternoon he sent Jones a detailed statement outlining the morning meeting and apologizing for his "importunate behavior" in pressing for swift action.[50]

Bentzon's was a virtuoso performance. Now there was every reason to believe that sometime during the summer the USS *John Adams* would escort a ship of Astor's on the long journey to the Columbia. Despite all his careful planning and public confidence, Astor really knew very little about the current state of the Pacific Fur Company. His information from London was fresher and more reliable. Until mid-June Astor was chasing black cats in a dark room. Some of that darkness lifted when letters carried by Robert Stuart's eastbound overlanders reached New York. Stuart and his companions had left Astoria in June 1812 and finally reached St. Louis at the end of April 1813. Their bundle of correspondence, including a letter from

Wilson Price Hunt, was nearly a year old. But Astor happily told Gallatin, "Everything has succeeded to our wishes thus far." It was only the cursed war that threatened "prospects of an extensive and beneficial trade." When Stuart himself reached New York on June 23, Astor was even more enthusiastic. Understating what seemed obvious, he told John Dorr that Stuart's account was "satisfactory."[51]

Astoria's future was forever held hostage to events and policies far beyond Astor's control. So it was in the spring and summer of 1813. In May Astor was certain that the *Adams* would soon carry sailing orders for the Pacific. But he had not counted on the needs of the navy in the Great Lakes. Oliver Hazard Perry's fleet in Lake Erie cried for sailors and officers. In the spring Commodore Isaac Chauncey required reinforcements for action on Lake Ontario. Although the *Adams* could not be used on the lakes, her captain and crew were available for transfer. At the end of June Secretary Jones gave Astor the bad news. Captain Crane and his men were heading for Lake Ontario. The *Adams* would not plough Pacific waters this season. Astor's response was polite but disappointed. "I have to thank you for the confidence which you were disposed to place in me." Robert Stuart had assured Astor that the Columbia post could be secured by twenty-five or thirty men against attackers ten times that number. And for want of one ship and crew, an empire appeared lost. Ever unwilling to let the prize slip from his grasp, Astor now proposed that he and the government jointly charter a "very fast sailing vessel" carrying a small troop contingent. Two ships currently available might suit the mission. One was the *Enterprise*, a ship that had been idle since her important 1809–12 voyage for Astor in the China trade. The second was a new, unnamed vessel built at Henry Eckford's shipyard to specifications from Astor's friend Captain John Whetten. Astor reported that this ship had the lines of a fast sailer and could be purchased for a mere fifteen thousand dollars. More important, she could be made ready for sea in five days. Supplies gathered for the *Adams* could be transferred to either ship once a decision was made. As always, Astor pleaded for a quick response.[52]

With the sailing season slipping away, Astor struggled to patch together some makeshift maritime expedition. The notion that Washington might charter the *Enterprise* or buy outright the new vessel seemed the only game in town. And Astor played it the best he could. On July 7 he wrote another letter to Jones. Captain John Ebbets, master of the *Enterprise*, had looked at the new ship on the ways at Eckford's yard. He was convinced that if she set sail before August 15 there might still be some chance of arriving at Astoria before the *Isaac Todd*. In his most compelling argument yet about the imperial meaning of Astoria, Astor portrayed the post on the Columbia River as "of great National Importancs in as much as it is not only the means of a wide and extensive trade on the coast but also a trade of grate value in the interior but one which will in a very few years give us a complete control over all the Indians on this side of the Mississippi and Mesure Rivers." Drawing on Robert Stuart's recent transcontinental journey, Astor concluded, "We know now from experience that by establishing a few posts as we intend to do on this siade the Rocky Mountains we can open a communication with the Pacific Ocean and connect and combine the trade of the interior with that on the coast to great extent and value." To the secretary, Astor appeared unfailingly optimistic, always ready with another variation on the theme of saving the Columbia country. But in a private letter to John Dorr there appeared a more subdued, pessimistic Astor. He confided to the Boston merchant that war would probably "ruin if not destroy us in that quarter." Angry at endless delays and unexpected reversals, he bitterly charged, "Our government ought to have afforded us some aid, but nothing has been done and nothing is to be expected."[53]

Despite that gloomy assessment, Astor could still tell Gallatin, "I have always some hopes." Those hopes freshened on July 16 when the latest news from London arrived. An unnamed correspondent reported that the *Phoebe* and the *Isaac Todd* had sailed under the cloak of "great secressy." Because the convoy moved slowly, there was plenty of reason to think that the British might not reach the Columbia until December. And if the ships laid over in Hawaii, they might not make Astoria until the spring of 1814. There was yet time to save the American presence. In a quick note to Jones, Astor insisted, "If the President as also yourself were well informed as to the importance of our having Columbia River some effort would be made to save it which I think can yet be Done." What Astor wanted now was a personal interview with the navy secretary. Perhaps then Jones could be persuaded to find a captain and crew for the USS *Constitution* riding at anchor in the Boston harbor.[54]

It was a desperate John Astor who traveled to Washington in late July. He must have known that this would be his last chance to gain federal aid for the Pacific Fur Company. If only the president could grasp the wider import of the western country, surely then there would be action. At the same time Astor recognized what his critics whispered. He sought, so they charged, official protection and status for a private venture. Although there is no firm evidence that Astor met with Madison, the president did at last give some sign that he wanted Astoria to remain American. On July 27 Astor wrote Madison a long, carefully worded letter outlining all that had been accomplished by the Pacific Fur Company. That selective history lesson—one that avoided any mention of troubles like the *Tonquin* disaster—concluded with a reference to Astor's 1808 meeting with Jefferson and several cabinet officers. Astor pointedly reminded Madison that defense against British attack had been "promised in a most desided and explicit manner." One voyage by the *Constitution* or a sister ship could preserve an empire. "The relinquishment of an object so great as the one here in question can not but be attended with bitter regret while an effort on the part of government to secure and save it can not but be attended with applause." If the smooth words and polite phrasing came from one of Astor's clerks, the sentiments were surely Astor's.[55]

The last weeks of July 1813 were hardly the best time to force a decision from the beleaguered Madison administration. Struggling with a war that seemed to threaten the very survival of the Republic, the president and cabinet had neither the patience nor the interest to deal with Far Western affairs. When the cabinet met on July 23, all

attention centered on Secretary of War John Armstrong's review of
current military operations. Though the Madison Papers contain no
hints about the decisions Astor sought, it is plain that something was
afoot. On the morning of July 30 Astor received a brief note from
the president. The communication has not survived, but it evidently
led Astor to believe that the government now understood the importance of the Columbia. Madison suggested that Astor pay a personal
call at the Navy Department as soon as possible.[56]

It was an invitation Madison did not have to repeat. Everything
depended on this meeting. With Bentzon on his way to Europe to
keep a close check on peace negotiations, Astor had to deal directly
with Jones. That sense of urgency led him to spin out a remarkable
tale filled with half-truths and outright lies. Astor began the interview by suggesting that the Pacific Fur Company was not his alone.
Many other unnamed investors, he assured the secretary, had put
money into the venture. Saving it would mean rescuing the fortune
of not just one American but many. When Jones asked about the
origins of the enterprise, Astor brought out an astounding falsehood. He claimed that in 1808 Jefferson had issued him a personal
invitation to plant a settlement on the Columbia. Astoria's entire
program had been, so he claimed, "submitted and approved by him
[Jefferson] and all the heads of departments." Surely, Astor argued,
the navy would not want to be guilty of scuttling an important
undertaking that had presidential origins. "If the object is now
abandoned which it must be if you do not give us aid it for many
years to come will discourage any Americans from entering in the
trade." But more than profit was at stake. Failure in the Columbia
country would prompt the Indians "to dispise us" and the Canadians
to "laugh at us and anyone who will hereafter venture." Neither
argument nor sarcasm immediately changed Jones's mind. Still un-
convinced, the navy secretary wondered if these were sufficient
reasons to withdraw a captain and crew from vital Great Lakes
operations and send them to the distant Pacific. The national interest did seem more compelling on Lake Erie than west of the Great
Divide. "I would beg reply," retorted Astor, "that I do believe that

there is no American who can Comprehend the object but what would applaud the measure and who would not be proud of the enterprise and the obtainment of the object."[57] Like Samuel Johnson's scoundrel, Astor had at last taken refuge in patriotism.

The first week of August found Astor back in New York, waiting impatiently for a decision from Washington. The navy was not about to send a ship of the line on so uncertain a venture. What Jones evidently settled on was the offer of a privateer to escort one of Astor's merchant ships. On the morning of August 8 a certain Mr. Parker appeared at Astor's New York office carrying news of the navy's proposal. Parker was either captain or first officer of the *Siren*, Jones's choice for the Columbia mission. Parker seemed ill informed about the journey, knowing only that his ship would be sailing for the Pacific in company with a merchantman.[58]

Once it was settled that his ship would have armed escort, Astor decided to send the *Enterprise* to the Columbia. Selecting a master and preparing the vessel for sea now became his most urgent concerns. For a captain, Astor turned to David Greene of New Haven, Connecticut. Greene's sailing reputation was of such dimensions that on two previous occasions Astor had tried to sign him for Pacific voyages. Saying little about plans for this venture except that a "friend" was preparing a fast ship for a Pacific journey, Astor asked Greene to consider taking the commission. While awaiting Greene's reply, Astor found dealing with Parker and the Navy Department a trying experience. Astor wanted to talk directly with the *Siren*'s master and owners to discuss supplies and sailing schedules. But Parker evidently refused to talk with Astor. Furious at all these complications, Astor pleaded with Jones to order Parker to be more cooperative. Orders for the *Siren* were proving to be maddeningly unclear. "Is it contemplated," queried Astor, "for government to fix a garrison at the River and is it intended that the *Siren* should proceed there?"[59]

Uncertain just what support he was really getting from Washington, Astor pushed ahead with preparations for the *Enterprise*'s voyage. In late August Captain Greene presented his financial terms for the proposed voyage. Officers and crew should share half the prize money from any enemy vessels as well as half the profits from furs sold at Canton. For himself, Greene required five thousand dollars if he reached the Columbia and twenty-five hundred dollars should he fail. The master also demanded a substantial commission on all fur profits.[60]

As Greene calculated his chances of eluding the Royal Navy, Astor busied himself with last-minute details. Captain Whetten located a first officer willing to sail on the *Enterprise*, and Astor urged Greene to hire as many experienced mariners as possible. Writing to Greene on August 27, Astor confidently predicted that the *Enterprise* and the *Siren* would sail very soon. Astor counseled patience for an anxious captain but his own stock of that commodity was running short. There had been delay after delay and he may have begun to doubt the government's good faith. Was the *Siren* just a sop designed to placate an important financier in wartime? Something of an answer came in the first week of September. For reasons that are now unclear, the *Siren*'s voyage was abruptly canceled. The *Enterprise* was half loaded, her captain and crew engaged, and now her escort had vanished. An exasperated Astor could only tell Greene, "The truth is, times are so extremely uncertain and change so frequent and quick that a man who wishes to adopt a plan today is obliged to change it tomorrow." Astoria had suffered so many changes and missed tomorrows. Writing a few days later to a man who sought a place on the *Enterprise* as supercargo, Astor reported, "At present nothing is doing."[61]

The motto on the coat of arms of the North West Company proclaims "Perseverance." Astor might have easily appropriated that word for his own. Where one plan failed, another might succeed. He remained convinced that a ship sailing before the end of the year might still reach the Columbia in time to fend off British attack. It was not yet time to concede the field. If the *Enterprise* had to sail unescorted, then Astor was willing to take the risk. The problem was the tightening British blockade of the New York port. No matter Greene's skill and the *Enterprise*'s speed, the Royal Navy could not be eluded. Astor now turned to Andrei Dashkov. The diplomat had been useful in providing the *Lark* with Russian papers. Why not, suggested Astor, try the same ploy again? During September the two men worked out details for a voyage by the *Enterprise* under Russian colors. The ship would fly the Russian ensign, carry a Russian passport, and have on board cargo invoices made out to the Russian-American Company. For his part, Dashkov promised that once the *Enterprise* was ready to put to sea, he would negotiate with senior British naval officers for the ship's safe passage. By the end of September Astor was all enthusiasm. The *Enterprise* would sail in two weeks, so he thought. Greene was told to hurry to New York to supervise final preparations. Astor was so confident that he wrote John Dorr asking for copies of Captain George Vancouver's charts of the Columbia. Everything had to be done, so he told Dorr, "as soon as possible." The on-again, off-again plan to save Astoria seemed at last ready to become reality.[62]

Mid-October found the *Enterprise* nearly loaded and Greene involved in dealings with customs officers. He suggested that customs men in New York might be more susceptible to "good management" than those in New England. Greene was sure that once things had been "managed," the proper clearances would be in hand.[63] No matter how carefully Astor and Greene dealt with American officials, the success of the scheme really depended on Dashkov and the willingness of the British navy to allow a somewhat suspect ship to pass the blockade. On November 17, as the *Enterprise* was just days from sailing, all seemed in order. Dashkov asked Astor to send the ship's papers to Nikolai Kozlov, the Russian legation secretary. The next step was for Dashkov to approach the Royal Navy. On November 23 he wrote an unnamed naval officer explaining that a ship currently in the New York harbor had been chartered by the Russian-American Company to carry trade goods for Russian merchants on the Northwest coast. The officer was asked to permit this neutral vessel to pass through the blockade. Knowing Russia's current role as mediator between Britain and the United States, Dashkov was confident that the British Navy would do nothing to damage relations with so important a neutral power.

At the end of November Dashkov and Astor got their reply. The answer effectively killed Astor's maritime strategy to defeat British moves against the Columbia. "No person," wrote an unnamed British naval officer, "is more ready to protect His Imperial Majesty's flag than myself . . . although New York is in a state of blockade." Despite international comity and courtesy, the answer was a firm no. The *Enterprise* could not pass because "the season of the year is such— that it appears to me it will be impossible for the vessel to approach the Northwest coast for some time to come." Just how much this officer knew or surmised about the *Enterprise*'s real mission is not clear. He might have guessed that she was something more than her colors and papers proclaimed. Whatever his suspicions, the answer kept the *Enterprise* tied up.[64]

Throughout 1813 Astor had struggled against events far beyond his control. At one point he bitterly complained that he was "working in the dark." As the sailing season ended, winter's dark closed in on Astor's dream. The *Enterprise* would not sail, Greene signed on with another ship, and Astor told the captain's son that the vessel was as the captain had left her and would "remain so for some time to come." Astor finished the troubled year wondering about Wilson Price Hunt, the *Lark*, and the *Forester*. Where was his chief field agent and what had become of those ships? In the last days of December Astor was handed a letter from Hunt dated July 17, 1813. The correspondence had come by way of the ship *New Hazard*, just put in to Boston after a long Pacific voyage. The ship's captain, David Nye, Jr., had entertained Hunt in Hawaii and had promised to carry his letters. Astor must have wondered what Hunt was doing so far from the Columbia. It was one more unsettling thought to ponder at the end of a grim year.[65]

9

Astoria in Retreat

A CONTINENT AWAY, the Astorians knew nothing about their employer's feverish efforts to fend off a British assault. As far as Duncan McDougall and Donald Mackenzie were concerned, Astoria and the company behind it were dead, early casualties of a distant war. Come the summer of 1813, partners, clerks, and voyageurs would pack their goods and seek passage out of the Columbia. But the Astorians might have guessed that in their world few things went as planned. April 11 was one more of those windy, rainy spring days when all outside work was a muddy chore. At ten in the morning the routine of gardening and blacksmithing was suddenly interrupted by the arrival of two canoes and eighteen men. After pitching camp in the bay below Astoria, several of the strangers paid a call at the post. These newest men on the Columbia turned out to be Nor'westers—John George McTavish, Joseph Larocque, Michel Bourdon, and their engagés. The Astorians had been expecting their arrival, but it was still something of a shock to see these Canadian traders and know that they might soon become Astoria's new proprietors.

McTavish and his companions were not turned away from the post as wartime enemies. Rather they were given a cool but cordial welcome. McDougall did not plan to defend Astoria against attack and saw no reason to treat fellow Scots with anything other than decent hospitality. For his part, McTavish expected that the *Isaac Todd* would arrive in Columbia within a few weeks. There seemed little cause for trouble. Relations between the two parties were so friendly that on April 12, the post's birthday, McTavish and his men were invited to the now traditional party. Food and liquor made it a festive time and it was easy to forget that Astoria's American days were numbered.[1]

Astorians and Nor'westers now settled in to wait for what all were sure would be the imminent arrival of British naval forces. Although the outcome seemed not in doubt—Astoria would become a trading center for the North West Company—the immediate future for McTavish and his men appeared less assured. It was not living under Astoria's cannons that troubled McTavish. Rather it was his slim store of provisions. In mid-April McTavish and McDougall struck an interesting bargain. The Nor'westers offered to exchange their trade goods, valued at about eight hundred dollars, for provisions from Astoria's larder. But the arrangement was more than just a goods-for-food swap. Both sides agreed not to trade against each other in the coming weeks. More important for the safety of all the traders, there was a general agreement not to reveal news about war or abandonment to either Indian neighbors or common laborers until the ships arrived.[2]

Throughout the rest of April and into May Astorians and Nor'westers shared a common life. There was much visiting and socializing. Yet each day anxious eyes scanned the Columbia expecting to see the *Isaac Todd* pass the bar and sail into the river estuary. Those eyes might have looked less intently had it been known that the *Todd* and the *Phoebe* were only beginning their long voyage. Expectations about the *Todd* were kept alive by Indians' repeated reports about ships and sails along the coast. But for all the stories, Astoria's anchorage remained empty.

Despite no certain evidence that the Royal Navy was knocking on their door, McDougall and Mackenzie decided to press ahead with their abandonment plans. Though news of the war was common knowledge at the post, the abandonment decision remained a closely guarded secret. On June 3, with the interior traders David Stuart and John Clarke not yet present, McDougall held a meeting with the clerks to discuss Astoria's future. He argued that Astor had failed to send them a relief ship. There could be no escape by sea. And even if an American vessel should come in the next few weeks, that would change nothing. McDougall asserted that the war and poor fur returns made abandonment inevitable. Although he had a point about the effect of war, the claim that the company had gathered a meager fur harvest was wide of the mark. On June 1 Astoria's clerks had compiled an account of furs at the main post and all satellite trading houses. That list showed the company had fared well both on the Columbia and at Okanogan and Spokane. Returns from Willamette and the Snake River, as well as the efforts of the free trappers Alexander Carson and Pierre Delauney, were respectable. In McDougall's defense it can be said that future trading prospects were uncertain. Without fresh supplies of goods, the fur business would die. McDougall insisted that there was no alternative: they should quit the post, pack everything of value, and head overland in July to St. Louis. The clerks agreed and everyone decided it was time to tell the company's men about their future. In early evening on June 3 all hands assembled to hear the news. They were warned against letting Indians know about the decision, fearing that their neighbors would take it as a sign of weakness and mount an attack.[3]

Once word of the decision to leave the Columbia was out, the pace of work at the post quickened. Furs had to be baled, remaining trade goods packaged, and personal property secured. All this business caught the attention of the Chinooks. They now began to ask about the bustle. Certain that the Indians suspected something, McDougall did his best to allay their suspicions.[4]

In the midst of all these hurried preparations, the interior trading parties arrived on June 12. David Stuart, John Clarke, Donald Mackenzie, and fifty-three employees suddenly swelled Astoria's population, straining the post's ability to feed its inhabitants. Over the next two weeks there was a greater strain as partners and clerks began to bicker about the wisdom of abandonment. Stuart and Clarke were especially unhappy about the decision. They criticized McDougall for rushing to judgment. The Shuswaps and Spokane traders insisted that their fur returns fully justified holding on to the country. Fort Astoria was well armed and could withstand anything short of a heavy naval bombardment. For his part McDougall charged that Stuart and Clarke had been too slow to follow orders requiring them to come to Astoria. Their unhurried pace had jeopardized the possibility of a July departure.

In an atmosphere filled with what Alexander Ross called "mutual recrimination," Donald Mackenzie proved the decisive figure. Experienced, energetic, and ambitious, Mackenzie had been attracted to the Pacific Fur Company by promises of wealth and advancement. But those promises, at least in his mind, had not been kept. He had expected to be something of a co-leader on the overland journey, but Astor had put Hunt firmly in command. Hunt and Mackenzie had argued, often rancorously, about hiring more Canadians. Disillusioned with the entire venture, Mackenzie used his considerable skill and prestige to push for abandonment. Addressing those who wanted to defend Astoria, he rhetorically asked: "Gentlemen, why do you hesitate so long between two opinions? Your eyes ought to have been opened before now to your own interests." Mackenzie argued that "in the present critical juncture" the only course was for the Astorians to save what they could before the British Navy came to destroy everything. But Mackenzie was not content to let his speech stop at support for a tactical withdrawal in the face of superior forces. Astor was his real target and he minced no words in what quickly became a bitter indictment of the Pacific Fur Company and its founder. "We have been long enough," he asserted, "the dupes of a vacillating policy." Mackenzie called the roll of troubles with Astor—arguments about hiring at Montreal, debates over Hunt's authority at Nodaway camp, and the unseemly promotion of Astor's nephew George Ehninger over the heads of older and more experienced clerks. And there was the old, not forgotten tensions between

Astor's ship captains and the Canadian partners. Necessity had forced Astor to give considerable power to men like Jonathan Thorn and Cornelius Sowle. What had been born of expediency was viewed in quite a different light by the partners. With ill-concealed anger, Mackenzie charged that Astor's private instructions to ship's masters "annihilate[d] the power and authority of the partners." There could be only one conclusion to this line of reasoning, and Mackenzie undoubtedly pressed it throughout the last days of June. "All these inauspicious circumstances taken together point out the absolute necessity of abandoning the enterprise as soon as possible." Whatever Mackenzie's personal motives, his arguments carried the day. By the time the partners prepared for a formal meeting at the end of June, Stuart and Clarke were won over to support abandonment.[5]

Although much had been settled in an informal way, the company agreement required a formal partners' meeting—certainly on an issue as momentous as quitting the country. That official proceeding began on June 25 and continued with some interruptions until July 1. Because of delays in leaving the interior trading houses and packing at Astoria, it was plain that any overland journey this season would be impossible. The Astorians would have to spend one more year in the Northwest. April 1814 was now set as a new departure date. The first session of the partners' meeting began with the frank admission that the store of goods at Astoria was unequal to the post's wants and was "distorted and unfit for the Trade of the Country, much less for Competition." Faced with the bleak prospect of being unable to trade for provisions during the coming winter, the Astorians hit on a remarkable course of action. Knowing that McTavish and the other Nor'westers might not be ready to launch a full-scale trade war in such uncertain times, McDougall proposed that the two companies divide the fur business until spring. The Astorians would keep Willamette, Okanogan, Shuswaps, and the Snake River while relinquishing Spokane and the Kutnais post. The store at Astoria would furnish McTavish with whatever trade goods were available, payable next spring in horses. McTavish was also requested to forward dispatches to Astor by way of the North West Company's winter express.[6]

For McTavish these proposals were a godsend. By now he was beginning to wonder if the *Todd* was going to appear at all. Perhaps she had been lost or the plan had in some other way gone awry. McDougall's offer gave the North West Company's party a means to survive the winter. In retrospect it was a most generous gift, one that McTavish was quick to accept. When the Astorians continued their meeting the following day it was plain that McTavish had agreed to the suggested division. Now the partners could settle on winter assignments. David Stuart was sent back to the Shuswaps post in the vicinity of present-day Kamloops, British Columbia. Alexander Ross was destined to spend another winter at Okanogan. John Clarke, formerly at Spokane, was now detailed to the Flathead country—a term the Astorians used to describe the Nez Perce homelands—to trade for horses. John Reed, four Canadian engagés, and two American free trappers were sent on a similar mission to the Snake River plains. Although there was no expectation that horses could be had along the Willamette, Donald Mackenzie and twelve men were sent to Wallace House in an effort to put less strain on Astoria's provisions. Finally, there was the touchy question of the future of the company's clerks. In these reduced circumstances Astoria no longer needed the services of men like Ross Cox, Donald McGillis, and Donald McLennan. Those three, all fairly recent arrivals with little seniority and experience, were given permission to seek places with McTavish.[7]

By the first of July 1813 all the important decisions had been made. The arguing was over but the explaining had just begun. The partners knew they would be required to justify their actions first to Hunt whenever he returned and later to Astor. On July 1 McDougall and his fellows put their defense in the company's letter book. The statement was a careful blend of honest evaluation and less-than-truthful argument. Because it reflects so well the view from Astoria, the entire entry deserves attention.

> We are now destitute of the necessary supplies to carry on the Trade, and we have no hopes of receiving more. We are yet entirely ignorant of the coast, on which we always had great dependence. The interior

parts of the country turn out far short of our expectations. Its yearly produce in furs is very far from being equal to the expenses the trade incurs; much less will it be able to recover the losses already sustained, or stand against a powerful opposition and support itself. In fine, circumstances are against us on every hand; and nothing operates to lead us into a conclusion, that we can succeed.

The Astorians would pack their traps, fold their tents, and steal away from the Northwest.[8]

The first week of July found both Astorians and Nor'westers busy preparing for voyages into the interior. On July 5 McTavish's men headed toward Spokane. Three days later the first of the Pacific Fur Company brigades pushed up the Columbia.[9] The rest of Astoria's summer was as quiet as Astor's was busy. While he struggled against the navy's bureaucracy and the federal government's indifference, his employees gardened, trapped, and counted the days of sun and storm.

The steady rhythm of a summer on the river was abruptly halted on August 20 when a ship appeared off the Columbia's bar. Thinking this might be the *Todd*, McDougall took a boat and hurried to take a closer look. The vessel proved to be the *Albatross*, an American trader under the command of Captain William Smith. The ship had just come from Hawaii and carried on board none other than Wilson Price Hunt. Once back inside the post, Hunt told one more chapter in the long volume of Astoria's misadventures. After leaving the Columbia on board the *Beaver* in early August 1812, Hunt and Captain Sowle had made for the Russian settlements. When it came to hard bargaining and hard drinking, Hunt was no match for Alexander Baranov. The Russian-American Company's manager at New Archangel subjected Astor's man to an endless round of negotiations, punctuated by drunken brawls. Hunt's journal, available to Irving but now apparently lost, contains a vivid description of those difficult days with Baranov. "He is continually giving entertainments by way of parade, and if you do not drink raw rum, and boiling punch as strong as sulphur, he will insult you as soon as he gets drunk, which is very shortly after sitting down to table."[10]

Throughout September Hunt struggled to make trade arrangements with the Russians. When terms were finally settled on, the *Beaver's* goods were to be paid in seal skins. Since the warehouses at New Archangel currently held none of those skins, Hunt and Sowle were obliged to sail to the island of St. Paul in the Bering Sea. It was not until the end of October 1812 that the *Beaver* could begin loading skins at St. Paul. Astoria's stock of good fortune was always thin, and in the first week of November it ran out for Hunt and the *Beaver*. While Hunt and some of the crew were busy at St. Paul, the *Beaver* was caught in a fierce storm. Sowle was able to save the *Beaver*, but she was severely damaged and needed repairs before sailing for Canton.

Hunt and Sowle now faced a difficult decision—a decision today made more difficult to evaluate because Hunt's journal dropped from sight after Irving used it. Hunt plainly wanted to return to Astoria as quickly as possible. Writing later and using generally reliable sources, Alexander Ross reported that Hunt and Sowle had a serious argument. The *Beaver's* captain finally settled the issue by producing a letter of instruction to him from Astor.

That document gave Sowle all power to regulate the movements of his vessel. Sowle insisted that the *Beaver* needed to get its cargo to Canton as fast as possible. Every captain in the China trade knew how volatile that market could be. Whatever their differences, Hunt and Sowle now laid plans for the *Beaver* to sail for Hawaii. Once there the ship could be repaired and Hunt might take passage back to Astoria on the next company vessel bound for the Columbia. Had there been no war between Britain and the United States, this plan might have been successful. But its execution kept Hunt away from Astoria during a crucial period and stranded him in Hawaii until midsummer 1813. Once again Astoria's genie had proved a fickle, troublesome spirit.[11]

Once the *Beaver* sailed for Canton on January 1, 1813, Hunt was left to fend for himself and wait for Astor's next ship. That vessel should have been the *Lark*, scheduled to sail from New York in September 1812. But wartime delays had kept her in port and she did not stand out to sea until March 1813. Toward the end of June 1813 Hunt began to hear rumors about a war now a full year old. Those stories were confirmed when the ship *Albatross*, fresh from Canton, brought sure news of the war. Realizing immediately that Astoria was in grave danger, Hunt negotiated a charter agreement with Captain Smith. Having traveled across the continent east to west and voyaged to Russian America and Hawaii, Hunt would at last be pointed back to the Columbia.[12]

Hunt certainly expected that once at Astoria he and the partners would begin preparing to defend the Columbia against any attack. What he found instead were evacuation plans already agreed on. Gabriel Franchère admitted that Hunt was "astonished when he learned of the decision to leave the country . . . and was extremely critical of us for making it so suddenly."[13] The measure of Hunt's anger became clear the following week when all the partners assembled for a formal meeting. At the August 25 meeting Hunt renewed his criticism of McDougall and the others, arguing that the hasty abandonment decision should be rescinded. Astoria was no fortress, but the post could surely be defended against most assaults. And there was growing doubt that any British naval force would appear on the Columbia. Hunt insisted that both the coastal and interior fur trades were promising. But his was one voice against many, and the decision to leave the Columbia the next spring was reaffirmed.

The resolutions passed on August 25 suggest how much Astoria had fallen under the sway of McDougall and Mackenzie. They maintained that the supply of goods brought by the *Albatross* was insufficient to service another trading year. Plainly distorting Hunt's report, the partners passed a resolution proclaiming that his reconnaissance demonstrated the poor state of the coastal trade. And once again the interior trade was branded as discouraging. No matter Hunt's objections, abandonment stood as the ruling policy.

Because the *Albatross* was already under contract to sell Hawaiian sandalwood in China, the ship could not be used to carry the company's employees to an American port. Captain Smith did agree to give Hunt passage back to Hawaii where he might charter another vessel. That ship was expected back on the Columbia sometime in January 1814. Astorians could take passage on her after depositing the company's goods at New Archangel. But by now everyone at Astoria knew that even the most carefully laid plans seemed to fail at the last moment. "Having already experienced so many unforeseen disasters in the prosecution of our plans and Human life being so uncertain, it is hereby agreed and concluded that Wilson Price Hunt draw three sets of exchange on John Jacob Astor of New York to the amount of $20,000 to be left with Duncan McDougall in case of being disappointed in said Wilson Price Hunt's return, to meet the demands of our people at St. Louis or elsewhere." Far from being Astor's chief agent in the West, Hunt had now been reduced to errand boy. Real power at Astoria rested with McDougall and Mackenzie. Once Hunt left the post, McDougall was in full command with sole power "to conclude any arrangements we may be able to make with whoever may come forward on the part of the North West Company."[14]

When Hunt left Astoria on board the *Albatross* on August 26 he must have realized that the days of an American empire on the Columbia were numbered. He might have been even more depressed had he known the tragic fate of the *Lark*. On August 13, running in heavy seas off Maui, the ship was hit by a sudden gale that knocked her on her side. "The Ship was almost keelout," recalled Captain Samuel Northrop. "Being destitute of experinect offercers and a greate parte of the Crew young and unacquainted with any kind of Seaman Ship," he reported, "we ware in greate Confusion and disorder." After considerable effort the crew was able to cut away the masts and rigging. The survivors now built a makeshift deck on the derelict *Lark*. That "sort of stage" became a precarious perch for the crew as the *Lark* drifted for some sixteen days. Members of the crew repeatedly swam into the submerged cabin, bringing up wine and water-soaked provisions. On August 29 the ordeal was finally over when the wreck beached at Maui. The shattered vessel had joined the *Tonquin* in Astoria's ocean graveyard.[15]

With Hunt once again at sea, the Astorians expected a quiet

winter before leaving the country in early spring. For yet another time, expectations did not match reality. In May 1813 Angus Shaw, a partner in the North West Company, had sent an urgent message to John George McTavish, alerting him to the sailing schedule of the *Todd* and her escort. Despite delays, the British force was indeed coming to "take and destroy everything that is American on the North West Coast." When the North West Company's wintering partners had met at Fort William in July 1813 they had followed that message up with renewed action. Alexander Henry the younger, Alexander Stuart, and James Keith were ordered across the Rockies to augment forces already in the West. Express messages and fresh forces were about to change Astoria's destiny in an unexpected way.[16]

It was not to be a quiet fall at Alexander Ross's lonely post on the Okanogan River. Sometime in September the trader was surprised by the unannounced arrival of some seventy-five Nor'westers. Led by McTavish and Stuart, the expedition was headed toward Astoria. McTavish now had the May letter from Shaw and was determined to lay siege to the American post. The winds of war had shifted, and whatever agreements had been made between McDougall and McTavish were no longer in force. McTavish had succeeded in luring John Clarke into the North West Company's fold with promises of quick promotion. Perhaps other Astorians might follow. Whatever schemes had been plotted before, McTavish now sensed victory at last.[17]

On October 5 Donald Mackenzie met McTavish's canoe flotilla on the Columbia. Two days later the canoes drew up to the Astoria wharf. The sudden arrival of so many Nor'westers stunned McDougall and others at the post. This was a most unexpected turn of events. There was even more alarm when McTavish produced his letter from Montreal. The *Isaac Todd* was on the way and could be expected any day. Having been burned once before by McTavish's tales, the Astorians decided to wait behind their log walls for something more than paper evidence.[18]

Perhaps surprised that McDougall did not immediately surrender the post, McTavish and his men camped in the bay beneath Astoria. With winter coming on, their situation was uncertain. Food shortages forced them to purchase provisions from the American fort. It did not take McTavish long to see that his party could not stay the winter at so exposed a camp. On October 8 the Nor'wester approached McDougall with an astonishing offer. The North West Company would buy all the holdings of the Pacific Fur Company— everything from kitchen utensils and blacksmith tools to furs and buildings. McTavish's argument was simple but powerful. Why risk death and destruction at the hands of the Royal Navy when lives and investments could be saved by selling at a fair price?[19]

Resolving to leave Astoria by means of honorable retreat was one thing, but to sell the entire enterprise to the opposition seemed quite another matter. Article sixteen of the company agreement allowed the partners to abandon the venture, but nowhere in the document was there any statement about selling the company's assets without Astor's permission. How the Astorians decided to accept McTavish's offer is not now clear. Between October 8 and October 12 there are no entries in McDougall's journal that bear on the decision. But there are two surviving clues that suggest why the offer was accepted. The most important comes from Franchère. "Situated as we were," he wrote in his diary, "expecting every day to see a warship arrive to deprive us of what little we had, we listened to those proposals and after several consultations set a price upon our furs and our remaining merchandise."[20]

McDougall's explanation did not come until some years later. In 1817 he was on the Columbia at Fort George, the new name for Astoria. There already had been considerable criticism of his leadership, and now in a draft of his will McDougall sought not so much to explain as to defend his actions. Turning over business and personal papers to his uncle, McDougall hoped that his executor might know "how much and how unjustly my character and reputation has suffered and been injured by the malicious and ungenerous conduct of some of my late associates in the late Pacific Fur Company—And I here declare in the most solemn manner that I did every thing in my power to do the utmost justice to the trust and confidence reposed in me by John Jacob Astor . . . and the charge that devolved upon me in consequence of Wilson Price Hunt's absence, agreeable to and in conformity with the Resolves of the Company, passed and signed by my Associates and myself in the months of June, July, and August, 1813, and the meaning and tenor of our agreement with the aforesaid John Jacob Astor."[21] However the decision to sell out had been reached, McDougall wanted posterity to know that the deciding had not been his alone.

On October 12 McDougall told McTavish that the partners were interested in taking up the Nor'wester's offer. McDougall let it be known that much remained to be settled. Prices and arrangements had not yet been specified. Those discussions began the next day and quickly sank into a mire of confusion and recrimination. The focus of the trouble was price—the prices for goods and furs at the various Pacific Fur Company posts. McDougall was willing to sell the company's assets but at a fairly high rate. When McTavish and Stuart asked what discounts might apply, they were abruptly told that full New York and Montreal prices were being asked. At the end of the day on October 13 the Nor'westers left Astoria in a huff. Worried about a possible surprise attack, McDougall put the fort on full alert throughout the night.[22]

The Astorians need not have worried about a midnight assault. McTavish had no plans for such a foolhardy maneuver. And besides, McDougall's recent marriage alliance to one of Comcomly's daughters suggested that an attack on the post might prompt retaliation by the Indians. More to the point, McTavish wanted to conclude arrangements before winter set in. The next day both parties gathered at Astoria to settle accounts. Goods and furs had to be inventoried and priced. Passage home for the Hawaiians also had to be arranged. By now most of the islanders were heartily sick of the Northwest. McTavish promised that his company would be responsible for both their wages and their transportation. To forestall any hard feelings, each Hawaiian was given a new gun, supplies of powder and shot, and three pounds of tobacco.[23]

With the islanders satisfied, McDougall and the Nor'westers could turn their attention to a formal bill of sale. On October 16 that document was presented for McDougall's signature. The most complete copy, containing four detailed articles, survives today in the Foreign Office Papers at the British Public Record Office. The first article spelled the death sentence for the Pacific Fur Company. The Astorians promised that as soon as proper inventories were complete, they would turn over "all establishments, furs, and stock." A payment schedule for this transfer was spelled out in the second article. McDougall had always expressed real concern for the future of the company's men, whether they were clerks or common laborers. The bill of sale provided for either employment at North West Company posts or safe passage back to the American states.

The final portion of the bill of sale was the longest and proved to be the most complex. This section laid out in precise detail how much the North West Company would pay for various kinds of goods, equipment, and furs. During lengthy talks on these points, McDougall claimed that the New York and Montreal invoices showing original prices had been lost on the *Tonquin*. McTavish would simply have to trust McDougall's memory. As Alexander Henry the younger observed later, McDougall had "a convenient memory to answer his own ends."[24] As events later revealed, McDougall kept his mind fresh by surreptitious peeks at secret invoice copies. Dry goods, tobacco, and powder went at 50 percent of the prime cost while lead, iron, and steel items fetched their full original value. New boats were priced at ten pounds Montreal currency. Roussel's blacksmith shop was rated at twenty-five pounds. Furs drew special attention. Ordinary beaver pelts were set at ten shillings per pound. Valuable sea otter pelts were placed at sixty shillings each. All told, the North West Company agreed to pay in three installments for all of Astoria's empire. To the end of his life McDougall believed he had made a good bargain for Astor.[25]

A continent away, John Astor had a less charitable view of the proceedings. Writing in late 1814 to William McGillivray, he bitterly complained: "I think the price at which Mr. McDougall made sale to your agents was not such as under all circumstances it ought to have been. The loss to me was as you must be aware of very heavy." The full weight of that loss was spelled out in Astor's 1823 letter to Secretary of State John Quincy Adams. Astor reported that McDougall had sold more than eighteen thousand pounds of beaver pelts at two dollars per pound. He claimed that the going rate at Canton in 1813 was between five and six dollars per pound. Astor insisted that he had taken an even greater loss on sea otter skins. McDougall sold 907 sea otters at fifty cents a skin. Astor maintained that those same skins would have fetched five or six dollars each at Canton. As Astor exclaimed in 1814, "We have been sold."[26]

Two days after signing the final documents, McDougall and his men got down to the real business of transferring Astoria to the North West Company's ownership. While clerks prepared inventories of goods and supplies, McTavish and his Nor'westers broke camp and made ready to occupy Britain's westernmost outpost. On October 22 McDougall handed over to McTavish the keys to Astoria's storehouse. More important than what flag snapped at the fort's pole or what name the post carried, those keys symbolized true power on the Columbia. Whoever controlled the warehouse held Astoria's future.[27]

More pieces of Astoria's troubled future fell into place late in 1813. A year earlier Astor had schemed with two of his captains to launch a secret Pacific rescue mission. The *Forester* adventure had all the marks of a suspense thriller. Covert agents, bribery, false flags, and an undisclosed destination made the voyage both dramatic and a high-stakes gamble. In the early fall months of 1813 that gamble seemed to be paying off. The *Forester*, flying British colors, had outsailed the English convoy in the race for the Columbia. But as the ship neared the Hawaiian Islands in early November, there was sudden trouble. On November 9 Captain Jennings and Astor's agents Pigot and Ebbets learned that there were American vessels at Oahu. Because the *Forester* still flew British colors, her officers decided to sail for Hilo on the island of Hawaii. There they heard tales of the *Lark*'s disaster. Hard on the heels of this unsettling news came

the unexpected arrival of the armed brig *Tamaahamaah*. That ship
had been chartered by Boston merchants in an effort to protect their
maritime fur trade assets. The *Tamaahamaah*'s presence in mid-
December sparked a sudden mutiny among the *Forester*'s sailors.
Evidently some of those seamen wanted to hand their ship over to
the American privateer. Jennings was forced to open fire on the
mutineers. It remains unclear if there were any casualties, but Pigot
quickly took charge of the troubled ship. Faced with an unruly crew,
Pigot decided to abandon efforts to sail for Astoria. Instead, he
directed the *Forester* on a trading voyage to Spanish California and
Russian Alaska.

When Pigot wrote to Richard Ebbets in late March 1814 explaining these events, the ship still carried British papers and colors.
Pigot chose his words carefully so that should the report fall into
English hands, the *Forester* would still appear to be what her flag
proclaimed. Pigot wrote that the exact reasons for the mutiny were
"out of my power at present" to relate, but information obtained
later from Captain Jennings by Peter Corney, a mariner with the
North West Company, suggests two possible causes for the trouble.
The ship's crew may have contained some American sailors who had
been trapped in Britain by the war. Patriotism and the desire to
return home may have been the motives behind the mutiny. On the
other hand a less noble impulse might have caused the violence.
Had the *Tamaahamaah* succeeded in seizing the *Forester*, there would
have been shares of prize money for all those who aided the capture.
Whatever the motive, the mutiny and its consequences doomed
Astor's most daring strategy to save his western empire.[28]

Tales of mutiny and false flags seemed remote to the lives of
traders living at Astoria in the fall of 1813. Astorians and Nor'westers, now sharing rooms at the overcrowded post, settled in to prepare for the coastal winter. Amid the daily chores there must have
been plenty of time to wonder about when the Royal Navy might
finally come to the Columbia. Those speculations intensified in mid-
November with the arrival of a second party from the North West
Company. This expedition, led by Alexander Henry the younger,

Alexander Stuart, and James Keith, had left Fort William in July with the latest news and fresh reinforcements. For the Astorians the news was anything but reassuring. Newspapers bearing early June 1813 dates were filled with stories of American defeats at the hands of British and Canadian forces. And the new arrivals reconfirmed plans for an attack on Astoria by the Royal Navy. In fact, Henry was quite surprised to learn that the *Isaac Todd* was not already riding at the Astoria anchorage.[29]

At the end of November questions about the Royal Navy and war on the Columbia were finally answered. Early on the morning of November 30 a ship running under full sail was seen heading for the anchorage inside Cape Disappointment. Because the vessel fired no signal guns and her flags could not be seen, everyone at Astoria worried over the ship's true identity. The Nor'westers were concerned that the vessel might be an American privateer. A Yankee force might return Astoria to the Pacific Fur Company's ownership and send McTavish and his men packing. If it was a British ship, both Astorians and Nor'westers wondered how to explain to its captain that the American post was already British property. No naval officer would want to hear that he had come on a fool's errand.

At midmorning it was decided to send McDougall, John Halsey, and several other former Pacific Fur Company men in a canoe headed for Cape Disappointment. Depending on the ship's flag, they would pass themselves off either as Americans or as crown subjects. As an extra precaution, McTavish filled two canoes with North West Company furs and sent them up the Columbia to safety at Tongue Point. Confusion at Astoria was complete when the sometime mariner Joseph Ashton reported that the unidentified vessel was flying a white ensign. Such a flag, he explained, was used by both British and American ships along the coast. By the time darkness closed in, Astoria's past and present proprietors could only watch across the water and count the tense hours.

That tension was suddenly broken at about 9:30 P.M. when the night air was filled with songs, shouts, and the splash of canoe paddles. Out of the darkness came Halsey and several Astorians all quite drunk from wine served on board a ship they identified as the HMS *Racoon*. Those at the fort could get few details from their tipsy friends. The *Racoon*'s mission and the whereabouts of the *Todd* were questions whose answers would have to wait until morning.[30]

On the following day, December 1, a longboat from the *Racoon* reached Astoria. On board were John McDonald of Garth, a partner with the North West Company, and the *Racoon*'s first officer. Both men were suffering from serious burns received when one of the ship's guns had hung fire and then exploded. In conversation during the day McDonald of Garth explained how the *Racoon* had come to Astoria before the *Todd*. After sailing from Portsmouth in late March 1813, the *Todd* and her convoy had made their way across the Atlantic to the British naval base at Rio de Janeiro. There, in early June 1813, the ships joined the squadron commanded by Rear Admiral Manley Dixon. Concerned about possible attack from the American warship *Essex*, then operating in Pacific waters, Dixon detached the HMS *Racoon* and the HMS *Cherub* to bolster the *Todd*'s protective cover. After some delay the four vessels left Rio on July 6 but parted company to double Cape Horn. By prearrangement, all would rendezvous at Juan Fernández Island, in the Pacific opposite present-day Valparaíso, Chile. James Hillyar, captain of the *Phoebe* and commodore of the convoy, waited for the *Todd* to arrive, but to no avail. Because the *Todd* had proven so "dull" a sailer, it had been arranged to have McDonald of Garth transfer to the *Phoebe* at Rio. Now, at Juan Fernández, all waited for the *Isaac Todd*.

While watching for the slow merchantman, Captain Hillyar took time to question Spanish officials about the nature of the Columbia River. They reported on the deadly bar at the entrance to the river as well as the many shallows that made navigation difficult. Hillyar found those observations confirmed when he examined a chart of the Columbia made in 1792 by Royal Navy Lieutenant W. R. Broughton. At the same time, Hillyar got fresh intelligence about Captain David Porter and the USS *Essex*. That American ship had successfully taken twelve British whalers as prizes. Learning that the *Essex* was sailing along the Chilean coast, Hillyar decided to give chase. He transferred the North West Company contingent to the lighter *Racoon* while the *Phoebe* and the *Cherub* went in search of the American ship. That search ended in March 1814 in the Valparaíso harbor when Hillyar's ships decisively defeated Porter's *Essex* and reestablished British naval superiority in the Pacific.[31]

The *Racoon*'s arrival and the flurry of activity at Astoria were not lost on Comcomly and the Chinooks. The headman had learned about war between Britain and the United States, but he did not know that Astoria and its surrounding posts had been sold. In Comcomly's mind the "fort men" were still reasonably reliable trading partners. That commitment had been cemented earlier when Duncan McDougall had taken one of Comcomly's daughters as a wife after "the custom of the country." Sometime during the first week of December, before any large landing party had come from the *Racoon*, Comcomly and some of his men had visited Astoria. They came decked out in full war dress ready for action. In a long speech Comcomly repeatedly pledged his readiness to defend Astoria against any British attack. The headman suggested that the best way to thwart any hostile advance was to ambush the ship's landing party. When McDougall promptly rejected Comcomly's advice, the Indian was both shocked and confused. Perhaps the Chinook guessed that power had somehow shifted at the fort. Now he might have to realign his own trade and diplomatic alliances.[32]

Bad weather kept Captain William Black and his crew on board the *Racoon* until the evening of December 12. Although Black now knew that Astoria was the property of the North West Company, he was still determined to take formal possession of the post for king and country. At dusk on the twelfth, Black and a party of officers, marines, and sailors made their way to Astoria. After dinner— Franchère reported "we gave them the best we had"—Black organized a proper conquest ceremony. Armed traders and sailors marched to Astoria's flagpole. The Union Jack was run up the pole, and in a dramatic gesture Black smashed a bottle of Madeira against the pole to signify that Astoria was now Fort George. Then, in words that would someday come back to haunt British diplomats, Black claimed Astoria and the country all around for Britain by right of wartime conquest. Amid the cheers, toasts, and artillery salutes, a bewildered Comcomly was heard to mutter that the Americans had sold themselves into slavery without a fight.[33]

Admiralty officials in England had always imagined Astoria to be a substantial military establishment. Years of lobbying by the North West Company had done much to foster such an impression. Captain Black had certainly thought Astoria was America's Gibraltar on the Columbia and had been ready to reduce it by naval bombardment if necessary. Because it was after dark when Black took possession of the post, he did not see its true character. That revelation was saved until the next morning. John McDonald of Garth had already been disappointed. He recalled later finding "only a few stores and barracks surrounded by a few imperfect stockades with two or three swivels mounted near the gate." Black was even more unhappy when he saw Astoria in the morning light. Turning to McDougall, he asked if this was *the* fort. When told that what he saw was the entire establishment, Black nearly doubled over in laughter. As Franchère recorded it, Black said: "What, is this the fort I have heard so much of? Great God, I could batter it down with a four-pounder in two hours!" Washington Irving believed that Black was more angry than amused. Irving maintained that Black felt robbed of the prize money that might have come to him by the sale of confiscated furs. There surely was some displeasure with the sale on the part of naval officers. Francis Phillips, a clerk on the *Racoon*, wrote, "Our grand attack and expectations were totally frustrated." Phillips argued that the purchase of American property in wartime amounted to illegal support of the enemy. The clerk hinted that a conspiracy of Scots, regardless of company or country, had robbed the *Racoon* of its rightful glory. John McDonald of Garth, writing after the publication of Irving's *Astoria*, pointedly disputed such charges. He insisted that Black had never spoken about prize money. Whatever Black's disappointments, he now readied his ship for sea. What he left behind was a curious act of conquest, one that had changed nothing and would eventually change everything.[34]

When Wilson Price Hunt had left Astoria on board the *Albatross* in late August 1813 he had grudgingly accepted abandonment plans. Now he sought a ship to provide passage for company employees back to New York. After encountering the USS *Essex* at the Marquesas Islands in late November, the *Albatross* steered for the Hawaiian Islands. Hunt arrived in Hawaii on December 20 and met Samuel Northrop, captain of the ill-fated *Lark*. Together the two men decided to buy a ship, hire a crew, and sail for the Columbia. The ship they set upon was the *Pedlar*, a Boston vessel then on the market for ten thousand dollars. A month later the *Pedlar* put to sea bound for Astoria. Hunt's plan was to take the company's goods to New Archangel for safekeeping before returning employees to New York.[35]

Astoria's new flag and name meant little to those living at the post. The daily rituals of cooking, cleaning, hunting, and trading continued, no matter what company or country claimed the community. Astoria celebrated New Year's 1814 with customary jubilation, although all noted the short supplies of liquor and flour. There were the inevitable squabbles that had always been part of Astorian life. McDonald of Garth argued with other Nor'westers about command of the fort. Dealings with native neighbors seemed unchanged. Comcomly and other headmen cared little about questions of sovereignty and imperial policy so long as trade remained on terms favorable to them. And there was the usual round of accidents, troubles, and complaints. The Fort George of 1814 seemed much like the Astoria of 1811.[36]

Late on the afternoon of February 28 that predictable rhythm suffered a severe jolt. Alexander Henry the younger, standing on the post's stockade platform, spotted two Indians waving at a distant object. Moments later some Indian women at the gate told Henry that a ship had been seen outside the river bar. That news flashed through Astoria and soon a dozen traders ran down to the shore for a closer look. Three shots were fired from one of the fort's guns but the ship did not reply and remained unidentified. As dark came to the Columbia, everyone at the post wondered about the ship and some even bet hats and furs on her true colors.

Although Henry and others at the fort did not know it until the following day, that ship was the *Pedlar*. On March 1 Henry and others walked down to Point George hoping for another look at the vessel. They even set signal fires to catch the ship's attention. Her lines—a brig with black sides and a white bottom—and the lack of any flag convinced those at the post that the vessel was an American privateer. Fort George had few packs of beaver for the taking, so no effort was made to send them to safety at Tongue Point. At the same time, the Nor'westers were plainly worried about a possible attack and prepared accordingly.

That evening Chinooks brought positive identification of the ship in a letter from Hunt to his fellows with the Pacific Fur Company. Worried about his own safety, he asked them to meet on board the *Pedlar*. McDougall declined but a delegation including McDonald of Garth, Thomas McKay, and Donald Stuart did visit with Hunt later that night. The next day, March 2, talks continued on board the *Pedlar*. Hunt now learned that instead of abandoning the post, his colleagues had sold it to the opposition. Franchère put Hunt's reaction in forceful terms. "One may imagine Mr. Hunt's surprise on finding Astoria under the British flag and in foreign hands."[37]

Duncan McDougall, who had made quiet arrangements in late December 1813 to join the North West Company, refused to deal with Hunt on board the *Pedlar*. Hunt had little choice but to leave the ship and venture to Fort George. On March 4 talks began between Hunt and the Nor'westers. Though Hunt challenged the valuations placed on various goods in the original bill of sale, his real strategy seemed to be to lure as many men as possible away from the North West Company's employ. The Nor'westers were just as fixed on preserving their work force. The Hawaiian laborers were a special bone of contention. Astoria's new owners prized Hawaiian maritime skill but at the same time recognized that the islanders were quite homesick. By the time Hunt left Fort George at the end of the day, four former Pacific Fur Company clerks had agreed to sail on the *Pedlar*. The touchy matter of the Hawaiians was yet unresolved.[38]

For the next few days Hunt remained on board the *Pedlar*. At Fort George the Nor'westers must have wondered about his next move. That move came on March 8 when discussions resumed. The atmosphere was anything but friendly. Hunt insisted that the Pacific Fur Company's goods had been sold at too cheap a price. Henry described the meeting as filled with "much talk, argument, and altercation." When Hunt demanded that the original New York and Montreal invoices be produced, he was told that they had been lost on the *Tonquin*. This was the same story McDougall had told during sale proceedings in October 1813. In truth, McDougall had a full set of papers from the *Tonquin* and the *Beaver* and had secretly consulted them throughout the sale talks. That fact now came to light and sparked even more hard feelings.[39]

Somehow Hunt got his hands on those papers and the following day produced them for all to see. Franchère and Halsey certified them as genuine, and Hunt and John Stuart began a close study of the evidence. Soon both Hunt and Stuart found striking differences between original price and later valuation. Some goods were pegged far too high, whereas others were posted inexplicably low. The result, wrote Henry, was predictable trouble. "Many disagreeable altercations took place between the parties concerned." Their arguments notwithstanding, Hunt and the Nor'westers were faced with few alternatives. They could agree to the flawed accounts made in October 1813 or they could try to renegotiate the entire sale. There was even the remote possibility that the sale might be declared void and the post turned back to the Astorians. The Nor'westers were not about to hand over the Columbia after struggling so long against Astor. Adjusting the original sale terms seemed the best way to avoid what Henry described as "pushing matters to extremes."[40]

Between March 10 and 12 Hunt and the Nor'westers worked to iron out their differences. The value of John Reed's Snake River trading expedition was cut in half and the price of fur and merchandise readjusted to fit inventory documents. At midday on March 12 Henry confidently wrote in his journal, "Every point being now settled to the satisfaction of Mr. Hunt, the accounts are balanced and closed." But at Astoria nothing was ever balanced or closed. As part of the revised agreement Hunt was to provide passage for some of the North West Company's furs. Later that evening, when the packaged skins were presented to him, he refused to accept delivery. Quite suddenly Hunt "objected to any terms." The Nor'westers now thought that an armed assault on the fort was in the offing. Because Hunt's journal and letters are now lost, it is unclear just what the Astorian had in mind. Whatever Hunt was thinking, his refusal to accept the furs put all plans off track.[41]

For the next several days there were lengthy meetings with Hunt on board his ship. Henry characterized those conferences as tense and angry. Each gathering saw "former plans being laid aside, others objected to, [and] new proposals made and entered upon." It was not until March 20 that the two sides finally reached agreement. Reevaluations settled upon days earlier were reaffirmed, four clerks and several free trappers were promised passage on the *Pedlar*, and four Hawaiians boarded for the trip home. Bad weather and high seas kept the ship from crossing the bar until April 2. Hunt and the *Pedlar* would not finally reach New York until mid-October 1816.[42]

* * *

In distant New York, Astor learned about Pacific events piecemeal. By mid-July 1814 he knew by means of newspaper accounts of the defeat of the *Essex* by Captain James Hillyar's ships. Thanks to Captain David Porter's published records Astor realized that Hunt had been to the Columbia on the *Albatross*. Hunt had evidently told Porter during their encounter at the Marquesas Islands that the Russian supply trade was not nearly so profitable as once imagined. More important, Astor learned that Hunt planned to abandon the post and move its goods to New Archangel. Astor may have agreed with such a course, since Porter also reported that the HMS *Racoon* was well on her way to seize the Columbia River post.[43]

Throughout the rest of the summer and into the fall of 1814 Astor heard no more from the Northwest. There was no news from the Columbia and only rumors from Montreal. In July partners of the North West Company had approved the purchase of Astoria, and perhaps Astor had that word secondhand. September found him almost ready to draft the Pacific Fur Company's obituary. Writing to Ramsay Crooks, he lamented, "Was there ever an undertaking of more merit, of more hazard and more enterprizing, attended with a greater variety of misfortune?"[44]

Two weeks later Astor knew all the grim details. An overland party that had left Fort George in early April 1814 reached Montreal late in August. Among those in that canoe convoy were Gabriel Franchère and Donald Mackenzie. Astor soon heard the worst. Writing to his old ally Andrei Dashkov, he reported that Astoria was in British hands and "the whole property gone." With remarkable equanimity Astor reminded the Russian diplomat of a timeless proverb. "This makes good the old saying, that one misfortune seldome comes alone." By the fall of 1814 every voice seemed to announce the death of Astoria's empire. From St. Petersburg the Russian-American Company advised Dashkov that Astor's game was over. "That is the end of it," declared the Russian company. And on November 12 readers of the *New-York Gazette and General Advertiser* were told simply, "The firm of the Pacific Fur Company is dissolved." From inception to collapse, America's first Far Western empire had lasted barely seven years.[45]

Astoria: The Legacy

DESPITE A FORMAL, newspaper obituary announcing the death of the Pacific Fur Company, Astor was not about to give up his Columbian enterprise. Diplomacy might restore what bad fortune had snatched away. In late March 1814, as the American and British governments moved closer to a negotiated peace, Astor confided his diplomatic hopes to Gallatin. "If matters go right," he wrote, "I am sure you will not forget the object in which I am so much interested and which sooner or later will and must become of great national importance." Whether Astor knew it or not, his views on the future of the Columbia were at last shared by some members of the Madison administration. Perhaps years of lobbying were now paying off. On the same day that Astor wrote Gallatin, Secretary of State James Monroe sent instructions to John Quincy Adams and other American peace negotiators. Monroe reminded Adams that when talks to end the war reached the point that exchanges of captured territory were under discussion, "you will have it in recollection that the United States had in their possession at the commencement of the war a post at the mouth of the River Columbia which commanded the river." Monroe assumed that Astoria had been captured during the conflict and now expected the post to be promptly returned. He was especially firm in rejecting any British claim to territories on the Pacific coast. Monroe's letter and the confusion about sale and seizure eventually put Astoria at the center of a diplomatic controversy that would determine the imperial shape of the West.[1]

Not privy to these diplomatic moves, Astor forged ahead with his own plans during the summer of 1814. By mid-July, newspaper reports had told him something about Hunt, the *Albatross*, and the movements of the HMS *Racoon*. September found Astor in possession of a distorted report that British forces had destroyed Astoria. At the same time he knew, thanks to news from Montreal, that the North West Company now held what was left of his post. Astor was desperate for reliable news, and when he heard that Donald Mackenzie was in Montreal, the entrepreneur began to arrange a meeting.

In late September Astor wrote both Monroe and Richard Forrest, a State Department clerk, asking that an American passport be issued to Mackenzie. Playing loose with the facts, Astor insisted that Mackenzie was a British subject but that he had "become a citizen of the U.S. four years ago." Repeating the news that British forces now had taken the Columbia, Astor declared that information from Mackenzie was critical to determine any future course of action. "It's important," he concluded, "that I should see Mr. Mackenzie here."[2]

Just how important Astor imagined that meeting was plain when he wrote Mackenzie on September 27. Astor urged his former partner to come "without delay." He hinted that plans were afoot to recover Astoria. With a dramatic flourish quite uncharacteristic of his usual no-nonsense temperament, Astor exclaimed, "While I breathe and so long as I have a dollar to spend I'll pursue a course to have our injuries repaired and when I am no more I hope you'll act in my place." Clearly Astor did not know the central role Mackenzie had played in the sale of the post. McDougall was Astor's choice as villain. Mackenzie was simply told, "Come here and we will soon act."[3]

Efforts to obtain a passport for Mackenzie dragged on, and it was not until October 8 that Astor could send the document enclosed in a letter for Robert Stuart.[4] What must have been a tense meeting between Astor and Mackenzie took place in New York sometime in late October. When Astor wrote to Mackenzie on November 1, he alluded to the meeting but gave no details. What is known about the encounter comes from an 1827 letter Mackenzie wrote to Wilson Price Hunt. The two Astorians kept in touch over the years, and in one letter Hunt evidently expressed considerable fondness for Astor and nostalgia over the Pacific Fur Company. Mackenzie's reply suggested what had happened in the fall of 1814. Astor was looking for scapegoats. McDougall was one and Hunt became another. At the New York meeting Astor evidently openly questioned Hunt's honesty and ability. Mackenzie recalled that Astor's "uncharitable questions" seemed to picture Hunt as "an outcast or a criminal." Mackenzie insisted that he had hurried to Hunt's defense. "It was with infinite ado that I managed to set his [Astor's] mind at ease." If Hunt eventually came back to Astor's good graces, Mackenzie soon fell from them. According to the Canadian, the two men had an angry parting.[5] Whatever plans Astor had in mind to revive Astoria, Mackenzie would have no part in them.

As was so often the case, Astoria's future was held in distant hands. In the fall of 1814 British and American diplomats met at Ghent to discuss an end to hostilities. Recent American military successes and a gloomy evaluation of British prospects from the Duke of Wellington made negotiators for the crown ready to talk. When British proposals were offered at the end of November, an unexpected and quite unofficial diplomat showed special interest in them. Adrian Bentzon had long been his father-in-law's most adept agent. Bentzon dealt with everyone from an American secretary of the navy to Russian merchants and bureaucrats. Early on a November morning, Bentzon showed up at John Quincy Adams's lodging "as inquisitive about the state of negotiations as he could indirectly be." Adams had already been directed to oppose any British claims to Pacific coast territories, but Bentzon heard none of that. Cold-shouldered by a wary Adams, Astor's man got a warmer welcome later in the day from Albert Gallatin. In conversation with Gallatin,

Bentzon reported that a vessel of Astor's then at Canton was ready to leave for the Columbia the moment peace was declared. The vessel's mission was "to renew the settlement there before the British will have time to anticipate" Astor's daring move. Bentzon insisted that the entire enterprise was in the public interest and asked to be kept posted on all diplomatic arrangements. Bentzon went further, presenting Astor's ideas in a formal report. Adams, Gallatin, and several other American diplomats discussed the Astor request and decided that what they were being asked to do was quite improper.[6]

The Treaty of Ghent ending the War of 1812 was signed on Christmas Eve, 1814. The treaty's provisions said little about the explosive issues that had sparked the war. The document simply proclaimed the conflict over and referred difficult boundary questions to four joint commissions. But article one of the treaty did bear directly on Astoria. It provided that lands captured during the war be restored to their former owners.[7] Astor and many American diplomats soon began to argue that because Captain Black had formally seized and occupied Astoria in 1813 the treaty now required the immediate return of the property to American hands. That position politely ignored Astoria's earlier and quite legal sale to the North West Company. The view advanced by the Nor'westers was quite the opposite. In the coming years they repeatedly insisted that Fort George was theirs by right of legal sale. For now no one was quite sure what would happen next.

By March 1815 Astor knew that the war was over. Whatever plans he had fancied about a fast ship bound for the Columbia seemed forgotten. Instead he wrote to his cousin George Ehninger lamenting "the damn'd War [by which] I have lost my business on the coast." At the same time Astor was convinced that the treaty would restore what had been lost. "By the peace," he declared, "we shall have a right to the Columbia river and I rather think, that I shall again engage in that business."[8]

Astor's selective reading of the Treaty of Ghent led him again to press his case with Monroe. Astoria had to be repossessed and only federal force could accomplish such a mission. In early summer

1815 Monroe and Astor corresponded on that question. Only a fragment of a June letter survives, but it does reveal the direction of Astor's thoughts. He continued to believe that had the post remained in American hands, "it would have shown itself to be of very great importance to this country." With all its promise still intact, the enterprise now required a genuine commitment from the government. Turning to more immediate concerns, Astor questioned Monroe about the Columbia's short-term future. Would the government demand the return of the post under the recent treaty and did the secretary think there might be any British opposition? Astor hoped the administration would send a naval force to recover the post. If so, he promised to again pick up and direct the whole venture.[9]

Astor's prompting evidently caught Monroe's attention. A month after receiving Astor's letter, the secretary of state took time to write the British chargé d'affaires, Anthony St. John Baker, on the subject of the Northwest coast. Monroe accepted Astor's version of events on the Columbia, telling Baker that a British force had captured Astoria during wartime. The United States now sought proper restitution under the Treaty of Ghent. Although no plans had yet been laid for that repossession, Monroe told Baker, "Measures therefore will be taken to reoccupy it without delay." The British diplomat was asked to notify authorities of the crown as well as to pass word to Astoria's current commander.[10]

Monroe was certain that the restoration of Astoria would spark no British response. He confidently told John Quincy Adams, "No objection is anticipated." The American secretary of state may not have predicted trouble, but he certainly got some from Baker and various Canadian officials. Two days after getting Monroe's note, Baker fired off a reply designed to block Yankee moves and buy time. Claiming ignorance of western affairs, Baker said he had no guidance from London on which to act. Sending a letter to Astoria would prove fruitless, so he claimed, since he thought the post "was broken up, and the persons found there brought away."[11] At the same time, Baker wrote an urgent letter to Sir Gordon Drummond, then governor-general of Canada. Baker asked for any information bearing on the current state of Astoria and the Northwest in general. Drummond relayed Baker's request to the North West Company's partner William McGillivray. Knowing that Astoria was now the company's Fort George, McGillivray sensed real danger to Nor'wester interests. His concerns were quickly communicated to his brother Simon. Simon McGillivray was one of the most astute Nor'westers. He had long been a leading proponent of western exploration and grasped the vital connection between the fur trade and imperial expansion. Simon had just returned from London and discussions with crown officials on the future of the Northwest.[12]

McGillivray used Baker's inquiry as an occasion to present a major statement on the North West Company's Pacific ambitions. He began by arguing the case for British sovereignty in the Northwest. Britain's claims, so he asserted, were based on the right of discovery—a string of discoveries that had begun with Sir Francis Drake and had culminated in the voyages of Mackenzie, Cook, and Vancouver. Subjects of the crown were not only explorers but settlers as well. Alluding to trading posts built by the North West Company, McGillivray insisted that Canadians had occupied the West long before Lewis and Clark and the Astorians. The key to McGillivray's argument was the current status of Astoria, or Fort George. The Nor'wester insisted that the post had been properly sold and thus was not liable for restoration under the recent treaty.[13]

While the McGillivrays and other Canadians scurried to defeat any American plans, company agents were also at work in London. Although evidence is sketchy, it does seem plain that men like William and Edward Ellice were busy lobbying crown officials on the Astoria question. Sometime in the early spring of 1815 Simon McGillivray believed he had assurances from Lord Bathurst that Britain viewed the entire Pacific coast as under the protection of the crown. But by the end of July, Canadians in London were not quite sure where the government stood. Writing to Henry Goulburn, Edward Ellice sought assurances against any hostile invasion of the Northwest. More important, Ellice asked that any American move to reclaim Astoria be stoutly resisted. The government's reply hardly

satisfied the company. Neither Bathurst nor Goulburn saw any real
value for Britain in places so remote as the Columbia River. Goulburn's letter to William Ellice and Ellice's reply suggest that by
August 1815 London was once again as uninterested in the West as
had been the case in the years before 1812.[14]

Just how much John Astor knew about events in Washington,
London, and Montreal during the summer of 1815 is unclear. It is
plain that Astor had now launched a major effort to have Astoria
restored. In mid-August he sent Monroe a general report on the
course of events at Astoria. That statement carefully avoided any
mention of the Pacific Fur Company's reverses, dwelling instead on
promises of wealth and national power. Astor argued that his post
had been fraudulently sold by McDougall who had then allowed the
Royal Navy to conquer it. Though admitting that there had indeed
been a sale of the property, Astor insisted that the entire transaction
was invalid. In his mind the Treaty of Ghent absolutely required that
Fort George once again become Astoria. Astor pressed his diplomatic offensive by appealing to his friend and ally Albert Gallatin.
Soon after Gallatin returned from Europe, Astor addressed him on
the Astoria question. Astor plainly had not given up his imperial
vision. "I am confident," he wrote, "that had we not been interrupted we should have done extremely well by combining the trade
of the interior and that of the coast and from these to Canton in
China." Although Astoria had changed flags, Astor did not think the
situation beyond hope. He wanted the government to send a naval
force to the Columbia to ensure prompt restoration of the post. And
Astor hoped that to bolster American claims, the army would establish one or two permanent garrisons in the region. What had been
done so far were "mere matters of experiment." Now was the time to
take the initiative and forge a lasting American empire.[15]

Astor was not the only one urging that the United States become
a Pacific power. David Porter's exploits as captain of the USS *Essex*
had captured considerable attention in the newspapers during the
War of 1812. Those adventures had convinced the naval officer that
a Pacific presence was vital for American security. In late October

1815 Porter wrote President Madison detailing an ambitious plan for maritime exploration in the western ocean. Following the tradition of Cook and Vancouver, Porter understood that such explorations were part of a larger imperial design. No Madison reply has survived, but the president was evidently intrigued by the plan. An American naval presence in the Pacific could bolster national prestige. Those same vessels also might effect a prompt restoration of property at Astoria. To that end Secretary of the Navy Benjamin W. Crowninshield ordered the frigates *Java* and *Guerriere* to prepare for a Pacific voyage. Although those plans were abandoned by the end of 1815, they do suggest a national government increasingly aware of western interests.[16]

Since Porter's scheme did not become public knowledge until 1821, Astor probably knew nothing about the design. Despite what seemed continued federal inaction, Astor had not given up his quest to have Astoria once again in American hands. In early spring 1816 he met with Gallatin in Washington. Their conversation inevitably drifted to the future of the Northwest in general and Astoria in particular. As Gallatin remembered it some years later, Astor was "disposed once more to renew the attempt, and to re-establish Astoria." All that was lacking was reliable government protection. What Astor sought was a small infantry company, "a lieutenant's command," as Gallatin put it. This conversation was more than hopeful words. Astor asked that his suggestions be passed along to the president. Gallatin evidently did so. As he recalled later, "Mr. Madison said he would consider the subject, and although he did not commit himself, I thought he had received the proposal favorably."[17]

Gallatin was right. For reasons that are not fully clear, the Madison administration now decided to make some show of force in the Pacific. Perhaps Porter's suggestions or Gallatin's words had come at just the right time. In June 1816 Captain Charles Morris was given orders to prepare for a Pacific mission. Those orders directed Morris to take the USS *Congress* on a cruise that would touch at Astoria as part of a larger plan to assert American sovereignty along the coast.

Morris and his ship were about to sail for the Pacific when unexpected events in the Gulf of Mexico suddenly changed all plans.
While patrolling in the gulf off Veracruz, the USS *Firebrand* was
attacked by Spanish naval forces. That assault altered Morris's orders and soon he and the *Congress* were bound for Mexican waters.[18]

The plans for the *Congress* did not escape Astor's attention. In
early September, before the ship's orders were changed, Astor wrote
a hurried note to Monroe asking about the vessel's sailing plans.
"Has any farther demand," he queried, "ben made by our government of the British for that Post?"[19] Although no clear evidence
survives, Astor must have been disappointed to finally learn that no
American ship would soon force Fort George to once again become
Astoria.

Even though Astor had not given up on recovering his Columbia
River empire, there was little he could accomplish without active
federal support. Writing to Gallatin in early June 1817, he gloomily
reported, "We have no settlement on the Columbia." It was even
more painful for Astor to acknowledge that both the Russians and
the Canadians were making good profits along the coast. "They are
doing that which I wish to have and wanted to do but you know why
I did not succeed—I think it was not my fault."[20] That despair was
short-lived. As the winds of international relations had so often
worked against Astor, now those currents suddenly advanced his
cause. Tensions in the Mediterranean had lessened by the fall of
1817, as had difficulties with Spain over the future of the Floridas.
Those shifts, coupled with the expansionist views of the newly elec-
ted president, James Monroe, and his aggressive secretary of state,
John Quincy Adams, put a Pacific voyage high on the administration's priority list.

In late September, plans were fixed for such an enterprise. The
USS *Ontario*, commanded by Captain James Biddle, was selected for
the voyage. Chosen as the official American agent was Judge John
B. Prevost. Prevost was handed a number of South American duties
as well as his Columbia River charge. Just what he was to accomplish
on the Columbia was made plain in precise directions from Adams.

Prevost was ordered "to proceed to the Columbia River with a view to assert there the claim of sovereignty in the name and on the behalf of the United States, by some symbolical or other appropriate mode of setting up a claim to national authority and dominion." Although Adams showed no interest in announcing the *Ontario*'s journey to British authorities, he did caution Prevost and Captain Biddle to avoid any force against the crown's citizens or property. Though English diplomats were kept in the dark, Monroe saw to it that Astor knew what was under way. "It is the desire of the President," wrote Richard Rush, "that Mr. Astor of New York be informed of the measure contemplated in relation to Columbia River."[21]

When the *Ontario* weighed anchor out of the New York harbor on October 4, her sailing sparked another crisis for Astoria. Adams might have guessed that such a mission would provoke some British protest. He later insisted that the failure to notify either Ambassador Charles Bagot or the Foreign Office was a simple oversight. On the other hand Adams was increasingly determined to expand American influence across the continent at the expense of any imperial rival. Whatever Adams's intentions, the *Ontario*'s sailing did not escape British attention. A month after the ship put to sea Bagot began to hear rumors that the vessel had a Pacific mission that perhaps included a stop at the Columbia. Although the ambassador was uncertain just what the *Ontario* might do at Fort George, the whole business did worry him. In fact, he decided to relay his fragmentary information to Canadian authorities so that they could alert the North West Company.[22]

In mid-November Bagot got the details he sought. Simon McGillivray was then in New York on his way from London to Montreal. From what he labeled "a private source" the Canadian had learned that the *Ontario* was indeed bound for the Columbia. McGillivray was convinced that the ship's real mission was to "seize or destroy the Establishments and Trade of the North West Company upon that coast." In his mind this was yet another move in the never-ending Yankee drive to dominate the entire continent. McGillivray urged

Bagot to challenge the *Ontario*'s mission or at least obtain some sort of American explanation.[23]

Disturbed by these confusing events, Bagot decided to confront Secretary Adams directly. On November 24 the two men had a spirited exchange on the matter.[24] Bagot began the discussion by pointedly asking about the nature of the *Ontario*'s voyage. After what the British ambassador later described as a moment of embarrassed silence, Adams admitted that the vessel was destined for the Columbia. But Adams hurriedly assured Bagot that she had no orders "to destroy or disturb the trade of the North West Company." When Bagot then questioned the secretary about what the ship sought to accomplish, Adams offered what would become a familiar American argument in the following years. Astor's post, so he asserted, was the first permanent settlement in the region. It had been captured in the recent war and was now due back in its owner's hands under the provisions of the Treaty of Ghent. Adams further insisted that a proper request for restoration had been made in 1815. And, as a lame afterthought, the secretary claimed that the *Ontario*'s mission had gone unannounced by a mere slip of memory.

Bagot may have doubted that facile explanation, but he was plainly alarmed by what he heard next. Hardly missing a step, Adams launched into a detailed explanation of American claims to the entire Northwest. He airily dismissed the explorations of Mackenzie, Cook, and Vancouver, focusing instead on the voyage of Robert Gray's *Columbia*, Lewis and Clark, and the Astorians. When Bagot pressed Britain's case, Adams brushed that aside saying that England and the United States should not quarrel about "so remote a territory."

This meeting, with all its excuses and imperial rhetoric, was promptly reported to London authorities. Bagot also took time to alert Canadian officials, urging them to make sure the Nor'westers were indeed in possession of the post when the American warship arrived. Because Bagot knew so little about events at Astoria, he also worried that Canadian traders might take matters into their own hands, using force either to evict Americans already at the post or to resist a landing party from the *Ontario*. With all this confusion, deception, and imperialist language abroad, Astoria suddenly gained even greater symbolic meaning in the contest for empire.

Bagot expected that London would soon hand Washington a stiff protest. There might even be naval moves to support the crown's claims to the Northwest. But when the ambassador's report reached London in January 1818 the response was quite different. Despite years of lobbying by the North West Company, royal officials still saw little value in the Northwest. More important, the political climate discouraged any forceful action. The Foreign Office pursued a diplomacy that Lord Castlereagh described as "to appease controversy, and to secure if possible for all states a long interval of Repose." Although not accepting any American claims to territorial sovereignty, the crown decided to return Astoria to its original owners. Lord Bathurst broke the news to the Nor'westers in a late January 1818 letter. The company's men were ordered to cooperate in every way with the restoration.[25]

While British and American diplomats were moving toward what would be the first in a series of joint occupation treaties for the Oregon country, the USS *Ontario* pressed her mission. In January 1818 the vessel was off Valparaíso, bound up the western coast of South America. Quite by accident Biddle and his ship stumbled into an armed revolutionary conflict between Chile and Spain. Because the spreading violence endangered American ships and crews, Biddle spent much of the early months of 1818 shuttling between Lima and Valparaíso. When the captain suggested that it might be time to press on to the Columbia, Judge Prevost offered a surprising response. As Biddle reported Prevost's argument, "[The administration] did not regard the object of our visit to the Columbia as of importance, and . . . our going there was intended only to divert attention from the really important object of the voyage, which was Chili and Peru." Biddle strongly disagreed, insisting that his orders required a voyage to the river as soon as possible. When neither man appeared ready to compromise, Biddle left Prevost in Chile and pointed the *Ontario* north to the Columbia.[26]

On August 19 the American vessel approached the treacherous bar of the Columbia. Unlike the foolhardy Jonathan Thorn, Captain Biddle realized that any attempt to force passage over the bar would put his ship in grave danger. Biddle sent three longboats and more than fifty officers and men across the bar and toward Cape Disappointment. Landing near a Chinook village on the north side of the river, Biddle now executed his mission. But the captain's notion of that mission was not the same as the one held by Secretary Adams or British officials. Diplomats on both sides expected the *Ontario* to effect a simple transfer of ownership at Astoria. Instead, Biddle followed the unfortunate example of William Black, the Royal Navy captain. Evidently Biddle thought he was in the Northwest to claim the entire region for the United States. To that end he raised the American flag and put a lead plate on a nearby tree proclaiming all the surrounding lands for the American republic. Biddle then took his crew to Fort George. After a brief interview with North West Company men—an exchange Biddle did not even bother to record in his official report—the American party left the river. Fort George still had its royal name and Union Jack. Little appeared to have changed.[27]

At the same time that Biddle was making his Columbia sojourn, Prevost evidently began to have second thoughts about his role in the whole enterprise. When the British government decided to return Astoria to America, correspondence was directed to Royal Navy officers ordering them to provide "all necessary support" for the transfer. In early July the HMS *Blossom*, under the command of Captain Frederick Hickey, appeared at Santiago de Chile. Hickey and his ship were on their way to the Northwest, perhaps to observe the transfer of Astoria. By now Prevost was eagerly looking for passage to Astoria. When the American diplomat proposed that he become a passenger on the *Blossom*, Hickey agreed. It was the kind of strange arrangement that now seemed so much a part of Astoria's twisted history.[28]

On October 6, 1818, Prevost was at Fort George to undertake an extraordinary diplomatic ceremony. While the North West Company's chief trader, James Keith, and his employees looked on, an American flag was hoisted up the flagpole. But that flag had little practical meaning. Upon application from Keith, Prevost agreed to allow the Canadian company to continue to occupy the post. Once again nothing had changed. Fort George remained a British outpost and the Nor'westers continued to pursue their imperial designs.[29]

The diplomatic historian Frederick Merk once described events at Astoria in 1818 as having "a strange haphazardness." Indeed, the crooked course of the *Ontario*'s mission was matched by the failure of Britain to secure its formal title to territory when American officials came knocking at the Columbia. As Merk noted, British diplomats and agents both in Washington and on the Columbia neglected "to register proof of reservation of British title." Such confusion would eventually weaken British claims while strengthening American assertions to Pacific sovereignty. But for Astor it seemed all too late. When news of the 1818 Joint Occupation Treaty reached him, he bitterly complained to Gallatin that his interests had been shamefully neglected. "If I was a young man," he lamented, "I would again resume that trade—as it is I am too old and I am withdrawing from all business as fast as I can."[30]

* * *

Astoria was born in an era that linked exploration to scientific inquiry. In the Age of Enlightenment, voyages of geographic discovery advanced all branches of human understanding. Alexander Ross, one of the most articulate Astorians, saw that connection. "The progress of discovery," he wrote, "contributes not a little to the enlightenment of mankind; for mercantile interest stimulates curiosity and adventure, and combines with them to enlarge the circle of knowledge." But from the beginning, Astoria's chroniclers doubted that the Pacific Fur Company's employees did much to advance learning. Washington Irving set the tone by insisting that company records were "kept by men of business little versed in science, or curious about matters not immediately bearing upon their interests." Ross and other Astorians would have lodged a stiff protest against such a judgment.[31] Although the Astorians did not actively seek scientific discoveries as did Lewis and Clark, men like Robert Stuart, Gabriel Franchère, Ross Cox, and Alexander Ross did make important observations. And the journeys to Astoria attracted professional naturalists like John Bradbury and Thomas Nuttall. Considered in sum, the Astorian venture compiled an enviable record of scientific achievement.

That record began when Wilson Price Hunt led his overlanders up the Missouri in 1811. Quite by accident the party had with it the first two professional naturalists to study the trans-Mississippi West. John Bradbury had come to the United States in 1809 on a botanizing trip partially funded by the Liverpool Botanic Garden. After a brief stay with Jefferson at Monticello, Bradbury had gone west to St. Louis to begin fieldwork. There he met Hunt and soon became part of the overland adventure.

As a scientist Bradbury was part of the eighteenth-century natural history tradition. That approach focused on collecting, categorizing, and describing plants and animals new to science. Natural history was at root a pragmatic science, one that sought useful knowledge about soils, climates, and plant life. Bradbury proved to be an astute observer of Missouri River life. His superb *Travels in the Interior Parts of America*, published in 1819, is filled with perceptive comments on river flora and fauna. Like other naturalists, Bradbury cast his net widely. Indian cultures fascinated him and he devoted considerable space in *Travels* to detailed descriptions of Omaha, Arikara, and Mandan customs and rituals. Everything from sacred ceremonies to domestic architecture attracted him, and his writing sparkles with wit and grace.

At the end of his American sojourn Bradbury planned to return to England. There he hoped to study his specimens and publish his findings. But some of that Astorian bad luck seemed to rub off on the naturalist. The War of 1812—the same war that doomed Astoria—stranded him in America. By the time Bradbury returned to England, Frederick Pursh had already published his encyclopedic *Flora Americae Septentrionalis*. Pursh had scooped not only Lewis and Clark but Bradbury as well. Despite this setback, Bradbury pressed ahead with his *Travels*. That determination produced a remarkable scientific and personal record. Here were the natural and native worlds of the Missouri just before disease and massive white settlement forever changed those river bottoms and grasslands.[32]

Bradbury's scientific companion on the journey up the Missouri was Thomas Nuttall, another gifted English botanist. Sent west on an overambitious and underfinanced expedition, Nuttall was just beginning a distinguished scientific career when he joined the Astorians. Although he was hardly an adept frontiersman—he sometimes used a gun barrel to dig up plant specimens—his Missouri expedition evidently yielded important results. The precise character of those results is now difficult to evaluate, since whatever written records he kept on the trip have disappeared. But two sources do survive to suggest what Nuttall accomplished during his Missouri River summer. A number of the specimens collected during the journey were consigned to be sold in London by Fraser's Nursery. The catalog issued for that sale lists forty-six plants collected along the Missouri. Nuttall identified a number of them as new to science, including several kinds of alliums and vetches.[33]

A fuller discussion of Nuttall's botanizing on the Missouri River came when he published his two-volume *Genera of North American Plants with a Catalogue of the Species through 1817*. That work put Nuttall in the front rank of American botanists. As one recent scholar put it, the appearance of *Genera* in 1818 made plain Nuttall's "greatness as a taxonomist." Although many of his discoveries were first published by Pursh, Nuttall's name remains connected to several plants.[34]

Because neither Bradbury nor Nuttall was a full-fledged employee of the Pacific Fur Company, it has been easy for scholars to dismiss the connection between their important work and the Astorian enterprise. But Astor's company did provide vital support for their efforts. As early as 1806 Hunt had shown an interest in the scientific discoveries made by Lewis and Clark. Now, in his position as Astor's chief field agent, he could use his influence to promote natural history. Hunt encouraged Bradbury and Nuttall, serving in the process as an important patron of science in the West.

Robert Stuart. From anonymous photograph in Philip Ashton
Rollins, ed., *The Discovery of the Oregon Trail* (1935).

There was at least one company employee, a partner in fact, who proved to be an astute naturalist in his own right. Well-educated and with an eye for the world of plants and animals, Robert Stuart deserves attention as the company's most able field naturalist. Stuart's epic eastward trek from Astoria to St. Louis in 1812–13 is most often discussed as an important journey of geographic discovery. But that venture also yielded detailed observations about plants and animals in parts of present-day Oregon, Idaho, Wyoming, Nebraska, Kansas, and Missouri. Stuart did not employ the Linnean system. Instead he used descriptive common names like sagebrush (*Artemisia tridentata*) or serviceberry (*Amelanchier alnifolia*). Despite this taxonomic deficiency, he produced valuable botanical descriptions.

Stuart's skills as a naturalist can be seen in his remarkable survey of the Platte River valley. After spending the winter of 1812–13 at a camp near present-day Torrington, Wyoming, Stuart, Ramsay Crooks, Robert McClellan, and several hunters prepared to launch canoes on the North Platte River. Stuart and his companions soon discovered what every traveler on the Platte learned. The river was often shallow and choked with sandbars. Canoes quickly ran aground and the party was reduced to walking along the Platte's sandy banks. Rough ground and prickly-pear spines blistered the men's feet and made the going painfully slow. Despite the struggle, Stuart took time on most days to record in his traveling notebook important details about the landscape.[35]

Typical of his observations was the entry for March 22, 1813. Camped that night near present-day Bridgeport, Nebraska, Stuart drafted a memorable portrait of the Platte world. "Nothing but a boundless Prairie plentifully stocked with animals appears before us, and the river runs East South East so shallow as makes us happy at having abandoned our canoes for its bed is for the most part upwards of a mile wide and the sandbars so numerous and flat that it would require more water than we have any right to expect." Herds of buffalo, creeks fringed with cottonwoods, and a scattering of wild horses—all found a place in Stuart's notebook. Early in April, with the travelers near what is today Grand Island, Nebraska, Stuart paused to note the complex biological community that called the river home. Stuart recorded the presence of cottonwood, elm, white willow, and box elder. The banks of the Platte were choked with what he called arrow wood, perhaps dogwood or Osage orange, and low willows. This dense ground cover invited large bird populations. Stuart spotted long-billed curlews, prairie larks, sharp-tailed grouse, and prairie chickens.[36]

While Bradbury, Nuttall, and Stuart made important contributions to the natural history of the West, other Astorians were busy recording the lifeways of native peoples. Like Alexander Mackenzie, David Thompson, and Lewis and Clark, several Astorians became participant-observers of Indian cultures. Gabriel Franchère, Alexander Ross, and Ross Cox all filled their journals with detailed ethnographic notes on Indian life in the Northwest. These ethnographers did not presume to offer a systematic or objective study of native peoples. Rather, in the tradition of the period, they described material culture and daily customs in language familiar to Euro-Americans.

Gabriel Franchère spent much of his time in the Northwest at Astoria. The slow pace of life at the post gave the naturally inquisitive young Canadian time to study the lives of his lower Chinookan neighbors. Sometime during the winter of 1811–12 Franchère wrote a long, detailed essay outlining the principal features of Chinookan culture. Like his contemporaries, Franchère began his ethnographic work by observing and recording material culture. Chinookan clothing, domestic utensils, food, and housing all found a place in his journal. He was equally interested in fishing techniques and the construction of remarkably seaworthy canoes.

But Franchère's comments went well beyond a simple catalog of cedar-bark clothing, sturgeon nets, and massive plank houses. He also sought to describe social customs and cultural values. From their earliest contacts with the Chinooks, Europeans were both fascinated and repelled by the practice of head-flattening. Franchère described the process with considerable accuracy. More important, he grasped its significance as a mark of social status. Other social patterns also drew his attention. Franchère commented on the place of gender in determining work and the differing economic roles of men and women. The rituals of marriage attracted his attention. Franchère also learned something about Chinookan social structure and political organization. He recognized the place of slavery and the sharp distinctions between masters and bondsmen. Like most non-Indians, Franchère did not fully comprehend the consensual nature of the natives' politics. Raised in a world rooted in coercive authority, he could only note that village chiefs seemed to have little real power.

Unlike many traders-turned-ethnographers, Franchère sought to learn something about the spiritual lives of his native neighbors. Perhaps he expected to find some form of idol worship. And indeed the Chinooks did possess small carved statues, but Franchère soon discovered that these figures had no special religious significance. Only gradually did he learn something about the rituals and stories that formed the spiritual foundation of Chinookan life. Shamans and healing ceremonies quickly drew Franchère's attention. Although he easily branded the native healers as "charlatans," he did take careful note of the rituals employed in curing illness. Just how much of the Chinook language or the trade jargon Franchère learned is unclear, but evidence in his journal suggests that he could converse with Indians on subjects well beyond the going price of fish or fur. On a number of questions he turned to one of Comcomly's sons, "an intelligent and talkative young man." It was from this informant that Franchère gathered important creation stories. Comcomly's son also revealed beliefs about life after death. Villagers who treated their friends and families well, so the Indian explained, "would live in bliss after death in a country well stocked with fish and fruit." Those who were rough and rowdy in this life would be banished after death "to a land of famine where they would eat bitter roots and drink salt water."[37]

Franchère's Chinookan ethnography concluded with a generally positive evaluation of his neighbors across the Columbia. Although their regular practice of picking up any goods not nailed down troubled him, the clerk was impressed by the Chinooks' sense of dignity, family responsibility, and care for the elderly. He approvingly recounted the story of one of Comcomly's sons who had drunk too much Astoria liquor. "The old chief came to scold us," he wrote, "saying that we had dishonored his son by making him the laughingstock of the slaves and begging us henceforth not to give him strong drink." Impressed by Chinookan material culture and quite taken by the personalities of his neighbors, Franchère paid them what he imagined was the ultimate compliment. "With all their faults," he asserted, "they seem to me more amenable to civilization than most Indians living east of the mountains."[38] It was a sentiment that well fit the underlying assumptions of Enlightenment ethnography. Comcomly's people might not have appreciated the judgment.

Ross Cox, another company clerk, had a quite different evaluation of Chinookan peoples. In 1831 Cox published his Astoria memoir. Drawing on his own notes as well as the published version of Franchère's narrative and Nicholas Biddle's edition of Lewis and Clark, Cox drew a most unflattering picture of the river Indians. Lacking Franchère's eye for detail and the Canadian's sympathetic nature, Cox fell back on traditional stereotypes. He labeled the Tillamooks "roguish" and the Chinooks "incontinent" while the Clatsops were "most honest" and the Cathlamets "tranquil." Head-flattening drew Cox's scorn and he described it as an "inhuman" and "abominable custom." Cox found the Indians physically repulsive, insisting that their "deformity" was "unredeemed by any peculiar beauty either in features or person." Though he grudgingly admitted that many Indians were honest, he insisted that their vices far outweighed any virtues. In a burst of angry rhetoric the clerk branded the river peoples as thieves, hypocrites, liars, and cruel torturers of the innocent.[39]

Perhaps the company's most thorough ethnographer was Alexander Ross. The former schoolmaster used his quick mind and deft pen to make an enduring record of the Indians he lived among at Fort Okanogan. Those Indians were the Kartar band of the Sinkaietks. Ross made a simple dictionary of their language and in 1813 married a daughter of a prominent headman. When the trader published his *Adventures of the First Settlers on the Oregon or Columbia River* in 1849, he included four detailed chapters on Sinkaietk life and culture. Those chapters amount to a remarkable survey of everything from the objects of daily life to creation stories and healing rituals. From Indian trading partners and his wife, Ross gathered information on hunting, housing, and patterns of leadership. He managed to record all these with sharp accuracy and a remarkably dispassionate eye.[40]

Geographic discovery was an essential part of Astoria's scientific world. Patrons of exploration like Jefferson and Banks expected their parties to find new mountain ranges, passes, and rivers. The overland Astorians surely qualify as important explorers of the American West. Hunt's expedition was the second United States transcontinental crossing. That troubled enterprise took a route through parts of present Wyoming, Idaho, and Oregon yet untracked by whites. Surely the most notable geographic accomplishment for the Astorians came in 1812 when Robert Stuart and his eastbound party came upon South Pass in Wyoming's Wind River range. South Pass became an essential part of the Oregon Trail. It was rediscovered in the 1820s by Jedediah Smith, but the Astorians deserve credit as the initial European discoverers.[41]

Although Astorians like Hunt, Robert Stuart, Ramsay Crooks, and David Stuart made significant geographic discoveries, the lack of cartographic records from the company's journeys makes a fuller evaluation difficult. Information from the various Astoria expeditions was recorded in only a handful of maps. William Clark's master map of the West contains a dotted line marked "Mr. W. P. Hunt's rout in 1811." From a source now unknown, Clark traced Hunt's overland journey from the Arikara villages into present-day Wyoming. He also named a tributary of the mythical Rio del Norte after Crooks. Although he must have learned about additional travels by Astorians, especially the journeys of Robert Stuart, little of that important knowledge found its way into his map.[42]

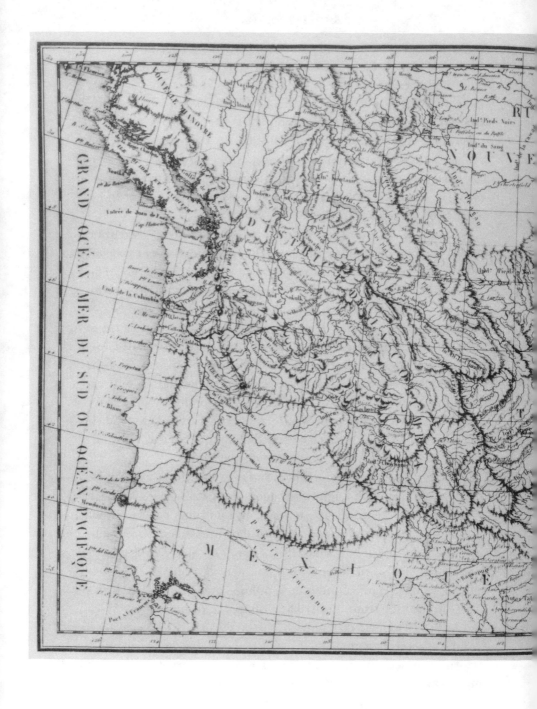

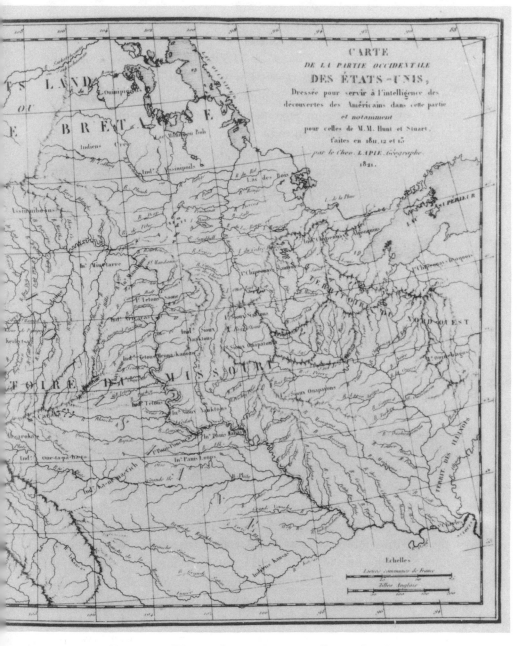

The routes of Hunt and Stuart. From *Nouvelles Annales*, 1821.
Collection of the author.

When Astor and Gallatin arranged for important Pacific Fur Company records to be published in the *Nouvelles Annales des Voyages de la Géographie et de l'Histoire* (1821), the documents were accompanied by a modest map. Drafted by an unknown cartographer, the map claimed to illustrate the journeys of Hunt, Stuart, and other Astorians. Bearing both English and French place-names, the map did reflect some exploration by the overlanders. Hunt's journey is traced, noting such features as the Mad, or Snake, River and the Grand Tetons, cited on the map as the Pilot Knobs. Stuart's important eastward passage is also treated, but South Pass is virtually lost in a clutter of hills and mountains. Though the map may well be the earliest to contain extensive information recorded by the Astorians, its small scale and limited distribution did little to enhance the standing of the company's men as western explorers.[43]

When Washington Irving published *Astoria* in 1836, the first edition contained a simple sketch map. If any Astorian had drawn a detailed map of the West, Irving would have been the person to see it. But no company man ever mentioned such a project, and the map of the Astorians' routes is plainly based on information Irving got from B.L.E. Bonneville. Entitled "Sketch of the Routes of Hunt and Stuart," it follows those paths but offers little else. In fact, it was quite inferior to those available as early as 1814. The map in *Astoria* perpetuated the image of the Rockies as narrow ranges of mountains easily traversed on foot or by wagon. It goes so far as to show one branch of the Missouri actually piercing the Continental Divide. The Astorians saw much of the West, but little of what they experienced found formal cartographic expression.

Joseph Charless, pioneer editor of the *Missouri Gazette*, saw clearly the scientific dimensions of the Astorian enterprise. Writing soon after the departure of Hunt's overlanders, the journalist confidently predicted that the venture was bound to produce "a rich scientific harvest, gratifying to the philosopher, and probably useful to society in general."[44] If a modern appraisal of Astoria's contribution to science is somewhat less enthusiastic, Charless's judgment remains close to the mark. Laboring within the confines of Enlightenment science, Astorians both in and out of the company's employ produced a remarkable body of western knowledge. Botany, ethnography, and geography were strengths of the Astorian enterprise, which yielded formal published studies like those done by Nuttall and Bradbury as well as important personal memoirs. Books by Ross, Franchère, and Cox added to a growing literature making the West less a land of fantasy and more a territory marked and defined.

* * *

Writing two decades after the official death of Astoria, Washington Irving argued that the enterprise could become "the watchword in a contest for dominion on the shores of the Pacific." Jefferson would have agreed. In a memorable 1813 letter to Astor, he predicted that Astoria would become "the germ of a great, free and independent empire." And the former president flattered Astor, comparing him to empire builders like Columbus and Ralegh. At a time when the journeys of Robert Gray, Meriwether Lewis, and William Clark were receding from the national imagination, Astoria was rapidly becoming the preeminent public symbol for American expansion to the Pacific. Fueled by both diplomatic wrangling and political expansionism, Astoria took on a symbolic life quite apart from Astor's original venture.[45]

No single political figure was more important in making Astoria a symbol for American imperial dreams than Thomas Hart Benton. In the years after 1820 Benton repeatedly offered legislation calling for a forceful reassertion of American sovereignty along the Columbia. Speech after speech portrayed Astoria as the first American western settlement, a colony on the great River of the West. Even before coming to the Senate in 1819, Benton used Astoria as the grounds for a grand empire stretching from the Missouri River to the Pacific. A series of St. Louis newspaper essays published by Benton in 1818 and 1819 presented the case for an American West. And Benton saw the Oregon country not only as a fur empire but as a place for agriculture as well.[46] These sentiments echoed much of what Astor had plotted years before. And the parallels were no

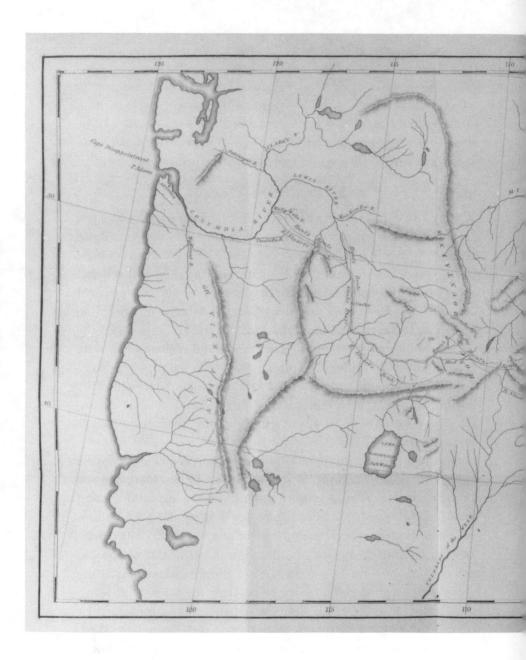

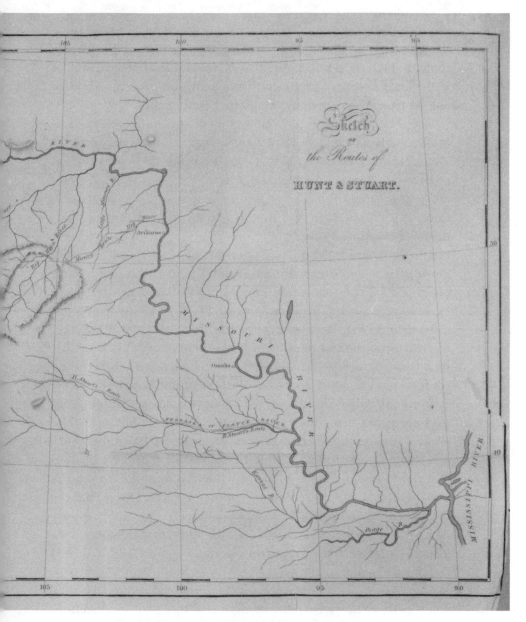

Sketch of the routes of Hunt and Stuart. From Irving, *Astoria*
(1836). Collection of the author.

accident. The new senator from Missouri would prove to be one of the American Fur Company's best Washington allies in the years to come. Benton liked to imagine that he had inherited the mantle of leadership in western expansion from Jefferson. Heir apparent or not, he gave Astor's notions yet another lease on life.

When Benton came to Washington in the winter of 1820 to assume his Senate seat, he took up residence at the popular Brown's Hotel. He quickly discovered that two former Astorians were staying at Brown's. Ramsay Crooks and Russel Farnham were still employees of Astor's, though now in the service of the American Fur Company. They were in Washington as lobbyists working to dismantle the government's Indian trading-house system. Benton was eventually to prove helpful in that effort. Also at Brown's was John Floyd, a Democratic representative from Virginia. A distant relative of Sergeant Charles Floyd, the only member of the Lewis and Clark expedition to die on the great journey, Floyd had long been interested in the West. Benton, Crooks, Farnham, and Floyd met regularly during the last months of 1820. Benton recalled later that their conversation, "rich in information upon a new and interesting country, was eagerly devoured by the ardent spirit of Floyd."[47]

Although the evidence is not wholly clear, it was probably Benton who suggested that these talks take on legislative substance. The senator strongly opposed joint occupation of the Oregon country and found Floyd a willing ally. On December 19, 1820, Floyd moved that the House of Representatives name a committee "to inquire into the situation of the settlements upon the Pacific Ocean, and the expediency of occupying the Columbia River." Floyd was promptly named to head the committee. The two additional members were Thomas Metcalf, a Democrat from Kentucky, and Floyd's Virginia colleague Thomas Swearingen.[48]

The report issued by the committee at the end of January 1821 and legislation proposed to further the report plainly revealed Benton's influence. Floyd and his committee insisted that the Northwest coast offered great wealth in fur, whales, and the ever attractive China trade. The region's promise had been unrealized, so ran the report, until John Astor had developed a systematic program to exploit the fur trade. Astoria itself was described as "this little colony." That emphasis on colonization fit the real goal of the report. Floyd and Benton were interested in permanent agricultural settlement along the coast. Fur trade posts like Astoria would become full-fledged farming communities. Such towns would eventually demand territorial status and perhaps even statehood. With the Floyd report the conception of American empire moved from Jefferson's St. Louis–based trade system to a farmers' frontier politically linked to the national union. The imperial implications were unmistakable.

Floyd's report was backed up by a legislative proposal designed to advance what Benton and others had in view. The draft bill was an astounding attack on the 1818 joint-occupation agreement. It authorized the president immediately to occupy lands along the Columbia, extinguish Indian title, and create formal governmental relations. If the bill's supporters were to have their way, Jefferson's Astoria "germ" was about to come alive.[49]

The report and its proposals for the occupation of the Columbia came at a time of increased interest in exploration and expansion. Secretary of War John C. Calhoun had already experimented with the use of federal troops as explorers in the ill-fated Missouri Expedition of 1819. Though that effort was largely unsuccessful, the venture did mark the renewal of official western activity after the War of 1812. Nationalism and resentment over the 1818 treaty with Great Britain prepared the ground for Benton and Floyd. Within a day after the report was issued, the *National Intelligencer* was full of comments about the revival of American enterprise in the West. Observations by a number of politicians suggested that the bill was just the beginning for a vigorous nation destined to spread its influence from Atlantic to Pacific waters.[50]

No one studied these reports with more attention than the British ambassador, George Canning. What worried him was the evident determination of the American government to establish a colony on the Columbia. He read accounts of Floyd's proposal in the *National Intelligencer*, accounts that emphasized claims of American sovereignty on the Pacific. Thinking that there had been a profound shift in federal foreign policy, Canning decided to pay a call on the secretary of state. Although John Quincy Adams did not openly support the Benton-Floyd plan, he did have a large vision of the Republic. Astoria's place in that vision was about to be sharply challenged.

When Canning came to Adams's office on the evening of January 26, he was filled with indignation over the reports in the *Intelligencer*.[51] The ambassador believed that the newspaper reports reflected official policy, a policy he now thought was bent on forming "a new settlement on the South Sea." Adams smoothly replied that he had not read those press accounts. Instead of stopping with this polite rebuttal, Adams suddenly decided to add his own expansionist views to the conversation. "It was very probable," he later recalled telling Canning, "that our settlement at the mouth of the Columbia would at no remote moment be increased." When Canning asked if this was a statement of official American policy, Adams quickly backed off and insisted that these were his own notions. But Canning guessed otherwise and insisted that any American moves on the Columbia would violate the 1818 treaty. Adams's response was to stride over to his office bookshelf and find a printed copy of the convention. When the secretary of state began to lecture Canning on the 1818 treaty, telling him as well that all future communications on the subject had to be in written form, the British diplomat lost any semblance of cool reserve. Adams remembered Canning's saying, "with great vehemence," that he was not about to be dictated to on the means of official communication. The meeting ended in a torrent of argument and loud voices.

Neither Canning's temper nor Adams's expansionist rhetoric cooled overnight. When the two met the next day, Astoria was still at the center of the storm. Pressed by Canning to define the extent of American claims in the West, Adams asserted that the nation was bound to stretch "to all the shores of the South Sea." But there was more. The secretary also rejected any British claims, thus striking at the very heart of the 1818 treaty. When Canning asked if the United

States would protest a British settlement in the region, Adams snapped, "I have no doubt we should."

Had Canning known how much support the Benton-Floyd proposals were generating in Congress, he might have protested even louder. In printed circular letters sent home to their constituents, many congressmen voiced approval for a reassertion of American sovereignty on the Pacific. William Hendricks, a Democrat from Indiana, couched his support in typically Jeffersonian language. "It will be gratifying to the friends of philanthropy and liberty," he exclaimed, "to see the mild and salutary influence of the Republic extended beyond the summit of the Rocky Mountains, to the Columbia, on the shores of the Pacific Ocean."[52]

When the House of Representatives resumed debate on the Floyd Bill in December 1822, the measure appeared to have considerable backing. Floyd's speech urging approval revealed both the growing power of Manifest Destiny and the symbolic place that Astoria now had in expansionist thinking. Astoria, Floyd argued, was the foundation of an American empire. Reclaimed and rebuilt, it would become the center of a vast domain. "The settlement on the Oregon [the Columbia]," he trumpeted, "connecting the trade of that river and the coast with the Missouri and Mississippi, is to open a mine of wealth to the shipping interests and the western country, surpassing the hopes even of avarice itself." That "mine of wealth" would enhance the fortunes not only of traders and sailors but of settlers as well. The Benton-Floyd approach saw farming communities as the result of the two men's labors. "The lands of the Oregon," Floyd claimed, "are well adapted to the culture of rye, corn, barley, and every species of grain."[53]

On December 19 the House passed a resolution asking the executive branch to provide all available documents bearing on Astoria and American claims in the West. Five days later Adams wrote Astor requesting any materials he might have. Astor quickly seized on this moment as an opportunity once again to advance his Pacific dreams. On January 4, 1823, he sent Adams a number of important Pacific Fur Company documents, including correspondence and post inventories. He also included a long, detailed history of Astoria. That self-serving account emphasized Astoria's promise, a promise betrayed, as Astor told it, by Duncan McDougall's "misuse of confidence." But in the right hands, Astoria's empire could be reborn to yield personal profit and national glory.[54]

Whatever the favorable signs, when the Floyd Bill came to a vote on January 27 it was defeated. Regional interests, combined with fears of disunion, doomed the measure.[55] No sooner had the Floyd Bill been lost in the House than Benton introduced a similar measure in the Senate. Benton's February 17 speech remains a classic statement of American imperialist thought and Astoria's ideological significance. Astoria was, so he asserted, "an American settlement." The post was no mere trading house but a genuine colony that qualified for primacy in the contest for Pacific sovereignty. The creation of Astoria was the act by which "the title of the United States was consummated." Astoria in British hands would mean the "destruction of the commerce of all other powers." From Astoria, Britain could hold hostage all western North America. Playing on Anglophobia, Benton insisted, "Not an American ship will be able to show itself beyond Cape Horn, but with the permission of England." To give up Astoria was to surrender the entire West and the Pacific to John Bull. To retake Astoria was to bring the United States to its rightful place in the world of nations.[56]

The Benton-Floyd proposals served many purposes. They provided a platform for imperialist rhetoric and they kept alive the dream of American empire. Equally important, the speeches established Astoria as the principal symbol of America's western dominion. John Quincy Adams surely saw Astoria in that light. Reporting on the Floyd Bill to Ambassador Richard Rush, Adams predicted, "There cannot be a doubt that in the course of a very few years it must be carried into effect." In Adams's words, "the finger of Nature" pointed to Astoria and empire.[57]

John Astor may have hoped that the London Conference of 1826–27 would finally resolve Astoria's future. But the meeting simply reaffirmed the principle of joint occupation. Writing to Gal-

Astoria in the late 1830s. Courtesy of the Montana Historical
Society

latin early in 1827, Astor seemed both bitter and resigned. "I am however sorry to see that nothing is to be done about the subject relative to the western coast. I never had but one opinion—our government ought in 1815 or 16 taking possession [to have] placed a post of 50 men which would have been as good as 5000—our people would have gone to trade and got the Indians with them." That American diplomats had failed to press Astoria's claims infuriated Astor. In a rare moment of anger with Gallatin, he charged, "The convention you yourself made gave them [the British] the country."[58]

* * *

By the time Astor began negotiations with Washington Irving in 1834 to write the history of the Pacific Fur Company, Astoria had been abandoned by British traders. Henceforth the center for British commerce would be Fort Vancouver. Travelers found Astoria's gardens choked with weeds and the buildings crumbling to ruin.[59] But Astoria had long since moved from the world of beaver pelts and ledger books to the realm of national destiny. When the soldier and explorer Theodore Talbot visited Astoria in 1849, he found a scattering of log houses that marked the beginnings of a modest fishing village. But the most important thing to come out of that brief visit was the telling phrase he wrote in a letter to his sister. Both had read Irving's *Astoria* and both accepted the place of Astoria in American claims to the West. Astoria, wrote Talbot, was that place "of which we have all heard and read so much."[60] Astoria had become a cultural commonplace, a national expression for the drive to forge an American West.

APPENDIX

After Irving: Astoria's Chroniclers

DESPITE A SHORT LIFE and an unfortunate end, Astoria and the Pacific Fur Company have never wanted for chroniclers. The Astorians themselves sensed that their errand along the Columbia meant something beyond pelts and profits. Gabriel Franchère, Ross Cox, and Alexander Ross wrote book-length accounts of their service in the Northwest. Two other clerks—Alfred Seton and William W. Matthews—also set down brief recollections of their days with Astor's company. Taken with the diary of Alexander Henry the younger, these traders' narratives make for a richly personal version of Astoria's empire.

That empire got its first comprehensive treatment from the pen of Washington Irving. In April 1832, Irving returned to his native New York and acclaim as the premier American man of letters. Seventeen years in Europe—years filled with business affairs and diplomatic service—had been Irving's literary apprenticeship. Even before leaving home in 1815 he had tilled the field of letters with such productions as the satirical *History of New York*, ostensibly the work of a scholar named Knickerbocker. But it took European landscapes and a friendship with Sir Walter Scott to spark Irving's love of romance and drama. Beginning with *The Sketch Book* (1819),

Irving wrote half a dozen books and collections of essays on everything from the life of Christopher Columbus to English Christmas customs. Having so long celebrated the European experience, Irving was now ready to take on American subjects.

That intention found print in his *Tour on the Prairies*. The occasion for Irving's first western book was a chance meeting with Henry L. Ellsworth, a federal commissioner headed west to oversee the resettlement of Indians under President Andrew Jackson's Indian-removal program. Friendship between Irving and Ellsworth led to an offer for the author to serve as the commissioner's secretary. The journey (September–November 1832) through present-day Missouri, Kansas, Oklahoma, and Arkansas was Irving's initiation into the world of rough-handed frontiersmen, western Indians, and a vast prairie landscape. Publication of *Tour on the Prairies* in 1835 announced Irving as an important writer about the western scene.

But even before *Tour* appeared, Irving and John Astor began talks that would eventually lead to *Astoria*. Sometime during the summer of 1834 Astor approached Irving about writing a history of the Pacific Fur Company. Astor's motives for wanting a public recounting of an apparently failed enterprise have always been obscure. It was not the first time he had sought publication of Astoria materials. In 1821 Astor and Gallatin had arranged for a French translation of Hunt's overland journal and a summary of parts of McDougall's Fort Astoria diary. Irving thought that Astor seemed bored by retirement and perhaps would enjoy reliving Astoria's halcyon days. More important, the author guessed the merchant was intent on securing a place in the history of his adopted country. Jefferson had once ranked Astor with Columbus and Ralegh. Irving was now to ensure that place.

What Astor offered Irving was a treasure trove of documents of the Pacific Fur Company. Among the items were Hunt's journals and letters, McDougall's Fort Astoria diary, Robert Stuart's overland journal, the company's ledger books, and correspondence with everyone from Captain Jonathan Thorn to Charles Gratiot. Added to this was the promise of interviews with surviving Astorians like

Ramsay Crooks and Robert Stuart. Here was an embarrassment of riches, and Irving was plainly tempted. As he saw it, the book Astor had in mind could be filled with "curious and entertaining matter, comprising adventurous expeditions by sea and land, scenes beyond the Rocky Mountains, incidents and scenes illustrative of Indian character, and of that singular and but little known class, the traders and voyageurs of the Fur Companies."[1] Busy working on drafts of his *Tour on the Prairies* and *The Crayon Miscellany*, Irving doubted that he had the time to sift through Astoria's voluminous records. That assignment he offered to his nephew, Pierre Munro Irving. Pierre was to be a research assistant, gathering and comparing documents and perhaps preparing convenient summaries. Pierre accepted the offer and by the spring of 1835 he was hard at work.

Irving originally assumed that he would simply take Pierre's summarizing and "dress it up advantageously, and with little labor, for the press."[2] But by the summer of 1835 Irving was increasingly fascinated by the story and its arresting characters. Spending weeks on end at Hellgate, Astor's estate along the Hudson, Irving gave the narrative his full attention. He now envisioned *Astoria* as a great American romance, a dramatic tale that might reveal the spirit of a daring and heroic West. For Irving, Astor's employees were neither simple traders nor agents of national destiny. Crooks, Mackenzie, the Stuarts, and their hardy companions were western Launcelots and Galahads. In a theme perfected in *The Adventures of Captain Bonneville, U.S.A.* (1837), Irving cast the fur traders as an American chivalry, a noble band of westering knights. Irving intended to do for the American West what Sir Walter Scott had done in the Waverley novels for the Scottish border. Both Irving and Scott would have nodded in approval on seeing Alfred Jacob Miller's sketch of Jim Bridger wearing armor and a plumed helmet.

By December 1835 the manuscript was nearly complete. In late October 1836 the Philadelphia firm of Carey, Lea, and Blanchard published *Astoria; or, Anecdotes of an Enterprise beyond the Rocky Mountains*. Irving predicted commercial success for the book and he was quickly proved right. In addition to American printings there were soon English, French, German, Dutch, and Swedish editions. By the time Irving's *Collected Works* appeared in 1849, *Astoria* had become an American literary perennial. In fact, *Astoria* became synonymous with Astor's entire project. Astoria and *Astoria* seemed one and the same.[3]

Because *Astoria* did so much to foster an idealized vision of the Far West, modern historians have been quick to criticize Irving. Over the years more has been written about Fort Astoria's literary namesake than about the original venture. Indeed, there is much to fault in Irving's work. *Astoria* is filled with heroes and villains, bold deeds and sinister betrayals. Irving cared little for the subtleties of diplomacy or social history. Modern readers familiar with the surviving original sources often find Irving guilty of copying directly from those records, sometimes without attribution. But Irving wrote in an age innocent of today's scholarly conventions. More important, he wrote about the past not as history but as dramatic romance. No other scholar has more carefully studied Irving's use of sources than Edgeley W. Todd. In his superb critical edition of *Astoria*, published in 1964, Todd painstakingly compared those surviving sources available to him with Irving's text. Todd found that Irving generally respected the integrity of the original sources. Long before rules of quotation and citation were set in place, Irving used document summaries as a means to lend authenticity to his work. Only when he drifted from those records did the book go astray. *Astoria* was and remains what Irving intended it to be: a compelling tale of romance and adventure.

Even though Irving emphasized drama and color, he did sense that what had happened at Astoria meant more than something out of the pages of Sir Walter Scott. *Astoria* concluded with a memorable line, one that would later spark fresh interest in Astoria's wider meaning. Writing with an eye toward future Anglo-American tensions in the Northwest, Irving predicted that a renewal of the Oregon Question could well make Astoria "the watchword in a contest for dominion on the shores of the Pacific."[4] Irving understood that contest to be a political and diplomatic one pitting an American empire against its Anglo-Canadian rival. That the struggle might also be for cultural dominion, with combatants from many different backgrounds, largely eluded Irving. The tacked-on phrase about "contest for dominion" did not reflect *Astoria's* essentially romantic thrust. And in the years that followed, it was that romantic perspective that dominated literary visions of Astor's enterprise. When popular writers from Mayne Reid and Karl May to Ned Buntline and Agnes Laut depicted the West after Lewis and Clark, they found a ready-made cast and script in Irving's books. Here was all the drama and excitement American and European audiences had come to expect from any western tale. Perhaps it was only an oversight that no Astorian was ever listed among the stalwarts portrayed in Buffalo Bill Cody's Wild West shows.

It was not until 1902 that Astoria enjoyed a discussion that began to escape Irving's definition of the subject. At the beginning of the century, American historians found eastern subjects more rewarding than western ones. Ignored by professional scholars, western themes were considered the province of journalists and novelists. Captain Hiram M. Chittenden was one who did not share that contempt for western history. Years of western travel in the service of the Army Corps of Engineers had taught him the larger significance of the region. Chittenden coupled that travel with careful research in neglected regional archives. His *American Fur Trade of the Far West* was the first serious study of the subject. Chittenden read all the published accounts of Astoria as well as the important Astor-Gratiot correspondence. This research convinced him that the rise and demise of the Pacific Fur Company was both a good tale and important history. Chittenden devoted seven chapters to the planning of Astor's venture, the various land and sea expeditions, and a measured evaluation of the enterprise. Chittenden was convinced that Astor's plan to engross the entire western fur trade was essentially sound. What doomed the venture, so he argued, was a deadly combination of war, inept leadership, and bad luck.

In his book Chittenden also took upon himself the task of defending Washington Irving against charges of plagiarism. Writing in his

History of the Northwest Coast, Hubert Howe Bancroft had asserted that Irving had lifted large portions of the Franchère, Ross, and Cox narratives for use in *Astoria*. This was done, so Bancroft insisted, without any proper bibliographic references. Chittenden correctly noted in reply that Irving had indeed acknowledged his debt to Franchère and Cox. And the redoubtable Captain Chittenden could not resist pointing out that Ross's book had appeared more than a dozen years after *Astoria*.

Much of Chittenden's pioneering scholarship focused on fur companies and their violent trade wars. Despite his concern with the genealogies of rival Rocky Mountain trading firms, Chittenden did give some attention to Astoria's larger diplomatic consequences. He realized that Astor's employees had taken part in a struggle that would determine the political future and imperial shape of the Northwest. "If the Astorian enterprise had succeeded," he speculated, "the course of the empire on the American continent would have been altogether different than it has been."[5] Chittenden recognized that the venture had been central to the clash of empires but paid little attention to any of Astoria's Canadian, Russian, and Indian rivals. For Chittenden and so many of those who followed his example, Astoria's meaning rested with Astor's men, not their political and cultural adversaries.

Chittenden's effort to edge Astoria out of Irving's shadow was largely unnoticed by other historians. The most popular school history texts of the teens and twenties either ignored the Astorians or dismissed them as colorful failures. And many writers, like David L. Muzzey in 1911, continued to repeat the tired claim that the post was surrendered to a powerful British naval force.[6] Astoria fared little better at the hands of professional historians. Frederic L. Paxson's standard *History of the American Frontier* (1924) gave Astoria only a few scant lines; three years earlier Constance L. Skinner had offered an extended paraphrase of Irving.[7]

What the historiography of Astoria needed was not so much a new interpretation as some fresh evidence. So long as scholars studied Astoria only by reading Irving, little would change. The much-

needed documentary transfusion came in 1931 with the publication
of Kenneth W. Porter's two-volume biography of Astor. Porter was
interested in examining economic development and business enterprise in the young Republic. No businessman had been more deeply
involved in that growth than John Astor. Porter was the first scholar
to use the Astor Papers as well as a number of other important
archival sources. *John Jacob Astor, Business Man* not only cast new light
on the early national economy but also put Astoria firmly within the
context of Astor's other commercial dealings. Porter was not interested in the comings and goings of western traders and their Indian
partners. Questions of geographic discovery and natural history
were left to others. Porter's angle of vision was from the countinghouse. However that limited the scope of his analysis, Porter's Astoria had moved far from Irving's romantic celebration of high
adventure on a distant frontier.

Porter's discussion of Astoria should have prompted a full-scale
history of the enterprise. Although no scholar in the decades immediately after Porter took up that formidable challenge, interest in the
subject did grow. More important, historians began to see that Astoria had a life and a meaning separate from Irving's book. Frederick
Merk's essays, collected in *The Oregon Question* (1967), probed the
ways in which Astoria became a center of controversy in Anglo-
American diplomacy. Philip Ashton Rollins carefully edited and
annotated Robert Stuart's overland journal as well as the fragmentary materials of Hunt and McDougall. Ramsay Crooks enjoyed an
extended biographical treatment in David Lavender's *The Fist in the
Wilderness* (1964). The accounts by Franchère, Cox, and Ross all
underwent serious scholarly scrutiny and emerged in new formal
editions. The publication of important documents from Russian
archives showed for the first time Astoria's reach toward Russian
America. Equally significant was the rediscovery of Duncan Mc-
Dougall's journal. That source, not used since Irving had paged
through it, illuminated the daily lives of otherwise unknown Astorians.

Explorers of Astoria's empire have found kingdoms of adventure, commerce, and diplomacy. The Astorians have been portrayed as daring trappers, diligent clerks, and diplomats in buckskin. Astoria has long represented the dreams of policy planners and entrepreneurs. In a West where national boundaries and cultural destinies were yet to be fixed, Astoria also symbolized the struggles of ordinary French-Canadian engagés, Indian traders, and Hawaiian laborers. Fort Astoria's mixture of tongues and habits hinted at a richly diverse West. In that West, Astoria was indeed the watchword of a powerful contest for cultural dominion. Astoria held the dreams of John Astor and all his influential rivals. It was also home ground for men as different as Paul Denis Jérémie, Ignace Shonowane, and Dick Paou. Astoria's empire represented many dreams and voices. All demand an attentive hearing.

Abbreviations in the Notes

Astor Papers, Beinecke-CtY
: John Jacob Astor Papers, Western Americana Collection, Beinecke Rare Book and Manuscript Library, Yale University, New Haven, Connecticut.

Astor Papers, MD-BA
: John Jacob Astor Papers, Baker Library, Harvard University Graduate School of Business Administration, Boston, Massachusetts.

Dip. Docs.
: W. R. Manning, ed., *Diplomatic Correspondence of the United States: Canadian Relations, 1784–1860.* 4 vols. Washington, D.C.: Government Printing Office, 1940–45.

DLC
: Library of Congress, Washington, D.C. Cited with appropriate collection name.

DNA
: National Archives, Washington, D.C. Always preceded by an RG (record group) number.

Gallatin Papers, NHi
: Albert Gallatin Papers, New-York Historical Society, New York City.

McDougall, Journal
: Duncan McDougall, Journal at Astoria, 1811–1813, 3 vols. Rosenbach Library and Museum, Philadelphia, Pennsylvania.

MoSHi
: Missouri Historical Society, St. Louis, Missouri. Always preceded by the appropriate collection name.

PAC
: Public Archives of Canada, Ottawa, Ontario, Canada. Always preceded by the appropriate MG (management group) number or collection name.

PRO
: Public Record Office, London, England. Always preceded by the appropriate manuscript class identification.

Russ. Docs.
: Nina N. Bashkina and David F. Trask, eds. *The United States and Russia: The Beginnings of Relations, 1765–1815.* Washington, D.C.: Government Printing Office, 1980.

Notes

CHAPTER 1

1. McDougall, Journal, July 4, 1812.

2. Astor to De Witt Clinton, New York, January 25, 1808, De Witt Clinton Papers, 4:5–6, Butler Rare Book and Manuscript Library, Columbia University, New York. A complete discussion of Astor's early correspondence with Clinton, Jefferson, and Gallatin can be found in chapter 2.

3. Gabriel Franchère, *Journal of a Voyage on the North West Coast of North America during the Years 1811, 1812, 1813, and 1814*, ed. W. Kaye Lamb (Toronto: Champlain Society, 1969), pp.42–43; Washington Irving, *Astoria; or, Anecdotes of an Enterprise beyond the Rocky Mountains* (1836), ed. Edgeley W. Todd (Norman: University of Oklahoma Press, 1964), pp.28–30; Alexander Ross, *Adventures of the First Settlers on the Oregon or Columbia River* (1849), reprinted with an introduction by James P. Ronda (Lincoln: University of Nebraska Press, 1986), pp.34–37.

4. Bernard DeVoto, *The Course of Empire* (Boston: Houghton, Mifflin Co., 1952), p.539.

5. Hamilton to Colonial Office, Quebec, April 9, 1785, CO 42/47/667–68, PRO.

6. Pond's recollections for the years 1740–76 are printed in Charles M. Gates, ed., *Five Fur Traders of the Northwest* (St. Paul: Minnesota Historical Society, 1965), pp.18–59. Also valuable for Pond's career are Daniel Francis, *Battle for the West: Fur Traders and the Birth of Western Canada* (Edmonton: Hurtig Publishers, 1982), pp.42–47; Harold A. Innis, *Peter Pond: Fur Trader and Adventurer* (Toronto: Irwin and Gordon, 1930); Henry R. Wagner, *Peter Pond: Fur Trader and Explorer* (New Haven: Yale University Library, 1955). W. Stewart Wallace's essay "Was Peter Pond a Murderer?" in his *The Pedlars from Quebec and Other Papers on the Nor'Westers* (Toronto: Ryerson Press, 1954), pp.19–26, discusses the violent side of Pond's nature.

7. J. C. Beaglehole, ed., *The Journals of Captain James Cook. The Voyage of the "Resolution" and the "Discovery," 1776–1780* (Cambridge, England: Hakluyt Society, 1967), pt. 1:cxxviii, 367. See also Glyndwr Williams, "Myth and Reality: James Cook and the Theoretical Geography of North America," in Robin Fisher and Hugh Johnston, eds., *Captain James Cook and His Times* (Seattle: University of Washington Press, 1979), pp.59–80.

8. James K. Munford, ed., *John Ledyard's Journal of Captain Cook's Last Voyage* (1783; reprint, Corvallis: Oregon State University Press, 1963), pp.80–81; John Rickman, *Journal of Captain Cook's Last Voyage to the Pacific Ocean* (London: E. Newbery, 1781), p.253. See also Barry M. Gough, "James Cook and the Origins of the Maritime Fur

Trade," *American Neptune* 38 (1978): 217–24.

9. Reproductions of Pond's maps can be found in Wagner, *Pond*, map portfolio. Wagner does not print the Pond map published in March 1790 by *Gentleman's Magazine*.

10. North West Company to Haldimand, Montreal, October 4, 1784, MG 11, Q Series, vol.24–2, pp.405–8, PAC.

11. Pond, "A Map Presented to Congress, New York, March 1, 1785," in Wagner, *Pond*, map 1.

12. Hamilton to Colonial Office, Quebec, April 9, 1785, CO 42/47/667–68, PRO; North West Company to Hamilton, Quebec, April 18, 1785, CO 42/47/649–51, PRO. The map Pond gave to Hamilton can be found in Wagner, *Pond*, map 2.

13. Hamilton to Colonial Office, Quebec, April 9, 1785, CO 42/47/667–68, PRO. See also Hamilton to Sidney, Quebec, June 6, 1785, MG 11, Q Series, vol.24–2, pp.403–4, PAC.

14. Wagner, *Pond*, map 3.

15. Patrick Small to Simon McTavish, Montreal, February 24, 1788, MG 19, Masson Collection, PAC.

16. Mackenzie, undated note, in W. Kaye Lamb, ed., *The Journals and Letters of Sir Alexander Mackenzie* (Cambridge, England: Hakluyt Society, 1970), p.19.

17. Diego Maria de Gardoqui to Conde de Floridablanca, Philadelphia, June 25, 1789, in A. P. Nasatir, ed., *Before Lewis and Clark: Documents Illustrating the History of the Missouri, 1785–1804*, 2 vols. (St. Louis: St. Louis Historical Documents Foundation, 1952), 1:130–31.

18. Isaac Ogden to David Ogden, Quebec, November 7, 1789, MG 11, Q Series, vol.49, pp.357–59, PAC.

19. *Gentleman's Magazine*, March 1790, 197–99; Instructions to Captain George Vancouver, March 8, 1791, in W. Kaye Lamb, ed., *The Voyage of George Vancouver, 1791–1795*, 4 vols. (London: Hakluyt Society, 1984), 1:284.

20. Nooth to Banks, Quebec, November 4, 1789, Sir Joseph Banks Papers, Sutro Library, San Francisco, California.

21. Mackenzie to Simcoe, York, September 10, 1794, in Lamb, *Sir Alexander Mackenzie*, pp.455–56. See also Simcoe to Privy Council for Trade and Plantations, York, early September 1794, in E. A. Cruikshank, ed., *The Correspondence of Lieut.-Gov. John Graves Simcoe, with Allied Documents*, 5 vols. (Toronto: Ontario Historical Society, 1923–31), 3:68–69.

22. Mackenzie to Hobart, London, January 7, 1802, in Lamb, ed., *Sir Alexander Mackenzie*, pp.503–7; Mackenzie to Sullivan, Montreal, October 25, 1802, ibid., pp.509–11; Mackenzie to Castlereagh, London, March 10, 1808, ibid., pp.516–19; Mackenzie to Board of Trade, London, April 1810, ibid., p.516. The 1810 petition was a copy of the 1808 memorial with added anti-American sentiments reflecting Mackenzie's worries about Astor's Pacific Fur Company.

23. Henry to Hamilton and Reid, Montreal, December 21, 1792, in Grace P. Morris, ed., "Some Letters from 1792–1800 on the China Trade," *Oregon Historical Quarterly* 42 (1941): 52–53.

24. Hallowell to Simon McTavish, Montreal, May 23, 1795, in ibid., pp.60–61. See also Joseph Frobisher to McTavish, June 12, 1793, ibid., p.54, and Hallowell to McTavish, Montreal, August 21, 1794, ibid., pp.54–55.

25. Mackenzie to McTavish, Fraser, and Co., New York, February 12, 1798, in ibid., pp.68–69; John Fraser to Simon McTavish, London, April 4, 1798, ibid., p.75. The quotation is from McTavish, Fraser, and Co. to McTavish, Frobisher, and Co., London, December 14, 1799, ibid., p.85.

26. Arthur S. Morton, ed., *The Journal of Duncan McGillivray of the North West Company, 1794–1795* (Toronto: Macmillan of Canada, 1929), p.65.

27. Victor G. Hopwood, ed., *David Thompson: Travels in Western North America, 1784–1812* (Toronto: Macmillan of Canada, 1971), p.216; Hugh A. Dempsey, "A History of Rocky Mountain House," *Canadian Historic Sites: Occasional Papers in Archaeology and History*, 6 (Ottawa: National Historic Sites Service, 1973), pp.8–13.

28. Hopwood, *Thompson Travels*, pp.222–26.

29. Thompson wrote two reports of this journey. Frederic W. Howay, ed., "David Thompson's Account of his First Attempt to Cross the Rockies," *Queen's Quarterly* 40 (1933): 333–56, and the narrative in his journal, Hopwood, *Thompson Travels*, pp.226–35.

30. Howay, "Thompson's Account," p.356.

31. Marjorie W. Campbell, *The North West Company* (Toronto: Macmillan of Canada, 1957), pp.119–45.

32. W. Kaye Lamb, ed., *The Letters and Journals of Simon Fraser, 1806–1808* (Toronto: Macmillan of Canada, 1960), p.15.

33. Ibid., p.96.

34. Ibid., pp.69, 108–9.

35. Richard Glover, ed., *David Thompson's Narrative, 1784–1812* (Toronto: Champlain Society, 1962),

pp.273–93; Hopwood, *Thompson Travels*, pp.236–73.

36. Duncan McGillivray, "Some Account of the Trade carried on by the North West Company, 1808," *Report of the Public Archives of Canada, 1928* (Ottawa: F. A. Acland, 1929), pp.70–71.

37. Fur Trade Agreement between John Jacob Astor and Rosseter Hoyle, Montreal, September 30, 1788, Notarial Records of John Gerband Beek, CN 601–296, Archives nationales du Quebec à Montreal; Kenneth W. Porter, *John Jacob Astor, Business Man*, 2 vols. (Cambridge, Mass.: Harvard University Press, 1931), 1:30–31; Journal of Joseph Frobisher, Montreal, September 8, 1806, Astor Papers, MD-BA; Journal of Samuel Bridges, Montreal, September 17, 1806, Astor Papers, MD-BA.

38. Mackenzie to McTavish, Fraser, and Co., New York, January 30, 1798, in Lamb, *Sir Alexander Mackenzie*, p.463; North West Company to McTavish, McGillivrays, and Co., Kaministiquia, July 18, 1807, Private Collection of Warren Baker, Montreal.

39. Alexander Henry, *Travels and Adventures in Canada and the Indian Territories between the Years 1760 and 1776* (1809; reprint, Edmonton: Hurtig Publishers, 1969). There is a considerable amount of Henry's business correspondence in Milo M. Quaife, ed., *The John Askin Papers*, 2 vols. (Detroit: Detroit Library Commission, 1928).

40. Henry, *Travels and Adventures*, pp.331–32.

41. James King to Banks, October 1780, in David Mackay, "A Presiding Genius of Exploration: Banks, Cook, and Empire, 1767–1805," in Fisher and Johnston, *Cook and His Times*, p.29.

42. Henry to Banks, Gravesend,

March 25, 1781, Banks Papers, Sutro Library.

43. Henry to Banks, Montreal, October 18, 1781, in Lawrence J. Burpee, *The Search for the Western Sea* (Toronto: Musson Book Co., 1908), pp.578–87.

44. Henry to Edgar, Montreal, September 1, 1785, March 5, 1786, North West Company Letters and Accounts Collection, Toronto Metro Reference Library.

45. Transfer Agreement between John Jacob Astor and Alexander Henry, Montreal, August 26, 1790, Notarial Records of John Gerband Beek, CN 601–49, Archives nationales du Quebec à Montreal; Protest of Richard Dobie against John Jacob Astor, Montreal, September 21, 1790, ibid., CN 601–54; Henry to Askin, Montreal, January 18, 1800, in Quaife, ed., *Askin Papers*, 2:275.

46. Henry to Simon McTavish, Montreal, November 23, 1794, in Morris, "Some Letters," p.56.

47. Lamb, *Sir Alexander Mackenzie*, pp.415–18; Donald Jackson, *Thomas Jefferson and the Stony Mountains* (Urbana: University of Illinois Press, 1981), p.121.

48. Jefferson to Lewis, Washington, June 20, 1803, in Donald Jackson, ed., *The Letters of the Lewis and Clark Expedition with Related Documents, 1783–1854*, 2d ed., 2 vols. (Urbana: University of Illinois Press, 1978), 1:61, 65.

49. Lewis to Jefferson, St. Louis, September 23, 1806, in ibid., 1:320–22.

50. Samuel L. Mitchill, *A Discourse on the Character and Services of Thomas Jefferson* (New York: Lyceum of Natural History, 1826), p.29.

51. Clark to ———, St. Louis, September 23, 1806, in Jackson, *Letters*,

1:327. The newspaper history of this important letter is traced in Henry R. Wagner and Charles L. Camp, eds., *The Plains and the Rockies: A Critical Bibliography of Exploration, Adventure, and Travel in the American West, 1800–1865*, 4th ed., ed. Robert H. Becker (San Francisco: John Howell-Books, 1982), pp.19–20.

52. Morris to John Jay, Philadelphia, May 19, 1785, quoted in Margaret C. S. Christman, *Adventurous Pursuits: Americans and the China Trade, 1784–1844* (Washington, D.C.: Smithsonian Institution Press, 1984), p.46. See also Jean G. Lee and Chadwick F. Smith, *Philadelphia and the China Trade, 1784–1844* (Philadelphia: University of Pennsylvania Press, 1984).

53. Frederic W. Howay, ed., *Voyages of the "Columbia" to the Northwest Coast, 1787–1790 and 1790–1793* (Boston: Massachusetts Historical Society, 1941), pp.v–xxvii; idem, "An Outline Sketch of the Maritime Fur Trade," *Reports of the Canadian Historical Association* (1932), 5–14; Mark D. Kaplanoff, ed., *Joseph Ingraham's Journal of the Brigantine "Hope" on a Voyage to the Northwest Coast of North America, 1790–1792* (Barre, Mass.: Imprint Society, 1971), p.1.

54. "Bold North-West Men," Western Americana Collection, Beinecke Rare Book and Manuscript Library, Yale University. See also Frederic W. Howay, "A Ballad of the Northwest Fur Trade," *New England Quarterly* 1 (1928): 71–79.

55. Samuel Shaw to Timothy Pickering, Canton, January 24, 1801, Consular Despatches, Canton, I, RG 59, DNA.

56. Thomas Randall to Alexander Hamilton, New York, August 14, 1791, in Harold G. Syrett, ed., *The Papers of*

Alexander Hamilton, 27 vols. to date (New York: Columbia University Press, 1961–), 9:49; Kaplanoff, *Ingraham's Journal,* p.178; Edmund Hayes, ed., *Log of the "Union": John Boit's Remarkable Voyage to the Northwest Coast and Around the World, 1794–1796* (Portland: Oregon Historical Society, 1981), p.88.

57. William Bayly, "Journal," quoted in Alexander Walker, *An Account of a Voyage to the North West Coast of America in 1785 and 1786,* ed. Robin Fisher and J. M. Bumsted (Seattle: University of Washington Press, 1982), p.228 n.83; Walker quoted in ibid., pp.40, 42; Kaplanoff, *Ingraham's Journal,* p.128.

58. This verse is taken from the version of the ballad in Widener Library, Harvard University, and quoted in Howay, "A Ballad of the Northwest Fur Trade," p.73. See also idem, "Indian Attacks upon Maritime Traders of the Northwest Coast," *Canadian Historical Review* 6 (1925): 287–309.

59. Astor to Thorn, New York, ca. September 5, 1810, quoted in Irving, *Astoria,* p.48; Kaplanoff, *Ingraham's Journal,* p.97.

60. Indian quotation from Robert Haswell, "Log of the Second Voyage of the 'Columbia,'" in Howay, *Voyages of the "Columbia,"* pp.342–43; Robin Fisher, *Contact and Conflict: Indian-European Relations in British Columbia, 1774–1890* (Vancouver: University of British Columbia Press, 1977), ch.1.

61. Ibid., pp.39, 99–100.

62. Orders given to Captain John Kendrick of the Ship Columbia for a Voyage to the Pacific Ocean, 1787, in Howay, *Voyages of the "Columbia,"* p.111. See also John Howell to Joseph Barrell, Canton, May 11, 1795, Consular Despatches, Canton, I, RG 59, DNA.

63. Sailing Orders for the Ship Argonaut, April 3, 1789, in Frederic W. Howay, ed., *The Journal of Captain James Colnett* (Toronto: Champlain Society, 1940), p.20; Boit quoted in Howay, *Voyages of the "Columbia,"* p.399.

64. Ross, *Adventures,* p.36.

CHAPTER 2

1. Astor to De Witt Clinton, New York, January 25, 1808, Clinton Papers, 4:5–6, Butler Library.

2. Ibid.

3. Astor to Jefferson, New York, February 27, 1808, Thomas Jefferson Papers, DLC.

4. Astor to George Clinton, New York, March 9, 1808, Astor Papers, Beinecke-CtY.

5. American Fur Company, Act of Incorporation, April 6, 1808, Porter, *Astor,* 1:413–20.

6. Jefferson to Dearborn, Washington, April 8, 1808, and Dearborn to Jefferson, Washington, April 8, 1808, Jefferson Papers, DLC.

7. Jefferson to John C. Breckinridge, Washington, August 12, 1803, ibid.

8. Everett S. Brown, ed., *William Plumer's Memorandum of Proceedings in the United States Senate, 1803–1807* (New York: Macmillan Co., 1923), p.520. The letter from Lewis to Jefferson, dated at St. Louis on September 23, 1806, is in the Jefferson Papers, DLC. The fullest account of Jefferson's western plans is Jackson, *Thomas Jefferson and the Stony Mountains.*

9. Jefferson to Astor, Washington, April 13, 1808, Jefferson Papers, DLC.

10. Astor to Madison, Washington, July 27, 1813, Astor Papers, Beinecke-CtY.

11. Gallatin to Astor, New York, August 5, 1835, Gallatin Papers, NHi.

12. Jefferson to Lewis, Washington, July 17, 1808, Jefferson Papers, DLC.

13. Minutes of the Beaver Club, Montreal, September 17, 1808, Astor Papers, MD-BA; Journal of Joseph Frobisher, Montreal, September 13, 1808, ibid.; Astor to Gallatin, Montreal, September 24, 1808, Gallatin Papers, NHi.

14. David Lavender, *The Fist in the Wilderness* (Garden City: Doubleday and Co., 1964), pp.110–11.

15. Reginald Horsman, *The War of 1812* (New York: Alfred A. Knopf, 1969), p.14; Astor to Gallatin, New York, September 28, 1809, Gallatin Papers, NHi.

16. Reginald Horsman, *The Diplomacy of the New Republic, 1776–1815* (Arlington Heights, Ill.: Harlan Davidson, 1985), p.111.

17. Astor to Gallatin, New York, May 16, 1809, Gallatin Papers, NHi.

18. See Astor-Gratiot Correspondence in Charles Gratiot Letterbook I, MoSHi.

19. Hunt and Hankinson's account books for this period have not survived, but Hunt's business dealings can be traced in his letters to John Wesley Hunt, in the John Wesley Hunt Papers, the Filson Club, Louisville, Kentucky. See also the Hunt-Gratiot Accounts, Charles Gratiot Collection, Box 1, MoSHi, and the Hunt-Chouteau Accounts, Chouteau Collection, Box 11, MoSHi.

20. James Wilkinson and Henry Dearborn, Cantonment Missouri, August 2, 1806, in Donald Jackson, ed., *The Journals of Zebulon Montgomery Pike, with Letters and Related Documents*, 2 vols. (Norman: University of Oklahoma

Press, 1966), 2:129; Wilkinson to Pike, Cantonment Missouri, August 6, 1806, ibid., 2:134.

21. Lewis to Dearborn, St. Louis, September 27, 1806, Jackson, *Letters*, 1:349; Hunt to John Wesley Hunt, St. Louis, October 14, 1806, Hunt Papers, Filson Club. For a full analysis of the letter, see Ronda, "Wilson Price Hunt Reports on Lewis and Clark," *Filson Club History Quarterly* 62 (1988): 251–59.

22. Astor to Gallatin, New York, May 16, 1809, Gallatin Papers, NHi.

23. Ibid.

24. Ibid.

25. *Louisiana Gazette*, June 21, 1809. This first St. Louis newspaper, edited by Joseph Charless, often carried the title *Missouri Gazette*; Lavender, *Fist in the Wilderness*, pp.112–17.

26. Gratiot to Astor, St. Louis, June 14, 1810, Gratiot Letterbook I:120–21, MoSHi; Thomas James, *Three Years among the Indians and Mexicans* (1846; reprint, Chicago: Lakeside Press, 1953), pp.18–19 (Since Crooks did become Astor's employee in 1810, James may have been off in his recollections by one year); Lavender, *Fist in the Wilderness*, p.441.

27. Astor to Gallatin, New York, July 10, 1809, Gallatin Papers, NHi; Horsman, *Diplomacy of the New Republic*, pp.111–12.

28. Astor to Gallatin, New York, September 28, 1809, Gallatin Papers, NHi.

29. North West Company, Minutes, Fort William, July 18, 1809, in W. Stewart Wallace, ed., *Documents Relating to the North West Company* (Toronto: Champlain Society, 1934), pp.262–63.

30. Astor to Gallatin, New York,

September 28, 1809, Gallatin Papers, NHi.

31. Memorial of the North West Company, Montreal, September 30, 1809, FO 115/20/3, PRO.

32. North West Company to Nathaniel Atcheson, Montreal, January 23, 1810, FO 115/20/3, No.1, PRO.

33. Richardson to Forsyth, New York, February 17, 1810, FO 115/20/3, No.3, PRO; Henry to Askin, Montreal, February 26, 1810, in Quaife, *Askin Papers*, 2:653–54.

34. Richardson to Forsyth, New York, February 17, 1810, FO 115/20/3, No.3, PRO.

35. Astor to Gallatin, New York, April 2, 1810, Gallatin Papers, NHi.

36. Ross, *Adventures*, p.9. For biographical details on the Canadian partners, see Wallace, *Documents*, pp.466, 473, 477.

37. Provisional Agreement, Pacific Fur Company, New York, March 10, 1810, Astor Papers, MD-BA.

38. Astor to Gallatin, New York, April 2, 1810, Gallatin Papers, NHi.

39. McGillivray to Liverpool, n.p., November 10, 1810, MG 11, Q Series, vol.113, pp.221–23, PAC; British North American Merchants to Wellesley, London, April 2, 1810, FO 115/20/3, No.4, PRO.

40. Mackenzie to Board of Trade, London, April 1810, in Lamb, *Sir Alexander Mackenzie*, p.516.

41. Horsman, *Diplomacy of the New Republic*, pp.112–14.

42. North West Company to Privy Council, London, June 30, 1812, CO 42/70/16, No.2, PRO; Forsyth, Richardson and Co. to Jacques Porlier, Montreal, June 8, 1810, in *Wisconsin*

Historical Society Collections 19 (1910): 337–38.

43. Astor to Gallatin, New York, May 26, 1810, Gallatin Papers, NHi. Hunt, then in New York, had hints in late April that negotiations with the Canadians were not going well. See Hunt to John Wesley Hunt, New York, April 28, 1810, Hunt Papers, Filson Club.

44. Final Agreement, Pacific Fur Company, New York, June 23, 1810, Pacific Fur Company Letterbook, American Fur Company Papers, MoSHi.

45. North West Company Wintering Partners to William McGillivray, Fort William, ca. July 18, 1810, Astor Papers, Beinecke-CtY.

46. Glover, *Thompson's Narrative*, p.L.

47. The initial attack on Thompson was mounted by Arthur S. Morton in "The North West Company's Columbian Enterprise and David Thompson," *Canadian Historical Review* 17 (1936): 266–88. In his edition of Thompson's *Narrative*, Richard Glover maintains that there was a race and that Thompson did his best to win it. Neither Morton nor Glover saw the wintering partners' July 1810 letter making it plain that Astor and at least some of the company's men were on the verge of a joint operation. The first historian to use that important document was David Lavender, in *Fist in the Wilderness*.

48. Thompson to McDougall, Tongue Point, July 15, 1811, Astor Papers, Beinecke-CtY.

49. T. C. Elliott, ed., "Journal of David Thompson," *Oregon Historical Quarterly* 15 (1914): 59.

50. Astor to Gallatin, New York, May 26, 1810, Gallatin Papers, NHi.

CHAPTER 3

1. Petition of Ivan I. Golikov and Gregorii I. Shelikhov, February 1788, *Russ. Docs.*, pp.246–49.

2. Ukase from Paul I to the Governing Senate, July 19, 1799, ibid., p.341. See also Report from the State College of Commerce, St. Petersburg, January 22, 1799, ibid., pp.321–25, and Mary E. Wheeler, "The Origins of the Russian-American Company," *Jahrbucher fur Geschichte Osteuropas* (1966), pp.485–95.

3. Rumiantsev to Emperor Alexander I, St. Petersburg, April 8, 1803, *Russ. Docs.*, pp.362–65.

4. Shelikhov to Governor Ivan A. Pil, Irkutsk, February 22, 1790, ibid., pp.268–73; Baranov to Emelian Larionov, August 4, 1800, ibid., pp.342–43; Rezanov to Rumiantsev, New Archangel, June 29, 1806, ibid., pp.455–57. See also James R. Gibson, *Imperial Russia in Frontier America* (New York: Oxford University Press, 1976), pp.153–58.

5. Baranov to Larionov, Kodiac, August 4, 1800, *Russ. Docs.*, pp.342–43; Memorial of the Russian-American Company, St. Petersburg, May 3, 1808, Consular Despatches, St. Petersburg, I, RG 59, DNA; Gibson, *Imperial Russia*, p.14.

6. Rezanov to Baranov, New Archangel, August 1, 1806, *Russ. Docs.*, pp.455–57.

7. Thomas H. Perkins to Baranov, Boston, July 20, 1805, ibid., p.424; Baranov to George W. Ayers, Kodiac, May 30, 1808, ibid., pp.511–16; John D'Wolf, "Recollections, April–May, 1805," ibid., pp.421–22. See also Basil Dmytryshyn and E.A.P. Crownhart-Vaughan, eds., *Colonial Russian America: Kyrill T. Khlebnikov's Reports, 1817–1832*

(Portland: Oregon Historical Society, 1976), p.11.

8. Harris to Madison, St. Petersburg, July 1806, Consular Despatches, St. Petersburg, I, RG 59, DNA.

9. Memorial of the Russian-American Company, St. Petersburg, May 3, 1808, ibid.

10. Rumiantsev to Harris, St. Petersburg, May 29, 1808, ibid.; Harris to Madison, St. Petersburg, 13 June 1808, ibid.

11. Russian-American Company to Dashkov, St. Petersburg, August 2, 1808, *Russ. Docs.*, pp.521–22; College of Foreign Affairs to Dashkov, St. Petersburg, August 30, 1808, ibid., p.532.

12. Dashkov to Rumiantsev, Philadelphia, August 23, 1809, ibid., pp.614–15.

13. Russian-American Company to Dashkov, St. Petersburg, September 1, 1808, ibid., p.523.

14. Irving, *Astoria*, p.31; Astor to Jefferson, New York, March 14, 1812, Jefferson Papers, DLC.

15. Dashkov to Baranov, Philadelphia, November 7, 1809, *Russ. Docs.*, pp.608–13. See also Dashkov to Rumiantsev, Philadelphia, November 15, 1809, ibid., pp.614–15. In his November 4, 1809, letter to Baranov, Astor confirmed that it was Dashkov who first suggested a commercial relationship between the two companies.

16. John Ebbets, Notes on *Enterprise* cargo, late October 1809, Astor Papers, MD-BA. Insurance on the *Enterprise* was arranged in Ebbets to Astor, New York, November 14, 1809, ibid.

17. Astor to Ebbets, New York, November 4, 1809, *Russ Docs.*, pp.601–3.

18. Astor to Ebbets, Philadelphia,

November 4, 1809, Astor Papers, MD-BA. There is some confusion about Astor's whereabouts on November 4. The document in Russian archives is dated at Philadelphia, whereas that in the Astor Papers was drafted in New York.

19. Astor to Baranov, New York, November 4, 1809, *Russ. Docs.*, pp.603–4.

20. Dashkov to Astor, Philadelphia, November 7, 1809, Astor Papers, MD-BA. The course of the *Enterprise* can be traced in Account of Sales of *Enterprise* Cargo, Sitka, July 1810, ibid., and Ebbets to Astor, Macoa, January 11, 1811, ibid. Russian views of their first dealings with Astor are in Vasilii M. Golovnin, "Recollections, July 1810," *Russ. Docs.*, pp.682–85, and Baranov to Astor, New Archangel, August 8, 1810, ibid., pp.687–89.

21. Dashkov to Rumiantsev, Philadelphia, November 15, 1809, ibid., pp.614–17. The fullest account of United States–Russian diplomacy in this period is Nikolai N. Bolkhovitinov, *The Beginnings of Russian-American Relations, 1775–1815* (Cambridge, Mass.: Harvard University Press, 1975).

22. Smith to John Quincy Adams, Washington, May 5, 1810, Diplomatic Instructions, All Countries, 7:90–92, RG 59, DNA; Smith to Dashkov, Washington, May 5, 1810, *American State Papers: I, Foreign Relations*, 5:441–42.

23. Smith to Adams, Washington, May 5, 1810, Diplomatic Instructions, All Countries, 7:91, RG 59, DNA; Dashkov to Smith, Philadelphia, April 24, 1810, Notes from Foreign Legations, Russia, I, ibid.

24. Astor to Gallatin, New York, May 26, 1810, Gallatin Papers, NHi.

25. Alexander I to Pahlen, St. Petersburg, January 8, 1810, *Russ. Docs.*, p.635.

26. Pahlen to Rumiantsev, Philadelphia, July 21, 1810, ibid., pp.677–79.

27. Bentzon to Astor, Washington, July 9, 1810, Astor Papers, MD-BA. See also Pahlen to Rumiantsev, Philadelphia, July 21, 1810, *Russ. Docs.*, pp.675–76, and Pahlen to Rumiantsev, Philadelphia, October 26, 1810, ibid., pp.677–79.

28. Bentzon to Astor, Washington, July 9, 1810, Astor Papers, MD-BA.

29. Gallatin to Madison, Washington, September 5, 1810, James Madison Papers, DLC. The course of Russian-American negotiations can be followed in Adams to Madison, St. Petersburg, August 31, 1810, Consular Despatches, St. Petersburg, I, RG 50, DNA; Adams to Smith, St. Petersburg, September 5, 1810, ibid.; Adams to Smith, St. Petersburg, October 12, 1810, ibid.

30. Madison to Gallatin, Montpelier, September 12, 1810, Madison Papers, DLC.

31. Astor to Gallatin, New York, December 27, 1810, including Gallatin's marginal notes, Gallatin Papers, NHi.

32. Gallatin to Madison, Washington, January 5, 1811, Madison Papers, DLC; Astor to Gallatin, New York, January 17, 1811, Gallatin Papers, NHi; Erving to Monroe, New York, March 18, 1816, James Monroe Papers, DLC.

33. Pahlen to Rumiantsev, Philadelphia, July 21, 1810, *Russ. Docs.*, p.678; Astor to Bentzon, New York, January 21, 1811, Astor Papers, MD-BA.

34. Smith to Adams, Washington, February 13, 1811, Diplomatic Instruc-

tions, All Countries, 7:149–53, RG 59, DNA; Adams to Monroe, St. Petersburg, August 9, 1811, Diplomatic Despatches, St. Petersburg, 2, ibid.

35. Russian-American Company to Rumiantsev, St. Petersburg, October 8, 1811, *Russ. Docs.*, pp.789–91. For problems that arose as a result of the *Enterprise* voyage, see Baranov to Astor, New Archangel, August 8, 1810, ibid., pp.687–89; Baranov to Astor, New Archangel, August 25, 1811, Astor Papers, MD-BA; Astor to Baranov, New York, October 10, 1811, *Russ. Docs.*, pp.793–94; Dashkov to Baranov, Philadelphia, October 12, 1811, ibid., pp.795–96.

36. Rumiantsev to Russian-American Company, St. Petersburg, October 16, 1811, *Russ. Docs.*, p.791.

37. Bentzon to Rumiantsev, St. Petersburg, October 26, 1811, ibid., p.798; Buldakov to Rumiantsev, St. Petersburg, October 31, 1811, ibid., pp.799–800.

38. Gur'ev to Rumiantsev, St. Petersburg, January 28, 1812, ibid., pp.813–14; Kozodavlev to Rumiantsev, St. Petersburg, January 28, 1812, ibid., pp.814–15.

39. Russian-American Company to Shareholders, St. Petersburg, February 13, 1812, ibid., p.817; Astor to Jefferson, New York, March 14, 1812, Jefferson Papers, DLC.

40. Rumiantsev to Bentzon, St. Petersburg, February 19, 1812, *Russ. Docs.*, p.820.

41. Agreement between the Russian-American Company and the American Fur Company, St. Petersburg, May 2, 1812, ibid., pp.841–42.

42. Dashkov to Astor, Philadelphia, November 7, 1809, Astor Papers, MD-BA.

CHAPTER 4

1. North West Company to Atcheson, Montreal, January 23, 1810, FO 115/20/3, No.1, PRO.

2. Hunt to Frederick Bates, New York, March 8, 1810, Bates Family Papers, MoSHi. See also Gratiot to Astor, St. Louis, November 12, 1809, Gratiot Letterbook, I, MoSHi.

3. Ross, *Adventures*, pp.40, 174.

4. Ibid.

5. Ibid., pp.40, 175.

6. Ibid., pp.41, 175.

7. Jean Baptiste Perrault, "Narrative of the Travels and Adventures of a Merchant Adventurer," *Michigan Pioneer and Historical Collections* 37 (1909–10): 583–84; John Reed Accounts Journal, 1:1–7, Astor Papers, MD-BA; Summary of Pacific Fur Company Employees, 1813, ibid. Although Reed did not begin making entries in the account book until the end of July 1810, the ledger is commonly called the Reed Journal. Entries before that time are in Hunt's hand.

8. Franchère, *Journal*, p.44.

9. Entries in the Reed Journal for July 5, 1810, contain notes on three money drafts from McKay to be drawn on Astor. There is also a detailed list of "Sundries furnished at different times by Mr. A. McKay," Reed Journal, 1:8–13, Astor Papers, MD-BA.

10. Franchère, *Journal*, p.44.

11. Ibid., p.45.

12. Registration No.402, August 23, 1810, RG 41, DNA; Edmund Fanning, *Voyages to the South Seas, Indian, and Pacific Oceans* (New York: William H. Vermilye, 1838), p.84; Pacific Fur

Company, Financial Accounts, Astor
Papers, MD-BA.

13. Registration No.242, May 20,
1807, RG 41, DNA; Subsequent registra-
tions: No.139, June 20, 1808, and
No.179, April 19, 1810, ibid. See also
Fanning, *Voyages*, pp.84–136.

14. Service Record of Jonathan
Thorn, 1800–1810, Office of Naval
Records and Library, RG 45, DNA.

15. Franchère, *Journal*, p.55.

16. Thorn to Secretary of the Navy,
New York, October 20, 1809, Office of
Naval Records and Library, RG 45,
DNA; Hamilton to Thorn, Washington,
May 18, 1810, ibid. Thorn continued to
be listed as a half-pay lieutenant until
1812, more than a year after his death;
see *American State Papers: VI, Naval Affairs*, 1:256.

17. Wilson Price Hunt's letter to his
cousin, dated April 28–30, 1810, indicates that he is on his way to Boston to
"procure a captain." Plainly Thorn was
hired later. Hunt to John Wesley Hunt,
New York, April 28–30, 1810, Hunt
Papers, Filson Club.

18. Invoice of Sundry Merchandise
delivered to David Stuart at Astoria,
July 22, 1811, Astor Papers, MD-BA.
See also Pacific Fur Company, Financial
Accounts, ibid.

19. Howay, *James Colnett*, p.40.

20. List of the Officers and Men
comprising the Crew of the Ship *Tonquin*, September 3, 1810, District and
Port of New York, RG 41, DNA.

21. Franchère, *Journal*, p.8.

22. Lewis's Astorian adventures are
given romantic treatment in Gilbert W.
Gabriel's colorful novel, *I, James Lewis*
(Garden City: Doubleday and Co.,
1935); Pacific Fur Company, Financial
Accounts, Astor Papers, MD-BA.

23. Franchère, *Journal*, p.130. A
careful search of Jackson's official correspondence has turned up no mention
of either this meeting or Astor's plans.

24. Astor to Monroe, New York, ca.
February 6, 1813, Astor Papers,
Beinecke-Cty.; Irving, *Astoria*, p.46.

25. Irving, *Astoria*, p.47.

26. Astor to Thorn, New York, ca.
September 5, 1810, quoted in ibid.,
p.48.

27. Astor to Pacific Fur Company
partners, New York, ca. September 5,
1810, quoted in ibid.

28. Ross, *Adventures*, p.44.

29. Franchère, *Journal*, p.50; Ross,
Adventures, p.44.

30. Franchère, *Journal*, p.49.

31. Ibid., p.50; Ross, *Adventures*,
p.43; Deck Log of the USS *Constitution*,
September 1810, RG 24, DNA.

32. Morier to Wellesley, Washington,
October 4, 1810, FO 5/70/59, PRO.

33. Franchère, *Journal*, p.50.

34. Ibid., p.51.

35. Ibid.

36. Ibid.

37. Thorn to Astor, undated but between October and December 1810,
quoted in Irving, *Astoria*, pp.51–52, 54,
60.

38. Ross, *Adventures*, p.45.

39. Franchère, *Journal*, p.53; Ross,
Adventures, p.50.

40. Franchère, *Journal*, pp.55–56;
Ross, *Adventures*, pp.52–53.

41. Thorn to Astor, ca. December
1810, quoted in Irving, *Astoria*, p.60;
Ross, *Adventures*, p.54.

42. Hayes, *Log of the "Union,"* pp.70–
79.

43. Harold W. Bradley, "The
Hawaiian Islands and the Pacific Fur
Trade, 1785–1813," *Pacific Northwest*

Quarterly 30 (1939): 275–99; Ralph S. Kuykendall, *The Hawaiian Kingdom, 1778–1854*, 2 vols. (Honolulu: University of Hawaii Press, 1938), 1:21–22.

44. Franchère, *Journal*, pp.58, 59.

45. Ibid., 59; Ross, *Adventures*, p.58.

46. Ibid., Ross, *Adventures* p.60.

47. Franchère, *Journal*, p.60.

48. Lamb, *George Vancouver*, 3:819–27; Kuykendall, *Hawaiian Kingdom*, 1:25, 35, 37.

49. Franchère, *Journal*, p.61.

50. Ibid., pp.62–63.

51. Ibid., p.63.

52. Ibid., p.69; Irving, *Astoria*, p.72.

53. Thorn to Astor, Oahu, February 1811, quoted in Irving, *Astoria*, p.73.

54. Franchère, *Journal*, p.70; Ross, *Adventures*, pp.57–58.

55. Ross, *Adventures*, pp.75–76; For a map of the Columbia bar before modern changes, see Captain Charles Wilkes, "Mouth of the Columbia River, Sheet No.1, 1841," in *Columbia's Gateway: A History of the Columbia River Estuary to 1920* (Vancouver: Pacific Northwest River Basins Committee, 1980), map 12.

56. Ross, *Adventures*, pp.76–77; Franchère, *Journal*, p.71.

57. Franchère, *Journal*, p.71.

58. Ross, *Adventures*, p.82.

59. Ibid.; Franchère, *Journal*, p.72.

60. Franchère, *Journal*, pp.73–74.

61. Ibid., pp.74–75.

CHAPTER 5

1. Reed Journal, 1:6, Astor Papers, MD-BA; Eric W. Morse, *Fur Trade Canoe Routes of Canada Then and Now*, 2d ed. (Toronto: University of Toronto Press, 1979), pp.22–24.

2. Reed Journal, 1:14, Astor Papers, MD-BA. The Astorians' route to Mackinac can be reconstructed by using a number of contemporary fur trade journals. Most valuable are W. Kaye Lamb, ed., *Sixteen Years in the Indian Country: The Journal of Daniel Williams Harmon, 1800–1816* (Toronto: Macmillan of Canada, 1957), pp.11–18; Henry, *Travels and Adventures*, pp.28–38. The best modern account is Morse, *Fur Trade Canoe Routes*, pp.48–65.

3. Reed Journal, 1:14, Astor Papers, MD-BA. Ross, *Adventures*, p.176, says that the journey from Lachine to Mackinac took seventeen days. A careful reading of Reed's journal seems to indicate that the Astorians were about twenty-six days on their travels. Since the typical brigade run from Lachine to Fort William was about thirty-five days, Robilliard and his crew did quite well.

4. Ross, *Adventures*, p.176. It should be recalled that Ross was not part of Hunt's overland party, but he did gather much information from men who were with Hunt and he corresponded with both Hunt and Donald Mackenzie after the Astorian years.

5. Irving, *Astoria*, pp.128–29.

6. Reed Journal, 1:16, 19, 22, 39, Astor Papers, MD-BA.

7. Grace L. Nute, *The Voyageur* (St. Paul: Minnesota Historical Society, 1931, 1955), p.60.

8. Reed Journal, 1:21–27, 32, Astor Papers, MD-BA; Statement showing the number of Clerks, Men, and Etc. in the Pacific Fur Company employ, 1813, Astor Papers, MD-BA.

9. Reed Journal, 1:109–14, 116–22, Astor Papers, MD-BA.

10. John S. Fox, ed., "Narrative of the Travels and Adventures of a Merchant Voyageur in the Savage Territories of Northern America 1783 to 1820

by Jean Baptiste Perrault," *Michigan Pioneer and Historical Collections* 37 (1909–10): 584–85; Statement showing the number of Clerks . . . 1813, Astor Papers, MD-BA.

11. Jeannette E. Graustein, *Thomas Nuttall, Naturalist: Explorations in America, 1808–1841* (Cambridge, Mass.: Harvard University Press, 1967), pp.14–41; Barton to Gallatin, Philadelphia, March 14, 1810, Benjamin Smith Barton Papers, B:B 284d, American Philosophical Society, Philadelphia.

12. Jeannette E. Graustein, "Manuel Lisa and Thomas Nuttall," *Bulletin of the Missouri Historical Society* 12 (1956): 249–52, reprints Nuttall's letter to Barton relaying information from Lisa.

13. The precise departure date is unclear. The last Mackinac entry in Reed's journal is for August 12. The dates in Nuttall's fragmentary travel diary are wide of the mark and do not jibe with other contemporary accounts. See Jeannette E. Graustein, ed., "Nuttall's Travels into the Old Northwest: An Unpublished 1810 Diary," *Chronica Botanica* 14 (1951): 1–88.

14. Reed Journal, 1:41–44, Astor Papers, MD-BA; Graustein, *Nuttall*, p.54.

15. Reed Journal, 1:45, Astor Papers, MD-BA; Clark to Eustis, St. Louis, September 12, 1810, in Clarence Carter, ed., *The Territorial Papers of the United States: The Territory of Louisiana-Missouri, 1806–1814* (Washington, D.C.: Government Printing Office, 1949), 14:414.

16. Ross, *Adventures*, p.178.

17. Reed Journal, 1:48, 50, 54, Astor Papers, MD-BA.

18. Ross, *Adventures*, pp.179–80.

19. Irving, *Astoria*, p.135; Reed Journal, 1:48–74, Astor Papers, MD-BA.

20. For the Morrison order, see Reed Journal, 1:136, Astor Papers, MD-BA; for the Moorhead order, see ibid., 1:133–35; and for the Smith order, see ibid., 1:123.

21. For Comegys, see ibid., 1:130–33; for the seamstresses, see ibid., 1:73; and for the Robidoux, see ibid., 1:66.

22. Reuben G. Thwaites, ed., *The Original Journals of the Lewis and Clark Expedition*, 8 vols. (New York: Dodd, Mead and Co., 1904–5), 5:374.

23. Jackson, *Pike*, 1:17–18; Lavender, *Fist in the Wilderness*, p.95.

24. Reed Journal, 1:75, 145, Astor Papers, MD-BA.

25. Hunt to John Wesley Hunt, St. Louis, October 14, 1806, Hunt Papers, Filson Club; Clark to Eustis, St. Louis, September 12, 1810, Carter, *Territorial Papers*, 14:414.

26. Thwaites, *Original Journals*, 5:319–20.

27. Burton Harris, *John Colter: His Years in the Rockies* (New York: Charles Scribner's Sons, 1952), pp.73–114.

28. *Louisiana Gazette*, April 8, 1811.

29. John Bradbury, *Travels in the Interior Parts of America in the Years 1809, 1810, and 1811* (Liverpool: Smith and Galway, 1819), pp.78–79. Clark's favorable appraisal of the Bighorn River is in Thwaites, *Original Journals*, 5:297.

30. *Missouri Gazette*, March 8, 1809.

31. Richard E. Oglesby, *Manuel Lisa and the Opening of the Missouri Fur Trade* (Norman: University of Oklahoma Press, 1963), pp.65–98.

32. Reuben Lewis to Meriwether Lewis, Three Forks, April 21, 1810, Meriwether Lewis Collection, MoSHi.

33. St. Louis Missouri Fur Company Ledger, 1:68–70, MoSHi; Clark to Eustis, St. Louis, September 12, 1810, Carter, *Territorial Papers*, 14:414.

34. Jefferson to Lewis, Monticello, August 16, 1809, Jefferson Papers, DLC; Susan D. McKelvey, *Botanical Exploration of the trans-Mississippi West, 1790–1850* (Jamaica Plain, Mass.: Arnold Arboretum of Harvard University, 1956), pp.107–112.

35. Reed Journal, 1:69–70, Astor Papers, MD-BA.

36. Ibid., 1:75–77; Irving, *Astoria*, p.137; Ross, *Adventures*, p.180; John C. Luttig, *Journal of a Fur-Trading Expedition on the Upper Missouri, 1812–1813*. ed. Stella M. Drumm, with additional notes by A. P. Nasatir (New York: Argosy-Antiquarian Books, 1964), pp.34–35.

37. Ross, *Adventures*, p.181; Irving, *Astoria*, p.137.

38. Bradbury, *Travels*, pp.45–46. The approximate location can be found on Missouri River Commission, *Map of the Missouri River from its Mouth to Three Forks, Montana, in eighty-four sheets*. (Washington, D.C.: Government Printing Office, for the Missouri River Commission, 1892–95), map 18.

39. Reed Journal, 1:84, 79–82, 99–137, Astor Papers, MD-BA.

40. Ibid., 1:160–65.

41. Lavender, *Fist in the Wilderness*, pp.73–75.

42. Irving, *Astoria*, p.138; McClellan to William McClellan, Nodaway camp, n.d. but probably December 1810, in Stella M. Drumm, "More about Astorians," *Oregon Historical Quarterly* 24 (1923): 348. David Lavender maintains that McClellan and the partners argued for six days before the trader accepted his share in the company. This is plainly a misreading of the 1810 letter and may be one more of Lavender's "imaginative reconstructions." Drumm says that McClellan joined the company without any argument. She gives no source for the McClellan letter, and it has not turned up in careful searches at the Missouri Historical Society and the Oregon Historical Society.

43. Reed Journal, 1:140, Astor Papers, MD-BA; Irving, *Astoria*, pp.138–39; T. C. Elliott, ed., "The Last Will and Testament of John Day," *Oregon Historical Quarterly* 17 (1916): 373–79.

44. Irving, *Astoria*, p.139; Ross, *Adventures*, p.181.

45. Quote in Irving, *Astoria*, pp.140–41; Bradbury, *Travels*, p.23.

46. Lewis to Hugh Heney, July 20, 1806, in Jackson, *Letters*, 2:310.

47. Irving, *Astoria*, p.142; Statement showing the number of Clerks . . . 1813, Astor Papers, MD-BA. This list seems to indicate that Dorion signed with Hunt on February 17, 1811.

48. Irving, *Astoria*, pp.142–43; Ross, *Adventures*, p.181–82.

49. Ross, *Adventures*, p.182.

50. Ibid., p.181; Lavender, *Fist in the Wilderness*, p.444.

51. Jackson, *Pike*, 1:291; Bradbury, *Travels*, pp.11–12; Oglesby, *Lisa*, pp.107–8.

52. Bradbury, *Travels*, pp.12–14.

53. Ibid., pp.17–21; Harris, *Colter*, pp.159–60.

54. Bradbury, *Travels*, pp.21–24.

55. Lisa to William Clark, St. Louis, July 1, 1817, printed in *Missouri Gazette*, July 5, 1817.

56. Henry M. Brackenridge, *Views of Louisiana; together with a Journal of a Voyage up the Missouri River in 1811* (Pittsburgh: Cramer, Spear, and Eichbaum, 1814), pp.200–201; St. Louis Missouri Fur Company Ledger, 1:83–84, MoSHi.

57. Bradbury, *Travels*, pp.26–31.

58. Brackenridge, *Views*, pp.201–2; *Louisiana Gazette*, April 11, 1811.

59. Bradbury, *Travels*, pp.37–40.

60. Ibid., p.43.

61. Brackenridge, *Views*, pp.208, 211.

62. Reed Journal, 2:15–17, Astor Papers, MD-BA.

63. Bradbury, *Travels*, pp.46–47.

64. Brackenridge, *Views*, p.214.

65. Bradbury, *Travels*, p.47.

66. Brackenridge, *Views*, p.220. Brackenridge also reports a curious and unexplained piece of trapper conversation. The traders insisted that Hunt had "informed them that they would meet us [Lisa's party] below the Grand River." Since there is no evidence to suggest that Hunt knew about Lisa's expedition, this remark is hard to explain.

67. Bradbury, *Travels*, pp.48–52.

68. Ibid., pp.52–53.

69. Ibid., pp.56–65.

70. Ibid., pp.69–71.

71. Brackenridge, *Views*, p.224.

72. Bradbury, *Travels*, pp.65–68; Reed Journal, 2:20–24, Astor Papers, MD-BA.

73. Bradbury, *Travels*, pp.68–69; Irving, *Astoria*, p.160. Irving saw letters from Hunt to Astor that evidently no longer survive. The May 14 letter from Hunt to Astor can be dated from postage records in Financial Accounts, Pacific Fur Company, Astor Papers, MD-BA.

74. Bradbury, *Travels*, pp.69–71.

75. Brackenridge, *Views*, pp.230–31.

76. Bradbury, *Travels*, pp.71–73.

77. Ibid., pp.73–76; Brackenridge, *Views*, p.234. Lisa got this news when his men rejoined him past the James River on May 26.

78. Irving, *Astoria*, p.256.

79. Irving, *Astoria*, pp.176–77; Bradbury, *Travels*, pp.78–79. A fuller sense of what Henry and his men believed to be the best route over the Continental Divide can be seen in Brackenridge's interview with Henry in the *Louisiana Gazette*, October 11, 1811. Henry's "Southern Pass" route is marked, probably too far north, on William Clark's master map. See Gary E. Moulton, ed., *The Journals of the Lewis and Clark Expedition*, 5 vols. to date (Lincoln: University of Nebraska Press, 1983–), atlas, map 125. See also Ralph E. Ehrenberg's treatment of John Dougherty's 1810–12 fur trade map in "Sketch of Part of the Missouri & Yellowstone Rivers with a Description of the Country, Etc.," *Prologue* 3 (1971): 73–78.

80. Brackenridge, *Views*, p.235.

81. This and the following information on Hunt's confrontation with the Sioux is from Bradbury, *Travels*, pp.82–89. Although the location of this encounter cannot be located with any precision, the stretch of the river on which the expedition found itself on May 31, is detailed in Missouri River Commission, *Map of the Missouri River*, maps 36 and 37. For a fuller discussion of northern plains trade relations see John C. Ewers, "The Indian Trade of the Upper Missouri before Lewis and Clark," *Bulletin of the Missouri Historical Society* 10 (1954): 429–46; W. Raymond Wood, "Contrastive Features of Native North American Trade Systems," *University of Oregon Anthropological Papers* 4 (1972): 153–69.

82. Brackenridge, *Views*, p.237.

83. Bradbury, *Travels*, p.92.

84. Ibid., pp.93–95.

85. Ibid., pp.96–100.

86. Ibid., pp.102–3; Brackenridge, *Views*, pp.241–42.

87. Bradbury, *Travels*, pp.103–9.

88. Roger L. Nichols, "The Arikara Indians and the Missouri River Trade: A Quest for Survival," *Great Plains Quarterly* 2 (Spring 1982): 77–93; James P. Ronda, *Lewis and Clark among the Indians* (Lincoln: University of Nebraska Press, 1984), ch.3.

89. Bradbury, *Travels*, p.109.

90. Annie Heloise Abel, ed., *Tabeau's Narrative of Loisel's Expedition to the Upper Missouri* (Norman: University of Oklahoma Press, 1939), pp.123–24, 129–37.

91. Bradbury, *Travels*, pp.110–15; Brackenridge, *Views*, pp.245–46.

92. Bradbury, *Travels*, pp.121–22, 126, 144, 148; Brackenridge, *Views*, pp.251, 259; Reed Journal, 2:66–68, Astor Papers, MD-BA.

93. Bradbury, *Travels*, pp.124–25.

94. Ibid.; Thwaites, *Original Journals*, 7:370.

95. Reed Journal, 2:35–66, Astor Papers, MD-BA; Brackenridge, *Views*, p.258.

96. Hunt to Astor, Arikara villages, July 17, 1811, paraphrased in Astor to Jefferson, New York, March 14, 1812, Jefferson Papers, DLC; *Louisiana Gazette*, August 8, 1811.

CHAPTER 6

1. Hunt to John Wesley Hunt, New York, April 28, 1810, Hunt Papers, Filson Club.

2. Wilson Price Hunt, Diary, in Philip A. Rollins, ed., *The Discovery of the Oregon Trail: Robert Stuart's Narrative of his Overland Trip Eastward from Astoria in 1812–1813* (New York: Edward Eberstadt, 1935), p.281; Reed Journal, 2:114, Astor Papers, MD-BA; Irving, *Astoria*, p.217. Hunt's original overland diary has been lost. What survives is a printed copy first published in 1821.

3. Hunt, Diary, p.281; Irving, *Astoria*, p.218.

4. Hunt, Diary, p.281; Reed Journal, 2:115–20 Astor Papers, MD-BA; Irving, *Astoria*, p.219.

5. Hunt, Diary, p.281. See also Joseph Jablow, *The Cheyenne in Plains Indian Trade Relations, 1795–1840* (Seattle: University of Washington Press, 1950), pp.51–58.

6. Gratiot to Astor, St. Louis, November 26, 1811, Gratiot Letterbook, I, MoSHi.

7. Hunt, Diary, pp.281–82.

8. Ibid., p.282.

9. Ibid., pp.282–83.

10. Ibid., p.283.

11. Ibid.

12. Ibid.

13. Ibid., pp.283–84.

14. Reed Journal, 2:123–24, Astor Papers, MD-BA; Hunt, Diary, p.284.

15. Hunt, Diary, p.284; Reed Journal, 2:124–30, Astor Papers, MD-BA.

16. Hunt, Diary, p.284; Willis Blenkinsop, "Edward Rose," in LeRoy R. Hafen, ed., *The Mountain Men and the Fur Trade of the Far West*, 9 vols. (Glendale, Calif.: Arthur H. Clark, 1962–75), 9:335–38.

17. Hunt, Diary, pp.284–85; Irving, *Astoria*, p.247.

18. Hunt, Diary, p.285; Reed Journal, 2:132, Astor Papers, MD-BA.

19. Hunt, Diary, pp.285–86.

20. Ibid., p.285.

21. Ibid., pp.286–87; Reed Journal, 2:135, Astor Papers, MD-BA.

22. Hunt, Diary, pp.287–88; Reed Journal, 2:136, Astor Papers, MD-BA.

23. Hunt, Diary, p.288; Reed Journal, 2:136, Astor Papers, MD-BA; Irving, *Astoria*, p.265.

24. Hunt, Diary, p.288.

25. Ibid.

26. Ibid., pp.288–89; Reed Journal, 2:146–50, Astor Papers, MD-BA.

27. Hunt's diary has the arrival on October 8. Reed's journal, generally more accurate on dates, records the day as October 9. Reed Journal, 2:151, Astor Papers, MD-BA.

28. Hunt, Diary, pp.289–90.

29. Pacific Fur Company Letterbook, MoSHI; Irving, *Astoria*, p.269.

30. Irving, *Astoria*, p.272 n.3.

31. Hunt, Diary, p.290.

32. Ibid., p.291; Reed Journal, 2:160, Astor Papers, MD-BA.

33. Hunt, Diary, p.292.

34. *Missouri Gazette*, October 26, 1811; Hunt, Diary, p.292.

35. Robert Stuart, "Overland Narrative, 1812–1813," in Rollins, *Discovery of the Oregon Trail*, pp.112–13; the Idaho Historical Society and the National Register of Historic Places provide the whirlpool's supposed location.

36. Hunt, Diary, p.292.

37. Ibid.; Reed Journal, 2:162–67, Astor Papers, MD-BA; Astor to Gratiot, New York, October 31, 1811, ibid.

38. McDougall, Journal, November 1, 1811; Hunt, Diary, p.292.

39. Irving, *Astoria*, p.280.

40. Hunt, Diary, p.293.

41. Ibid.

42. Ibid., p.294.

43. Ibid., p.295.

44. Ibid., p.296.

45. Ibid., p.297.

46. Ibid.

47. Ibid., pp.297–98.

48. Ibid., p.299.

49. Ibid., p.300.

50. Ibid.

51. Ibid., pp.300–301.

52. Franchère, *Journal*, p.107; McDougall, Journal, December 25, 1811; Astor to Gratiot, New York, December 24, 1811, Astor Papers, MD-BA.

53. Hunt, Diary, pp.301–2.

54. Ibid., p.302.

55. Ibid., pp.302–3.

56. Ibid., p.303. Clark's map is in Thwaites, *Original Journals*, 3:131.

57. McDougall, Journal, January 18, 1812; Franchère, *Journal*, pp.108–10.

58. Hunt, Diary, p.303.

59. Ibid., p.308; Duncan McDougall, "An Account of Events at Fort Astoria during more than a year (1811–1812)," in Rollins, *Discovery of the Oregon Trail*, p.278. McDougall's "Account" is a version of his Astorian journal, first published in 1821. It differs in some important ways from the original at the Rosenbach Library.

60. Reed Journal, 2:176–87, Astor Papers, MD-BA.

61. Astor to Gratiot, New York, February 28, 1812, Astor Papers, MD-BA; Astor to Gratiot, New York, December 26, 1812, ibid.

CHAPTER 7

1. Ross, *Adventures*, p.83.

2. McDougall, Journal, March 27, 28, 1811.

3. Ibid., April 1–3, 1811.

4. Franchère, *Journal*, p.75; Ross, *Adventures*, p.72; McDougall, Journal, March 27, 1811.

5. McDougall, Journal, April 10, 1811; Franchère, *Journal*, p.76.

6. McDougall, Journal, April 9, 1811.

7. Ross, *Adventures*, p.77.

8. Ibid.

9. Franchère, *Journal*, p.77.

10. Ross, *Adventures*, pp.77–80.

11. Ibid., pp.79–81; Franchère, *Journal*, pp.77–78.

12. McDougall, Journal, April 19, 22, 1811.

13. Ibid., April 30, May 2, 15, 1811; Franchère, *Journal*, pp.78–84.

14. McDougall, Journal, June 2, 20, 21, July 23, 1811; Franchère, *Journal*, pp.89–90.

15. Franchère, *Journal*, p.90.

16. McDougall, Journal, April 24, July 1, 2, 1811; Ross, *Adventures*, p.88.

17. McDougall, Journal, October 16, November 15, 20, December 31, 1811; Franchère, *Journal*, p.96; Elliott Coues, ed., *New Light on the Early History of the Greater Northwest: The Manuscript Journals of Alexander Henry and of David Thompson*, 3 vols. in 2 (1897; reprint, Minneapolis: Ross and Haines, 1965), 2:756, 891.

18. McDougall, Journal, March 30, May 1, 5, 8, 12, 21, 27, October 20, 1812.

19. Coues, *New Light*, 2:780, 869–70; Franchère, *Journal*, pp.95–96; Frederick Merk, ed., *Fur Trade and Empire: George Simpson's Journal, 1824–1825*, rev. ed. (Cambridge, Mass.: Harvard University Press, 1968), p.111.

20. Franchère, *Journal*, p.97.

21. Ibid., p.108; McDougall, Journal, November 25, 1811.

22. Franchère, *Journal*, pp.110–11; McDougall, Journal, February 24, 1812.

23. Franchère, *Journal*, p.116; McDougall, Journal, October 1, 20, 1812.

24. Invoice of Merchandise shipped on board the *Beaver*, October 16, 1811, Astor Papers, MD-BA; Provisions and Stores delivered at Astoria, October 1813, in *Message from the President Com-*municating the Letter of Mr. Prevost and other Documents Relating to an Establishment made at the Mouth of the Columbia River, 17th Cong. 2d sess., H. Doc. 45 (Washington, D.C.: Gales and Seaton, 1823), p.63. Hereafter cited as *Message*, 1823.

25. Because of restrictions placed on McDougall's journal by the Rosenbach Library, I am not free to quote directly from the document. The library has permitted unrestricted paraphrasing.

26. Glyndwr Williams, ed., *Andrew Graham's Observations on Hudson's Bay, 1767–1791* (London: Hudson's Bay Record Society, 1969), p.243.

27. Lamb, *Indian Country*, pp.47, 126.

28. Franchère, *Journal*, p.117.

29. Invoice of Merchandise shipped on the *Beaver*, October 16, 1811, Astor Papers, MD-BA. I am especially grateful to Hildegard Schnuttgen for her help in reconstructing Astoria's reading list.

30. Mackenzie to Hunt, Fort Nez Perces, April 20, 1821, Astorians Collection, MoSHi.

31. Coues, *New Light*, 2:875.

32. Summary of Pacific Fur Company Employees, 1813, Astor Papers, MD-BA.

33. Coues, *New Light*, 2:889–90.

34. Ibid., 2:890; Ross, *Adventures*, p.92; McDougall, Journal, May 15, 1812.

35. Coues, *New Light*, 2:825, 840.

36. McDougall, Journal, May 12, 1811, July 6, September 22, November 9, 1812.

37. Ibid., June 4, 1811, September 27, 1812; Coues, *New Light*, 2:837–38.

38. McDougall, Journal, June 28, October 17, 1811.

39. Ibid., June 28, 1811.

40. Ibid., July 26, 1811.

41. Ibid., November 10, 24, 1811; Franchère, *Journal*, pp.93–96.

42. Franchère, *Journal*, p.135; Coues, *New Light*, 2:773.

43. These last pieces of evidence about Jérémie come from an anonymous note, ca. 1818, attached to Astor to Prevost, New York, November 11, 1817, Astor Papers, MD-BA. There is no mention of Jérémie in either Prevost's official correspondence or Captain Biddle's special report on the voyage.

44. McDougall, Journal, July 4, 1811, April 12, July 4, 1812, April 12, 1813.

45. Ibid., March 29, 1812.

46. Lamb, *Sir Alexander Mackenzie*, p.248; Moulton, *Lewis and Clark Expedition*, 3:266–67.

47. McDougall, Journal, January 1, 1812. See also the entry for January 1, 1813.

48. Ibid., October 27, 1812.

49. Coues, *New Light*, 2:861.

50. Thwaites, *Original Journals*, 4:128.

51. McDougall, Journal, May 19, 1811.

52. Thwaites, *Original Journals*, 3:278. McDougall, Journal, June 2, 20, 22, July 20, 1811; Franchère, *Journal*, pp.96–97.

53. Verne F. Ray, "Lower Chinook Ethnographic Notes," *University of Washington Publications in Anthropology* 7 (1938): 110–11.

54. McDougall, Journal, June 6, 14, October 27, 1811; Franchère, *Journal*, pp.96–97.

55. McDougall, Journal, June 13, 22, 1811.

56. Abstract of Returns from Columbia River, Pacific Fur Company, 1811–12, Astor Papers, MD-BA.

57. Anon. note quoting P. D. Jérémie, in Astor to Prevost, New York, November 11, 1817, Astor Papers, MD-BA; Ross, *Adventures*, pp.86–87.

58. McDougall, Journal, June 3, 1811; Ross, *Adventures*, pp.89–90.

59. Astor to Jones, Washington, April 19, 1813, Astor Papers, Beinecke-Cty.

60. Astor to Monroe, New York, ca. February 6, 1813, ibid.

61. McDougall, Journal, May 16, 1811.

62. Ibid., May 18, 1811.

63. Paul Kane, *Wanderings of an Artist among the Indians of North America* (1859; reprint, Edmonton: Hurtig Publishers, 1968), p.130; McDougall, Journal, July 12, 23, 1811.

64. McDougall, Journal, July 23, 29, 30, 31, August 3, 1811; Franchère, *Journal*, pp.88–89.

65. McDougall, Journal, August 4, 12, 14, 17, 1811.

66. Franchère, *Journal*, pp.90–91.

67. McDougall, Journal, August 23, 1811; McDougall, "Account," pp.275–76.

68. Thwaites, *Original Journals*, 3:239.

69. McDougall, Journal, July 6, 1811, February 22, 1813, November 24, 1812; Coues, *New Light*, 2:868, 871–75.

70. Coues, *New Light*, 2:835–36, 859, 888, 890–91.

71. For a fuller discussion see Ronda, *Lewis and Clark among the Indians*, p.172.

72. McDougall, Journal, June 10, 11, 1811.

73. Ibid., June 12, 18, July 26, 1812.

74. McDougall, "Account," p.273.

75. Glover, *Thompson's Narrative*, p.367; Ross, *Adventures*, p.101.

76. McDougall, Journal, June 15, 1811; Franchère, *Journal*, pp.85–86; McDougall, "Account," pp.273–74. W. Kaye Lamb notes that there was no post named Fort Estekatadene. The trader John Stuart was then at Stuart Lake, a place with the Indian name Nakazeleh. Lamb thinks that McDonald sent the Indians on a snipe hunt to be rid of them. It is equally possible that Estekatadene is a garbling of Nakazeleh.

77. McDougall, Journal, July 1, 1811; Ross, *Adventures*, p.101.

78. Ross, *Adventures*, pp.101–2.

79. Ibid.; Franchère, *Journal*, pp.87–88; Thompson to McDougall, Stuart, and Stuart, Tongue Point, July 15, 1811, Astor Papers, Beinecke-Cty. This letter survives only in a copy made by the Astorians for Astor.

80. Ross, *Adventures*, p.102.

81. McDougall, Stuart, and Stuart to Thompson, Astoria, July 16, 1811, Astor Papers, Beinecke-Cty. McDougall's Journal contains no comments on Thompson until July 22, the day Thompson left the post. On that day McDougall notes that he replied to Thompson on July 16, but the nature of his reply is heavily crossed out in the journal.

82. Ross, *Adventures*, p.102; Elliott, "Journal of David Thompson," p.57.

83. Elliott, "Journal of David Thompson," p.106; Invoice of Goods delivered to David Stuart, Astoria, July 22, 1811, Astor Papers, MD-BA.

84. McDougall, Robert Stuart, and David Stuart to Astor, Astoria, July 22, 1811, Astor Papers, MD-BA.

85. Franchère, *Journal*, p.85; Ross, *Adventures*, p.98.

86. McDougall, Journal, August 11, 1811, notes those July rumors. They were not recorded in the post's journal in July. See also Franchère, *Journal*, pp.88–89; Ross, *Adventures*, p.163; Stephen Reynolds, *The Voyage of the "New Hazard,"* ed. Frederic W. Howay (Salem, Mass.: Peabody Museum, 1938), p.33.

87. P. J. Schurer and R. H. Linden, "Results of a Sub-Bottom Acoustic Survey in a Search for the *Tonquin*," *International Journal of Nautical Archaeology and Underwater Exploration* 13 (1984): 305–9.

88. Franchère, *Journal*, pp.123–26, quote at p.126. The earliest printed account of the *Tonquin* appeared in the *Missouri Gazette*, May 15, 1813, based on a report carried to St. Louis by Robert Stuart. Stuart's own views on the incident can be found in a letter summarizing Stuart's 1831 lecture on the event. See Elisha Loomis to Chester Loomis, Mackinac, April 2, 1831, in Kenneth A. Spaulding, ed., *On the Oregon Trail: Robert Stuart's Journey of Discovery* (Norman: University of Oklahoma Press, 1953), pp.174–77. The most thorough review of all the accounts of the *Tonquin* is Frederic W. Howay, "The Loss of the *Tonquin*," *Washington Historical Quarterly* 13 (1922): 83–92.

89. McDougall, Journal, January 1, 18, 1812; Franchère, *Journal*, pp.108–10, 112.

90. McDougall, Journal, June 6, 24, October 5, 1811; Franchère, *Journal*, p.99; Ross, *Adventures*, pp.154–59.

91. Pacific Fur Company Letterbook, March 1, 1812, MoSHi.

92. McDougall, Journal, March 22, 1812; McDougall, "Account," p.278;

Ross, *Adventures*, p.199; Franchère, *Journal*, pp.111–12.

93. Franchère, *Journal*, pp.112–14; Irving, *Astoria*, pp.338–47.

94. Articles of Agreement between John Jacob Astor and the Clerks and Men to go out on the *Beaver*, October 8, 1811, Astor Papers, MD-BA; Invoice of Merchandise shipped by John Jacob Astor on the *Beaver* to the Northwest Coast, October 1811, ibid.

95. McDougall, Journal, June 21, 1812. The fullest account of the June meeting is in Ross, *Adventures*, pp.194–95, quoting a document now lost.

CHAPTER 8

1. North West Company, Petition, London, June 30, 1812, CO 42/70/16, No.2, PRO; Astor to State Department, Philadelphia, April 4, 1813, Astor Papers, MD-BA; Memorandum for Secretary of the Navy William Jones, Washington, April 19, 1813, Astor Papers, Beinecke-CtY.

2. Astor to Clinton, New York, January 25, 1808, Clinton Papers, Butler Library; Astor to Madison, Washington, July 27, 1813, Astor Papers, Beinecke-CtY.

3. Astor to Dashkov, New York, April 13, 1811, Astor Papers, MD-BA.

4. North West Company, Memorial, Montreal, September 30, 1809, FO 115/20/ encl. in No.3, PRO.

5. North West Company to Atcheson, Montreal, January 23, 1810, FO 115/20/3, No.1, ibid.

6. McGillivray to Liverpool, London, November 10, 1810, MG 11, Q Series, vol.113, pp.221–23, PAC.

7. Atcheson to Wellesley, London, April 2, 1810, FO 115/20/ encl. in No.3, PRO.

8. Atcheson to Wellesley, London, June 20, 1810, MG 11, Q Series, vol.113, p.244, PAC; Wellesley to Morier, London, June 29, 1810, FO 115/20/3 and all encls., PRO.

9. North West Company Wintering Partners to McGillivray, Fort William, mid-July 1810, Astor Papers, Beinecke-CtY.

10. Morier to Wellesley, Washington, October 4, 1810, FO 5/70/59, PRO; McGillivray to Liverpool, London, November 10, 1810, MG 11, Q Series, vol.113, pp.221–22, PAC.

11. North West Company, Petition, Montreal, May 1811, CO 42/61/12, encl., PRO.

12. Wallace, *Documents*, pp.265–68.

13. Astor to Monroe, New York, ca. February 6, 1813, Astor Papers, Beinecke-CtY.

14. The best recent survey of the origins of the War of 1812 is Horsman, *Diplomacy of the New Republic*, pp.86–125.

15. Astor to Gratiot, New York, March 17, 1812, Gratiot Letterbook I, MoSHi; Astor to Gratiot, March 31, 1812, ibid.; Astor to Gallatin, New York, May 13, 1812, Gallatin Papers, NHi; Astor to Gallatin, New York, May 30, 1812, ibid. The "restrictions on commerce" Astor mentioned was a ninety-day embargo passed by Congress on April 4, 1812.

16. Astor to Gratiot, New York, June 12, 1812, Gratiot Letterbook I, MoSHi.

17. Gallatin to Daniel Jackson, New York, August 23, 1836, Gallatin Papers, NHi.

18. Astor to Gallatin, New York, June 27, 1812, Gallatin Papers, NHi; Astor to State Department, Philadelphia, April 4, 1813, Astor Papers, MD-BA.

19. Ships Entered at Canton, January 28, 1813, Consular Despatches, Canton, I, RG 59, DNA; Irving, *Astoria*, p.471.

20. Pigot to Astor, London, September 28, 1812, Astor Papers, MD-BA; Astor to State Department, Philadelphia, April 4, 1813, ibid.

21. Wallace, *Documents*, pp.271–72; John McDonald of Garth, "Autobiographical Notes, 1791–1816," in L. R. Masson, ed., *Les Bourgeois de la Compagnie du Nord-Ouest*, 2 vols. (1889–90; reprint, New York: Antiquarian Press, 1960), 2:42–43.

22. North West Company to Atcheson, Montreal, August 18, 1812, CO 42/149/95, PRO.

23. Pigot to Astor, London, September 28, 1812, Astor Papers, MD-BA.

24. Pigot to Astor, London, January 24, 1813, ibid.; Pigot to Astor, London, February 8, 1813, ibid. Astor's knowledge of the *Forester*'s adventure can be seen in his letter to the State Department, Philadelphia, April 4, 1813, ibid.

25. Atcheson to Castlereagh, London, September 24, 1812, CO 42/70/16, PRO; Atcheson to Castlereagh, London, September 25, 1812, CO 42/149/87 and encls., ibid.; North West Company to King-in-Council, London, October 1, 1812, CO 42/149/97, ibid.

26. Atcheson to Bathurst, London, October 9, 1812, CO 42/149/93, ibid.; Atcheson to Goulburn, London, October 29, 1812, CO 42/149/137, ibid.; Atcheson to Bathurst, London, November 19, 1812, CO 42/149/141, ibid.

27. Simon McGillivray to Goulburn, London, December 29, 1812, CO 42/149/197, ibid.

28. Orders to Capt. James Hillyar, Admiralty Office, February 16–March 12, 1813, Adm. 2/1380/368–75, ibid.

29. John McDonald of Garth, "Notes," in Masson, *Les Bourgeois*, 2:44–45.

30. Admiralty to Adm. Bickerton, London, March 24, 1813, Adm. 1/1108/221–22, PRO; Bickerton to Admiralty, Portsmouth, March 25, 1813, Adm. 1/1215/A. 788, ibid. Information on the *Forester*'s sailing can be found in Pigot to ———, Coast of California, March 22, 1814, Astor Papers, MD-BA.

31. Ross, *Adventures*, pp.234–35; Astor to Gratiot, New York, December 26, 1812, Astor Papers, MD-BA; Astor to Thomas Hart Benton, New York, January 29, 1829, General Collections, Beinecke-CtY.

32. Gallatin to Jones, Washington, January 10, 1813, Astor Papers, Beinecke-CtY.

33. Astor to Monroe, New York, ca. February 6, 1813, Astor Papers, Beinecke-CtY. The letter is not in Astor's hand, except for the signature. The document's language and phrasing suggest the influence of Adrian Bentzon.

34. Astor to Gallatin, New York, February 6, 1813, Gallatin Papers, NHi; Astor to Gallatin, New York, February 14, 1813, with attached note in Gallatin's hand, ibid.

35. Astor to Gallatin, New York, February 14, 1813, ibid.; Astor to Gallatin, New York, February 18, 1813, ibid.

36. Astor to Dashkov, New York, September 26, 1814, Astor Papers, MD-BA.

37. Astor to Hunt, New York, ca. March 6, 1813, quoted in Irving, *Astoria*, p.432.

38. Astor to Gallatin, New York, February 18, 1813, Gallatin Papers, NHi; Astor to Gallatin, New York, March 20, 1813, ibid.; Astor to Monroe, New York, March 22, 1813, Domestic Letters of the Department of State, 14, RG 59, DNA.

39. Dorr to Astor, Boston, March 30, 1813, Astor Papers, MD-BA.

40. Confidential Memorandum for John Jacob Astor, April 1813, Astor Papers, Beinecke-CtY.

41. Ross, *Adventures*, p.216; Irving, *Astoria*, p.444.

42. McDougall, Journal, January 1, 4, 1813.

43. Franchère, *Journal*, p.117; Ross, *Adventures*, p.216; Pacific Fur Company Agreement, 1810, Pacific Fur Company Letterbook, MoSHi. The precise date of Mackenzie's arrival at Astoria is in question. Ross and Franchère report January 15, whereas the usually reliable McDougall records January 16.

44. McDougall, Journal, January 25, 29, February 2, 1813; "Inventory of the Principal Articals of Provision and Merchandise on Hand at Astoria, 17 January 1813," Astor Papers, MD-BA.

45. McDougall, Journal, March 31, 1813.

46. Porter, *Astor*, 1:330–44.

47. Astor to Department of State, Philadelphia, April 4, 1813, Astor Papers, MD-BA.

48. Astor to Jones, Philadelphia, April 6, 1813, Astor Papers, Beinecke-CtY.

49. Jones to Madison, Washington, November 15, 1814, Madison Papers, DLC.

50. Memorandum for the Honorable William Jones, Secretary of the Navy, Washington, April 19, 1813, Astor Papers, Beinecke-CtY.

51. Astor to Gallatin, New York, June 19, 1813, Gallatin Papers, NHi; Astor to Dorr, New York, July 7, 1813, Astor Papers, MD-BA. For Stuart's arrival in St. Louis, see Gratiot to Astor, St. Louis, May 1, 1813, Gratiot Letterbook I, MoSHi; *Missouri Gazette*, May 8, 1813.

52. Astor to Jones, New York, July 6, 1813, Astor Papers, Beinecke-CtY.

53. Astor to Jones, New York, July 7, 1813, ibid.; Astor to Dorr, New York, July 7, 1813, Astor Papers, MD-BA.

54. Astor to Gallatin, New York, July 17, 1813, Gallatin Papers, NHi; Astor to Jones, New York, July 17, 1813, Astor Papers, Beinecke-CtY.

55. Astor to Madison, Washington, July 27, 1813, Astor Papers, MD-BA.

56. Astor to Jones, Washington, July 30, 1813, Astor Papers, Beinecke-CtY.

57. Astor to Jones, Washington, July 30, 1813, ibid.

58. Astor to Jones, Washington, August 8, 1813, ibid.

59. Astor to Jones, New York, August 23, 1813, ibid.

60. Greene, Terms for a Proposed Voyage, n.d. but probably late August–early September 1813, Astor Papers, MD-BA.

61. Astor to Greene, New York, 27 August 27, 1813, ibid.; Astor to Greene, New York, September 8, 1813, ibid.; Astor to E. G. Bartsch, New York, September 15, 1813, ibid.

62. Astor to Greene, New York, September 30, 1813, ibid.; Astor to Dorr, New York, October 1, 1813, ibid.

63. Greene to Astor, New Haven, November 10, 1813, ibid.; Astor to Greene, New York, October 18, 1813, ibid.

64. ——— to Dashkov, late Novem-

ber 1813, ibid. This is a copy in Astor's hand.

65. Astor to George Ehninger, New York, November 10, 1813, ibid.; Astor to William Greene, New York, December 25, 1813, ibid. Hunt's July 17, 1813, letter to Astor has not survived, but Astor alludes to it in his December 30, 1813, letter to John Dorr. On Hunt's dealings with the *New Hazard*, see Reynolds, *Voyage*, p.150.

CHAPTER 9

1. McDougall, Journal, April 11, 12, 1813; Franchère, *Journal*, pp.118–19.

2. McDougall, Journal, April 15, 1813; Astoria Financial Journal, June 15, 1813, Astor Papers, MD-BA.

3. McDougall, Journal, June 3, 1813; Account of Furs and Goods at Astoria and other Columbia River Posts, June 1, 1813, Astor Papers, MD-BA; Astoria Financial Journal, June 15, 1813, ibid.

4. McDougall, Journal, June 4, 5, 7, 1813.

5. Mackenzie's speech is quoted in Ross, *Adventures*, pp.237–38. Ross was at Astoria during this period before heading back to his usual Okanogan post.

6. Astoria Partners' Meeting, June 25, 1813, Pacific Fur Company Letterbook, MoSHi. McDougall's journal summarizes all these decisions in its July 1, 1813, entry.

7. See both sources cited in the preceding note.

8. Abandonment Resolution, July 1, 1813, Pacific Fur Company Letterbook, MoSHi. See also Abstract of Fur Returns, July 10, 1813, Astor Papers, MD-BA.

9. McDougall, Journal, July 5, 8, 1813.

10. Irving, *Astoria*, p.465.

11. Evidence for Hunt's travels during this period is scanty. Irving clearly used Hunt's journal, now lost. Business dealings with the Russian-American Company can be traced in two important documents: Account of Sales of the ship *Beaver* to A. Baranoff, September 25–November 14, 1812, Astor Papers, MD-BA; Barter Account of the ship *Beaver*, September 20–December 24, 1812, ibid. Something of Hunt's affairs in Hawaii can be seen in Invoice of Goods landed at Woahoo [Oahu] from on board the ship *Beaver*, December 29, 1812, ibid. Irving's discussion is in *Astoria*, pp.465–70. Ross's remarks are in *Adventures*, pp.234–35.

12. Reynolds, *Voyage*, pp.145, 146, 150.

13. Franchère, *Journal*, p.123.

14. Partners' Meeting, August 25, 1813, Pacific Fur Company Letterbook, MoSHi.

15. Northrop to Astor, Astoria, March 1814, Astor Papers, MD-BA.

16. Shaw to McTavish, Montreal, May 9, 1813, copied in the Pacific Fur Company Letterbook, MoSHi, on October 9, 1813, in an unknown hand; Wallace, *Documents*, p.274.

17. Ross, *Adventures*, p.244.

18. McDougall, Journal, October 7, 1813; Franchère, *Journal*, pp.128–29.

19. McDougall, Journal, October 8, 1813.

20. Franchère, *Journal*, p.129.

21. The Last Will and Testament of Duncan McDougall, Fort George, March 28, 1817, Office of the Court of King's Bench, Archives nationales du Quebec à Montreal.

22. McDougall, Journal, October 13, 1813.

23. Ibid., October 15, 1813.

24. Coues, *New Light*, 2:861.

25. Bill of Sale, Astoria, October 16, 1813, FO 5/208/156–58, PRO. The bill of sale does not specify a total sale amount. This was left for later negotiations.

26. Astor to William McGillivray, New York, October 27, 1814, Astor Papers, MD-BA; Astor to Adams, New York, January 4, 1823, in *Message*, 1823, p.12; Astor to Donald Mackenzie, New York, September 27, 1814, Astor Papers, MD-BA.

27. McDougall, Journal, October 18, 20, 22, 1813.

28. Pigot to Richard Ebbets, Coast of California, March 22, 1814, Astor Papers, MD-BA; Peter Corney, *Voyages in the Northern Pacific, 1813–1818* (1821; reprint, Fairfield, Wash.: Ye Galleon Press, 1965), pp.125–27. See also Kenneth W. Porter, "The Cruise of the *Forester*: Some New Sidelights on the Astoria Enterprise," *Washington Historical Quarterly* 23 (1932): 261–65.

29. McDougall, Journal, November 11, 1813; Franchère, *Journal*, p.131; Coues, *New Light*, 2:747.

30. The best accounts of the *Racoon*'s arrival are Franchère, *Journal*, pp.131–32, and Coues, *New Light*, 2:757–61. See also McDougall, Journal, November 30, 1813.

31. McDonald of Garth, "Notes," in Masson, *Les Bourgeois*, 2:48–50; Black to John Wilson Croker, Columbia River, December 15, 1813, in *Oregon Historical Quarterly* 17 (1916): 147–48. See also Barry M. Gough, "The 1813 Expedition to Astoria," *Beaver* (Autumn 1973): 44–51.

32. Ross Cox, *The Columbia River*, ed. Edgar I. Stewart and Jane R. Stew-

art (1831; reprint, Norman: University of Oklahoma Press, 1957), pp.147–48.

33. Ibid., pp.147–48; Franchère, *Journal*, pp.133–34; Coues, *New Light*, 2:770.

34. Franchère, *Journal*, p.134; McDonald of Garth, "Notes," Masson, *Les Bourgeois*, 2:50; Francis Phillips quoted in Gough, "Expedition to Astoria," p.50; Irving, *Astoria*, pp.490–91.

35. David Porter, *Journal of a Cruise made to the Pacific Ocean*, 2 vols. (Philadelphia: Bradford and Inskeep, 1815), 2:81; Irving, *Astoria*, p.479; Kenneth W. Porter, "The Cruise of Astor's Brig *Pedlar*, 1813–1816," *Oregon Historical Quarterly* 31 (1930): 224–25.

36. Because McDougall's journal ends with the arrival of the HMS *Racoon*, the best daily account of life at the post is the journal of Alexander Henry the younger, in Coues, *New Light*, 2:825ff.

37. Franchère, *Journal*, pp.144–45; Coues, *New Light*, 2:844–45.

38. Coues, *New Light*, 2:849.

39. Ibid., 2:851–52.

40. Ibid., 2:852.

41. Ibid., 2:851–53; Astoria Financial Journal, March 12, 1814, Astor Papers, MD-BA.

42. Coues, *New Light*, 2:856.

43. Astor to Dorr, New York, July 14, 1814, Astor Papers, MD-BA.

44. Astor to Crooks, New York, September 14, 1814, T. C. Elliott Collection, Oregon Historical Society, Portland.

45. Astor to Dashkov, New York, September 26, 1814, Astor Papers, MD-BA; Russian-American Company to Dashkov, St. Petersburg, October 28, 1814, *Russ. Docs.*, p.1094; *New-York Gazette and General Advertiser*, November 12, 1814.

CHAPTER 10

1. Astor to Gallatin, New York, March 22, 1814, Gallatin Papers, NHi; Monroe to Ministers Plenipotentiary, Washington, March 22, 1814, Diplomatic Instructions, All Countries, 7:351–52, RG 59, DNA.

2. Astor to Monroe, New York, September 26, 1814, Astor Papers, MD-BA; Astor to Forrest, New York, September 26, 1814, ibid.

3. Astor to Donald Mackenzie, New York, September 27, 1814, ibid.

4. Astor to Stuart, New York, October 8, 1814, ibid.; see also Astor to Forrest, New York, October 5, 1814, ibid.

5. Mackenzie to Hunt, Red River, June 25, 1827, Hunt Family Papers, MoSHi.

6. Charles Francis Adams, ed., *The Memoirs of John Quincy Adams*, 12 vols. (Boston: J. B. Lippincott, 1874–77), 3:90–91. See also Astor to Dorr, New York, 29 December 1814, Astor Papers, MD-BA.

7. Horsman, *War of 1812*, 127–29.

8. Astor to George Ehninger, New York, March 6, 1815, Astor Papers, MD-BA.

9. Astor to Monroe, n.p., early June 1815, Monroe Papers, DLC.

10. Monroe to Baker, Washington, July 18, 1815, *Dip. Docs.*, 1:230–31.

11. Monroe to Adams, Washington, July 21, 1815, Diplomatic Instructions, All Countries, 7:409–10, RG 59, DNA; Baker to Monroe, Washington, July 23, 1815, *Dip. Docs.*, 1:723–24.

12. These events are discussed in Simon McGillivray to Bagot, New York, November 15, 1817, FO 5/123/183–85, PRO.

13. Simon McGillivray, "Statement relative to the Columbia River and ad-joining Territory on the Western Coast of the Continent of North America, late summer 1815," FO 5/123/186–90, PRO.

14. Ellice to Goulburn, London, July 28, 1815, CO 42/164/499, PRO; Goulburn to Ellice, London, August 1, 1815, CO 42/164/500, ibid.; Ellice to Goulburn, August 2, 1815, CO 42/164/501, ibid.

15. Astor to Monroe, New York, August 17, 1815, Astor Papers, MD-BA; Astor to Gallatin, New York, October 6, 1815, Gallatin Papers, NHi.

16. Porter to Madison, Washington, October 31, 1815, Madison Papers, DLC; Frederick Merk, *The Oregon Question: Essays in Anglo-American Diplomacy and Politics* (Cambridge, Mass.: Harvard University Press, 1967), p.11.

17. Gallatin to Astor, n.p., August 5, 1835, Gallatin Papers, NHi.

18. William Sturgis to Morris, Boston, August 22, 1816, ibid.; Morris to John Graham, Boston, November 24, 1816, ibid. See also Merk, *Oregon Question*, pp.11–12.

19. Astor to Monroe, New York, September 5, 1816, Astor Papers, MD-BA.

20. Astor to Gallatin, New York, June 1, 1817, Gallatin Papers, NHi.

21. Adams to Prevost, Washington, September 29, 1817, Diplomatic Instructions, All Countries, 8:149, RG 59, DNA; Richard Rush: Re. John B. Prevost, Washington, September 25, 1817, *Dip. Docs.*, 1:262; Adams, *John Quincy Adams*, 4:11.

22. Bagot to Castlereagh, Washington, November 7, 1817, FO 5/123/104, PRO.

23. McGillivray to Bagot, New York, November 15, 1817, FO 5/123/183–85, ibid. In this same letter McGillivray of-

fered details on the 1815 restoration argument and also enclosed a copy of his thoughts on that subject.

24. The Bagot-Adams meeting can be reconstructed from several sources: Adams, *John Quincy Adams*, 4:24–25; Bagot to Adams, Washington, November 26, 1817, FO 5/123/192–93, PRO; Bagot to Shelburne, Washington, December 1, 1817, FO 5/123/194–95, ibid.; Bagot to Castlereagh, Washington, December 2, 1817, FO 5/123/179–81, ibid.

25. Castlereagh to Bagot, London, November 10, 1817, quoted in Merk, *Oregon Question*, p.20; Bathurst to North West Company, London, January 27, 1818, *Dip. Docs.*, 2:558.

26. James Biddle, Report of the Voyage of the USS *Ontario*, RG 45, DNA.

27. Ibid.; Biddle to Crowninshield, Columbia River, August 19, 1818, *Dip. Docs.*, 1:862.

28. Commodore William Bowles to Captain W. H. Shirreff, n.p., May 30, 1818, *Dip. Docs.*, 1:859–60; Prevost to Adams, Santiago de Chile, July 8, 1818, ibid., 1:858.

29. Keith to Prevost, Fort George, October 6, 1818, ibid., 1:888.

30. Merk, *Oregon Question*, p.26; Astor to Gallatin, New York, December 30, 1818, Gallatin Papers, NHi.

31. Ross, *Adventures*, p.34; Irving, *Astoria*, p.xlvii.

32. John C. Greene, *American Science in the Age of Jefferson* (Ames: Iowa State University Press, 1984), pp.207, 253–76.

33. Thomas Nuttall, comp., "A Catalogue of New and Interesting Plants, Collected in Upper Louisiana, and principally on the River Missouri, North America, by T. Nuttall, 1813," *Pittonia* 2 (1890): 116–19.

34. Thomas Nuttall, *A Journal of Travels into the Arkansas Territory During the Year 1819*, ed. Savoie Lottinville (1821; reprint, Norman: University of Oklahoma Press, 1980), p.xix.

35. Stuart, "Overland Narrative," in Rollins, *Discovery of the Oregon Trail*, pp.207–9.

36. Ibid., pp.210, 217–18.

37. Franchère, *Journal*, pp.106–7.

38. Ibid., p.107.

39. Cox, *Columbia River*, pp.164–79.

40. Ross, *Adventures*, pp.272–319.

41. William H. Goetzmann, *Exploration and Empire: The Explorer and the Scientist in the Winning of the American West* (New York: Random House, 1966), pp.34, 116–17.

42. Moulton, *Lewis and Clark Expedition*, Atlas, plate 125.

43. Rollins, *Discovery of the Oregon Trail*, map between pp.270 and 271.

44. *Missouri Gazette*, March 14, 1811.

45. Irving, *Astoria*, p.505; Jefferson to Astor, Monticello, November 9, 1813, Jefferson Papers, DLC.

46. Thomas Hart Benton, "Settlement on the Oregon River," 20th Cong., 1st sess., H. Doc. 139.

47. Thomas Hart Benton, *Thirty Years' View; or, A History of the Working of the American Government for Thirty Years, from 1820 to 1850*, 2 vols. (New York: D. Appleton, 1854), 1:13.

48. *Abridgment of the Debates and Proceedings of Congress, 1789–1856*, 16 vols. (New York: D. Appleton, 1857), 7:50.

49. Report of the Committee, to whom was referred a resolution of the House of Representatives . . . directing an inquiry into the situation of the settlements on the Pacific Ocean . . . 25 January 1821, *New American State Papers*, 1:72–86.

50. *National Intelligencer*, January 26, 1821.

51. For the Canning-Adams meetings, see Adams, *John Quincy Adams*, 5:243–46.

52. Noble E. Cunningham, Jr., ed., *Circular Letters of Congressmen to their Constituents, 1789–1829*, 3 vols. (Chapel Hill: University of North Carolina Press, 1978), 3:1138.

53. *Abridgment of the Debates and Proceedings*, 7:392–96, 398.

54. Astor to Adams, New York, January 4, 1823, in *Message*, 1823, pp.11–18.

55. *Abridgment of the Debates and Proceedings*, 7:421–22.

56. Ibid., 7:366–69; 8:188.

57. Adams to Rush, Washington, July 22, 1813, *Dip. Docs.*, 2:58.

58. Astor to Gallatin, New York, March 7, 1827, Gallatin Papers, NHi.

59. Thomas J. Farnham, *Travels in the Great Western Prairies* (Poughkeepsie: Killey and Lossing, 1841), p.99.

60. Robert V. Hine and Savoie Lottinville, eds., *Soldier in the West: Letters of Theodore Talbot During His Services in California, Mexico, and Oregon, 1845–1853* (Norman: University of Oklahoma Press, 1972), p.121.

APPENDIX

1. Irving to Pierre Munro Irving, New York, September 15, 1834, in Ralph M. Aderman, et al., eds., *The Complete Works of Washington Irving: Letters*, 4 vols. (Boston: Twayne Publishers, 1978–82), 2:798.

2. Ibid.

3. For the publishing history of *Astoria*, see Todd's edition of Irving, *Astoria*, pp.xxiii–xxvi.

4. Irving, *Astoria*, p.505.

5. Hiram M. Chittenden, *The American Fur Trade of the Far West*, 2 vols. (1902; reprint, Lincoln: University of Nebraska Press, 1986), 1:227–28.

6. David S. Muzzey, *An American History* (Boston: Ginn and Co., 1911), p.266.

7. Frederic L. Paxson, *History of the American Frontier, 1763–1893* (Boston: Houghton, Mifflin and Co., 1924), p.179; Constance L. Skinner, *Adventurers of Oregon* (New Haven: Yale University Press, 1921), pp.116–210. See also Cardinal Goodwin, *The Trans-Mississippi West, 1803–1853* (New York: D. Appleton, 1922), pp.123–24; Robert E. Riegel, *America Moves West* (New York: Henry Holt and Co., 1930), pp.153–55.

Bibliography

PRIMARY SOURCES

Manuscript Collections

American Philosophical Society, Philadelphia, Pennsylvania
    Benjamin Smith Barton Papers
Archives nationales du Quebec à Montreal
    Notarial Records of John Gerband Beek
    Office of the Court of King's Bench
Baker Library, Harvard University Graduate School of Business Administration, Boston, Massachusetts
    John Jacob Astor Papers
Beinecke Rare Book and Manuscript Library, Yale University, New Haven, Connecticut
    John Jacob Astor Papers, Western Americana Collection
    General Collections
Butler Rare Book and Manuscript Library, Columbia University, New York
    De Witt Clinton Papers
Filson Club, Louisville, Kentucky
    John Wesley Hunt Papers
Library of Congress, Washington, D.C.
    Thomas Jefferson Papers
    James Madison Papers
    James Monroe Papers
Missouri Historical Society, St. Louis, Missouri
    Astorians Collection
    Bates Family Papers
    Chouteau Collection
    William Clark Papers
    Charles Gratiot Collection
    Charles Gratiot Letterbooks
    Hunt Family Papers

Meriwether Lewis Collection
Pacific Fur Company Letterbook
St. Louis Missouri Fur Company Ledger
National Archives, Washington, D.C.
   RG 24: Records of the Bureau of Naval Personnel
   RG 41: Records of the Bureau of Marine Inspection and Navigation
   RG 45: Collection of the Office of Naval Records and Library
   RG 59: General Records of the Department of State
New-York Historical Society, New York City
   Albert Gallatin Papers
Oregon Historical Society, Portland, Oregon
   T. C. Elliott Collection
Private Collections of Warren Baker, Montreal
Public Archives of Canada, Montreal, Ontario, Canada
   MG 11, Q Series: British Colonial Office Transcripts
   Senator L. R. Masson Collection
Public Record Office, London, England
   Admiralty Office Papers
   Colonial Office Papers
   Foreign Office Papers
   Treasury Office Papers
Rosenbach Library and Museum, Philadelphia, Pennsylvania
   Duncan McDougall, Journal at Astoria, 1811–1813
Sutro Library, San Francisco, California
   Sir Joseph Banks Papers
Toronto Metro Reference Library
   North West Company Letters and Accounts Collection

Published Sources

Abel, Annie Heloise, ed. *Tabeau's Narrative of Loisel's Expedition to the Upper Missouri*. Norman: University of Oklahoma Press, 1939.

Abridgment of the Debates and Proceedings of Congress, 1789–1856. 16 vols. New York: D. Appleton, 1857.

Adams, Charles Francis, ed. *The Memoirs of John Quincy Adams*, 12 vols. Philadelphia: J. B. Lippincott, 1874–77.

Aderman, Ralph M., et al., eds. *The Complete Works of Washington Irving: Letters*. 4 vols. Boston: Twayne Publishers, 1978–82.

Bashkina, Nina N., and David F. Trask, eds. *The United States and Russia: The*

Beginnings of Relations, 1765–1815. Washington, D.C.: Government Printing Office, 1980.

Beaglehole, J. C., ed. *The Journals of Captain James Cook. The Voyage of the "Resolution" and the "Discovery," 1776–1780.* Cambridge, England: Hakluyt Society, 1967.

Benton, Thomas Hart. *Thirty Years' View; or, A History of the Working of the American Government for Thirty Years, from 1820 to 1850.* 2 vols. New York: D. Appleton, 1854.

Brackenridge, Henry M. *Views of Louisiana; together with a Journal of a Voyage up the Missouri River in 1811.* Pittsburgh: Cramer, Spear, and Eichbaum, 1814.

Bradbury, John. *Travels in the Interior Parts of America in the Years 1809, 1810, and 1811.* Liverpool: Smith and Galway, 1819.

Brown, Everett S., ed. *William Plumer's Memorandum of Proceedings in the United States Senate, 1803–1807.* New York: Macmillan Co., 1923.

Carter, Clarence, ed. *The Territorial Papers of the United States: The Territory of Louisiana–Missouri, 1806–1814.* Washington, D.C.: Government Printing Office, 1949.

Corney, Peter. *Voyages in the Northern Pacific, 1813–1818.* 1821. Reprint. Fairfield, Wash.: Ye Galleon Press, 1965.

Coues, Elliott, ed. *New Light on the Early History of the Greater Northwest: The Manuscript Journals of Alexander Henry and of David Thompson.* 3 vols. in 2. 1897. Reprint. Minneapolis: Ross and Haines, 1965.

Cox, Ross. *The Columbia River.* Edited by Edgar I. Stewart and Jane R. Stewart. 1831. Reprint. Norman: University of Oklahoma Press, 1957.

Cruikshank, E. A., ed. *The Correspondence of Lieut.-Gov. John Graves Simcoe, with Allied Documents.* 5 vols. Toronto: Ontario Historical Society, 1923–31.

Cunningham, Noble E., Jr. ed. *Circular Letters of Congressmen to their Constituents, 1789–1829.* 3 vols. Chapel Hill: University of North Carolina Press, 1978.

Douglas, Jesse S., ed. "Matthews' Adventures on the Columbia: A Pacific Fur Company Document." *Oregon Historical Quarterly* 40 (1939): 105–48.

Ehrenberg, Ralph, ed. "Sketch of Part of the Missouri & Yellowstone Rivers with a Description of the Country, Etc." *Prologue* 3 (1971): 73–78.

Elliott, T. C., ed. "Journal of David Thompson." *Oregon Historical Quarterly* 15 (1914): 39–63, 104–25.

———. "The Last Will and Testament of John Day." *Oregon Historical Quarterly* 17 (1916): 373–79.

Fanning, Edmund. *Voyages to the South Seas, Indian, and Pacific Oceans*. New York: William H. Vermilye, 1838.

Farnham, Thomas J. *Travels in the Great Western Prairies*. Poughkeepsie: Killey and Lossing, 1841.

Fox, John S., ed. "Narrative of the Travels and Adventures of a Merchant Voyageur in the Savage Territories of Northern America 1783 to 1820 by Jean Baptiste Perrault." *Michigan Pioneer and Historical Collections* 37 (1909–10): 508–619.

Franchère, Gabriel. *Journal of a Voyage on the North West Coast of North America during the Years 1811, 1812, 1813, and 1814*. Edited by W. Kaye Lamb. Toronto: Champlain Society, 1969.

Gates, Charles M., ed. *Five Fur Traders of the Northwest*. St. Paul: Minnesota Historical Society, 1965.

Glover, Richard, ed. *David Thompson's Narrative, 1784–1812*. Toronto: Champlain Society, 1962.

Graustein, Jeannette E., ed. "Nuttall's Travels into the Old Northwest: An Unpublished 1810 Diary." *Chronica Botanica* 14 (1951): 1–88.

Hayes, Edmund, ed. *Log of the "Union": John Boit's Remarkable Voyage to the Northwest Coast and Around the World, 1794–1796*. Portland: Oregon Historical Society, 1981.

Henry, Alexander. *Travels and Adventures in Canada and the Indian Territories between the Years 1760 and 1776*. 1809. Reprint. Edmonton: Hurtig Publishers, 1969.

Hine, Robert V., and Savoie Lottinville, eds. *Soldier in the West: Letters of Theodore Talbot During His Services in California, Mexico, and Oregon, 1845–1853*. Norman: University of Oklahoma Press, 1972.

Hopwood, Victor G., ed. *David Thompson: Travels in Western North America, 1784–1812*. Toronto: Macmillan of Canada, 1971.

Howay, Frederic W., ed. "David Thompson's Account of his First Attempt to Cross the Rockies." *Queen's Quarterly* 40 (1933): 333–56.

———. *The Journal of Captain James Colnett*. Toronto: Champlain Society, 1940.

———. *Voyages of the "Columbia" to the Northwest Coast, 1787–1790 and 1790–1793*. Boston: Massachusetts Historical Society, 1941.

Irving, Washington. *Astoria; or, Anecdotes of an Enterprise beyond the Rocky Mountains*. 1836. Edited by Edgeley W. Todd. Norman: University of Oklahoma Press, 1964.

Jackman, S. W., ed. *The Journal of William Sturgis*. Victoria, British Columbia: SonoNis Press, 1978.

Jackson, Donald, ed. *The Journals of Zebulon Montgomery Pike, with Letters and Related Documents*. 2 vols. Norman: University of Oklahoma Press, 1966.

————. *The Letters of the Lewis and Clark Expedition with Related Documents, 1783–1854*. 2d ed. 2 vols. Urbana: University of Illinois Press, 1978.

James, Thomas. *Three Years among the Indians and Mexicans*. 1846. Reprint. Chicago: Lakeside Press, 1953.

Kane, Paul. *Wanderings of an Artist among the Indians of North America*. 1859. Reprint. Edmonton: Hurtig Publishers, 1968.

Kaplanoff, Mark D., ed. *Joseph Ingraham's Journal of the Brigantine "Hope" on a Voyage to the Northwest Coast of North America, 1790–1792*. Barre, Mass.: Imprint Society, 1971.

Lamb, W. Kaye, ed. *The Journals and Letters of Sir Alexander Mackenzie*. Cambridge, England: Hakluyt Society, 1970.

————. *The Letters and Journals of Simon Fraser, 1806–1808*. Toronto: Macmillan of Canada, 1960.

————. *Sixteen Years in the Indian Country: The Journal of Daniel Williams Harmon, 1800–1816*. Toronto: Macmillan of Canada, 1957.

————. *The Voyage of George Vancouver, 1791–1795*. 4 vols. London: Hakluyt Society, 1984.

Luttig, John C. *Journal of a Fur-Trading Expedition on the Upper Missouri, 1812–1813*. Edited by Stella M. Drumm, with additional notes by A. P. Nasatir. New York: Argosy-Antiquarian Books, 1964.

McGillivray, Duncan. "Some Account of the Trade Carried on by the North West Company, 1808." *Report of the Public Archives of Canada, 1928*. Ottawa: F. A. Acland, 1929.

Manning, W. R., ed. *Diplomatic Correspondence of the United States: Canadian Relations, 1784–1860*. 4 vols. Washington, D.C.: Government Printing Office, 1940–45.

Masson, L. R., ed. *Les Bourgeois de la Compagnie du Nord-Ouest*. 2 vols. 1889–90. Reprint. New York: Antiquarian Press, 1960.

Merk, Frederick, ed. *Fur Trade and Empire: George Simpson's Journal, 1824–1825*. Rev. ed. Cambridge, Mass.: Harvard University Press, 1968.

Missouri River Commission. *Map of the Missouri River from its Mouth to Three Forks, Montana, in eighty-four sheets*. Washington, D.C.: Government Printing Office, for the Missouri River Commission, 1892–95.

Mitchill, Samuel L. *A Discourse on the Character and Services of Thomas Jefferson*. New York: Lyceum of Natural History, 1826.

Morris, Grace P., ed. "Some Letters from 1792–1800 on the China Trade." *Oregon Historical Quarterly* 42 (1941): 48–87.

Morton, Arthur S., ed. *The Journal of Duncan McGillivray of the North West Company, 1794–1795.* Toronto: Macmillan of Canada, 1929.

Moulton, Gary E., ed. *The Journals of the Lewis and Clark Expedition.* 6 vols. to date. Lincoln: University of Nebraska Press, 1983–.

Munford, James K., ed. *John Ledyard's Journal of Captain Cook's Last Voyage.* 1783. Reprint. Corvallis: Oregon State University Press, 1963.

Nasatir, A. P., ed. *Before Lewis and Clark: Documents Illustrating the History of the Missouri, 1785–1804.* 2 vols. St. Louis: St. Louis Historical Documents Foundation, 1952.

Nuttall, Thomas, comp. "A Catalogue of New and Interesting Plants, Collected in Upper Louisiana, and principally on the River Missouri, North America, by T. Nuttall, 1813." Fraser's Nursery Catalogue, London, 1813, reprinted in *Pittonia* 2 (1890): 116–19.

——. *A Journal of Travels into the Arkansas Territory During the Year 1819.* Edited by Savoie Lottinville. 1821. Reprint. Norman: University of Oklahoma Press, 1980.

Pierce, Richard A., ed. *Russia's Hawaiian Adventure, 1815–1817.* Berkeley: University of California Press, 1965.

Porter, David. *Journal of a Cruise made to the Pacific Ocean.* 2 vols. Philadelphia: Bradford and Inskeep, 1815.

Quaife, Milo M., ed. *The John Askin Papers.* 2 vols. Detroit: Detroit Library Commission, 1928.

Reynolds, Stephen. *The Voyage of the "New Hazard."* Edited by Frederic W. Howay. Salem, Mass.: Peabody Museum, 1938.

Rickman, John. *Journal of Captain Cook's Last Voyage to the Pacific Ocean.* London: E. Newbery, 1781.

Rollins, Philip Ashton, ed. *The Discovery of the Oregon Trail: Robert Stuart's Narratives of his Overland Trip Eastward from Astoria in 1812–1813.* New York: Edward Eberstadt, 1935.

Ross, Alexander. *Adventures of the First Settlers on the Oregon or Columbia River.* 1849. Reprint. With an introduction by James P. Ronda. Lincoln: University of Nebraska Press, 1986.

Sage, Walter N., ed. "The Appeal of the North West Company to the British Government to Forestall John Jacob Astor's Columbian Enterprise." *Canadian Historical Review* 17 (1936): 304–11.

Seton, Alfred. "Life on the Oregon." *Oregon Historical Quarterly* 36 (1935): 187–204.

Spaulding, Kenneth A., ed. *On the Oregon Trail: Robert Stuart's Journey of Discovery*. Norman: University of Oklahoma Press, 1953.

Syrett, Harold G., ed. *The Papers of Alexander Hamilton*. 27 vols. to date. New York: Columbia University Press, 1961–.

Tate, Vernon D., ed. "Spanish Documents Relating to the Voyage of the *Racoon* to Astoria and San Francisco." *Hispanic American Historical Review* 18 (1938): 183–91.

Thwaites, Reuben G., ed. *The Original Journals of the Lewis and Clark Expedition*. 8 vols. New York: Dodd, Mead and Co., 1904–5.

Walker, Alexander. *An Account of a Voyage to the North West Coast of America in 1785 and 1786*. Edited by Robin Fisher and J. M. Bumsted. Seattle: University of Washington Press, 1982.

Wallace, W. Stewart, ed. *Documents Relating to the North West Company*. Toronto: Champlain Society, 1934.

Williams, Glyndwr, ed. *Andrew Graham's Observations on Hudson's Bay, 1767–1791*. London: Hudson's Bay Company Record Society, 1969.

Government Documents

American State Papers. 38 vols. Washington, D.C.: Gales and Seaton, 1789–1838.

Message from the President communicating the Letter of Mr. Prevost and other Documents Relating to an Establishment made at the Mouth of the Columbia River. 17th Cong., 2d sess., H. Doc. 45. Washington, D.C.: Gales and Seaton, 1823.

Report of the Committee, to whom was referred a resolution of the House of Representatives of the 19th of December last, directing an inquiry into the situation of the settlements on the Pacific Ocean, and the expediency of occupying the Columbia River; accompanied with a bill to authorize the occupation of the Columbia River, 25 January 1821. *New American State Papers*. Vol 1. Wilmington, Del.: Scholarly Resources, 1972.

Report of the Select Committee, appointed on the 29th of December last, with instructions to inquire into the expediency of occupying the Mouth of the Columbia River. 18th Cong. 1st sess. Washington, D.C.: Gales and Seaton, 1824.

Report of the Select Committee on the Exploration of the Northwest Coast, January 16, 1826. 19th Cong., 1st sess., H. Doc. 35. Washington, D.C.: Gales and Seaton, 1826.

Newspapers and Magazines

Gentleman's Magazine (London) 1790

Missouri Gazette (St. Louis) 1809–17 (also published irregularly as the *Louisiana Gazette*

National Intelligencer (Washington, D.C.) 1809–25

New York Evening Post, 1809–26

New-York Gazette and General Advertiser, 1810–15

Niles' *Register*, 1810–28

SECONDARY SOURCES

Books

Bemis, Samuel F. *John Quincy Adams and the Foundations of American Foreign Policy*. New York: Alfred A. Knopf, 1949.

Bolkhovitinov, Nikolai N. *The Beginnings of Russian-American Relations, 1775–1815*. Cambridge, Mass.: Harvard University Press, 1975.

Burpee, Lawrence J. *The Search for the Western Sea*. Toronto: Musson Book Co., 1908.

Campbell, Marjorie W. *The North West Company*. Toronto: Macmillan of Canada, 1957.

Christman, Margaret C. S. *Adventurous Pursuits: Americans and the China Trade, 1784–1844*. Washington, D.C.: Smithsonian Institution Press, 1984.

Combes, John D. *Excavations at Spokane Houses—Fort Spokane Historic Site, 1962–1963*. Pullman: Washington State University, 1964.

Cook, Warren. *Flood Tide of Empire: Spain and the Pacific Northwest, 1543–1819*. New Haven: Yale University Press, 1973.

Davidson, Gordon C. *The North West Company*. Berkeley: University of California Press, 1918.

DeVoto, Bernard. *The Course of Empire*. Boston: Houghton, Mifflin Co., 1952.

Fisher, Robin. *Contact and Conflict: Indian-European Relations in British Columbia, 1774–1890*. Vancouver: University of British Columbia Press, 1977.

Fisher, Robin, and Hugh Johnston, eds. *Captain James Cook and His Times*. Seattle: University of Washington Press, 1979.

Foley, William E., and C. David Rice. *The First Chouteaus: River Barons of Early St. Louis*. Urbana: University of Illinois Press, 1983.

Francis, Daniel. *Battle for the West: Fur Traders and the Birth of Western Canada*. Edmonton: Hurtig Publishers, 1982.

Gibson, James R. *Imperial Russia in Frontier America*. New York: Oxford University Press, 1976.

Goetzmann, William H. *Exploration and Empire: The Explorer and the Scientist in the Winning of the American West*. New York: Random House, 1966.

Goldstein, Jonathan. *Philadelphia and the China Trade, 1682–1846: Commercial, Cultural, and Attitudinal Effects*. University Park: Pennsylvania State University Press, 1978.

Gough, Barry M. *Distant Dominion: Britain and the Northwest Coast of North America, 1579–1809*. Vancouver: University of British Columbia Press, 1980.

————. *The Royal Navy and the Northwest Coast of North America, 1810–1914: A Study of British Maritime Ascendancy*. Vancouver: University of British Columbia Press, 1971.

Graustein, Jeannette E. *Thomas Nuttall, Naturalist: Explorations in America, 1808–1841*. Cambridge, Mass.: Harvard University Press, 1967.

Greene, John C. *American Science in the Age of Jefferson*. Ames: Iowa State University Press, 1984.

Horsman, Reginald. *The Diplomacy of the New Republic, 1776–1815*. Arlington Heights, Ill.: Harlan Davidson, 1985.

————. *The War of 1812*. New York: Alfred A. Knopf, 1969.

Innis, Harold A. *The Fur Trade in Canada*. Rev. ed. Toronto: University of Toronto Press, 1956.

————. *Peter Pond: Fur Trader and Adventurer*. Toronto: Irwin and Gordon, 1930.

Jablow, Joseph. *The Cheyenne in Plains Indian Trade Relations, 1795–1840*. Seattle: University of Washington Press, 1950.

Jackson, Donald. *Thomas Jefferson and the Stony Mountains*. Urbana: University of Illinois Press, 1981.

Kuykendall, Ralph S. *The Hawaiian Kingdom, 1778–1854*. 2 vols. Honolulu: University of Hawaii Press, 1938.

Lavender, David. *The Fist in the Wilderness*. Garden City: Doubleday and Co., 1964.

Long, David F. *Nothing Too Daring: A Biography of Commodore David Porter, 1780–1843*. Annapolis: United States Naval Institute Press, 1970.

McKelvey, Susan Delano. *Botanical Exploration of the Trans-Mississippi West, 1790–1850*. Jamaica Plain, Mass.: Arnold Arboretum of Harvard University, 1955.

Meinig, Donald W. *The Great Columbia Plain: A Historical Geography, 1805–1910*. Seattle: University of Washington Press, 1968.

Merk, Frederick. *The Oregon Question: Essays in Anglo-American Diplomacy and Politics.* Cambridge, Mass.: Harvard University Press, 1967.

Meyer, Roy W. *The Village Indians of the Upper Missouri: The Mandans, Hidatsas, and Arikaras.* Lincoln: University of Nebraska Press, 1977.

Morgan, Theodore. *Hawaii: A Century of Economic Change, 1778–1876.* Cambridge, Mass.: Harvard University Press, 1948.

Morse, Eric W. *Fur Trade Canoe Routes of Canada Then and Now.* 2d ed. Toronto: University of Toronto Press, 1979.

Oglesby, Richard E. *Manuel Lisa and the Opening of the Missouri Fur Trade.* Norman: University of Oklahoma Press, 1963.

Oregon Historical Society. *Columbia's Gateway: A History of the Columbia River Estuary to 1920.* Vancouver, Washington: Pacific Northwest River Basins Commission, 1980.

Perkins, Bradford. *Castlereagh and Adams: England and the United States, 1812–1823.* Berkeley: University of California Press, 1964.

———. *Prologue to War: England and the United States, 1805–1812.* Berkeley: University of California Press, 1961.

Pethick, Derek. *First Approaches to the Northwest Coast.* Vancouver: J. J. Douglas, 1976.

———. *The Nootka Connection: Europe and the Northwest Coast, 1790–1795.* Vancouver: Douglas and McIntyre, 1980.

Phillips, Paul C. *The Fur Trade.* 2 vols. Norman: University of Oklahoma Press, 1961.

Porter, Kenneth W. *John Jacob Astor, Business Man.* 2 vols. Cambridge, Mass.: Harvard University Press, 1931.

Rich, E. E. *The Fur Trade and the Northwest to 1857.* Toronto: McClelland and Stewart, 1967.

———. *Montreal and the Fur Trade.* Montreal: McGill University Press, 1966.

Ronda, James P. *Lewis and Clark among the Indians.* Lincoln: University of Nebraska Press, 1984.

Ruby, Robert H., and John A. Brown. *The Chinook Indians: Traders of the Lower Columbia River.* Norman: University of Oklahoma Press, 1976.

———. *Indians of the Pacific Northwest: A History.* Norman: University of Oklahoma Press, 1981.

Stagg, J.C.A. *Mr. Madison's War: Politics, Diplomacy, and Warfare in the Early American Republic, 1783–1830.* Princeton: Princeton University Press, 1983.

Stuart, Reginald C. *United States Expansion and British North America, 1775–1871.* Charlotte: University of North Carolina Press, 1988.

Van Alstyne, Richard. *The Rising American Empire*. New York: Oxford University Press, 1960.

Wagner, Henry R. *Peter Pond: Fur Trader and Explorer*. New Haven: Yale University Library, 1955.

Wallace, W. Stewart. *The Pedlars from Quebec and Other Papers on the Nor'-Westers*. Toronto: Ryerson Press, 1954.

Articles

Barry, J. Neilson. "Astorians Who Became Permanent Settlers." *Washington Historical Quarterly* 24 (1933): 221–31, 282–301.

———. "Madame Dorion of the Astorians." *Oregon Historical Quarterly* 30 (1929): 272–78.

———. "Site of Wallace House, 1812–1814." *Oregon Historical Quarterly* 42 (1941): 205–7.

Blenkinsop, Willis. "Edward Rose." In LeRoy R. Hafen, ed., *The Mountain Men and the Fur Trade of the Far West*. 9 vols. Glendale, Calif.: Arthur H. Clark, 1962–75, 9: 335–38.

Bradley, Harold W. "The Hawaiian Islands and the Pacific Fur Trade, 1785–1813." *Pacific Northwest Quarterly* 30 (1939): 275–99.

Drumm, Stella M. "More about Astorians." *Oregon Historical Quarterly* 24 (1923): 335–60.

Ewers, John C. "The Indian Trade of the Upper Missouri before Lewis and Clark." *Bulletin of the Missouri Historical Society* 10 (1954): 429–46.

Fisher, Robin. "Arms and Men on the Northwest Coast, 1774–1825." *BC Studies*, number 29 (Spring 1976): 3–18.

Gough, Barry M. "The 1813 Expedition to Astoria." *Beaver* (Autumn 1973): 44–51.

———. "James Cook and the Origins of the Maritime Fur Trade." *American Neptune* 38 (1978): 217–24.

———. "The North West Company's 'Adventure to China.'" *Oregon Historical Quarterly* 76 (1975): 309–31.

Grabert, G. F. "The Astor Fort Okanogan." *University of Washington Reports in Archaeology* 2 (1968).

Graustein, Jeannette E. "Manuel Lisa and Thomas Nuttall." *Bulletin of the Missouri Historical Society* 12 (1956): 249–52.

Haeger, John D. "Business Strategy and Practice in the Early Republic: John Jacob Astor and the American Fur Trade." *Western Historical Quarterly* 19 (1988): 183–202.

Haines, F. D. "McKenzie's Winter Camp, 1812–1813." *Oregon Historical Quarterly* 37 (1936): 329–333.

Howay, Frederic W. "The Loss of the *Tonquin*." *Washington Historical Quarterly* 13 (1922): 83–92.

———. "An Outline Sketch of the Maritime Fur Trade." *Reports of the Canadian Historical Association* (1932), 5–14.

Morton, Arthur S. "The North West Company's Columbian Enterprise and David Thompson." *Canadian Historical Review* 17 (1936): 266–88.

Nichols, Roger L. "The Arikara Indians and the Missouri River Trade: A Quest for Survival." *Great Plains Quarterly* 2 (Spring 1982): 77–93.

Porter, Kenneth W. "The Cruise of Astor's Brig *Pedlar*, 1813–1816." *Oregon Historical Quarterly* 31 (1930): 223–30.

———. "The Cruise of the *Forester*: Some New Sidelights on the Astoria Enterprise." *Washington Historical Quarterly* 23 (1932): 261–85.

———. "John Jacob Astor and the Sandalwood Trade of the Hawaiian Islands, 1816–1828." *Journal of Economic and Business History* 2 (1930): 495–519.

———. "Joseph Ashton, Astorian Sailor, 1812–1815." *Oregon Historical Quarterly* 31 (1930): 343–50.

———. "More about the Brig *Pedlar*, 1813–1816." *Oregon Historical Quarterly* 33 (1932): 311–12.

———. "Roll of Overland Astorians, 1810–1812." *Oregon Historical Quarterly* 34 (1933): 103–12.

Ray, Verne F. "Lower Chinook Ethnographic Notes." *University of Washington Publications in Anthropology* 7 (1938): 29–165.

Rickett, H. W. "John Bradbury's Explorations in Missouri Territory." *American Philosophical Society Proceedings* 94 (1950).

Ronda, James P. "Astoria and the Birth of Empire." *Montana the Magazine of Western History* 36 (Summer 1986): 22–35.

———. "Wilson Price Hunt Reports on Lewis and Clark." *Filson Club History Quarterly* 62 (1988): 251–59.

Schurer, P. J., and R. H. Linden. "Results of a Sub-Bottom Acoustic Survey in a Search for the *Tonquin*." *International Journal of Nautical Archaeology and Underwater Exploration* 13 (1984): 305–9.

Van Alstyne, Richard W. "International Rivalries in the Pacific Northwest." *Oregon Historical Quarterly* 46 (1945): 185–218.

Wheeler, Mary E. "The Origins of the Russian-American Company." *Jahrbucher fur Geschichte Osteuropas* (1966), 485–94.

White, M. Catherine. "Saleesh House: The First Trading Post among the Flatheads." *Pacific Northwest Quarterly* 33 (1942): 251–63.

Wood, W. Raymond. "Contrastive Features of Native North American Trade Systems." *University of Oregon Anthropological Papers* 4 (1972): 153–69.

Index

Abandonment plans, 265–66, 278–82, 285, 297

Adams, John Quincy, xii, 77, 79–80, 82, 84, 291, 302, 304–5, 306, 310–12, 332–34

Aird, James, 127–28, 136, 146, 147

Aitken, Job, 98, 114, 115

Alaska, Russian fur trade in, 65–66

Albatross (ship), 283, 285–86, 297, 300, 303

All Saints' Day, 185, 218

American Fur Company, 42, 45, 47, 79, 210, 330

Ames, Edward, 97

Anderson, Peter, 97

Argonaut (ship), 35

Argus (later *Wasp*) (ship), 263

Arikara Indians, 129, 155–56, 157–64

Armstrong, John, 272

Ashton, Joseph, 293

Astor, John Jacob: American fur empire envisioned by, 1–2, 36, 223; creates Pacific Fur Co., 58–59, 62, 87; fears North West Co.–British alliance, 244; federal backing sought by, 38–46 passim, 52–53, 55; federal protection sought by, 243, 258–63, 266–73; Floyd Bill and, 333–34; hires Hunt, 50–51, 59, 87; Irving and, 335, 338–39; laments sale and loss of Astoria, 290–91, 300–301, 315, 334–35; Lewis and Clark and, 29, 31; Mackenzie and, 280–81, 304; meeting with Gallatin, 267; meeting with Jefferson, 45–47; meeting with Monroe, 259–60; in Montreal, 24–25, 29, 47, 55; offer to buy Michilimackinac Co., 46–49, 55–62 passim; overland route, 128, 164; planning for Astoria, 37–64; Porter's biography of, 343; restoration efforts, 302–11 passim; Russian strategies, 71–86 passim; schemes to save Astoria, 251–54, 258–63, 266–76 passim; and *Tonquin*, 94–96, 98–100; warns of Indians, 34, 100–101; War of 1812 and, 242, 249, 250–52; illus., 3

Astor, Magdalen, 78. *See also* Bentzon, Mrs. Adrian

Astoria: as diplomatic issue, 304–15, 327–35; as symbol, xii, 327, 334. *See also* Fort Astoria

Astoria (book by Irving), 326, 336, 338–42

Atcheson, Nathaniel, 56–57, 245–47, 253, 255–56

Athabasca Lake, 6–7, 27–28

Bagot, Charles, 311–13

Baker, Anthony St. John, 306–7

Baker Bay, 114–15, 197–99

Bancroft, Hubert Howe, 342

Banks, Sir Joseph, 12, 27–28, 133

Baranov, Alexander, 65, 66, 68–69, 72, 74–75, 242, 283

Barrell, Joseph, 32

Barton, Dr. Benjamin Smith, 122–23

Bartram, William, 122

Bathurst, Lord, 255–56, 307–8, 313

Bayly, William, 33

Beaver (ship), 208, 211, 236, 237, 240, 242, 250–51, 265, 283–84; illus., 241

Beaver Club, 25, 47, 55, 245
Bell, George, 98, 212
Belleau, Antoine, 216
Belleau, Jean Baptiste, 213, 216
Benton, Thomas Hart, 258, 327, 330–31, 334
Bentzon, Adrian Benjamin, 78–86, 267–68, 272, 304–5
Bentzon, Mrs. Adrian (née Magdalen Astor), 78, 81
Biddle, James, 310–11, 313–14
Big Elk (Omaha headman), 148
Bighorn Mountains, 170, 174
Big Man (Arikara chief), 158
Black, William, 295–96, 305
Blackfeet Indians, 129, 131, 143
Blossom (ship), 314
Boise River, 188, 190
Boit, John, 4, 33, 35, 106
Bonneville, B.L.E., 326
Books at Astoria, 211–12
Boone, Daniel, 140
Botany, Astorians and, 316–17, 319–20
Bourdon, Michel, 277
Brackenridge, Henry Marie, 142, 143, 151, 156, 157, 164
Bradbury, John, 124, 133, 138, 140–41, 142, 143–44, 146–47, 151, 153, 156, 157, 159, 162, 163, 164, 316–17
Breaux, Jean Baptiste, 120
Breckinridge, John C., 43
Broughton, W. R., 294
Brownson, John, 143
Bruguier, Regis, 213
Brule, Louis, 235
Buffalo, 169
Buldakov, Michael, 82–85

Caldron Linn, 182–83, 185; illus., 184
Calhoun, John C., 249, 331
Canadian Astorians, 91, 98–100, 101, 103, 104, 106, 111–12, 113, 119, 125–26, 178, 213–14

Canning, George, 331–33
Cannon, William, 120
Canoe River (Snake River), 179, 180–81, 182, 194
Cape Disappointment, 113, 293
Cape Verde Islands, 103
Carriere, Michel, 125, 134, 193, 195
Carson, Alexander, 149, 150, 151, 162, 177, 279
Cascades (Columbia River), 202–3
Cass, Martin, 179
Castlereagh, Lord, 255–56, 313
Catherine the Great, Empress of Russia, 65–66
Cathlamet Bay, 194
Cathlamet Indians, 219, 322
Caulk, Harry, 125, 139
Cayuse Indians, 191, 193
Celilo Falls, 194
Charbonneau, Toussaint, 143, 154
Charless, Joseph, 125, 131, 143, 164, 181, 326
Chehalis Indians, 222, 225
Cherub (ship), 294–95
Cheyenne Indians, 162, 167–68
China trade, profits and problems of, 32–33
Chinook Indians, 35, 115, 197, 202, 219–22, 226–30, 235, 279, 295, 298; culture viewed by Astorians, 320–22; sex in trade, 227–29
Chipewyan Indians, 27
Chittenden, Hiram M., 341–42
Chouteau, Pierre, 130
Chouteau family, 50, 51, 53
Christmas, 192, 208, 218
Clapp, Benjamin, 211
Clappine, Antoine, 182, 195
Clark, William, 53, 124, 125, 128, 129–30, 132–33, 134, 136, 141, 142, 148, 154, 165, 180, 220; map by, 129, 193–94, 323. *See also* Lewis and Clark expedition
Clarke, John, 241, 264, 266, 279–80, 281, 282, 287

Clatsop Indians, 197, 201, 202, 219–20, 226, 322; Astorian diplomacy and, 223–24

Clear Creek (Wyoming), 171

Clemson, Eli, 134, 143

Clerke, Charles, 6

Clerks at Astoria, 210–11, 279, 282

Clinton, DeWitt, 2, 38–42 passim, 244

Clinton, George, 38, 41–42

Coalpo (Clatsop headman), 203, 223, 229, 236, 238

Coles, John, 114, 115

Colnett, James, 35, 97

Colter, John, 116, 129–30, 131, 140–41, 180

Columbia (ship), xi, 8, 32, 33, 35, 312

Columbia River, 23, 29, 43–44; diplomatic implications of post on, *see* Astoria: as diplomatic issue; Fraser's River mistaken for, 22; trade post proposed, 30–31, 35

Comcomly (Chinook chief), 198, 222–30 passim, 295–96, 297, 322

Comegys, John G., 126–27

Committee of British North American Merchants, 60, 245–46

Congress (ship), 309–10

Constitution (ship), 100, 102, 271

Continental Divide, 11; Astorians cross, 175, 177

Cook, James, 4, 5, 27, 106, 111–12; illus., 5

Cook's River, 6–7, 9–10, 12–13, 27, 28–29, 30

Corney, Peter, 292

Côte sans Dessein, 141

Cowlitz River, 198

Cox, Edward, 197

Cox, Ross, 210, 236, 241, 282, 320, 322, 337

Crane, William M., 268, 269

Crazy Woman Creek (Wyoming), 172

Crooks, Ramsay, 53–54, 62, 119, 126, 128, 133, 137, 143, 162, 179, 301,

323; distrusts Lisa, 136, 142, 149, 156–57; on Henry's Fort Mission, 185–86; illness of, 167, 189–92 passim; as lobbyist, 330; side trip to Otos and Omahas, 146–47; on Snake River mission, 186–90

Crow Indians: trade route of, 171; visit Astorians' camp, 172

Crowninshield, Benjamin W., 309

Czartoryski, Prince Adam, 69

Daitshowan (Clatsop headman), 197–98, 223–24, 229

Dalles, The, 202, 207, 229, 234, 239–40

Dashkov, Andrei, 70–77, 86, 244, 261, 275–76, 301

Davis, Isaac, 109

Day, John, 137, 167, 178, 190, 240

Dearborn, Henry, 42, 45, 46

Delaunay, Pierre, 177, 279

Delorme, Jean Baptiste, 90

Denum, Otis, 122

Detaye, Pierre, 177

DeVoto, Bernard, 3–4

Diet at Fort Astoria, 204–9

Diplomatic activity, Astorian: among Clatsops and Tillamooks, 223–24; among Omahas, 148

Discovery (ship), 5–6

Dixon, George, 106

Dixon, Manley, 294

Dolly (ship), 97, 98, 208, 215

Dorion, Marie L'Ayvoise, 138, 140, 143, 144, 162, 166, 192

Dorion, Pierre, Jr., 138–39, 140, 141, 151–53, 156–57, 178, 213

Dorr, John, 263, 269, 270, 275

Drouillard, George, 116, 129, 131

Drummond, Sir Gordon, 306–7

Dubreuil, J. B., 190

Duchesne, Benjamin, 215

East India Company, 16, 57, 88, 245

Ebbets, John, 32, 72, 73–74, 95, 270

Ebbets, Richard, 252, 253–54, 258, 291–92
Edgar, William, 28–29
Ehninger, George, 280, 305
Eleanora (ship), 109
Ellice, Edward, 256, 257, 307–8
Ellice, William, 307–8
Ellsworth, Henry L., 338
Embargo repeal, 49
Empress of China (ship), 32
Enterprise (ship), 56, 72–75, 269, 270, 273–76
Erskine, David, 49
Erskine Agreement, 49, 55, 61
Erving, George W., 80–81
Essex (ship), 294–95, 297, 300, 308
Ethnographers, Astorian, 320–23
Eulachon (candlefish), 208
Eustis, William, 53, 125

Factory (trading-house) system, 53, 330
Fair American (ship), 109
Falkland Islands, 104–5
Fanning, Edmund, 94–95
Farnham, Russel, 92, 105, 239, 241, 330
Fictor, Adam, 97
Finley, Jaco, 23
Firearms trade. *See* Weapons trade
Firebrand (ship), 310
Firesteel Creek, 167
Flathead Indians, 174
Florez, Manuel Antonio, xi
Floyd, John, 330–31
Floyd Bill, 331–34
Forester (ship): in Astor's secret mission, 254, 267, 268, 276; mutiny aboard, 291–92
Forrest, Richard, 303
Forsyth, Richardson & Company, 61
Fort Astoria: abandonment plans, 265–66, 278–81; birthday of, 217–18, 278; building of, 200–202; complaints at, 215; described, 196; diet at, 204–9; diplomatic activity at, 222–24; fortification of, 225–26; fur trade at, 221–22; gardens at, 205–6; holidays at, 1, 185, 192, 208, 217–18; Indians visit, 202, 219–20; 228–29; injuries and illnesses at, 214–15, 219; library at, 211–12; livestock at, 206–7; occupations and trades at, 209–10, 212–14; overlanders arrive at, 194–95, 96; restoration efforts, 302–11 passim; returned, 313; sale of, 288–91; site selection, 197–99; social organization, 209–10, 212–14; theft at, 229–30; illus., 203, 335. *See also* Astoria
Fort Clatsop, 202, 204, 219–20
Fort George (formerly Astoria), 215, 228, 295–98, 299, 301; status dispute, 305–15 passim
Fort Mandan, 138, 204, 218
Fort Okanogan: plans for, 232–35, 281; returns from, 238–40, 279; Ross at, 265–66, 282, 287, 322
Fort Osage, 128, 134–35, 137, 143, 145
Fort Spokane (Pacific Fur Co.), 241, 264, 266, 279, 280, 281
Fort Vancouver, 206, 335
Fort William, 21, 23, 55, 57, 62, 88, 116, 118, 247, 248, 252, 287, 293
Foster, Augustus, 249
Fourth of July, 1, 217
Fox, John C., 97, 111, 113, 115
Franchère, Gabriel, 3, 91, 93–94, 301; in abandonment/sale activity, 265, 285, 288, 295–96, 298; at Astoria, 200, 203, 205–6, 208, 210–11, 216, 218, 232; background and career of, 91, 210–11; as ethnographer, 320–22; in Hawaii, 107, 111–12; journal mentioned, 112, 236, 337, 342, 343; on Thorn, 96, 101; *Tonquin* experiences, 101–5 passim, 115; illus., 90
Fraser, Simon, 22–23, 50
Fraser River, 22–23

Frobisher, Benjamin, 7
Frobisher, Joseph, 7, 25
Frobisher, Thomas, 25

Gallatin, Albert, 45, 46, 47–48, 52–53, 54–55, 56, 60, 62, 64, 77, 79–81, 87, 88, 123, 124, 250–51, 258–62, 266, 267, 269, 270, 302, 304–5, 308, 309–10, 315, 326, 334–35, 338
Gardapie, Jean Baptiste, 135
Gardoqui, Diego María de, 11
Garreau, Joseph, 158, 160
Geographic discoveries, Astorian, 323, 326
Ghent, Treaty of, 305–6, 308, 312
Gibbs, Elisha, 97
Gillespie, George, 59, 62, 121
Golikov, Ivan, 65
Goulburn, Henry, 255–56, 307–8
Graham, Andrew, 209
Grande Ronde River, 192
Grand River, 164, 166–67, 168–69
Grand River villages, 150, 156, 161
Grand Tetons, 175, 326
Gratiot, Charles, 50, 51, 54, 168, 185, 192, 195, 250–51, 258
Gray, Robert, xi, 77, 312
Great Slave Lake, 6–7, 9, 11
Greeley, Aaron, 122
Greene, David, 273–76
Green River, 176
Greenwood, Caleb, 135, 139
Grey Eyes (Arikara headman), 158, 161
Gros Ventre Range, 175
Guerriere (ship), 309
Gur'ev, Dmitrii, 84

Hallowell, James, 17–18
Halsey, John, 240, 293–94, 299
Hamilton, Henry, 4, 8–9, 13, 16
Hamilton, Paul, 96
Hankinson, John, 50, 53
Harmon, Daniel, 211
Harrington, Samuel, 125, 146, 147

Harrington, William, 146, 147
Harris, Levett, 69, 70
Harry (Hawaiian sailor), 114
Haswell, Robert, 35
Hawaiian Astorians, 111, 197, 201, 215, 218–19, 228, 289, 298, 300; in Columbia channel ordeal, 114–15; as gardeners, 205–6
Hawaiian Islands: Hunt in, 284–86, 297; *Tonquin* resupplies at, 106–11
Hells Canyon, 190
Hendricks, William, 333
Henry, Andrew, 116, 130–31, 132, 137, 150, 173
Henry's Fort, 178–79, 180, 185–86
Henry, Alexander the elder, 4, 16, 25–29, 57, 211; illus., 26
Henry, Alexander the younger, 214, 228, 287, 290, 292–93, 297–98, 299–300; diary mentioned, 337
Hickey, Frederick, 314
Hidatsa Indians, 155
Hill, Robert, 98
Hillyar, James, 256–57, 294–95, 300
Hoback, John, 149–50, 175, 179
Hoback River, 176–77
Holidays at Astoria, 1, 185, 192, 217–18, 208
Honolulu, Astorians visit, 109–11
Hope (ship), 32
Hornet (ship), 267
Horse trading, 159, 161–63, 167–68, 172, 187, 193
Hudson's Bay Company, 4, 13, 18, 21, 25, 209, 245, 249
Hughes, James, 19–20
Hunt, John Wesley, 51
Hunt, Wilson Price: as Astor's scapegoat in correspondence with Mackenzie, 304; Astor selects, 50–51, 59, 87; correspondence with Astor, 53, 262, 276; disputes with Mackenzie, 89–90, 119, 135, 139, 280; expedition of, 165–94, 323; ex-

Hunt, Wilson Price (*cont.*)
pedition preparations and recruitment, 53, 54, 88–90, 116–27 passim; expedition route (incl. maps),
123, 324–26, 328–29; expedition
route planning, 128–30, 150, 164,
165; in Hawaii, 284–86, 297; hires
botanists, 123, 133; hires traders
and mountain men, 149, 150;
horsetrading efforts, 159, 161–63,
167–68, 172, 187, 193; Indians and,
147, 151–62 passim, 167–68, 172,
174, 176, 181, 187–89, 191, 193;
journal mentioned, 283, 284, 338;
Lisa pursues, 142–45, 147, 149,
151, 154–55; objects to abandon-
ment/sale, 285, 297, 298–300;
reaches Astoria, 194, 238; Rose and,
172–74; and Russians, 283–84;
trade-expansion plans of, 240–42;
in Washington, 88
Hunters at Astoria, 213

Idaho Falls, 181
Indian cultures, Astorians observe, 144,
147–48, 163, 316, 320–23
Indians: Astor warns against, 34, 100–
101; as guides, 19–20, 178–79, 191;
route information from, 174, 175–
76, 178, 188–89, 191, 193. *See also*
Indian cultures; Indian trade; *names
of specific tribes*
Indian trade, 33–34; at Astoria, 219–
22; Crow, 172; items for, 121; sex
and, *see* Sex in commerce; and
Thorn-*Tonquin* disaster, 236–37
Ingraham, Joseph, 4, 32, 33, 34
Irving, Pierre, Munro, 339
Irving, Washington, xii, 3, 71–72, 99–
100, 119, 126, 137, 138, 179, 236,
296, 315, 326, 327, 335, 362; writes
Astoria, 338–40; career, 337–38;
work assessed, 340–42; mentioned,
283, 284

Isaac Todd (ship), 252–53, 255–66 passim, 278, 282, 283, 287, 293, 294

Jackson, Donald, 30
Jackson, Francis James, 99, 264
James, Thomas, 54
Java (ship), 309
Jefferson, Thomas: on Astoria, xii; cor-
respondence with Astor, 40–45, 72,
85, 327; correspondence with Lewis,
30–31, 46–47, 133; Lewis and Clark
expedition and, 29–31, 42–43;
meetings with Astor, 45–47, 244,
271, 272; views on expansion, 43;
mentioned, 69, 124, 316
Jennings, John, 254, 291–92
Jérémie, Paul Denis, 203, 215–17, 344
John Adams (ship), 80–81, 267, 268–69
Joint Occupation Treaty, 315, 330–34
Jones, Benjamin, 149, 150, 151, 167,
238
Jones, William, 223, 258–59, 263, 267–
73 passim

Kailua Bay, 108–9
Kalanimoku ("William Pitt") (Hawaiian
prime minister), 110
Kamaquiah (Chinook headman), 229,
230
Kamehameha, King of Hawaiian Is-
lands, 108–11
Kane, Paul, 225
Kealakekua Bay, 107–8
Keith, James, 287, 293, 315
Kendrick, John, 35
Kimoo, James, xii, 197, 203, 218
Koaster, Johann, 98, 202, 212–13
Ko-come-ne-pe-ca (Indian messenger),
231–32
Kootenay House, 23
Kozlov, Nikolai, 275
Kozodavlev, Osipp, 84–85
Kutenais trading area, 241, 281
Kyakhta, 68

La Chappelle, A., 192
La Charette, 140
Lachine, 62, 64; recruitment at, 88–93
Lady Washington (ship), 8, 32, 34
Laframboise, Michel, 202
La Liberte, Louis, 90
Landry, François, 119–20, 192
Lapensée, Ignace and Bazile, 90, 113, 115
Lapierre, Joseph, 202
Lark (ship), 261–63, 275, 276, 284; tragic fate of, 286, 291, 297
Larocque, Joseph, 277
Laurison, Daniel, 135, 139
Lavender, David, 53–54, 343
L'Ayvoise, Marie (Dorion's wife), 138, 140, 143, 144, 162, 166, 192
Le Clairc, François, 189, 238
Le Compte, Alexis, 125
Ledyard, John, 6
Le Gauche (Arikara chief), 158–61
Le Roux, Guillaume, 120
Lewis, James, 98, 210, 235
Lewis, Meriwether, 30–31, 43, 46–47, 88, 129, 131, 133, 163, 180, 219
Lewis, Reuben, 53, 130–32, 162–63
Lewis and Clark expedition: Astorians' route plans and, 128–30; with Arikaras, 156, 157–58, 161, 167; botanic samples from, 123; and Cheyennes, 168; at Ft. Clatsop, 202, 204, 205, 219–20, 227; Hunt learns from, 51, 128–30; supposed influence on Astor, 3–4, 29–31, 39, 42–44, 128; mentioned, 21, 127, 153, 166, 194, 208, 316, 317, 320
Lewis's River, 177. *See also* Snake River
Lisa, Manuel, 51, 53, 124, 131–33, 141–55 passim, 168, 173; and Dorion controversy, 138–39, 156–57; pursues Hunt, 142–45, 147, 149, 151, 154–55; travels with Hunt, 156; withdraws from Far West contest, 162

Little Missouri River, 169
Little Nemaha River, 145
Liverpool, Lord, 60, 247–48

McClellan, Robert, 53–54, 62, 153, 240; background and temperament of, 136–37; distrusts and despises Lisa, 136, 142, 149, 156–57; as explorer and scout, 176, 185–86, 190, 194, 319; quits company, 238–39; in Rose affair, 173
McDonald, Finan, 231, 240
McDonald of Garth, John, 252–53, 257, 294, 296, 297, 298
McDougall, Duncan, xii, 58, 59, 88, 98, 105, 109, 185, 192, 198–99, 201–3, 204, 209–10, 214–16, 219, 227–28, 231–36 passim, 238, 242, 259, 264, 283, 285–87, 293, 298; abandonment plans of, 265, 277–82, 285–86; Astor blames for sale, 303–4, 308, 334; criticism of, 202, 215, 280, 285, 288; defends actions, 282–83, 288–89; journal mentioned, 229, 338, 343; Indians and, 220, 221, 223–24, 226, 279, 289, 295; in negotiations and sale of Astoria, 286–91, 295, 299
McGill, James and Andrew, 61
McGillis, Donald, 92, 240, 282
McGillivray, Duncan, 4, 18–19, 21, 24
McGillivray, Simon, 246, 247–48, 256, 257, 307, 311
McGillivray, William, 57–58, 63, 233, 247, 290, 307
McKay, Alexander, 58, 59, 88, 91, 93, 98–99, 109, 114, 115, 120, 199, 209–10, 224, 235, 236, 237; challenges Thorn, 101; death of, 210, 237; as explorer, 197, 203
McKay, Thomas, 298
McKay, William, 252
Mackenzie, Sir Alexander, 4, 10, 12, 13, 16–18, 21, 22, 25, 29–30, 57, 58, 60; illus., 17

Mackenzie, Donald, 58, 59, 88, 122, 133, 264, 301; criticizes Astor, 280–81; disagreements with Hunt, 89–90, 119, 135, 139; at Fort Astoria, 212, 238, 239; hires Astorians, 89–91, 118–20, 125; meeting with Astor, 304; role in abandonment/sale, 265–66, 277–82 passim, 285–86, 287, 303–4

Mackenzie River, 6–7, 9, 12

Mackinac, recruiting at, 118–22

McLennan, Donald, 234, 241, 282

McMahon, Bernard, 122

McMillan, James, 240

McNair brothers (David, John, Thomas), 135, 139

McTavish, Donald, 252–53, 255, 256, 257

McTavish, John George, 247, 252, 264, 277–78, 281–83, 287–91, 293

McTavish, Simon, 10

McTavish, Fraser, and Company, 18, 246

McTavish, McGillivrays & Co., 61

Madison, James, 45, 61, 69, 70, 82, 88, 267, 309; Astor seeks support of, 46, 79–81, 249–50, 251, 262, 271–72

Madison administration, 260, 271–72, 302

Mad River, 176, 177, 180. *See also* Snake River

Mandan Indians, 155

Maps: from Astorian expeditions (incl. illus.), 323–26, 328–29; by Clark, 129, 193–94, 323; by Pond, 6–13 passim; Pond's 1790 map (illus.), 14–15

Marcial, François, 120

Marin, Francisco de Paula, 109

Martin, John, 97, 113

Mathews, William W., 202, 210, 215, 216, 239, 337

Menard, Pierre, 130, 142

Merk, Frederick, 315, 343

Metcalf, Thomas, 330

Methye Portage, 4

Michilimackinac Company, Astor seeks to buy, 46–49, 55–62 passim, 72

Miller, Joseph, 53–54, 62, 126, 179–80

Missouri Buttes, 169

Missouri Expedition, 331

Missouri Fur Company, 53, 124, 130–33, 135, 138, 141, 151, 173

Monroe, James, 262–63, 302–3, 305–6, 308, 310, 311; meets with Astor, 259–60

Montigny, Ovide de, 92, 203

Montour, Nicholas, 241

Montreal, Astor in, 24–25, 29, 47, 55

Moorhead, Forgus, 126–27

Morier, John Philip, 309–10

Morris, Robert, 32

Morrison, James, 126–27

Morrison, William, 130

Mumford, John, 215

Mumford, William P., 97, 107, 113–14

Murray, Dr. John, 143–44

Muzzey, David L., 342

Nadeau, Joseph, 113, 115

Nahwhitti, 235

Natural science, Astorians and, 316–17, 319–20

Neahkeluk (Clatsop village), 198, 224

New Archangel (Sitka), 65, 69, 262, 284, 286, 297, 300

New Hazard (ship), 235, 276

New Year's celebrations, 218, 237, 264, 297; Hawaiian, 218

Niobrara River, 148

Nodaway River, camp at, 134, 135–37, 140, 145

Nooth, Dr. John Mervin, 12–13

Nootka Indians, 225, 226–27

Northrop, Samuel H., 261, 286, 297

North West Company: exploration efforts of, 8–11, 13–21, 22–24,

248–49; negotiations with Astor, 46–49, 55–60, 61–64; pamphlet on, 24; partners reach cooperative arrangement with Astorians, 278, 281–82; petitions British government, 56–57, 60, 87–88, 244–49, 255–58; plans to acquire Astoria, 253, 277–79, 287–88; purchases Astoria, 288–91, 301

Northwest Passage, 10, 11

Nowood Creek (Wyoming), 174

Nuttall, Thomas, 122–24, 133, 140, 141, 142, 147, 317

Nye, David, Jr., 276

Oahu, *Tonquin* visits, 109–11

Ogden, Isaac, 11–12

Okanogan. *See* Fort Okanogan

Okanogan River, exploration along, 232–35

Okhotsk, 68

Omaha Indians, 147–48

Ontario (ship), 217, 310–15

Oregon Question, 56, 340; essay on, 343

Osage Indians, 141; scientists visit, 144. *See also* Fort Osage

Oto Indians, Astorians attempt to visit, 146–47

Ouvre, Jean Baptiste, 120

Overland express, Astorian, 238–39

Pacific Fur Company, xi, 1–3; Astor's business contacts and, 24–25; Astor's design for, 39–41, 243; Astor seeks official approval for, 39–44 passim, 52–53; Astor seeks protection for, 243, 258–63, 271–72; Astor seeks restoration of, 302–11 passim; Crooks and, 53–54; dissolved, 310 (*see also* Abandonment plans); field headquarters, 221 (*see also* Fort Astoria); first post, *see* Nodaway River, camp at; formal beginnings, 58–59, 62, 87, 88; Irving's history of, *see* Astoria; McClellan and, 136–37, 238–39; Miller joins, 126; Missouri Fur Co. rivalry with, 131–33, 141–42; North West Co. buys, 288–91, 301; North West Co. rivalry with, 45, 59, 62, 244–49; and North West Co. in supposed joint venture, 46–48, 55–60, 61–64, 232–34; records of, xiii; recruits Astorians, 89–93, 119–20, 125–26, 134–35; Russian American Co. and, 73, 283–84; sale terms questioned, 299–300; undercover rescue mission for, 252, 253–54, 267

Pahlen, Count Fedor, 77–79, 81, 82

Paou, Dick, 219, 344

Papin, Antoine, 134, 213

Parker, Mr. (ship's officer), 273

Parker, Gerrard and Ogilvie, 61

Paxton, Frederic L., 342

Peace River, 6

Pedlar (ship), 297, 298–99, 300

Perrault, Jean Baptiste, 91, 117, 121–22

Perrault, Joseph, 120, 136

Peter (Hawaiian sailor), 114

Phillips, Francis, 296

Phoebe (ship), 256–58, 262, 270, 278, 294, 295

Picotte, Pierre, 90

Pigot, William J., 32, 252, 253–54, 258, 259, 291–92

Pike, Zebulon, 128; expedition of, 140

Pillet, François, 92, 231, 232, 234, 241

Pillon, Jean Baptiste, 120

Plante, Antoine, 166

Platte River, 145–46; described by Stuart, 319–20

Plumer, William, 43–44

Point Adams, 198, 223

Point George, 199, 298

Ponca Indians, 149

Pond, Peter, 4–13, 25, 28; maps of Northwest by (illus.), 14–15

Pork: Astorians' disdain for, 207; Kamehameha's monpoly on, 108–9
Porter, David, 294–95, 300, 308–9
Porter, Kenneth W., 343
Portlock, Nathaniel, 106
Pothier, Toussaint, 121
Potts, John, 131
Powder River (Wyoming and Idaho), 171, 189
Powder River (Oregon), 192
Powder River Range, 169
Powrowie, Joseph, 218
Prevost, Jean Baptiste, 120, 190, 195
Prevost, John B., 310–11, 313–15, 217
Prince (ship), 244
Pryor, Nathaniel, 156
Pursh, Frederick, 123, 316–17

Quinault Indians, 222, 238

Racoon (ship), 217, 294–95, 296, 300, 303
Raft River, 181
Rampart River, 166
Ramsay, Jack ("Lamazu"), 236–37
Randall, Thomas, 33
Recruitment of Astorians: at Fort Osage, 134–35; at Lachine, 88–93; at Mackinac, 118–19; at St. Louis, 125–26
Reed, John, 120, 122; as explorer, scout, and trader, 178, 183, 185–86, 190, 194, 282, 299; clerical activity of, 121, 134–35, 137, 145, 148, 163–64, 166, 167, 172, 181, 195; and messenger service, 238; wounded, 239
Resolution (ship), 5
Restoration of Astoria, 313; Astor's efforts toward, 302–11 passim
Reynolds, Stephen, 235
Rezanov, Count Nikolai, 65, 68
Reznor, Jacob, 149–50, 175, 179
Rhtarahe (Arikara village), 158

Richardson, John, 57–58
Robert, François, 148
Robertson, Francis, 97
Robilliard, Joseph, 91, 117–18
Robinson, Edward, 149–50, 162, 166, 169, 170, 175, 177, 178, 179
Rocky Mountain House, 18–21, 23, 249
Rogers, John, 99–100
Rogers, William, 128, 146–47
Rollins, Philip Ashton, 343
Rook (Cree guide), 19–20
Roscoe, William, 133
Rose, Edward, 172–74
Ross, Alexander, 3, 58–59, 88–89, 91, 101, 106, 108, 109, 112, 113, 135, 139, 231; on Astor, 36, 258; books on Astoria by, 327, 337, 342, 343; on building Astoria, 199–202; clerk's duties of, 210; on discovery and enlightenment, 315–16; as ethnographer, 320, 322–23; on laborers' complaints and resentment, 209, 215; on prospective recruits, 118, 125; reports on abandonment/sale turmoil, 265, 280, 284; aboard *Tonquin*, 101–8 passim, 112, 113, 114; as trader and explorer, 203, 222, 232, 234, 238, 240, 282, 287; illus., 92
Roussel, Augustus, 90, 98, 203, 212, 214
Rumiantsev, Nikolai, 66, 70, 75, 81–85 passim
Rush, Richard, 311, 334
Russian-American Company, 8, 57, 66–86 passim, 242, 256, 275, 283–84, 301; flag of (illus.), 67

Sacagawea, 143
Sailors' lore, Astor and, 31–33
St. Amant, Joseph, 148, 213, 214
St. Charles, 140
St. Louis, 50, 124, 129; Astorians re-

cruited at, 125–26; Astorians depart, 134

St. Michael, Louis, 125, 177

Salmon: in Astorian diet, 207; Chinook ceremony, 220–21

Saskatchewan River path, 248

Sawa-haini (Arikara village), 158, 161

Sciatoga Indians, 191

Science, Astorians' contribution to, 316–17, 319–20

Seton, Alfred, 211, 240, 337

Sex in commerce: Arikara view of, 163; Astorians' enthusiasm for, 164, 228; Chinook women and, 227, 228; Omaha women and, 148

Shaw, Angus, 287

Sheheke (Mandan chief), 54, 131, 156

Shelikhov, Gregorii, 8, 65

Shonowane, Ignace, xii, 205, 213, 344

Shoshoni Indians, 174, 176, 178–79, 180, 181, 187, 188–89, 191, 193

Shuswap Indians, 239

Shuswap trading area, 240, 280, 281, 282

Sibley, George C., 134

Simcoe, John Graves, 13

Simpson, George, 207

Sinkaietk Indians, 232, 322–23

Sioux Indians: in Astorians' camp, 147; confrontation with, 151–55. *See also* Teton Sioux Indians; Yankton Sioux Indians

Siren (ship), 273–74

Skinner, Constance L., 342

Slaight, Aaron, 97

Slim Buttes, 169

Small, Patrick, 10

Smith, Jedediah, 323

Smith, John, 127

Smith, Robert, 76–77, 78

Smith, William, 283, 285

Smith Point, 196, 199

Snake River: Hunt expedition along, 176–91; in fur trade operations, 240, 279, 281, 282, 299

Solander, Daniel, 27–28

South Pass, 323, 326

South Seas Company, 35

Sowle, Cornelius, 240, 242, 251–52, 283, 284

Spokane House (North West Co. post), 231, 240, 264, 283

Stuart, Alexander, 287, 293

Stuart, David, 92, 97, 98, 105, 197, 198, 199, 232, 233, 234, 240, 241, 266, 279–81, 282, 323

Stuart, Donald, 298

Stuart, John, 231, 252, 264, 287, 299

Stuart, Robert, 92–93, 98, 203, 222, 225, 226, 232, 233, 235, 304, 339; at Caldron Linn, 182–83; challenges Thorn, 105–6, discovers South Pass, 323; journal mentioned, 183, 338, 343, 319–20; as naturalist, 319–20; routes (incl. maps), 323–26, 328–29; as trader and explorer, 198–99, 238, 239, 323; as transcontinental messenger, 240, 268–69, 270; illus., 318

Stuart-Ross Okanogan expedition, 232, 234–35

Swearingen, Thomas, 330

Tabeau, Jean Baptiste, 159

Talbot, Theodore, 336

Tamaahamaah (ship), 252, 292

Tavern Rock, 134

Teton Pass, 178

Teton River, 179

Teton Sioux Indians, 129, 136, 138, 148–49, 151–55. *See also* Sioux Indians

Thompson, David: early explorations by, 18–21, 23–24, 50, 55; and fabled "race" to Astoria, 63–64, 234; in joint venture, 232–35; letter by, mentioned, 259; mysterious Indian couple and, 231; mentioned, 227

Thompson River, 239, 241

Thorn, James C., 98

Thorn, Jonathan: Astor hires, 95–96, 281; Astor's instructions for, 100; authority challenged, 101, 105–6, 108, 112; at Baker Bay, 197–99; harsh command of, 96, 101, 103, 104–6, 112–15; in Hawaii, 107–12; Indians and, 34, 100, 236–37; last voyage and violent end, 235–37; prepares for voyage, 97–98

Thunder Basin, 170–71

Tillamook Indians, 223–24, 322

Todd, Edgeley W., 180, 340

Togwotee Pass, 150, 175, 177

Tongue Point, 199, 232, 293, 298

Tonquin (ship): Astor buys, 94; Astor hears of loss of, 250; at Baker Bay, 114–15, 197–99; Columbian passage of, 112–15; described, 94–95; final voyage and destruction of, 235–37; in Hawaii, 106–11; preparation and loading of, 96–100; voyage to Astoria, 101–15; illus., 95; mentioned, 34, 78, 80, 208, 225, 245

Tonwantonga (Omaha town), 146–47

Trade, Indian. *See* Indian trade

Trade jargon, 230

Trade rituals, in Northwest, 33–34

Trask, John, 139

Tuanna, Thomas, 228

Turcotte, J. B., 191–92

Tushepaw Indians, 193

Twin Falls (Idaho), 183

Umatilla River, 193–94

Union Pass, 150, 175, 177

Union (ship), 33, 106

United American Company, 66

Valle, André, 238

Vancouver, George, 6, 12; charts of, 275

Vancouver Island, 235–36

Vanderhoop, Egbert, 97, 213

Venereal disease, 227–28

Verstille, Peter, 97

Wahkiakum Indians, 202, 219

Waho-erha (Arikara village), 158

Walker, Alexander, 33

Wallace, William, 240

Wallace House, 240, 282

Walla Walla River, 193

Walula Indians, 64

War of 1812, 249, 251; Astorians learn of, 263–64; end of, 305

Wasco Indians, 239

Wasp (ship), 267

Waubuschon (Osage headman), 144

Weapons trade, in Russian America, 67–68, 71, 75–78 passim, 82, 83, 84, 86

Weeks, Henry, 97

Weeks, Stephen, 97, 114, 115

Weiser River, 188, 190, 191

Wellesley, Viscount, 102, 246–47

Whetten, John, 269, 274

White Cow (Omaha headman), 148

Whitehead, Robert, 125

Willamette trading area, 238, 239, 240, 265, 279, 281

Williams, Thomas, 97

Wilson, Thomas H., 252, 253–54, 259

Wind River, 174–75, 177

Windsor, John, 122

Wishram Indians, 239

Woodruff, Simon, 6

Yankton Sioux Indians, 148

Yelleppit (Walula chief), 234

Yellowstone River Route, 129–30, 141

Young, John, 108–9